O-Parts HunteR

SEISHI KISHIMOTO

CHARACTERS of O-Parts HUNTER

Satan is looking for an opportunity to take over Jio's body, but Ruby is holding Satan in check.

Ruby Crescent: A treasure hunter in search of the Legendary O-Part and her missing father. Currently, her body is with the Stea Government, and her soul is resting inside Jio's body.

Satan: An alternate personality that exists inside Jio's body. The ultimate weapon of the Kabbalah who holds earth-shattering powers.

Jio Freed: A wild O.P.T. boy whose dream is world domination. He has been emotionally hurt from his experiences in the past but has become strong after meeting Ruby. Ever since the Rock Bird incident, he has had Ruby's soul inside him.

Jio's Friends

Kirin: An O-Part appraiser and a master of dodging attacks. He trained Jio and Ball into strong O.P.T.s.

Ball: He is the mood-maker of the group and a kind person who cares about his friends.

Cross: He used to be the Commander in Chief of the Stea Government's battleship. His sister was killed by Satan.

Master Zenom & the Big Four
The Zenom Syndicate claims that their aim is to bring chaos and destruction upon the world, but...

Stea Government Leader Amaterasu Miko
The very person who turned the Stea Government into a huge military state. Rumor has it that she has been alive for at least a century...

KABBALAH

the keyword of 666

A legacy left by the Ancient Race who are said to have come from the Blue Planet. The Kabbalah is the Ultimate Memorization Weapon, which absorbs every kind of "information" that makes up this world, and evolves along with the passing of time! It consists of two counterparts, the Formal Kabbalah and the Reverse Kabbalah.

10i
Nahema
(Materialism)
9i
Lilith
(Instability)
7i
Baal
(Lust)
8i
Adramelech
(Avarice)
6i
Belphegor
(Odiousness)
4i
Astaroth
(Apathy)
5i
Asmodeus
(Cruelty)
2i
Beelzebub
(Stupidity)
3i
Lucifuge
(Rejection)
1i
Satan
(Atheism)

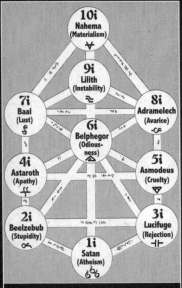

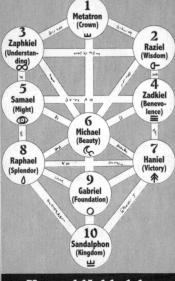

Reverse Kabbalah

The symbol of destruction with the names of the powerful archdemons listed on the sephirot from one to ten.

1
Metatron
(Crown)
3
Zaphkiel
(Understanding)
2
Raziel
(Wisdom)
5
Samael
(Might)
4
Zadkiel
(Benevolence)
6
Michael
(Beauty)
8
Raphael
(Splendor)
7
Haniel
(Victory)
9
Gabriel
(Foundation)
10
Sandalphon
(Kingdom)

Formal Kabbalah

The symbol of creation with the names of the great archangels listed on the sephirot from one to ten.

STORY

Ascald: a world where people fight amongst themselves to get their hands on mystical objects left behind by an ancient civilization...the O-Parts.

In that world, a monster that strikes fear into the hearts of the strongest of men is rumored to exist. Those who have seen the monster all tell of the same thing–that the number of the beast, 666, is engraved on its forehead.

***

Four years have passed since the incident at Rock Bird. Kirin, Amidaba, Cross and Ball have reunited with Jio and are now attempting to retrieve Ruby's body from the headquarters complex of the Stea Government. Ruby has not woken up since her soul went inside Jio's body to keep Satan at bay. Jio and the others figure they'll get a pretty rough reception, and they're not disappointed!

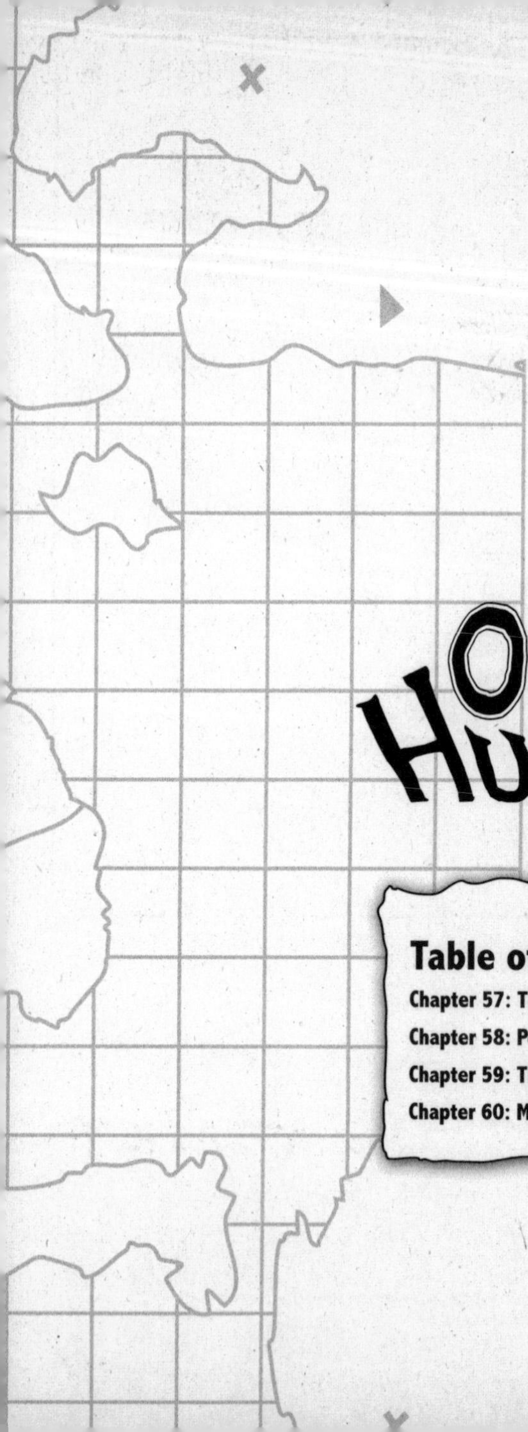

O-Parts Hunter

15

Table of Contents

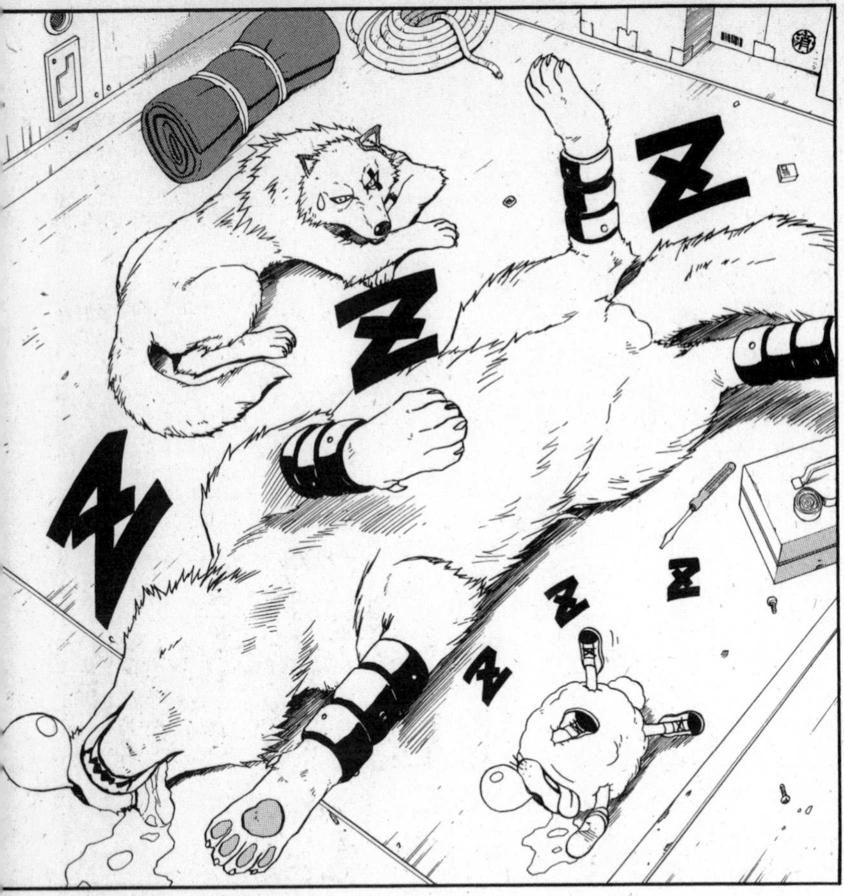
ZZZ
ZZZ

CHAPTER 57 THE ATTACK!!

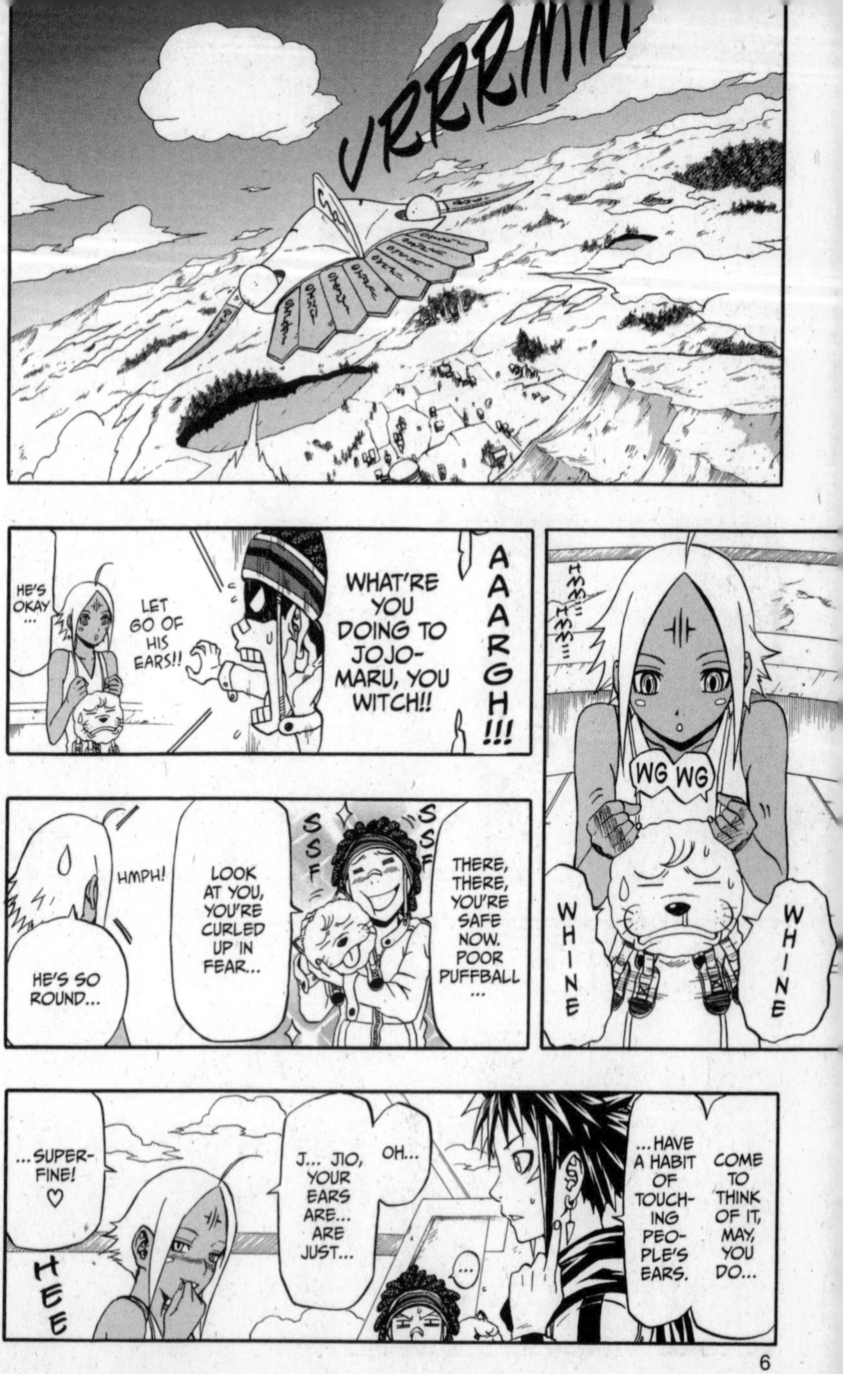
VRRRMM
HMM... HMM...
WG WG
WHINE
WHINE
AAARGH!!!
WHAT'RE YOU DOING TO JOJO-MARU, YOU WITCH!!
LET GO OF HIS EARS!!
HE'S OKAY...
SSF
SSF
THERE, THERE, YOU'RE SAFE NOW. POOR PUFFBALL...
LOOK AT YOU, YOU'RE CURLED UP IN FEAR...
HMPH!
HE'S SO ROUND...
COME TO THINK OF IT, MAY, YOU DO...
...HAVE A HABIT OF TOUCH-ING PEO-PLE'S EARS.
...
OH...
J... JIO, YOUR EARS ARE... ARE JUST...
...SUPER-FINE! ♡
HEE

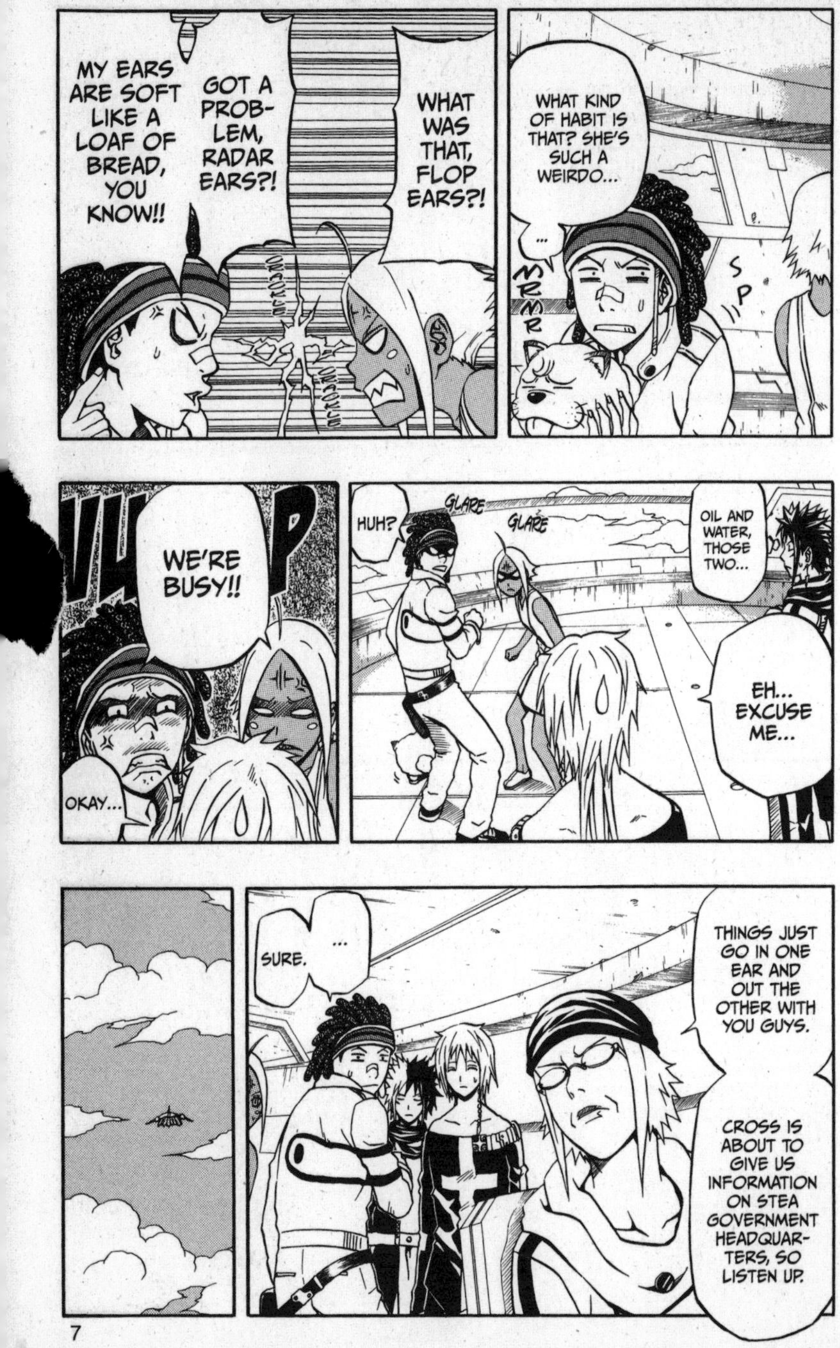
WHAT KIND OF HABIT IS THAT? SHE'S SUCH A WEIRDO...
...
MRMR
SP
WHAT WAS THAT, FLOP EARS?!
GOT A PROB-LEM, RADAR EARS?!
MY EARS ARE SOFT LIKE A LOAF OF BREAD, YOU KNOW!!
CRACKLE
CRACKLE
OIL AND WATER, THOSE TWO...
GLARE
GLARE
HUH?
EH... EXCUSE ME...
WE'RE BUSY!!
OKAY...
THINGS JUST GO IN ONE EAR AND OUT THE OTHER WITH YOU GUYS.
CROSS IS ABOUT TO GIVE US INFORMATION ON STEA GOVERNMENT HEADQUAR-TERS, SO LISTEN UP.
...
SURE.

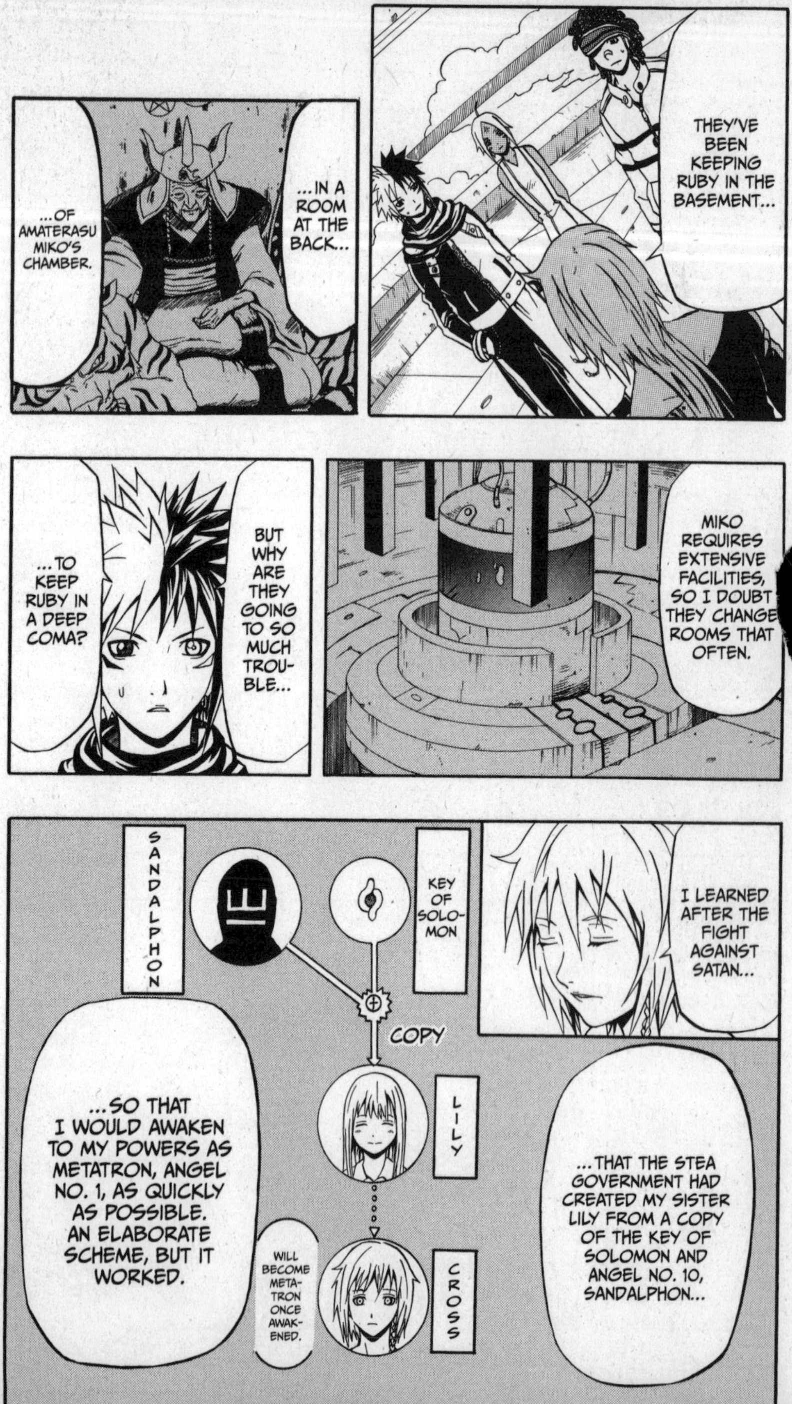
THEY'VE BEEN KEEPING RUBY IN THE BASEMENT...
...IN A ROOM AT THE BACK...
...OF AMATERASU MIKO'S CHAMBER.
MIKO REQUIRES EXTENSIVE FACILITIES, SO I DOUBT THEY CHANGE ROOMS THAT OFTEN.
BUT WHY ARE THEY GOING TO SO MUCH TROUBLE...
...TO KEEP RUBY IN A DEEP COMA?
I LEARNED AFTER THE FIGHT AGAINST SATAN...
KEY OF SOLOMON
SANDALPHON
COPY
LILY
CROSS
WILL BECOME METATRON ONCE AWAKENED.
...THAT THE STEA GOVERNMENT HAD CREATED MY SISTER LILY FROM A COPY OF THE KEY OF SOLOMON AND ANGEL NO. 10, SANDALPHON...
...SO THAT I WOULD AWAKEN TO MY POWERS AS METATRON, ANGEL NO. 1, AS QUICKLY AS POSSIBLE. AN ELABORATE SCHEME, BUT IT WORKED.

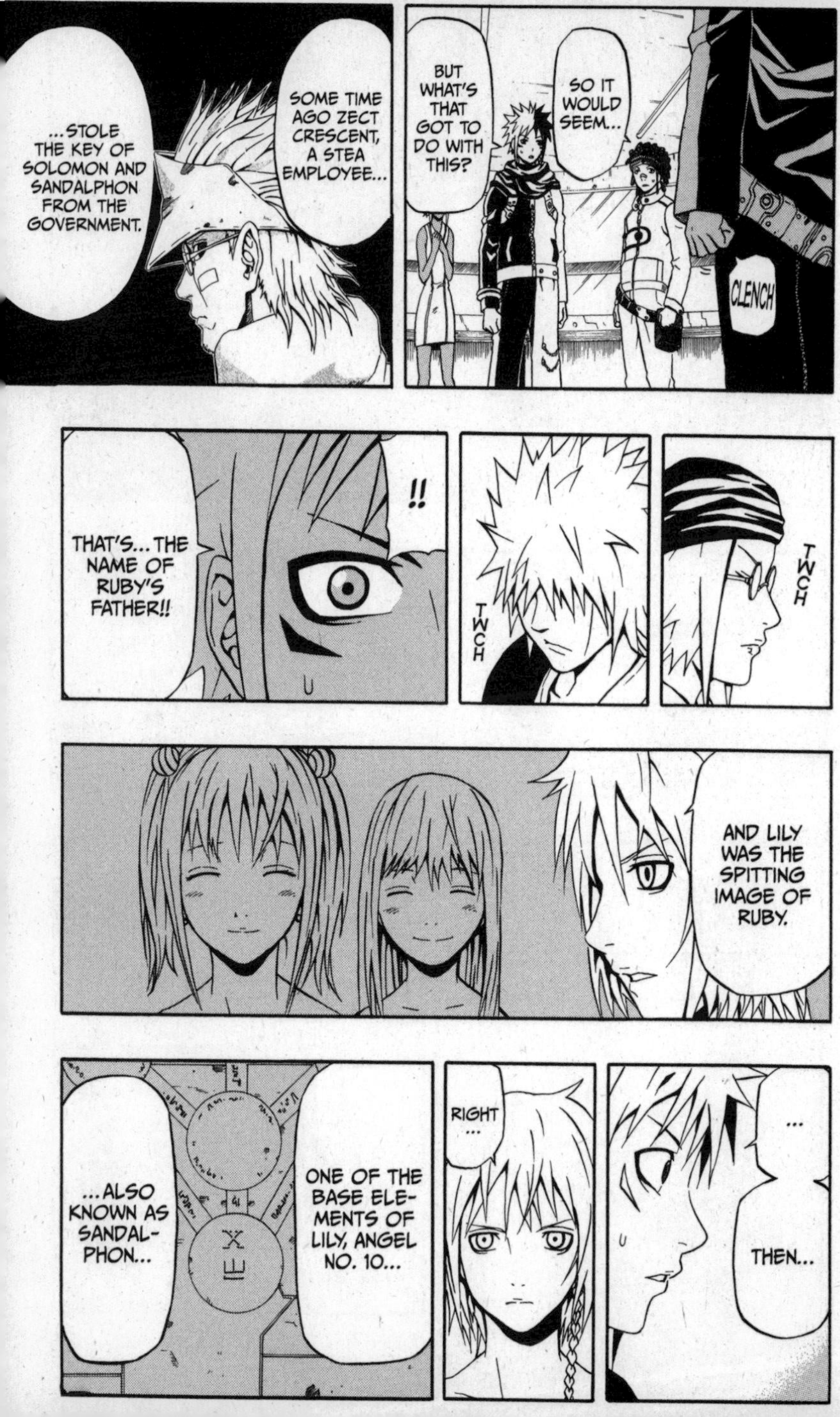
SO IT WOULD SEEM...
BUT WHAT'S THAT GOT TO DO WITH THIS?
CLENCH
SOME TIME AGO ZECT CRESCENT, A STEA EMPLOYEE...
...STOLE THE KEY OF SOLOMON AND SANDALPHON FROM THE GOVERNMENT.
TWCH
TWCH
!!
THAT'S... THE NAME OF RUBY'S FATHER!!
AND LILY WAS THE SPITTING IMAGE OF RUBY.
...
THEN...
RIGHT...
ONE OF THE BASE ELE-MENTS OF LILY, ANGEL NO. 10...
...ALSO KNOWN AS SANDAL-PHON...

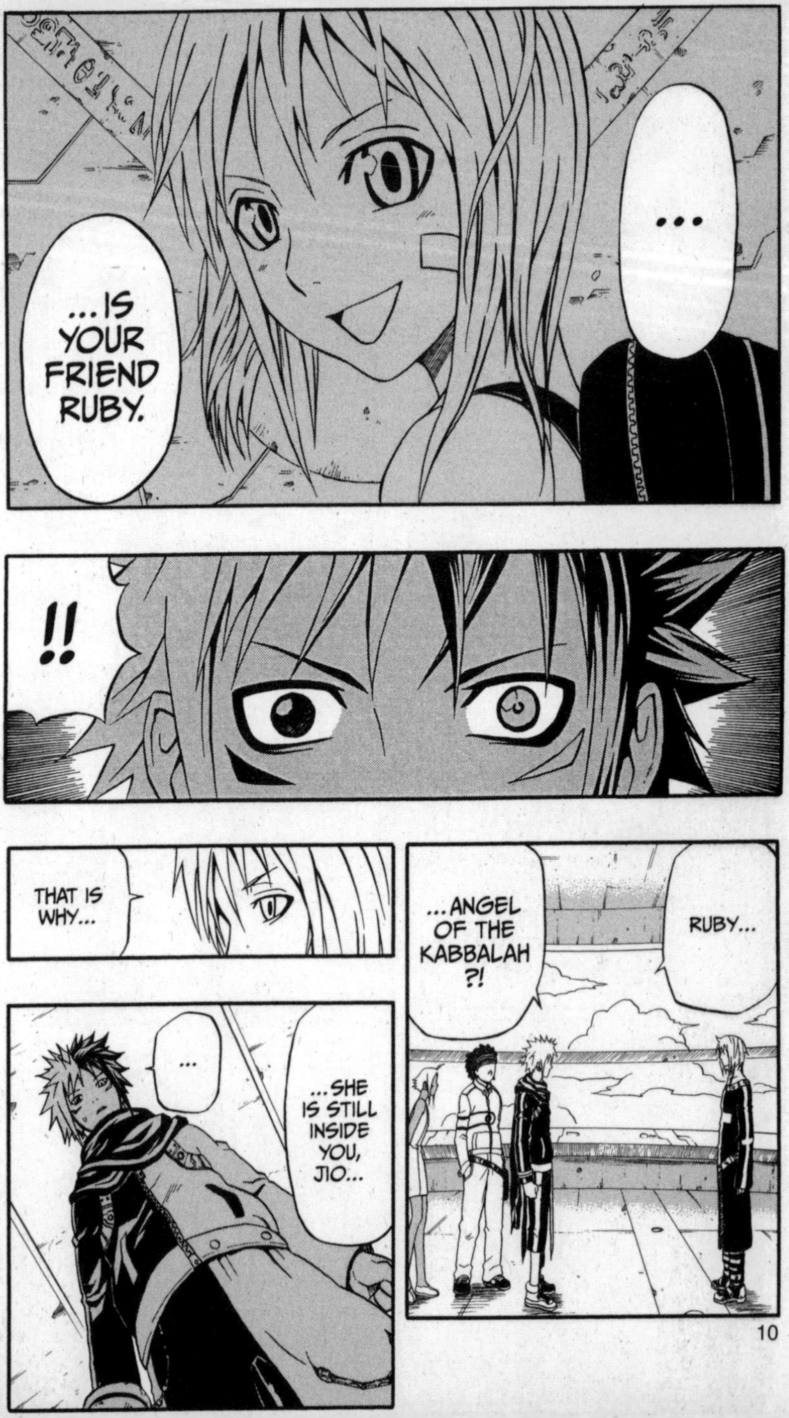
...
...IS YOUR FRIEND RUBY.
!!
RUBY...
...ANGEL OF THE KABBALAH ?!
THAT IS WHY...
...SHE IS STILL INSIDE YOU, JIO...
...

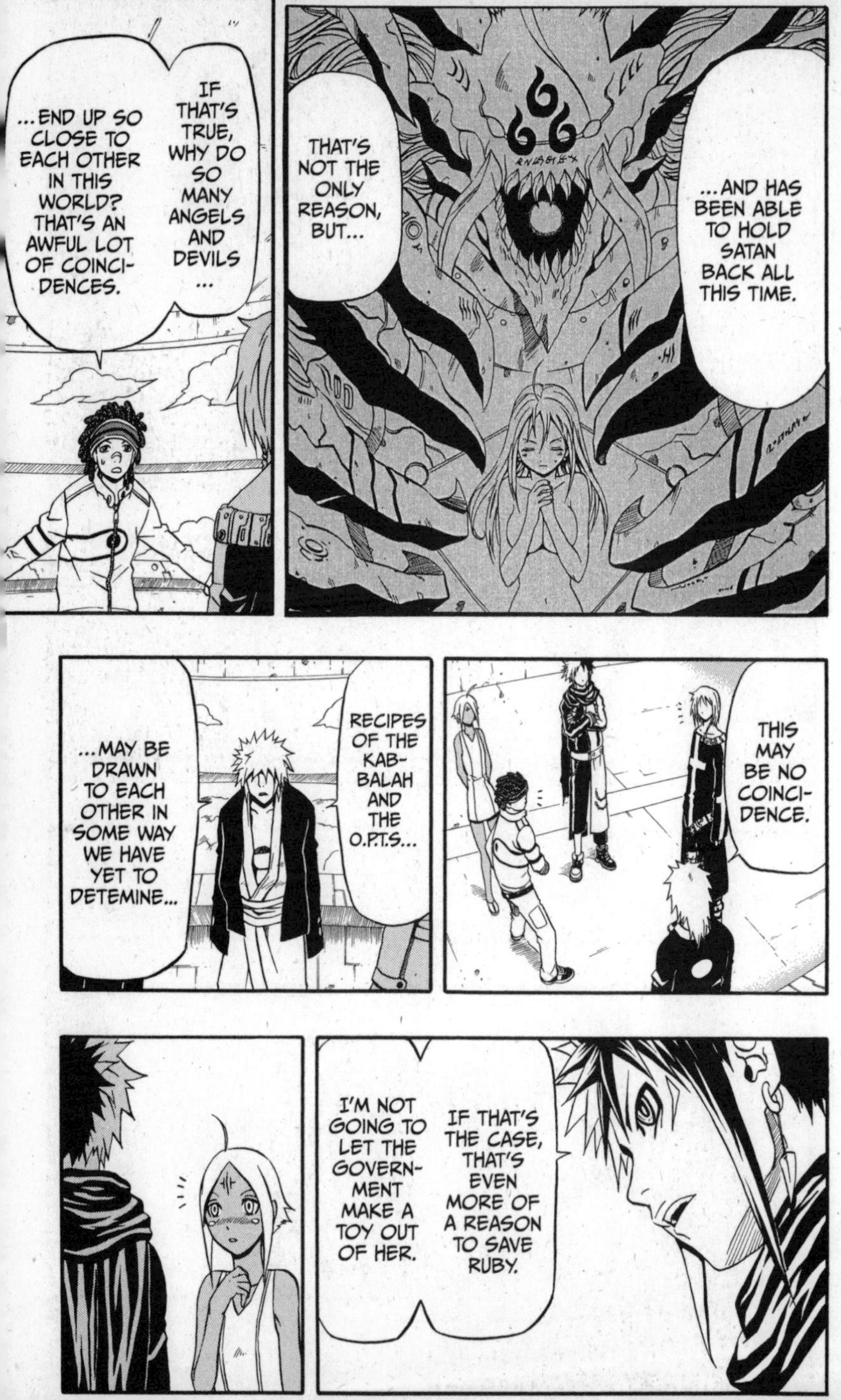

...AND HAS BEEN ABLE TO HOLD SATAN BACK ALL THIS TIME.
THAT'S NOT THE ONLY REASON, BUT...
IF THAT'S TRUE, WHY DO SO MANY ANGELS AND DEVILS...
...END UP SO CLOSE TO EACH OTHER IN THIS WORLD? THAT'S AN AWFUL LOT OF COINCIDENCES.
THIS MAY BE NO COINCIDENCE.
RECIPES OF THE KABBALAH AND THE O.P.T.S...
...MAY BE DRAWN TO EACH OTHER IN SOME WAY WE HAVE YET TO DETEMINE...
IF THAT'S THE CASE, THAT'S EVEN MORE OF A REASON TO SAVE RUBY.
I'M NOT GOING TO LET THE GOVERNMENT MAKE A TOY OUT OF HER.

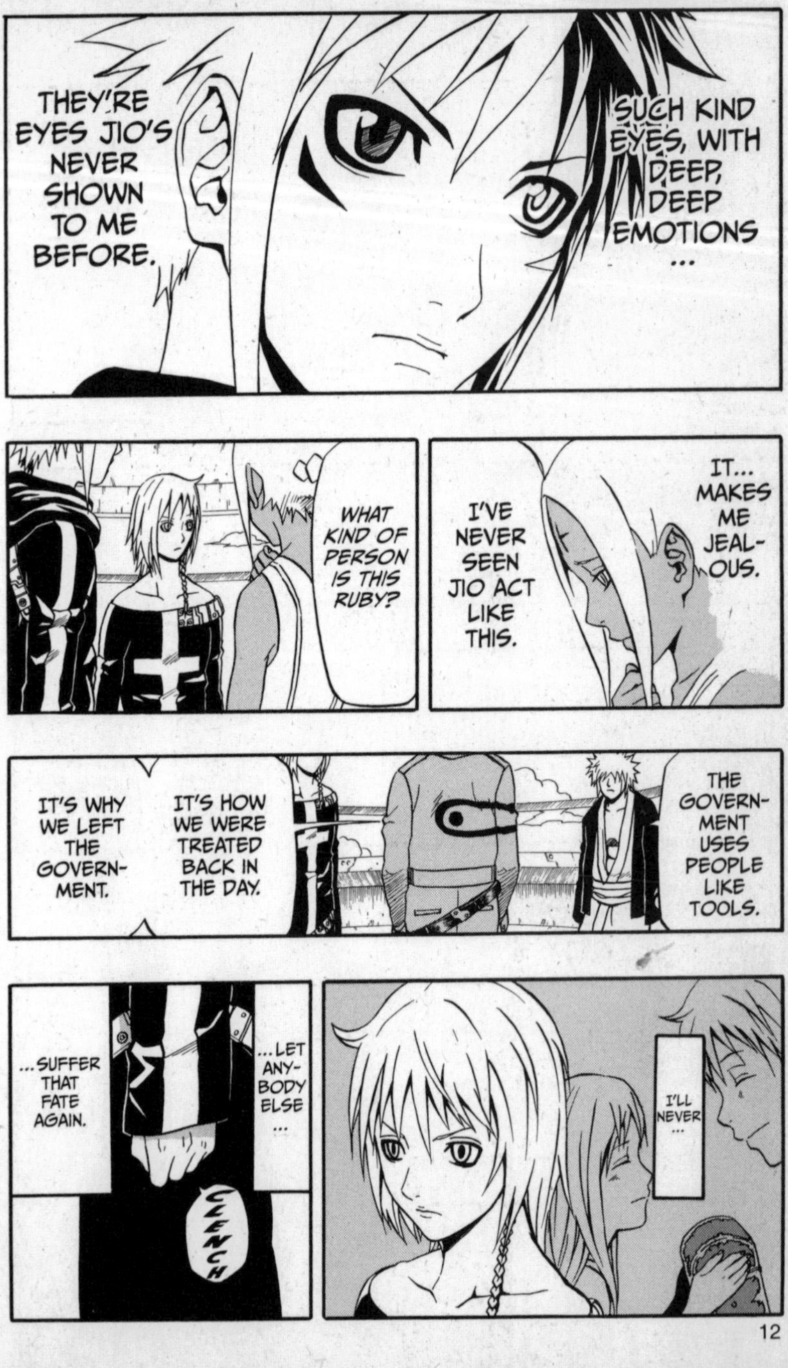
SUCH KIND EYES, WITH DEEP, DEEP EMOTIONS ...
THEY'RE EYES JIO'S NEVER SHOWN TO ME BEFORE.
IT... MAKES ME JEAL-OUS.
I'VE NEVER SEEN JIO ACT LIKE THIS.
WHAT KIND OF PERSON IS THIS RUBY?
THE GOVERN-MENT USES PEOPLE LIKE TOOLS.
IT'S HOW WE WERE TREATED BACK IN THE DAY.
IT'S WHY WE LEFT THE GOVERN-MENT.
I'LL NEVER ...
...LET ANY-BODY ELSE ...
...SUFFER THAT FATE AGAIN.
CLENCH

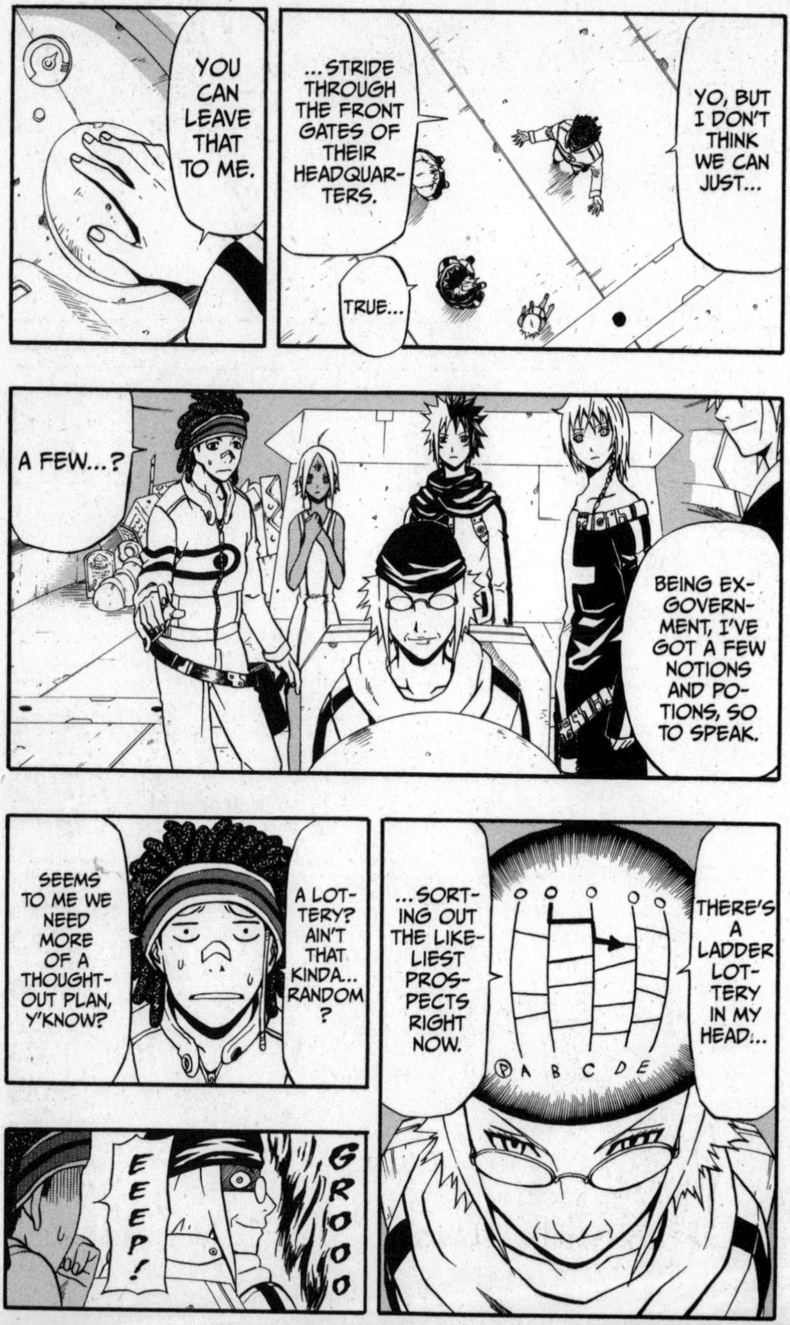
YO, BUT I DON'T THINK WE CAN JUST...
...STRIDE THROUGH THE FRONT GATES OF THEIR HEADQUARTERS.
TRUE...
YOU CAN LEAVE THAT TO ME.
BEING EX-GOVERNMENT, I'VE GOT A FEW NOTIONS AND POTIONS, SO TO SPEAK.
A FEW...?
THERE'S A LADDER LOTTERY IN MY HEAD...
...SORTING OUT THE LIKELIEST PROSPECTS RIGHT NOW.
P A B C D E
A LOTTERY? AIN'T THAT KINDA... RANDOM?
SEEMS TO ME WE NEED MORE OF A THOUGHT-OUT PLAN, Y'KNOW?
GROOOO
EEEEP!

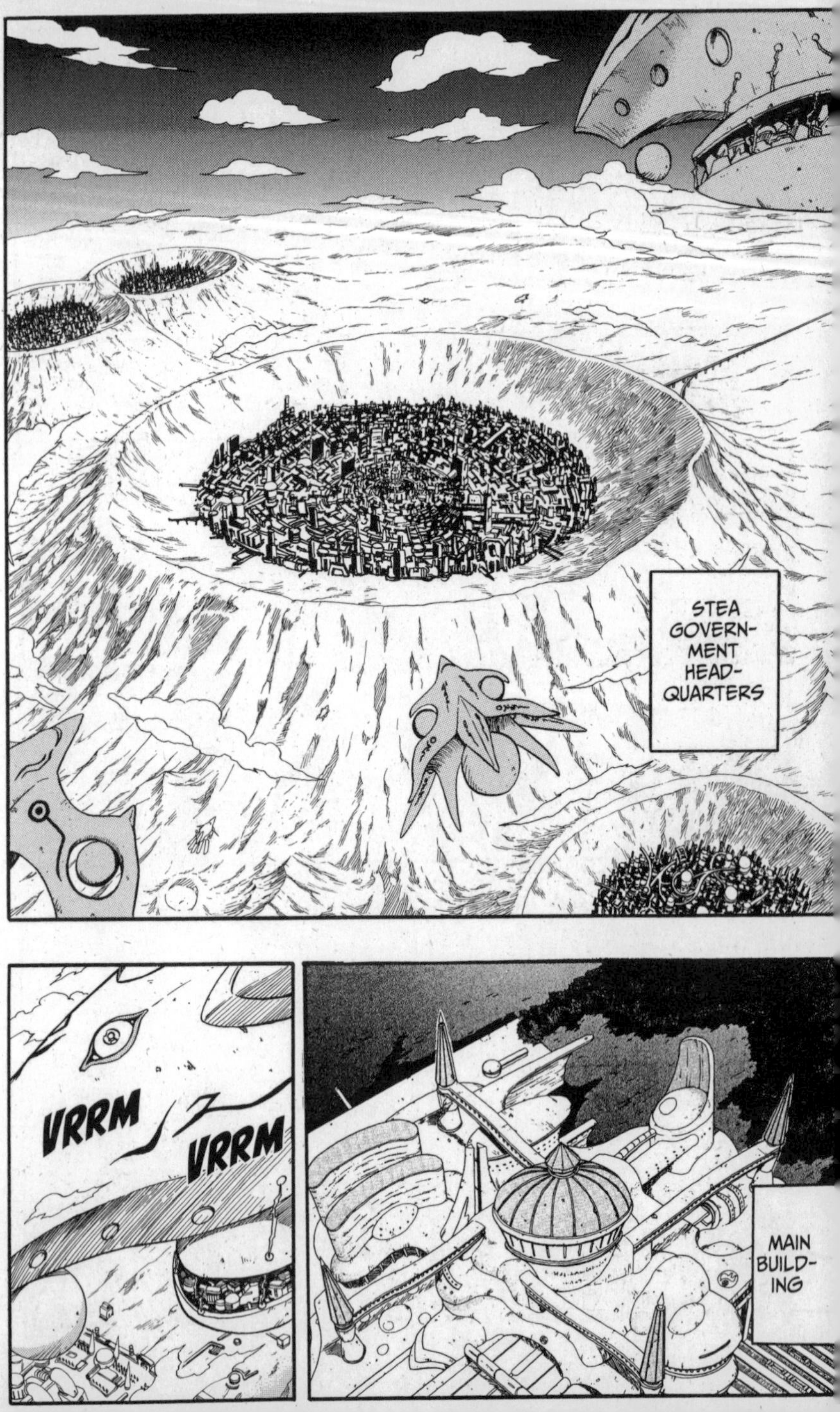
STEA GOVERNMENT HEADQUARTERS
MAIN BUILDING
VRRM
VRRM

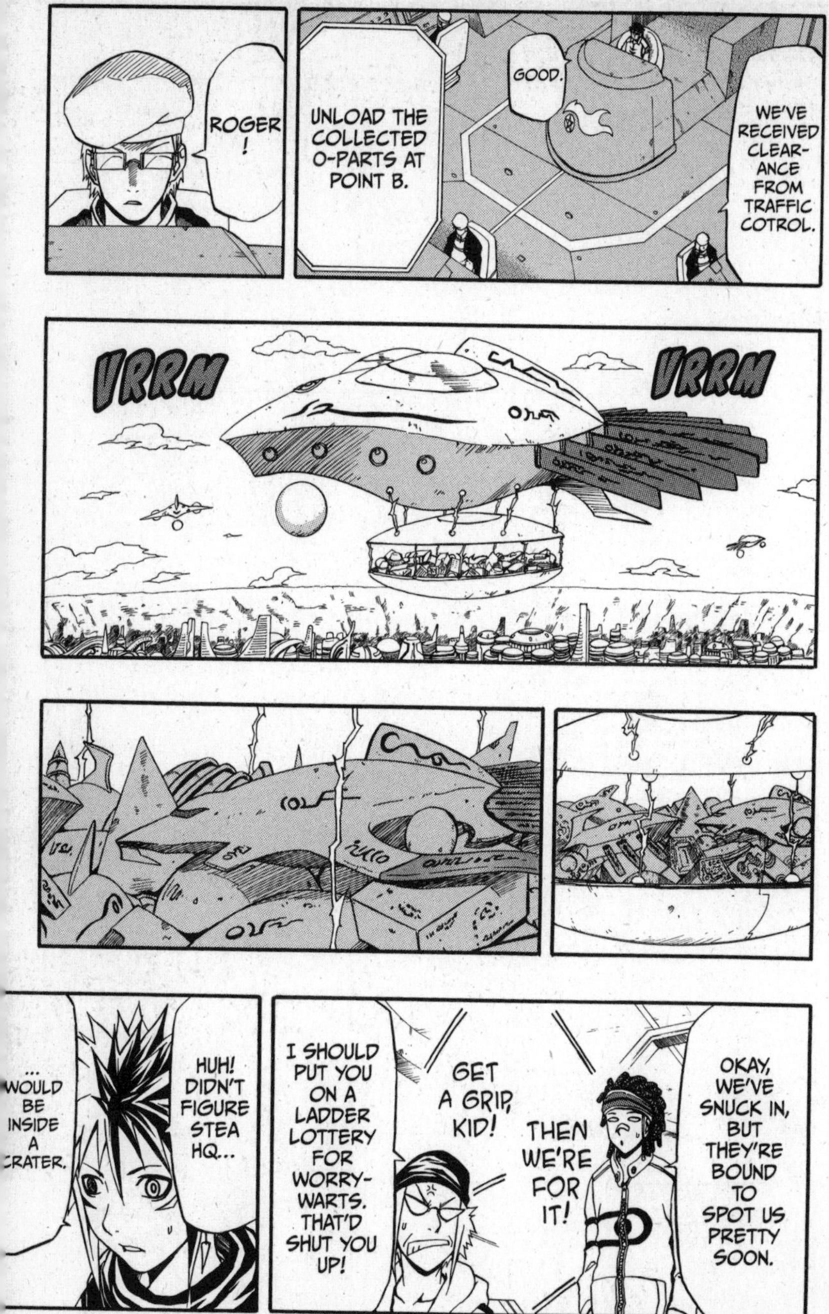
WE'VE RECEIVED CLEARANCE FROM TRAFFIC COTROL.
GOOD.
UNLOAD THE COLLECTED O-PARTS AT POINT B.
ROGER!
VRRM
VRRM
OKAY, WE'VE SNUCK IN, BUT THEY'RE BOUND TO SPOT US PRETTY SOON.
THEN WE'RE FOR IT!
GET A GRIP, KID!
I SHOULD PUT YOU ON A LADDER LOTTERY FOR WORRY-WARTS. THAT'D SHUT YOU UP!
HUH! DIDN'T FIGURE STEA HQ...
...WOULD BE INSIDE A CRATER.

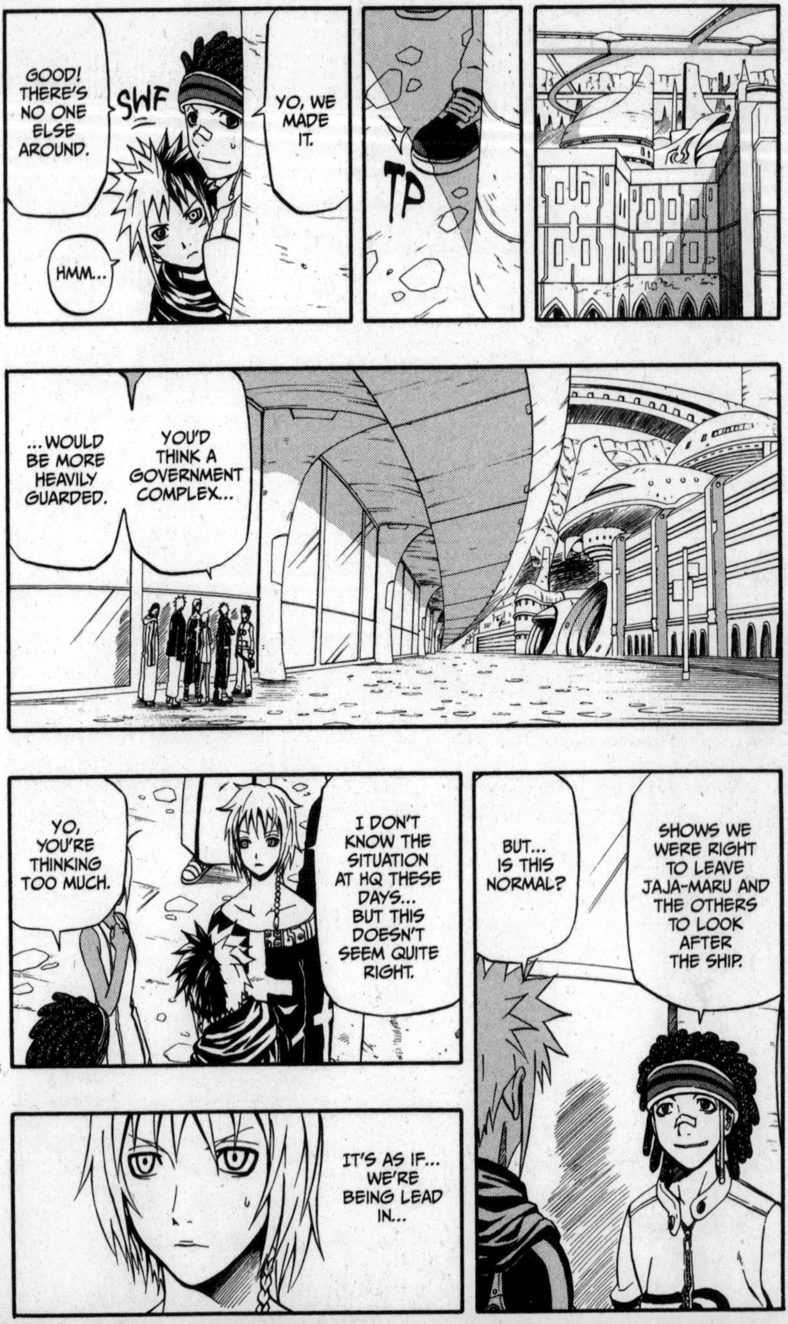
TP
YO, WE MADE IT.
SWF
GOOD! THERE'S NO ONE ELSE AROUND.
HMM...
YOU'D THINK A GOVERNMENT COMPLEX...
...WOULD BE MORE HEAVILY GUARDED.
SHOWS WE WERE RIGHT TO LEAVE JAJA-MARU AND THE OTHERS TO LOOK AFTER THE SHIP.
BUT... IS THIS NORMAL?
I DON'T KNOW THE SITUATION AT HQ THESE DAYS... BUT THIS DOESN'T SEEM QUITE RIGHT.
YO, YOU'RE THINKING TOO MUCH.
IT'S AS IF... WE'RE BEING LEAD IN...

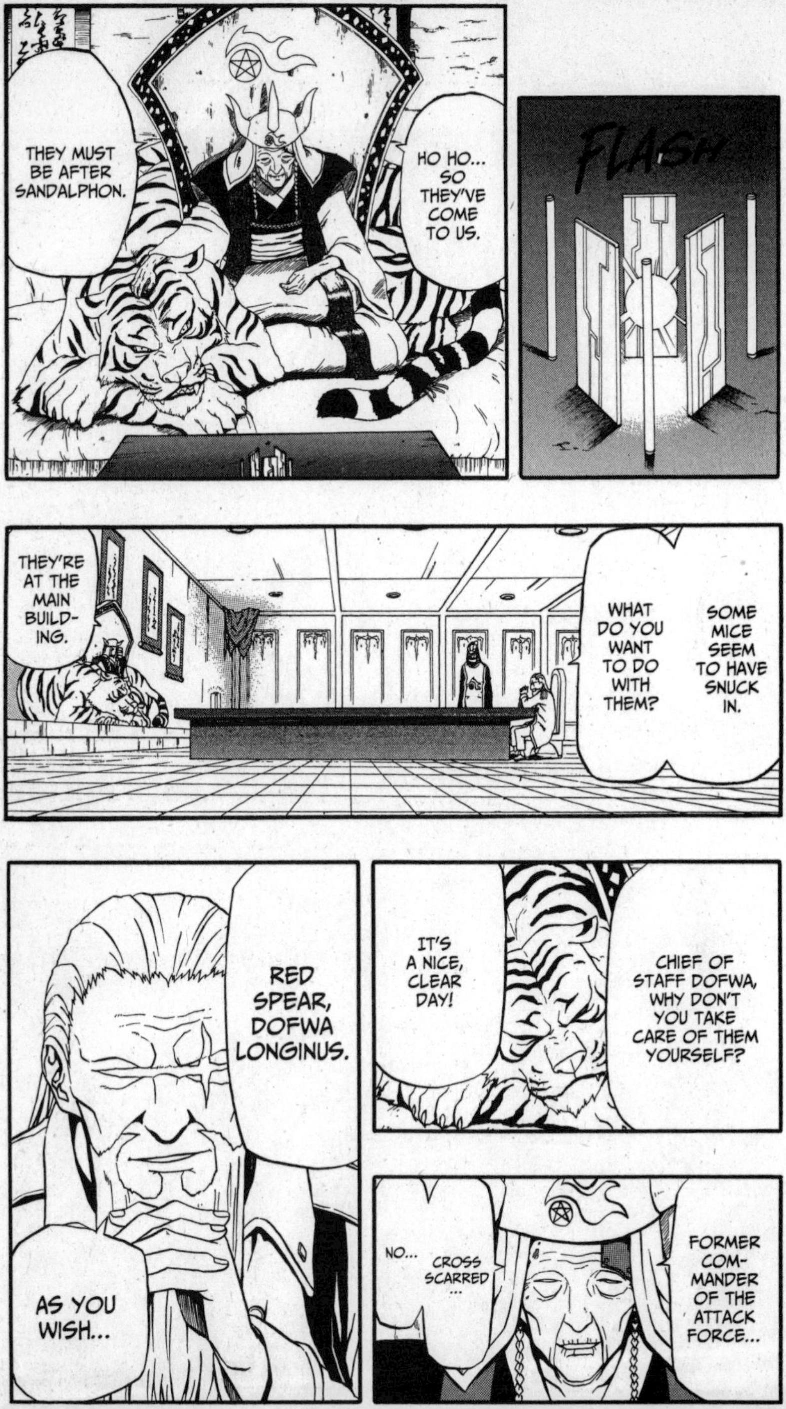
FLASH
HO HO... SO THEY'VE COME TO US.
THEY MUST BE AFTER SANDALPHON.
SOME MICE SEEM TO HAVE SNUCK IN.
WHAT DO YOU WANT TO DO WITH THEM?
THEY'RE AT THE MAIN BUILDING.
CHIEF OF STAFF DOFWA, WHY DON'T YOU TAKE CARE OF THEM YOURSELF?
IT'S A NICE, CLEAR DAY!
FORMER COMMANDER OF THE ATTACK FORCE...
CROSS SCARRED...
NO...
RED SPEAR, DOFWA LONGINUS.
AS YOU WISH...

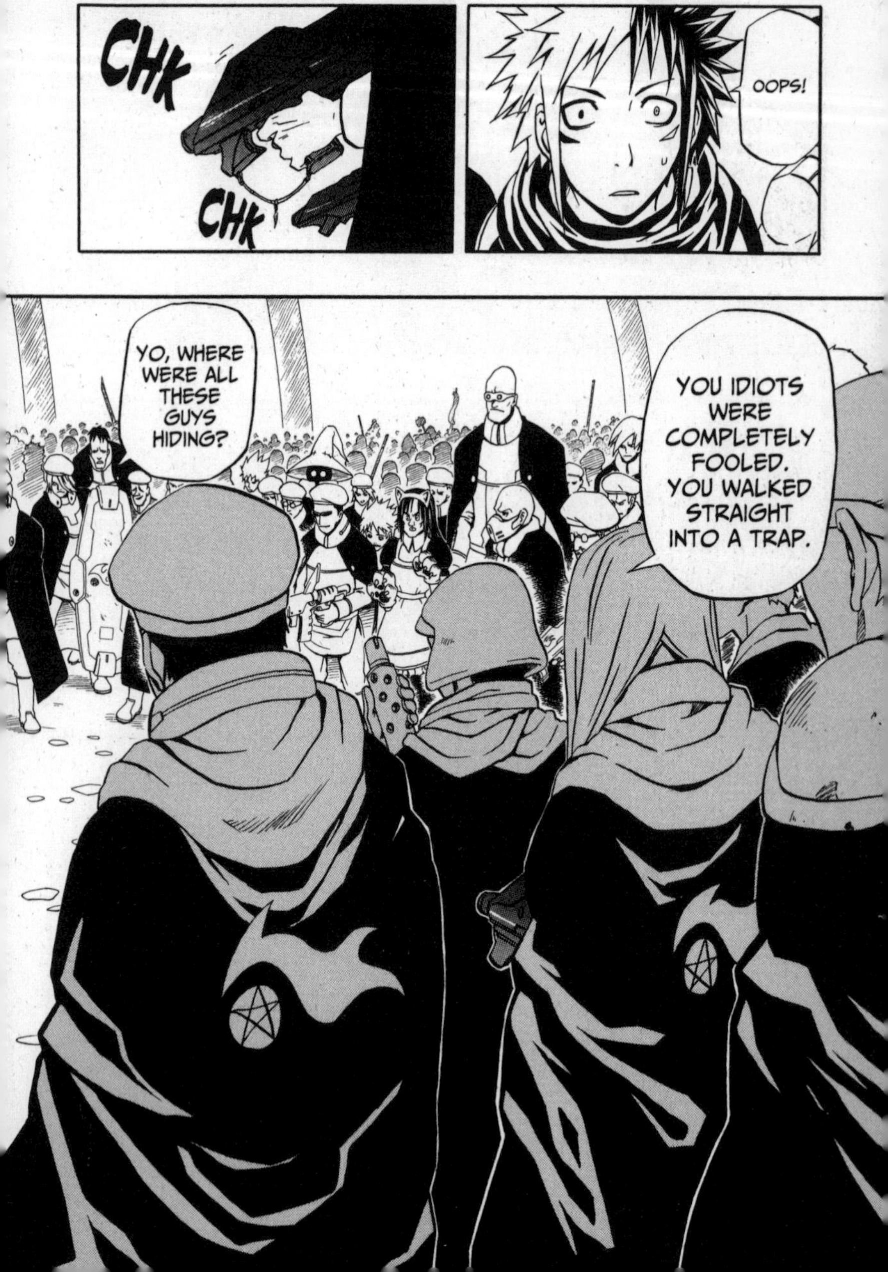
OOPS!
CHK
CHK
YOU IDIOTS WERE COMPLETELY FOOLED. YOU WALKED STRAIGHT INTO A TRAP.
YO, WHERE WERE ALL THESE GUYS HIDING?

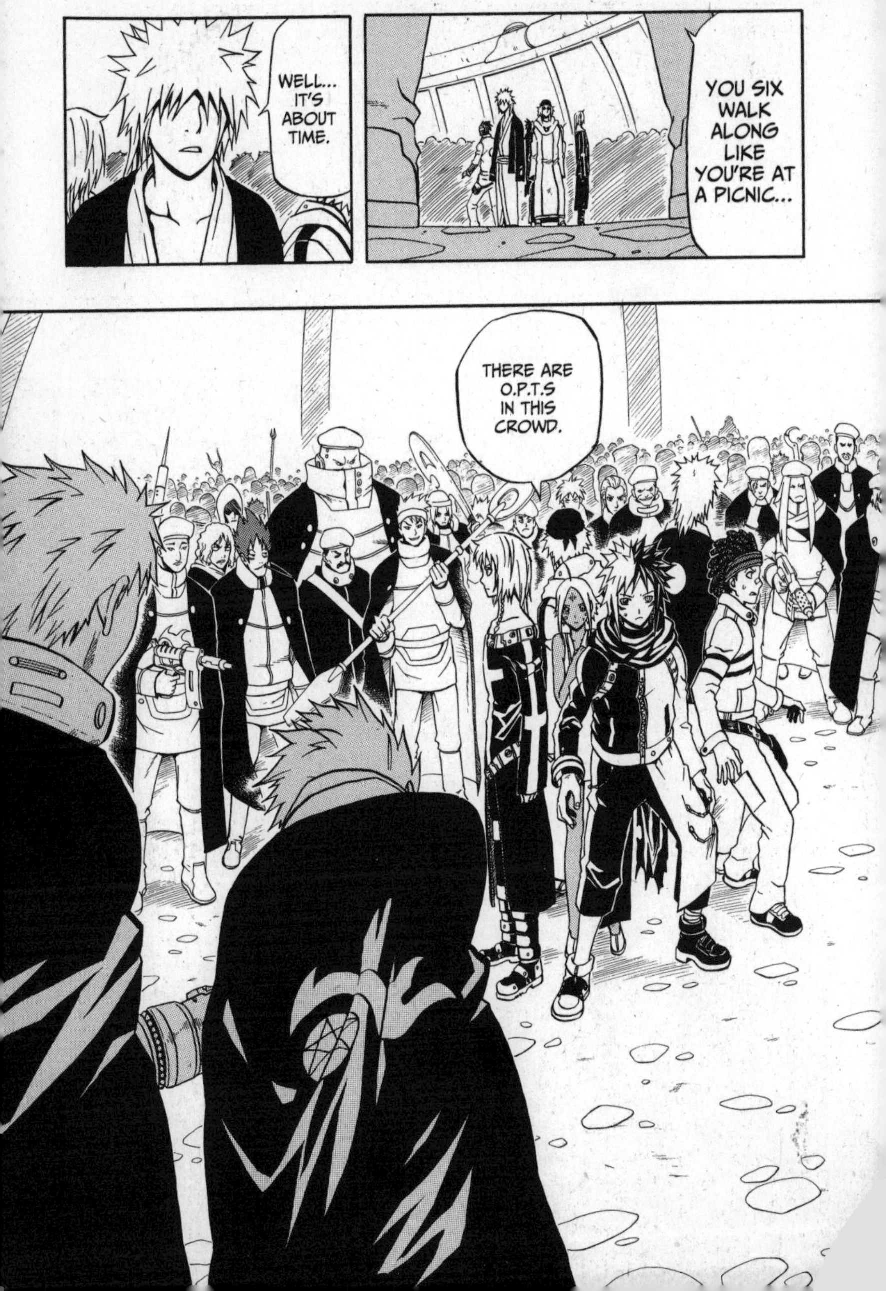
YOU SIX WALK ALONG LIKE YOU'RE AT A PICNIC...
WELL... IT'S ABOUT TIME.
THERE ARE O.P.T.S IN THIS CROWD.

AMIDABA AND I WILL DUCK OUT NOW. WE NEED TO MOVE ABOUT IN SECRECY.

YOU GO AHEAD AND TAKE CARE OF THESE GUYS.

HUH?

DON'T YOU NEED CROSS AS A GUIDE?!

WE USED TO WORK HERE, Y'KNOW.

WE KNOW OUR WAY AROUND BETTER THAN YOU MIGHT THINK.

SO YOU YOUNG-'UNS HAVE FUN, Y'HEAR?

ENOUGH OF THIS CRAP!! KILL THEM ALL! EXCEPT THE RECIPE, THAT IS!

GET 'EM!

RAAAAAAAAAH

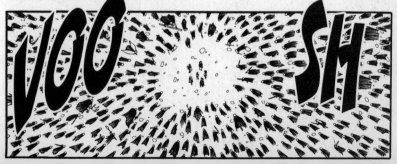

VOOSH

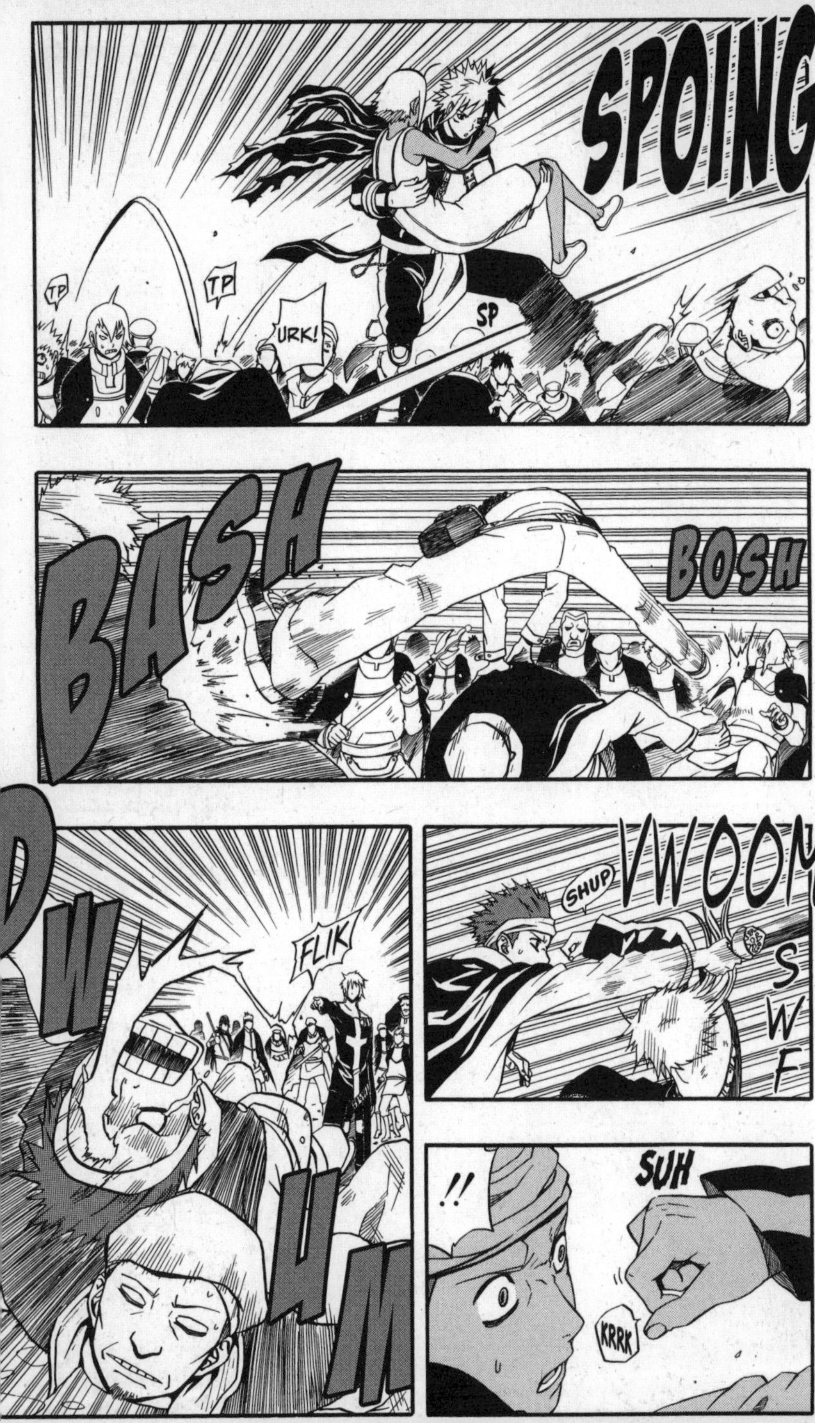
SPOING
SP
URK!
TP
TP
BOSH
BASH
VWOOM
SHUP
SWF
SUH
!!
KRRK
FLIK
DWHM

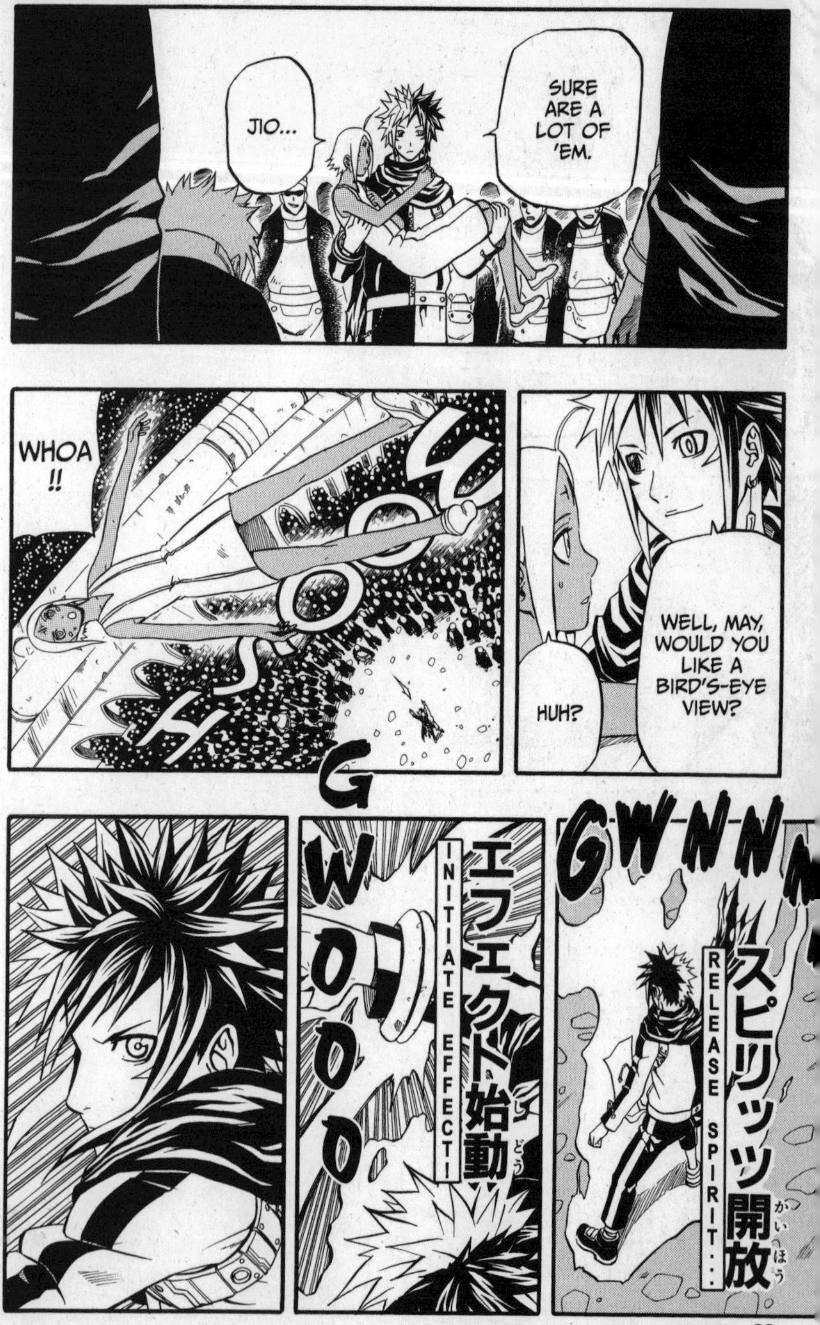
SURE ARE A LOT OF 'EM.
JIO...
WELL, MAY, WOULD YOU LIKE A BIRD'S-EYE VIEW?
HUH?
WOOSH
WHOA!!
GWNNN
スピリッツ開放
RELEASE SPIRIT...
G
WOOOO
エフェクト始動
INITIATE EFFECT!

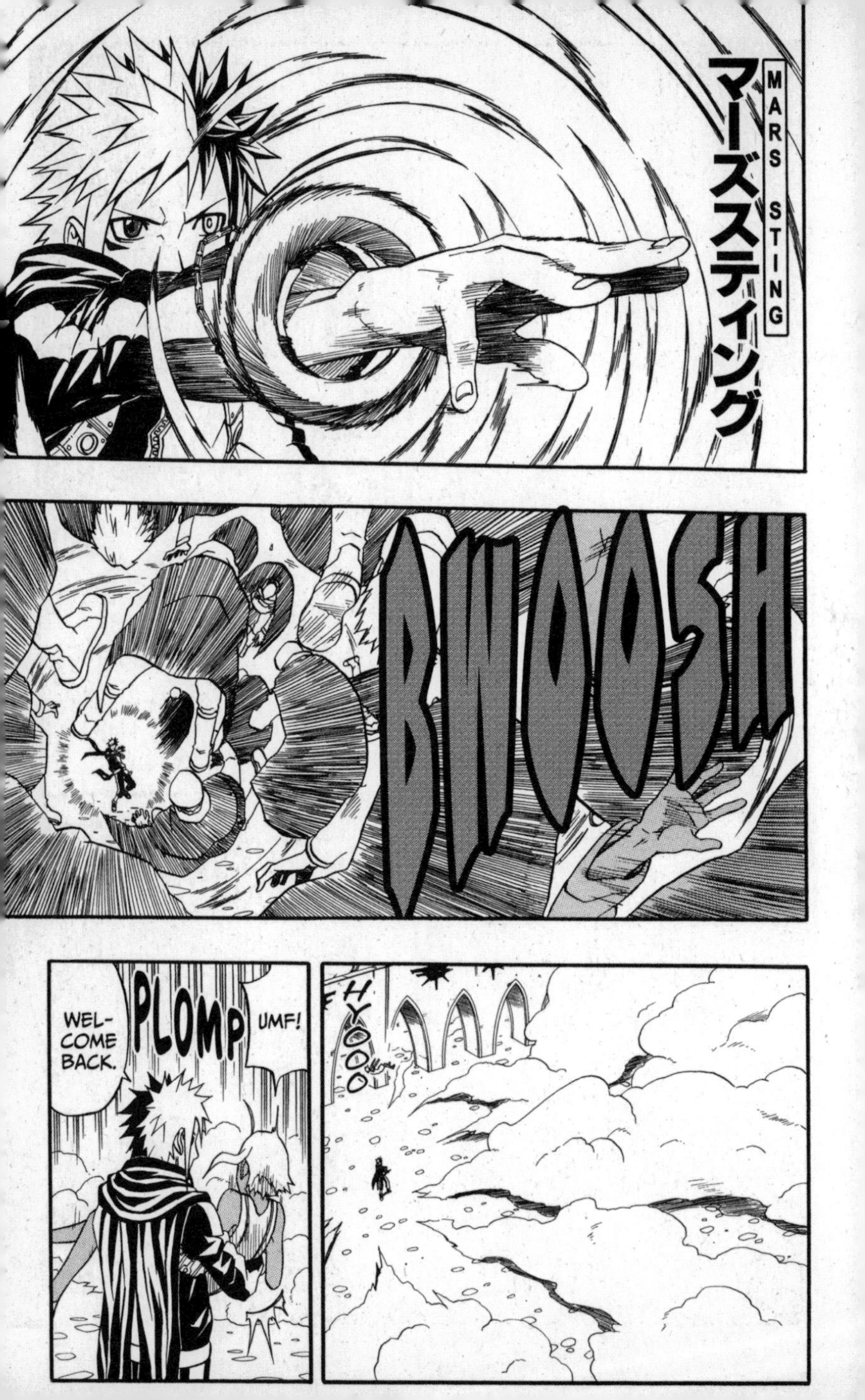
マーズスティング
MARS STING
BWOOSH
HYOOOO
UMF!
PLOMP
WEL-
COME
BACK.

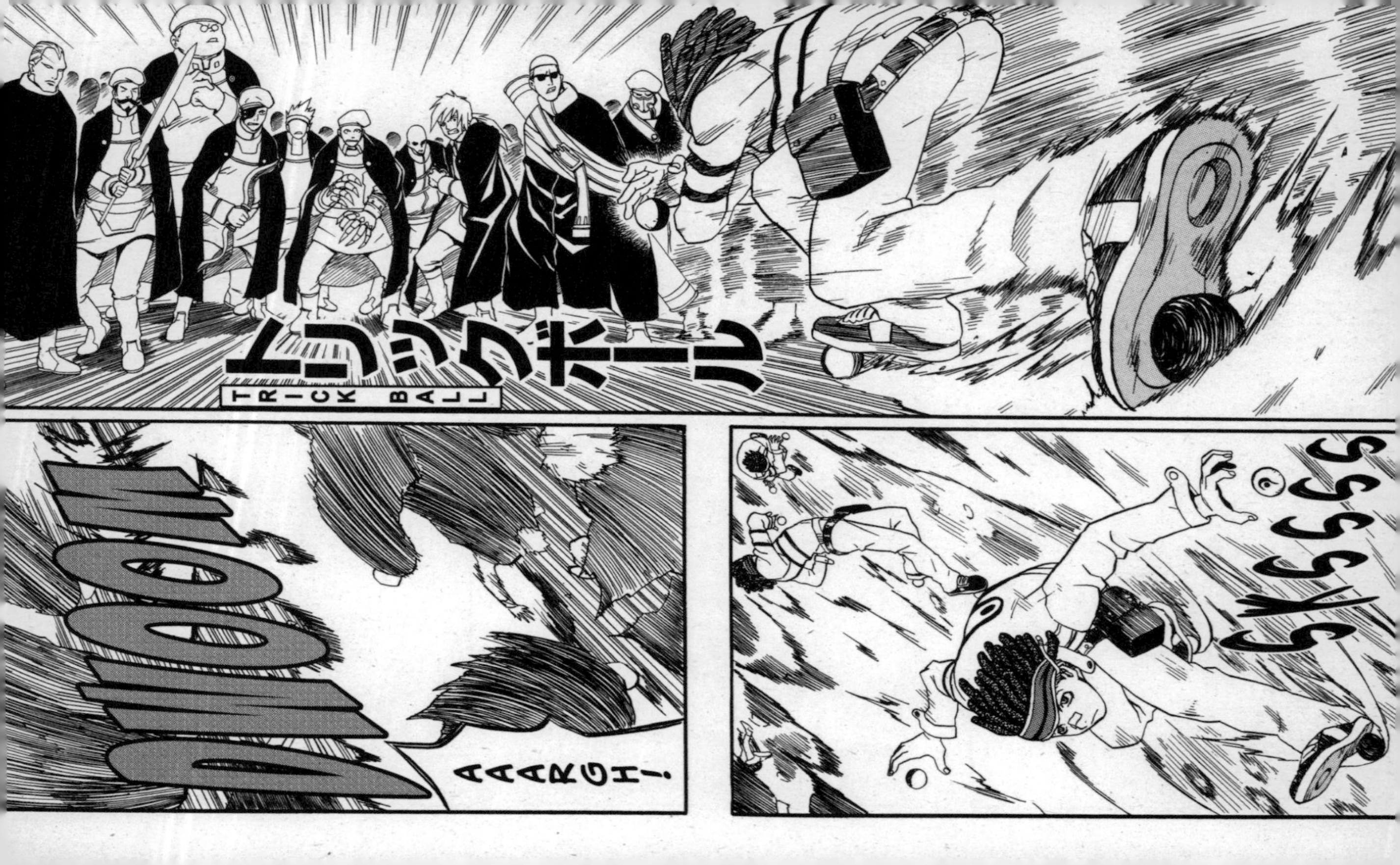
トリックボール
TRICK BALL
SKSSSS
DWOOM
AAARGH!

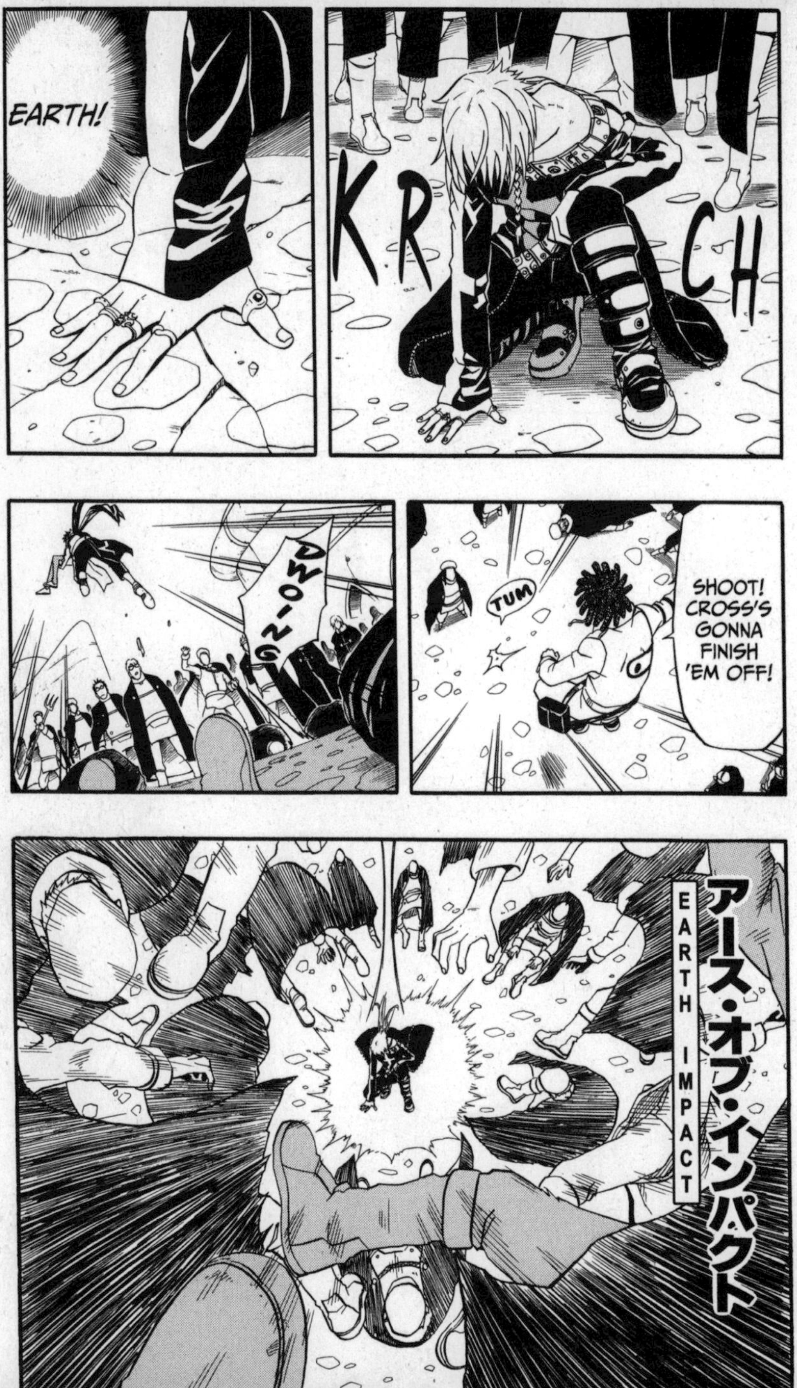
KR
CH
EARTH!
TUM
SHOOT! CROSS'S GONNA FINISH 'EM OFF!
DWO-I-NG
アース・オブ・インパクト
EARTH IMPACT

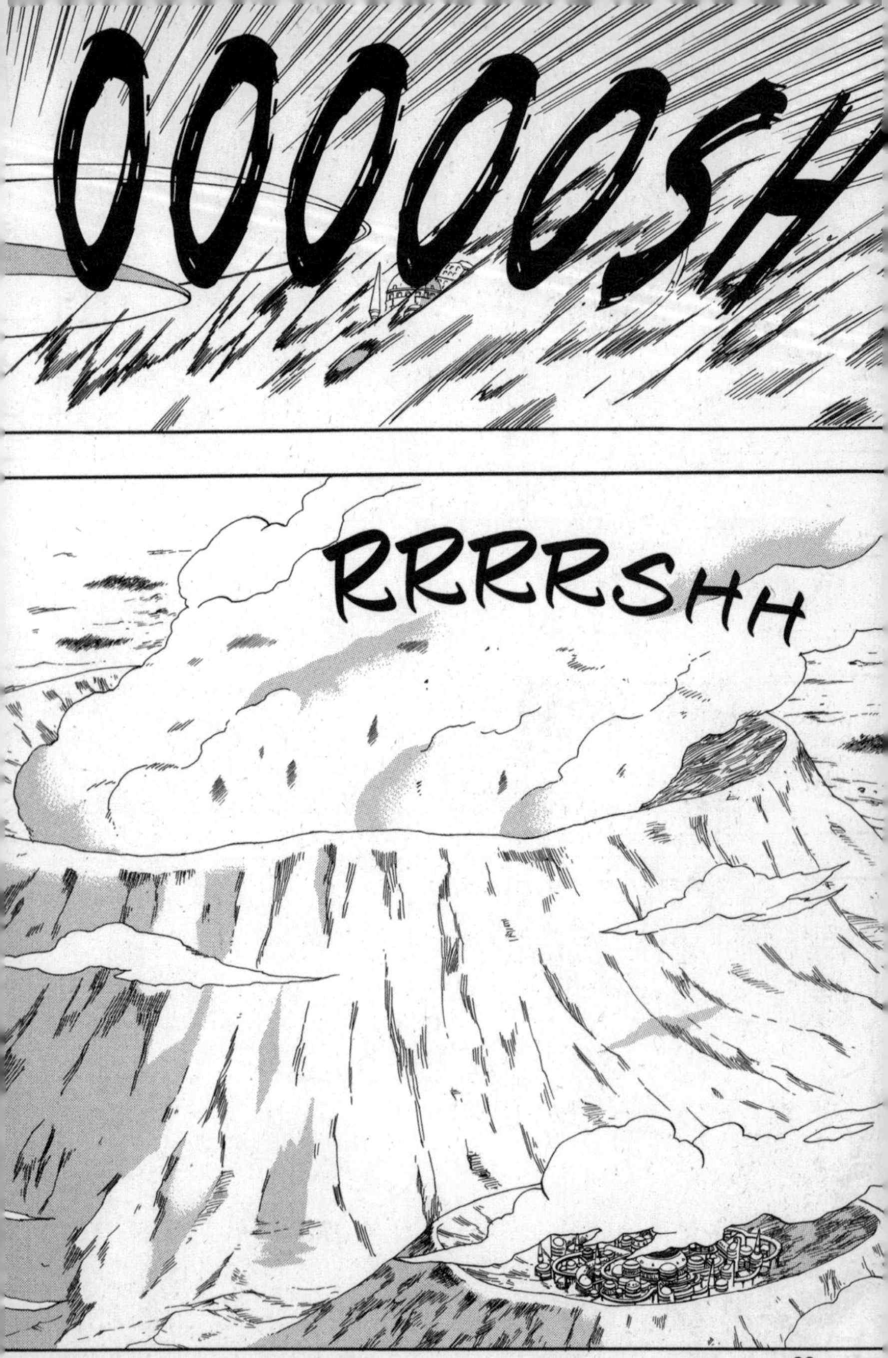
OOOOOSH
RRRRSHH

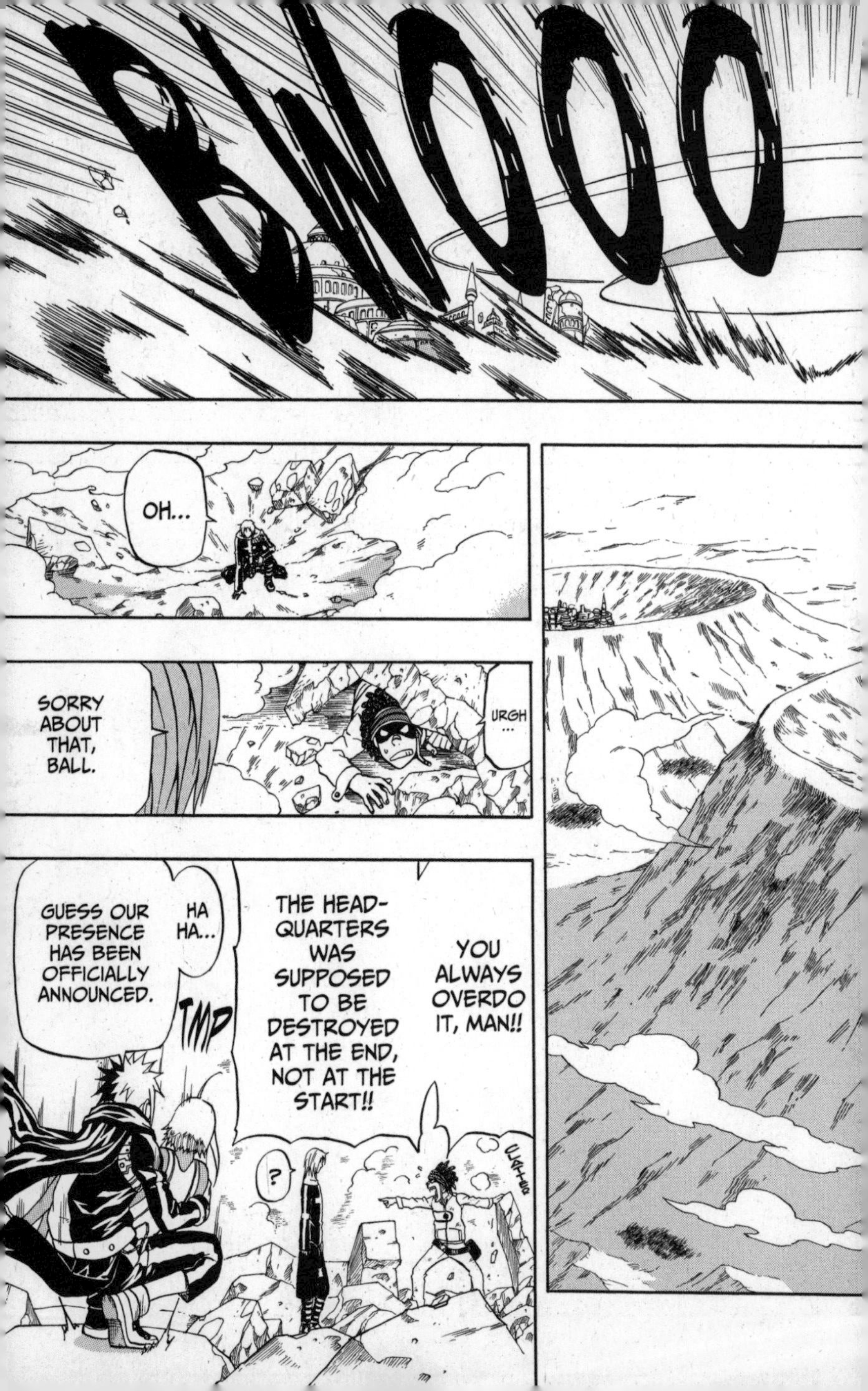
BWOOO
OH...
URGH...
SORRY ABOUT THAT, BALL.
YOU ALWAYS OVERDO IT, MAN!!
THE HEAD-QUARTERS WAS SUPPOSED TO BE DESTROYED AT THE END, NOT AT THE START!!
HA HA...
GUESS OUR PRESENCE HAS BEEN OFFICIALLY ANNOUNCED.
TMP
CLATTER
?

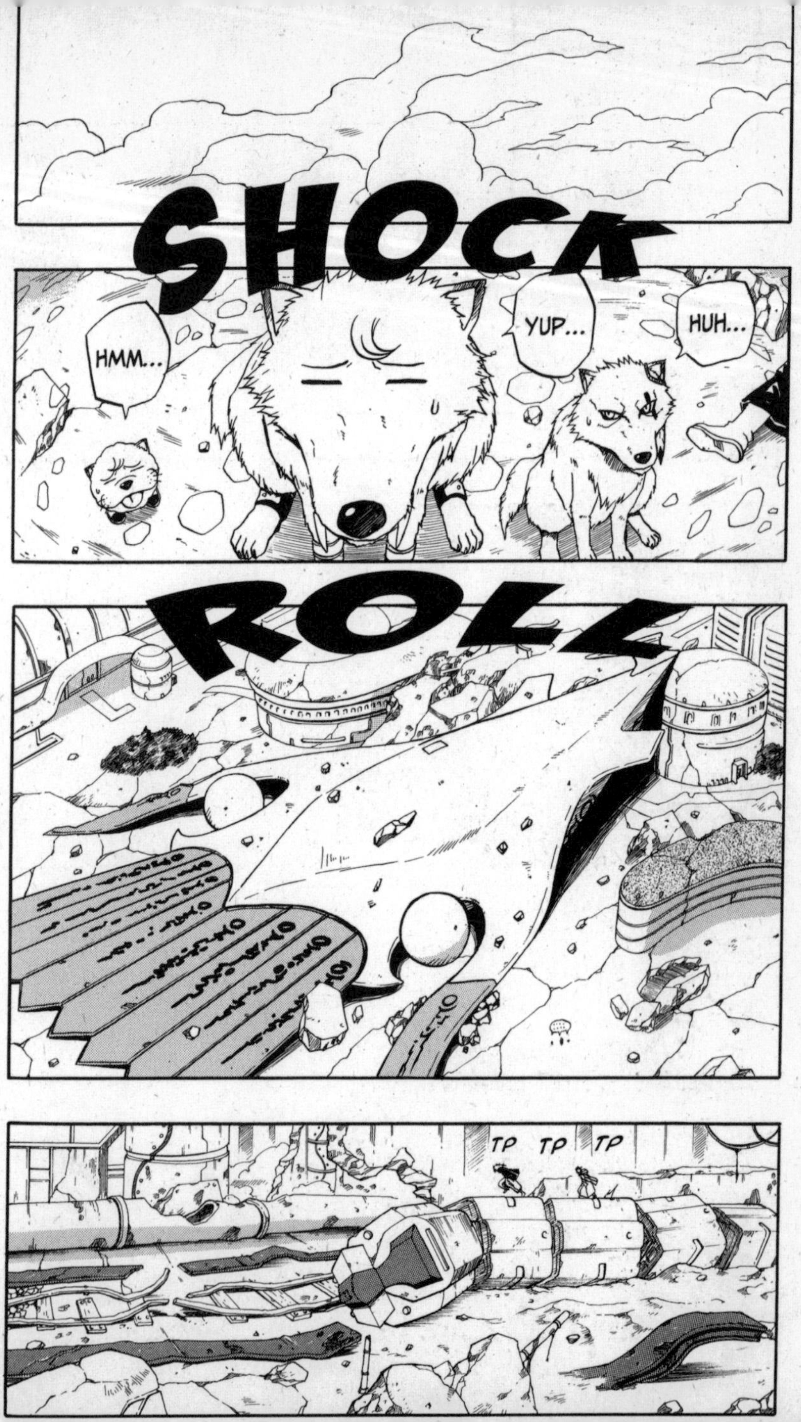
SHOCK
HUH...
YUP...
HMM...
ROLL
TP TP TP

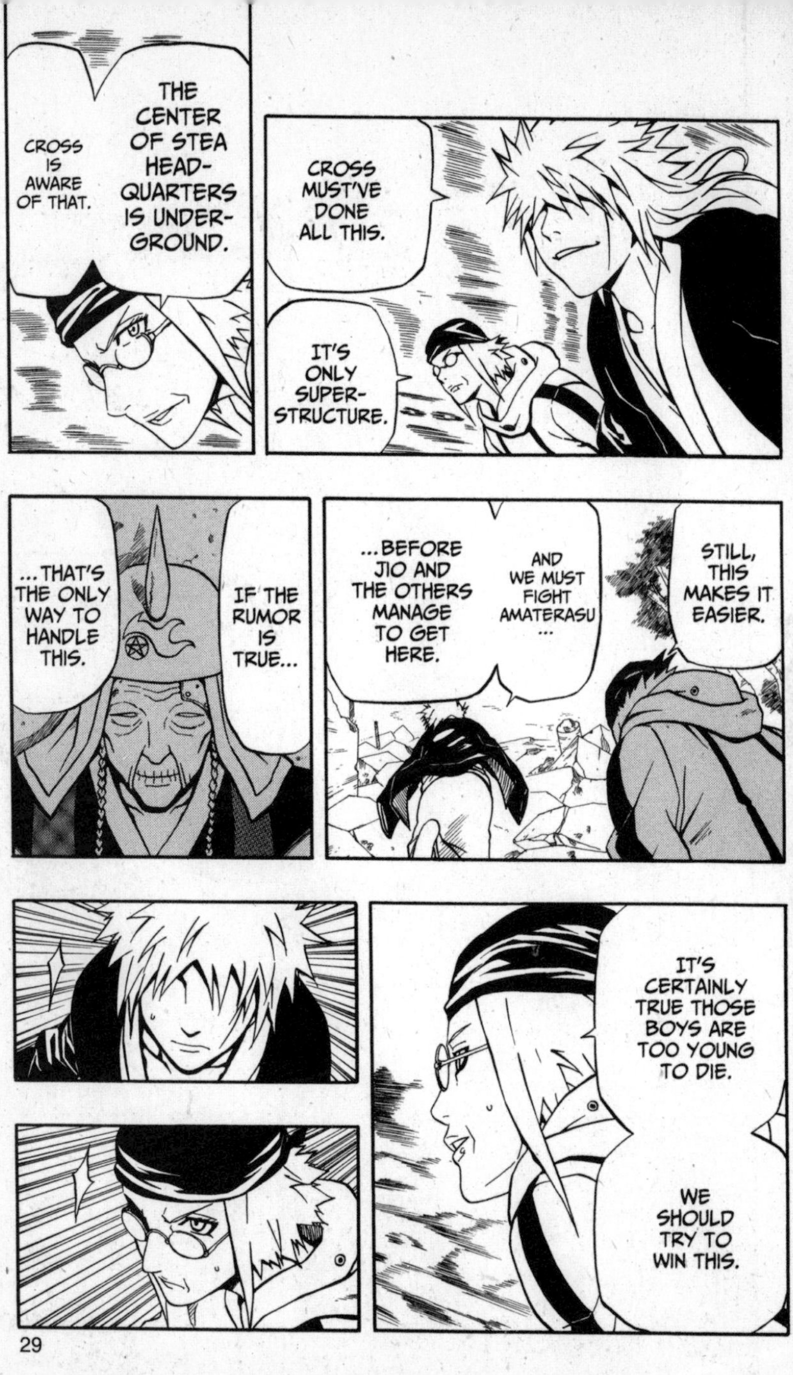
CROSS MUST'VE DONE ALL THIS.
IT'S ONLY SUPER-STRUCTURE.
THE CENTER OF STEA HEAD-QUARTERS IS UNDER-GROUND.
CROSS IS AWARE OF THAT.
STILL, THIS MAKES IT EASIER.
AND WE MUST FIGHT AMATERASU ...
...BEFORE JIO AND THE OTHERS MANAGE TO GET HERE.
IF THE RUMOR IS TRUE...
...THAT'S THE ONLY WAY TO HANDLE THIS.
IT'S CERTAINLY TRUE THOSE BOYS ARE TOO YOUNG TO DIE.
WE SHOULD TRY TO WIN THIS.

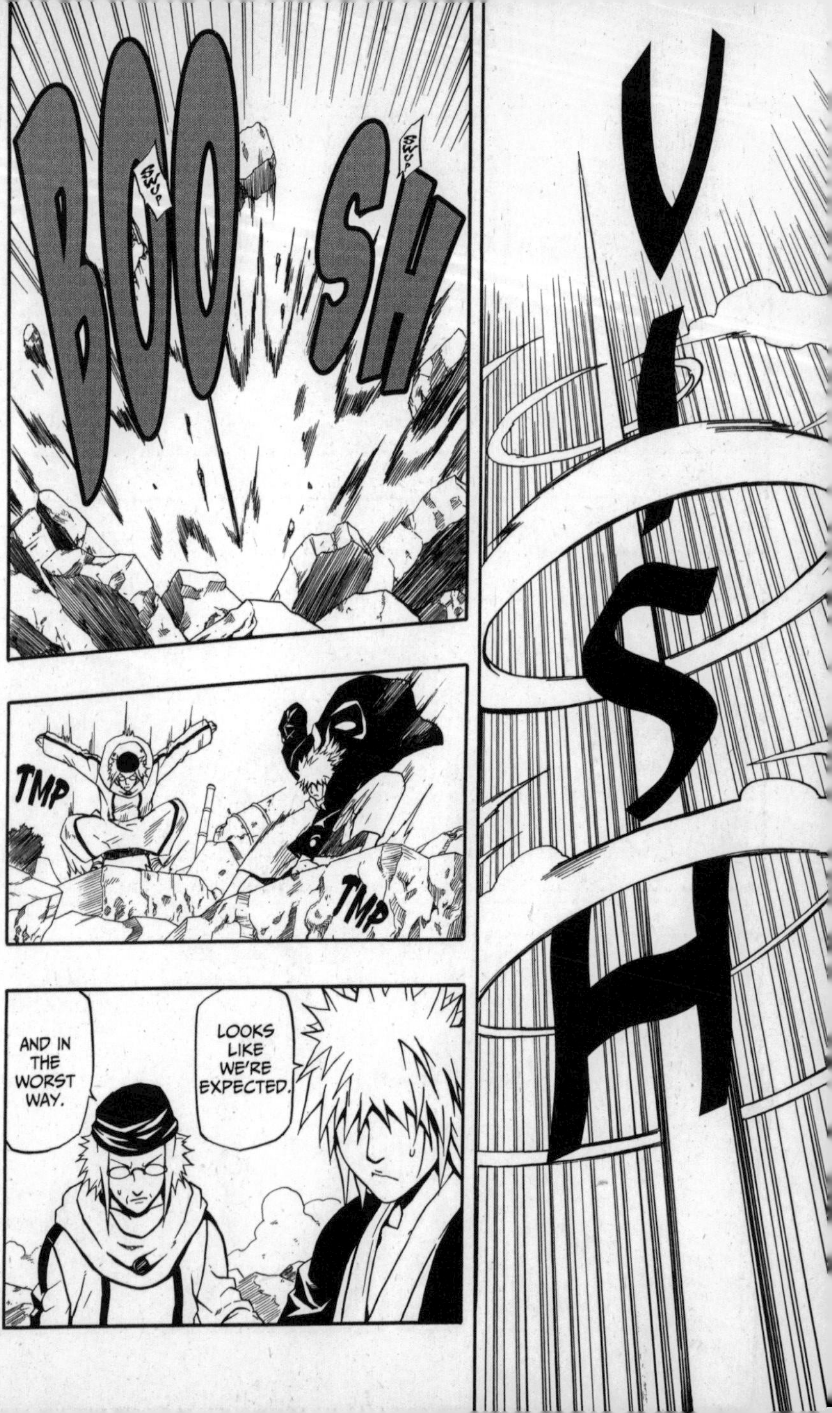

VISH
SWUP
SWUP
BOOSH
TMP
TMP
LOOKS LIKE WE'RE EXPECTED.
AND IN THE WORST WAY.

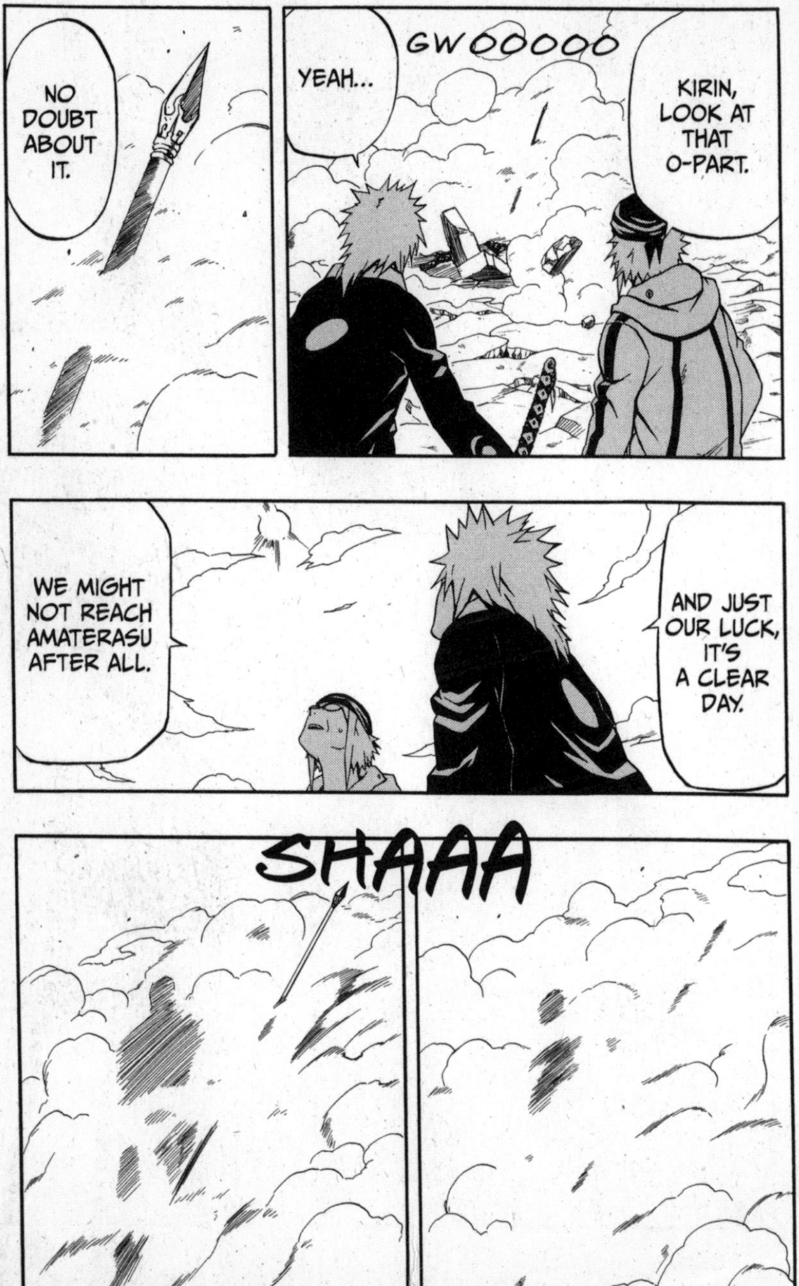
KIRIN, LOOK AT THAT O-PART.
GWOOOOO
YEAH...
NO DOUBT ABOUT IT.
AND JUST OUR LUCK, IT'S A CLEAR DAY.
WE MIGHT NOT REACH AMATERASU AFTER ALL.
SHAAA

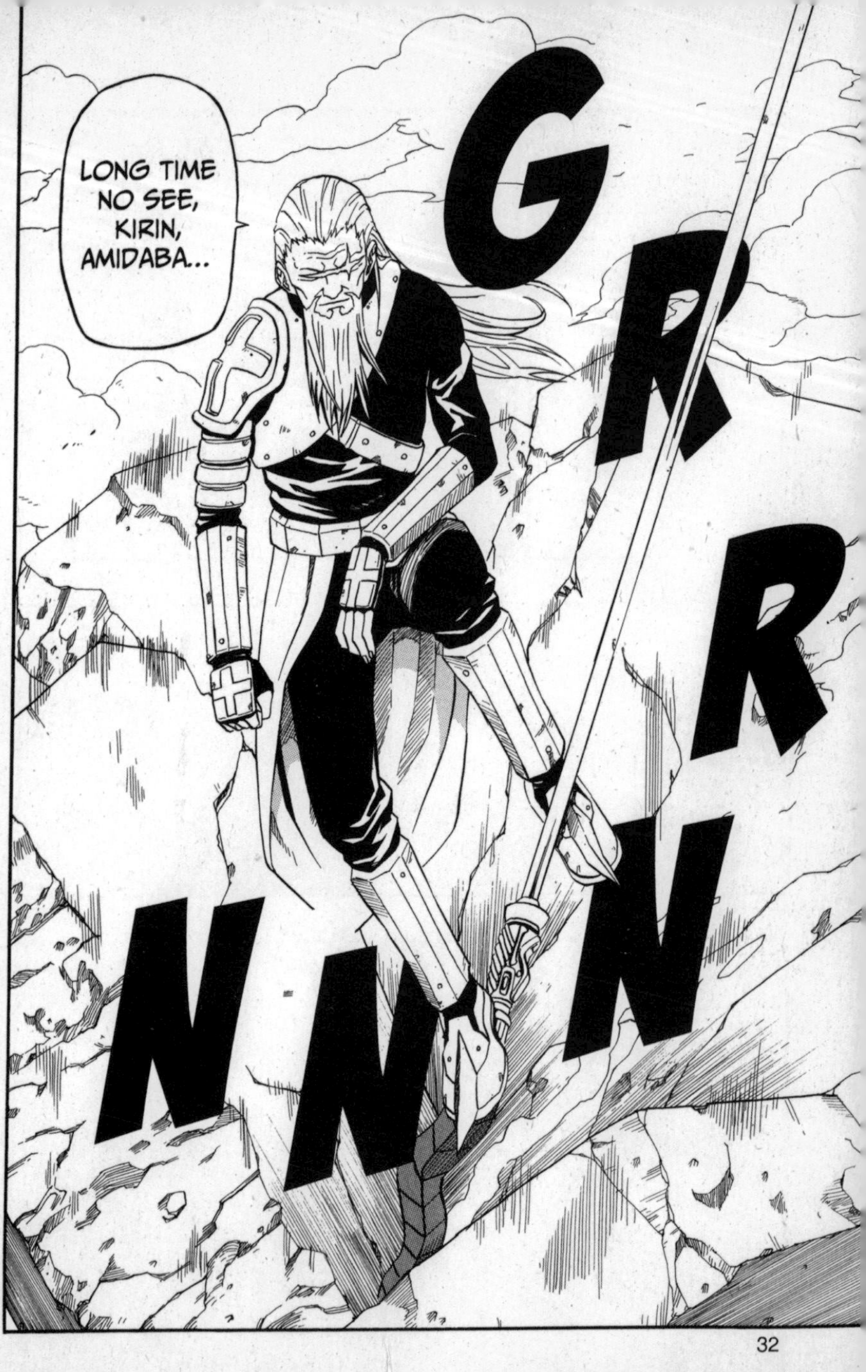
GRRNNN
LONG TIME NO SEE, KIRIN, AMIDABA...

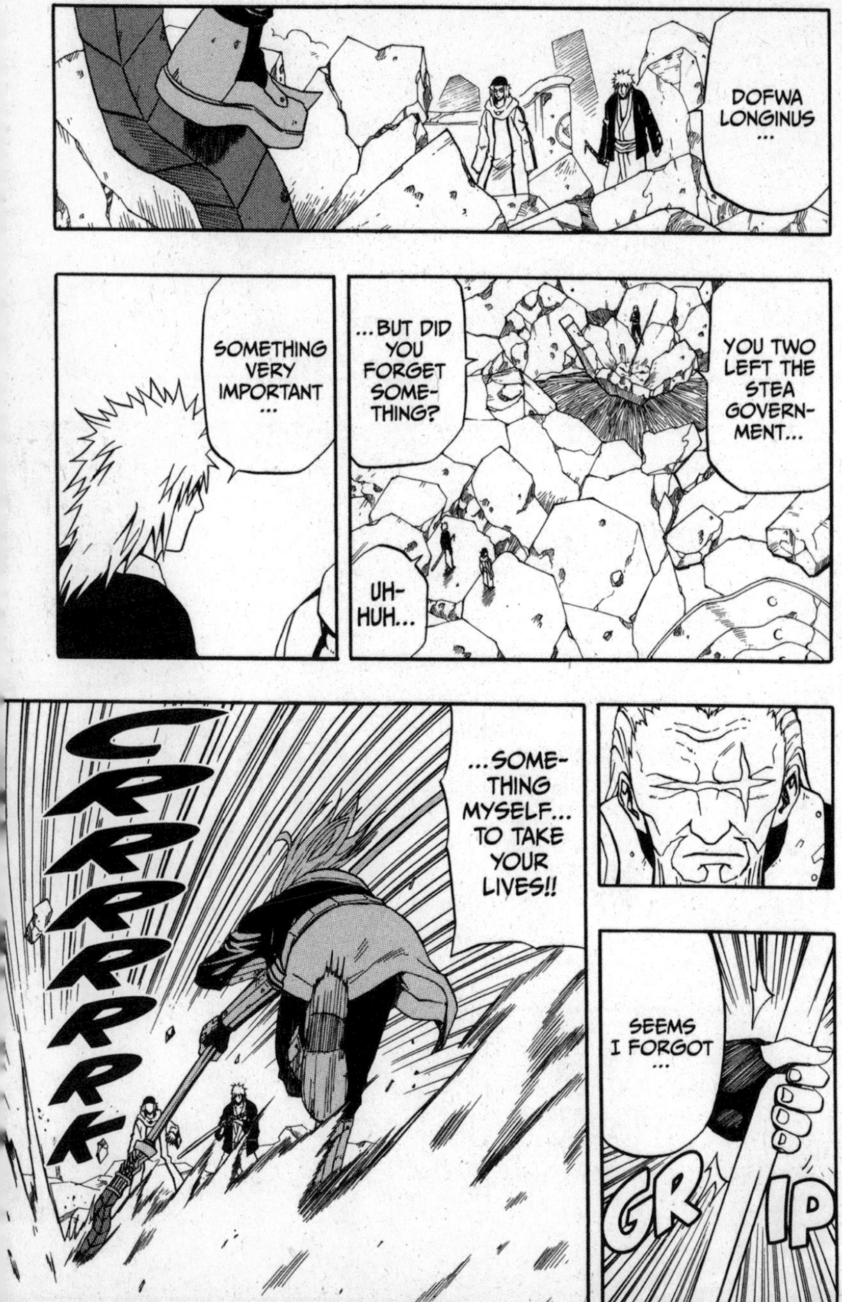
DOFWA LONGINUS ...
YOU TWO LEFT THE STEA GOVERNMENT...
...BUT DID YOU FORGET SOMETHING?
UH-HUH...
SOMETHING VERY IMPORTANT ...
SEEMS I FORGOT ...
GRIP
...SOMETHING MYSELF... TO TAKE YOUR LIVES!!
CRRRRRK

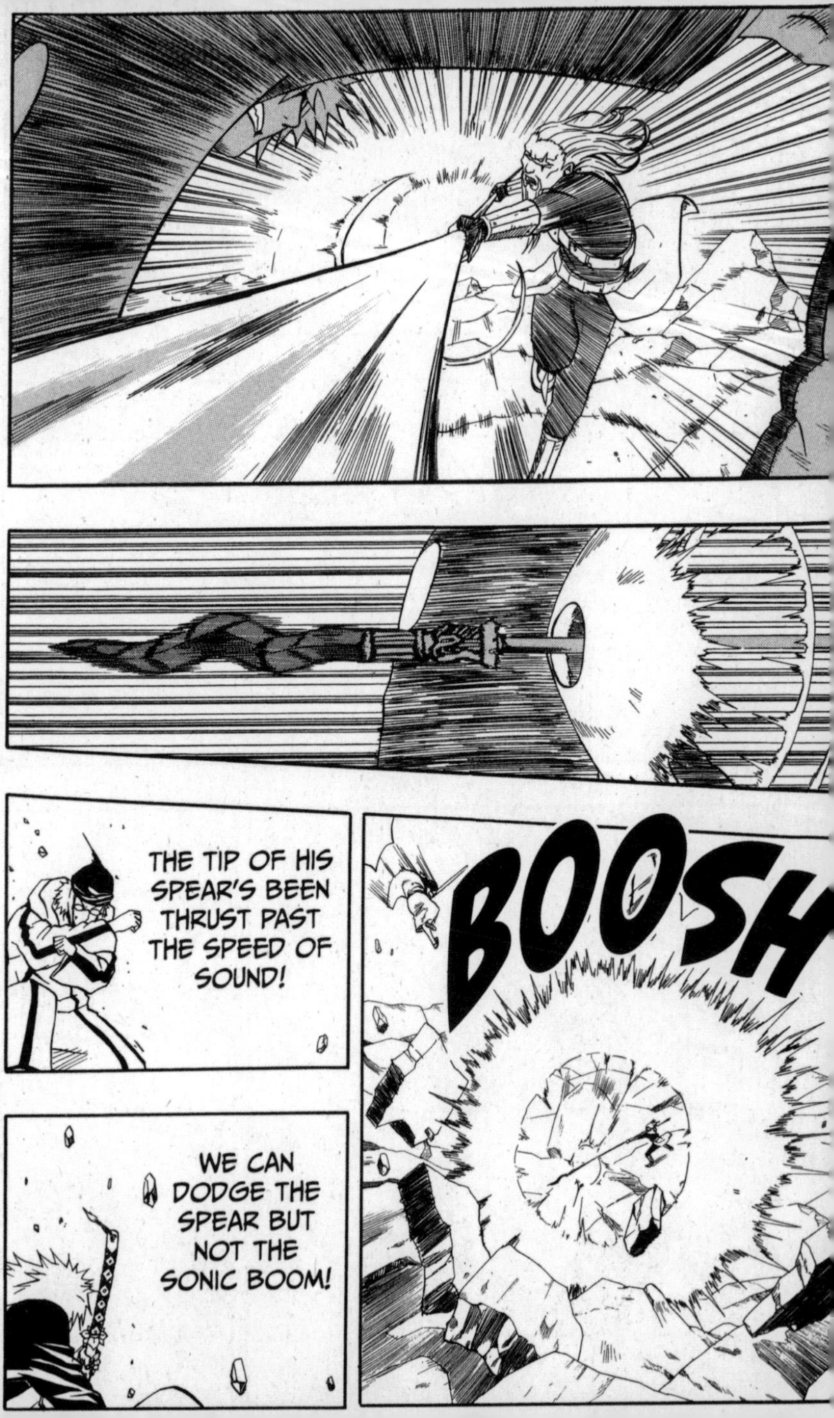
BOOSH
THE TIP OF HIS SPEAR'S BEEN THRUST PAST THE SPEED OF SOUND!
WE CAN DODGE THE SPEAR BUT NOT THE SONIC BOOM!

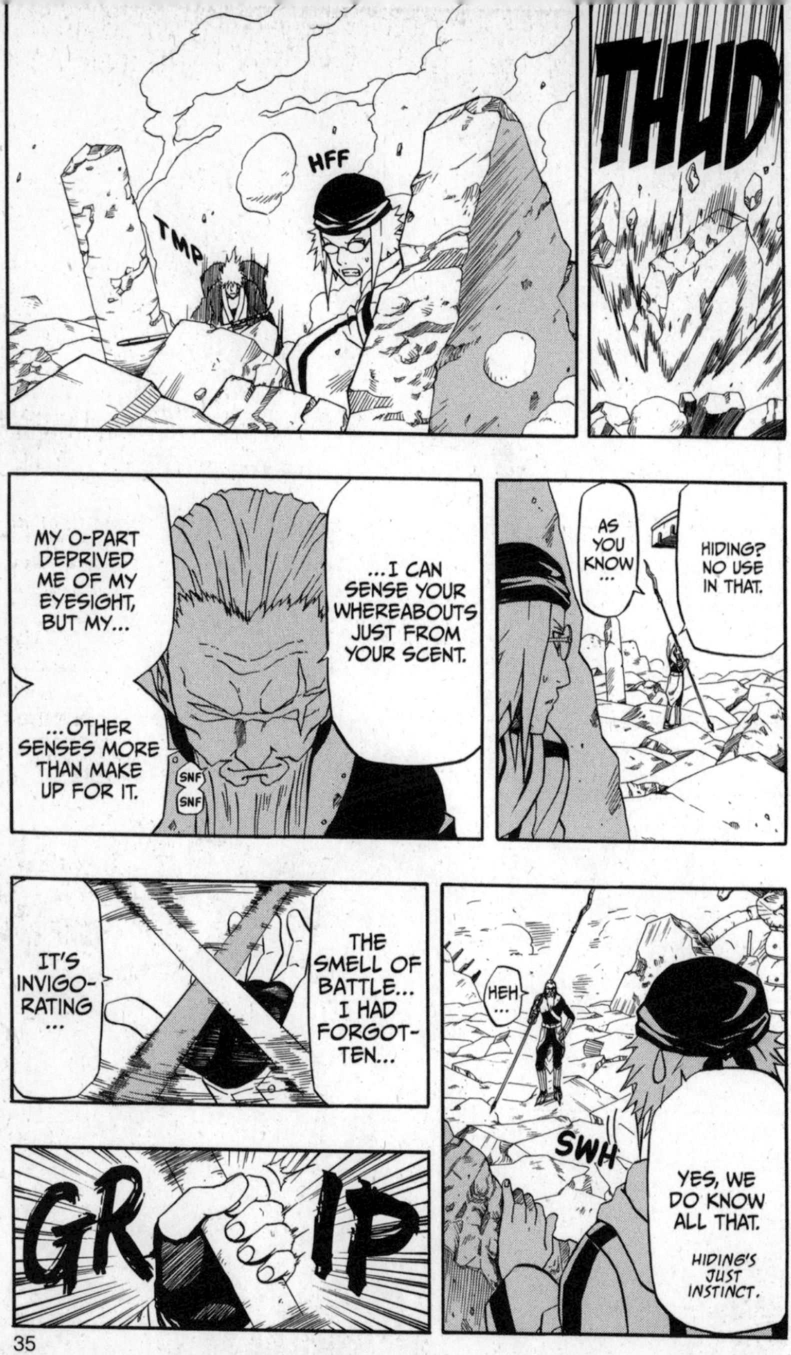
THUD
HFF
TMP
HIDING? NO USE IN THAT.
AS YOU KNOW...
MY O-PART DEPRIVED ME OF MY EYESIGHT, BUT MY...
...OTHER SENSES MORE THAN MAKE UP FOR IT.
SNF SNF
...I CAN SENSE YOUR WHEREABOUTS JUST FROM YOUR SCENT.
HEH...
SWH
YES, WE DO KNOW ALL THAT.
HIDING'S JUST INSTINCT.
THE SMELL OF BATTLE... I HAD FORGOT-TEN...
IT'S INVIGO-RATING...
GR IP

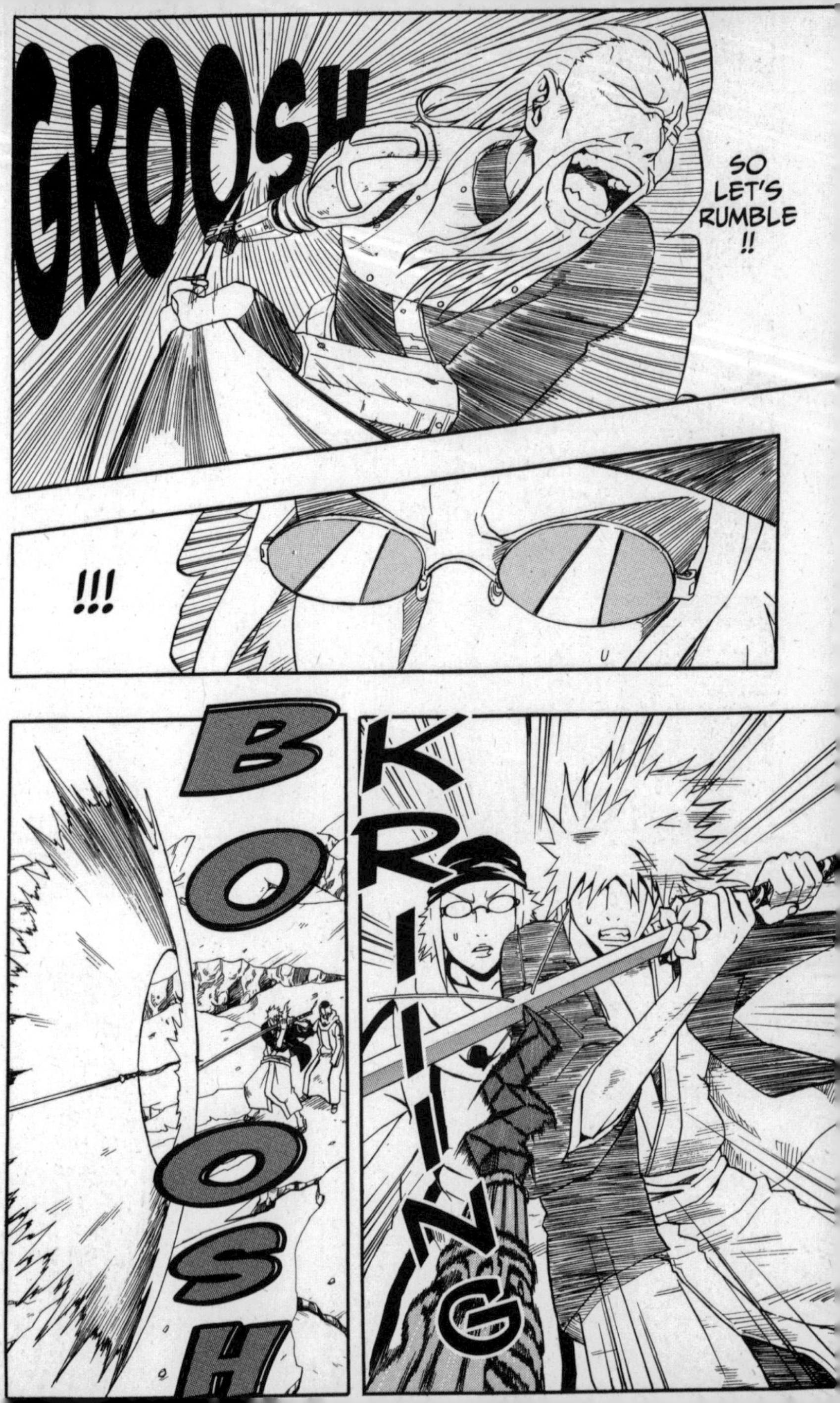
SO LET'S RUMBLE !!
GROOSH
!!!
KRIIING
BOOOSH

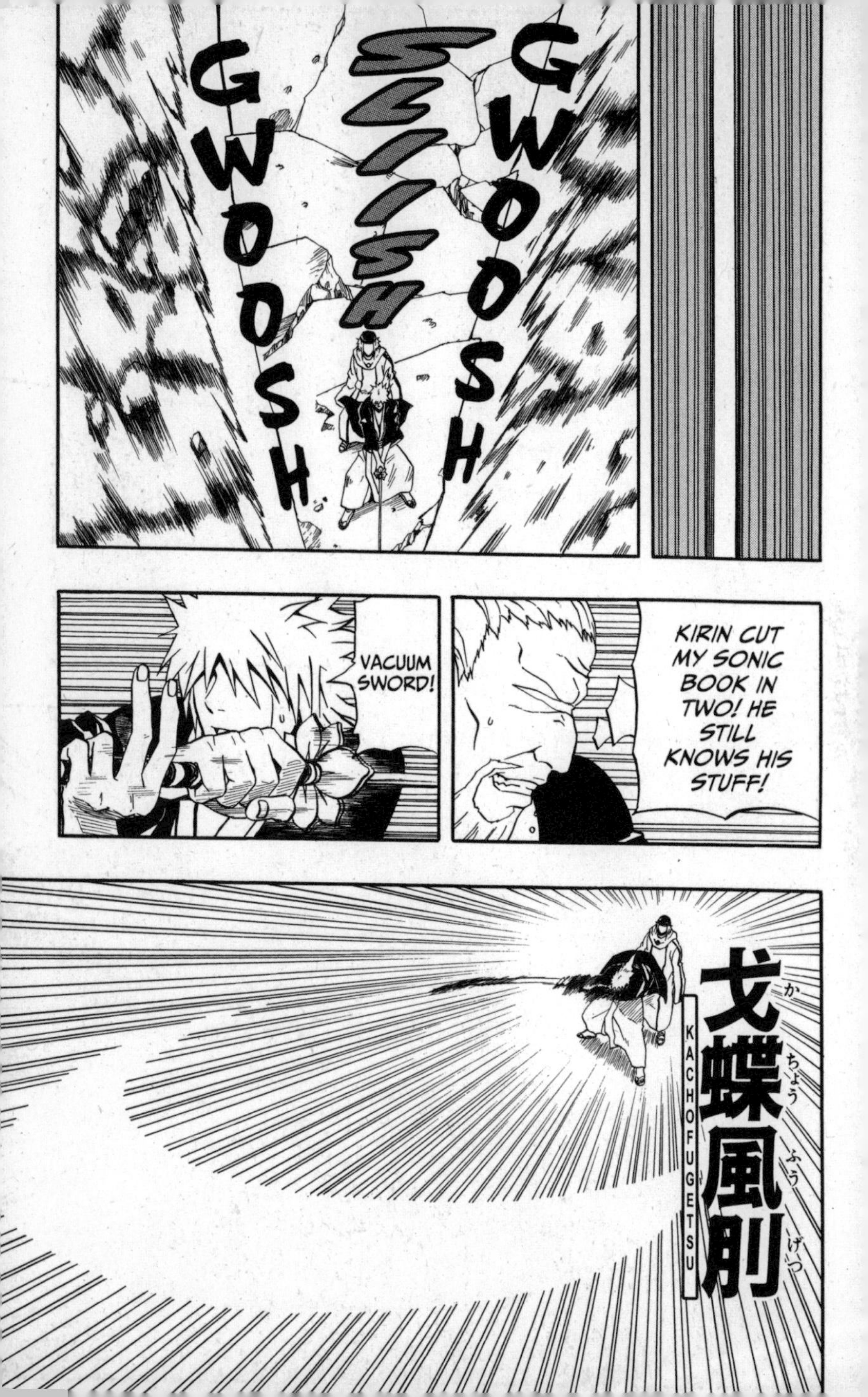
GWOOSH
SWIISH
GWOOSH
KIRIN CUT MY SONIC BOOK IN TWO! HE STILL KNOWS HIS STUFF!
VACUUM SWORD!
戈蝶風刖
かちょうふうげつ
KACHOFUGETSU

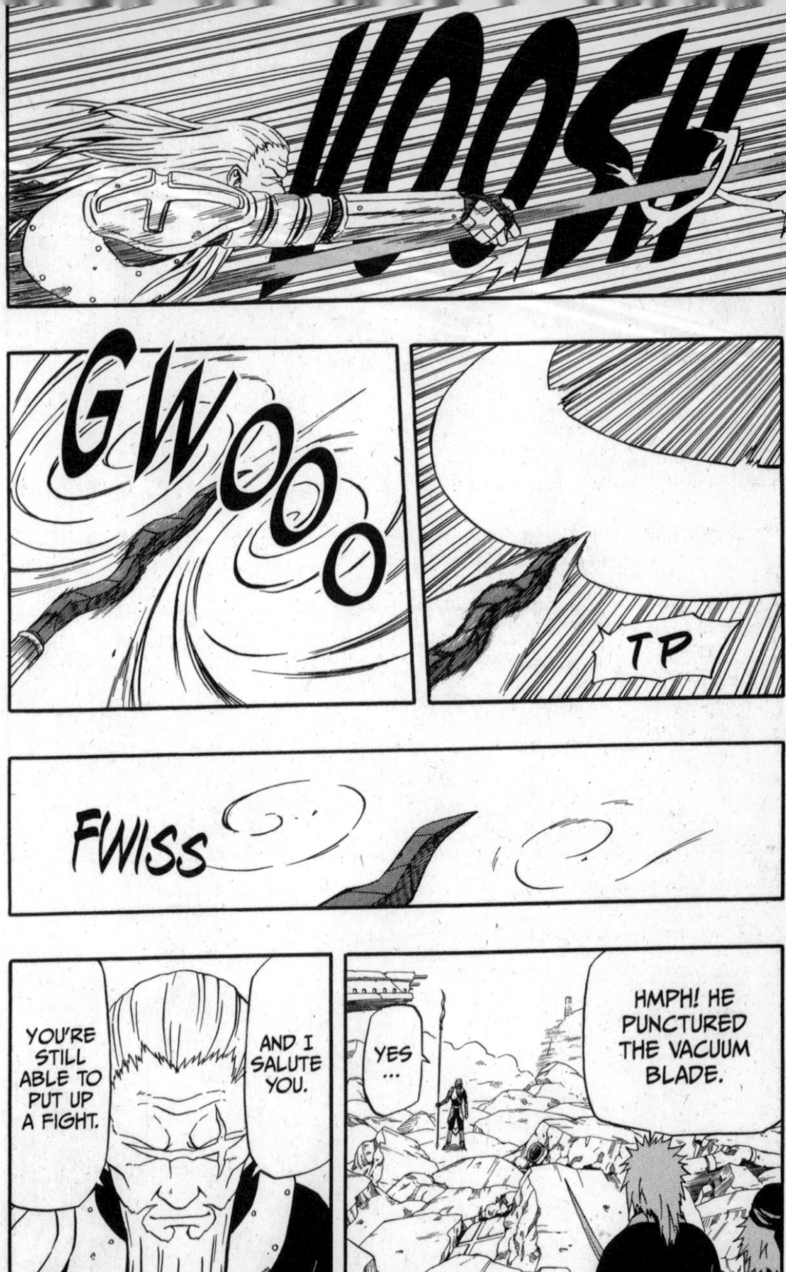
WOOSH
TP
GWOOOO
FWISS
HMPH! HE PUNCTURED THE VACUUM BLADE.
YES...
AND I SALUTE YOU.
YOU'RE STILL ABLE TO PUT UP A FIGHT.

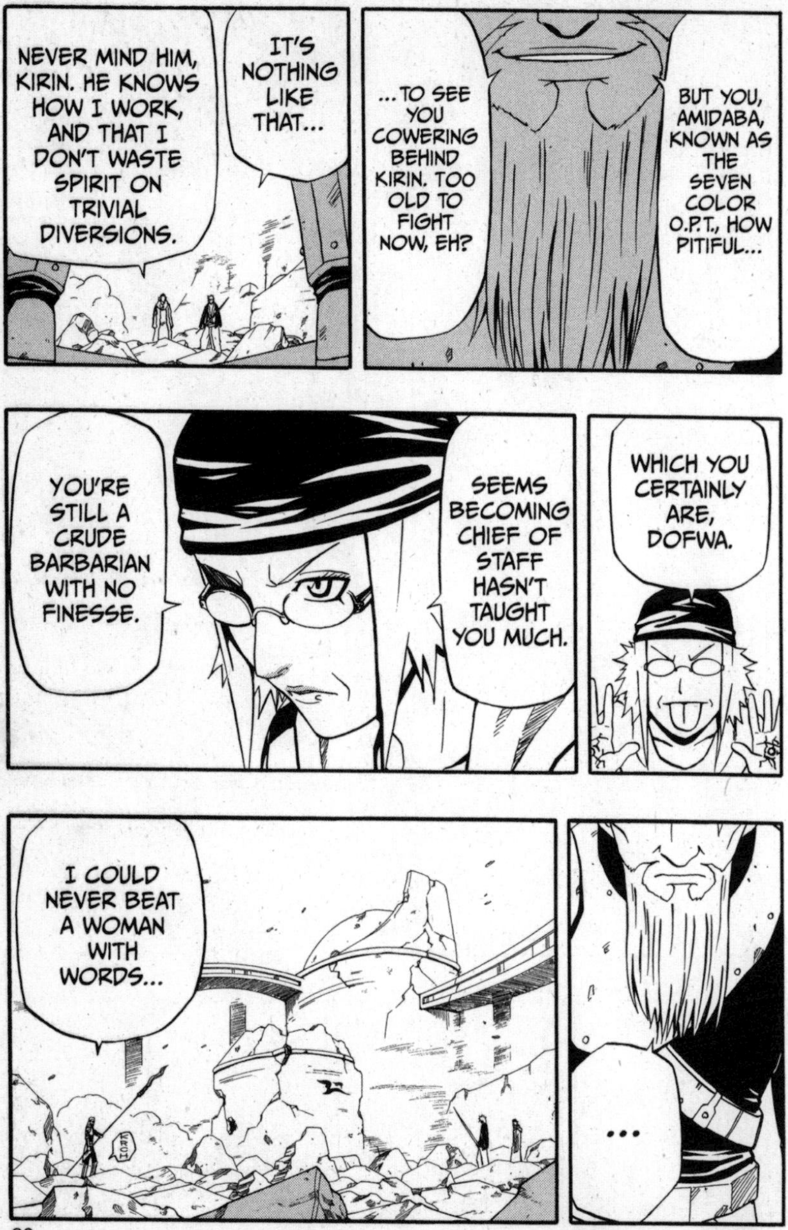
BUT YOU, AMIDABA, KNOWN AS THE SEVEN COLOR O.P.T., HOW PITIFUL...
...TO SEE YOU COWERING BEHIND KIRIN. TOO OLD TO FIGHT NOW, EH?
IT'S NOTHING LIKE THAT...
NEVER MIND HIM, KIRIN. HE KNOWS HOW I WORK, AND THAT I DON'T WASTE SPIRIT ON TRIVIAL DIVERSIONS.
WHICH YOU CERTAINLY ARE, DOFWA.
SEEMS BECOMING CHIEF OF STAFF HASN'T TAUGHT YOU MUCH.
YOU'RE STILL A CRUDE BARBARIAN WITH NO FINESSE.
...
I COULD NEVER BEAT A WOMAN WITH WORDS...
KRCH

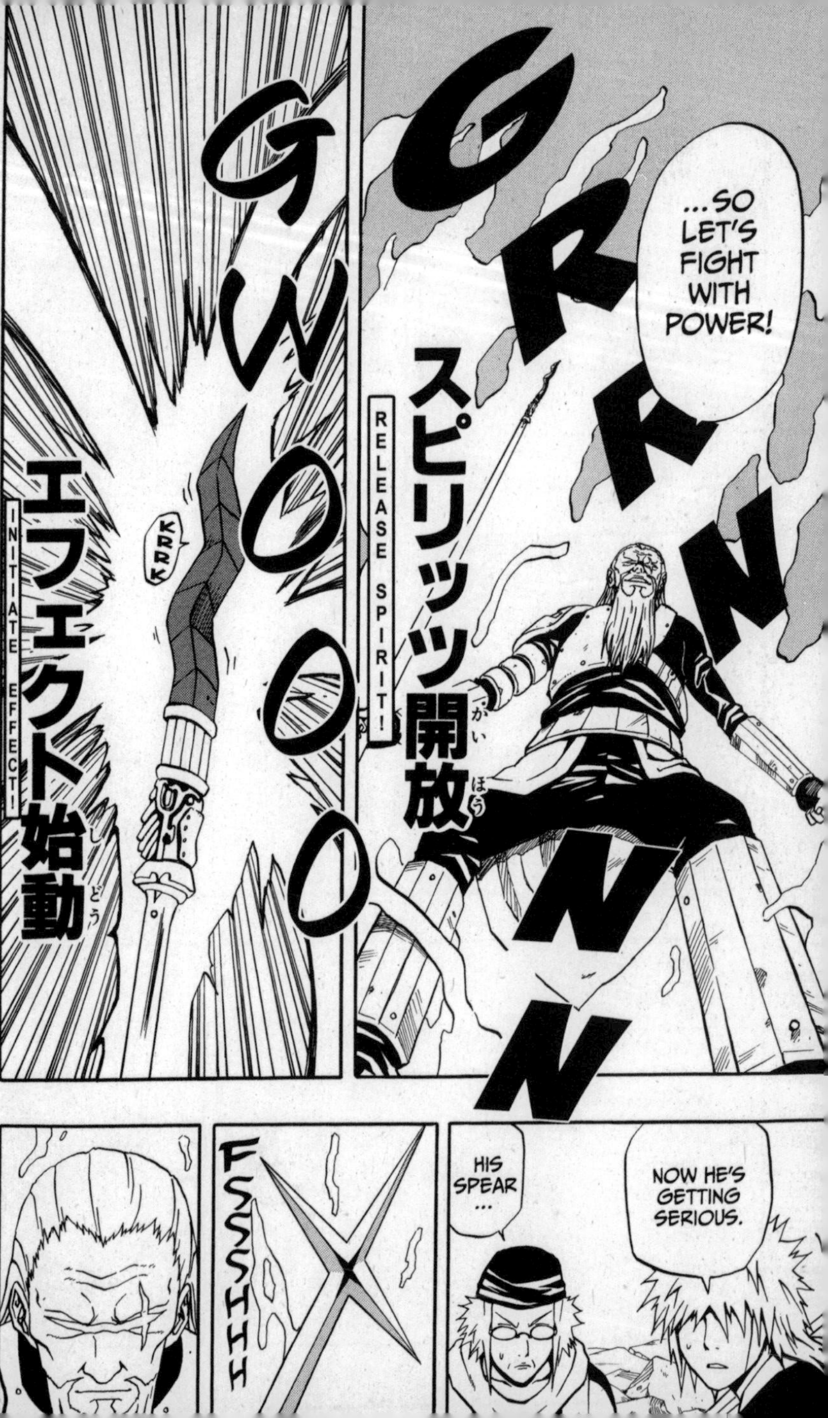
GRRNNNN
...SO LET'S FIGHT WITH POWER!
スピリッツ開放
RELEASE SPIRIT!
GWOOOO
KRRK
エフェクト始動
INITIATE EFFECT!
NOW HE'S GETTING SERIOUS.
HIS SPEAR...
FSSSHHH

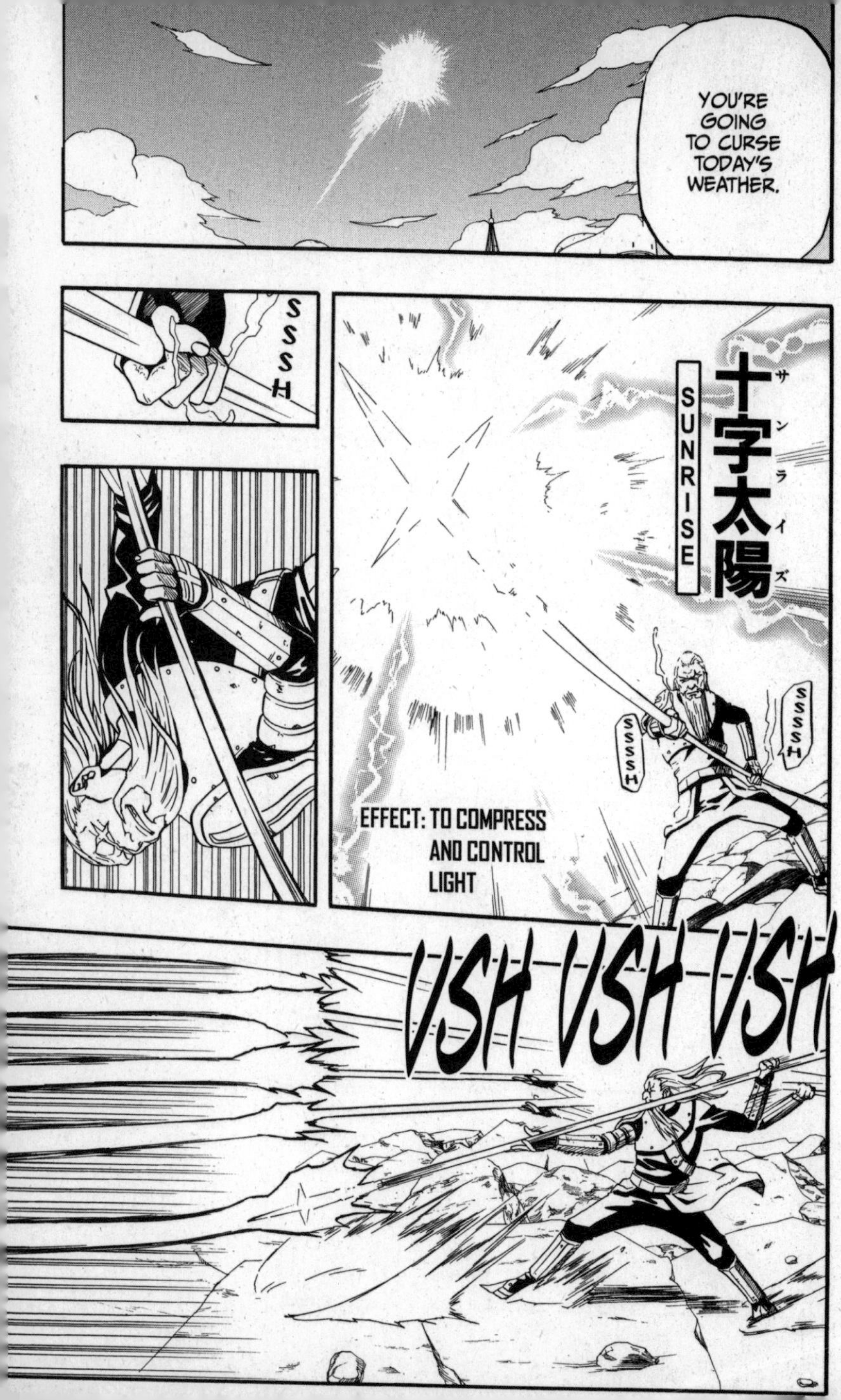
YOU'RE GOING TO CURSE TODAY'S WEATHER.
十字太陽
サンライズ
SUNRISE
SSSSH
SSSH
EFFECT: TO COMPRESS AND CONTROL LIGHT
SSSH
VSH VSH VSH

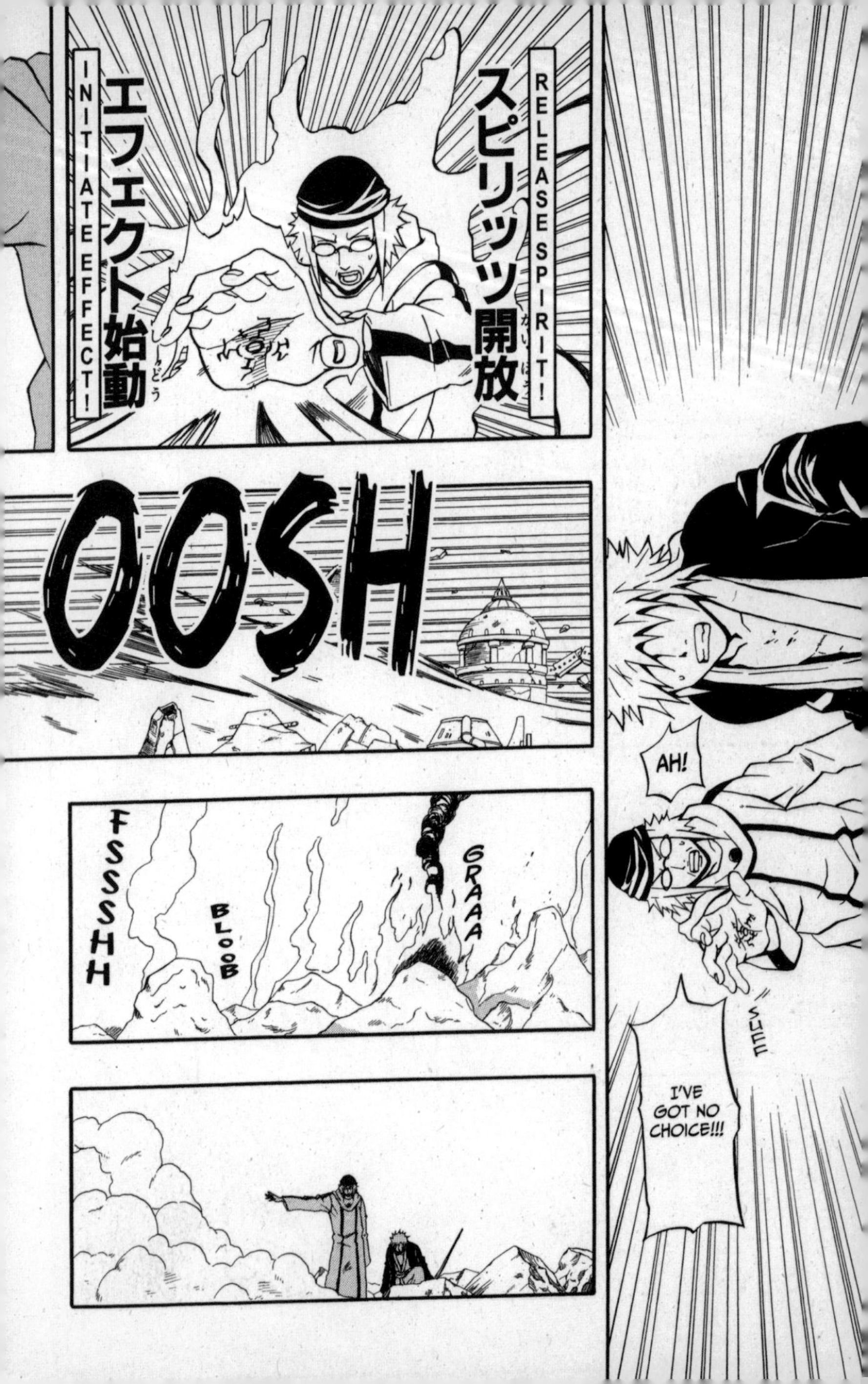
AH!
SUFF
I'VE GOT NO CHOICE!!!
RELEASE SPIRIT!
スピリッツ開放
INITIATE EFFECT!
エフェクト始動
OOSH
FSSSHH
BLOOB
GRAAA

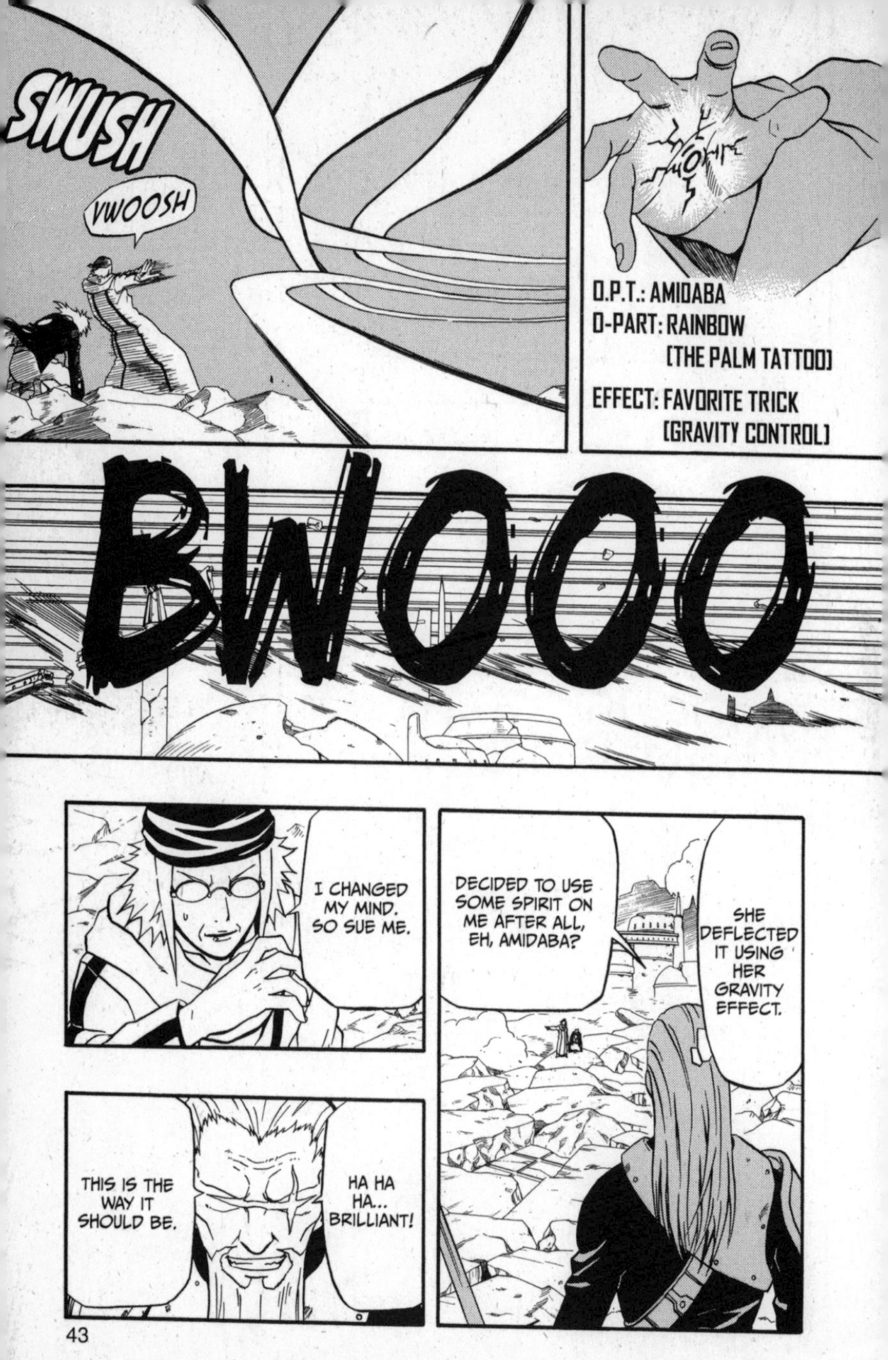
O.P.T.: AMIDABA
D-PART: RAINBOW [THE PALM TATTOO]
EFFECT: FAVORITE TRICK [GRAVITY CONTROL]
SWUSH
VWOOSH
BWOOO
SHE DEFLECTED IT USING HER GRAVITY EFFECT.
DECIDED TO USE SOME SPIRIT ON ME AFTER ALL, EH, AMIDABA?
I CHANGED MY MIND. SO SUE ME.
HA HA HA... BRILLIANT!
THIS IS THE WAY IT SHOULD BE.

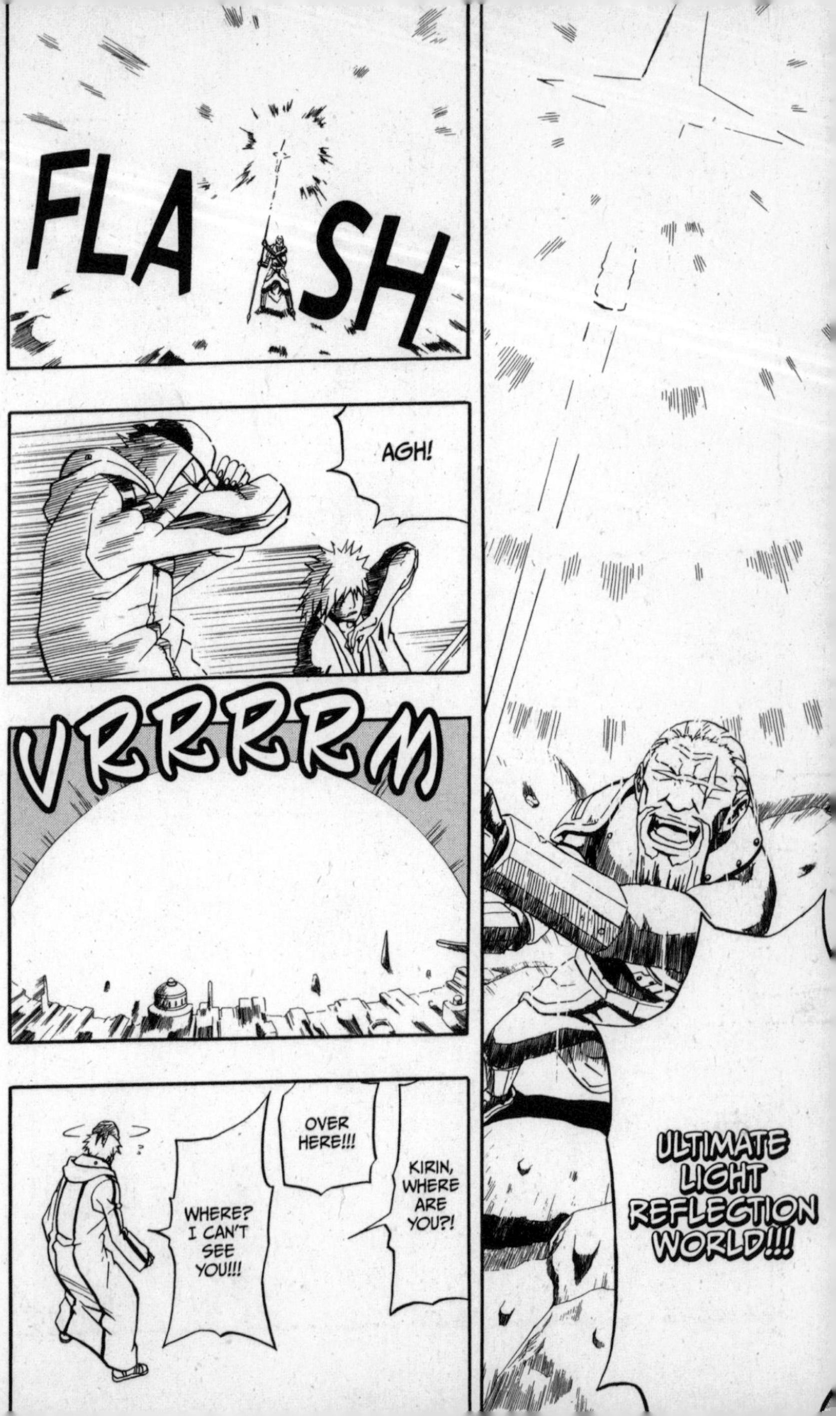
ULTIMATE LIGHT REFLECTION WORLD!!!
FLASH
AGH!
VRRRRM
KIRIN, WHERE ARE YOU?!
OVER HERE!!!
WHERE? I CAN'T SEE YOU!!!

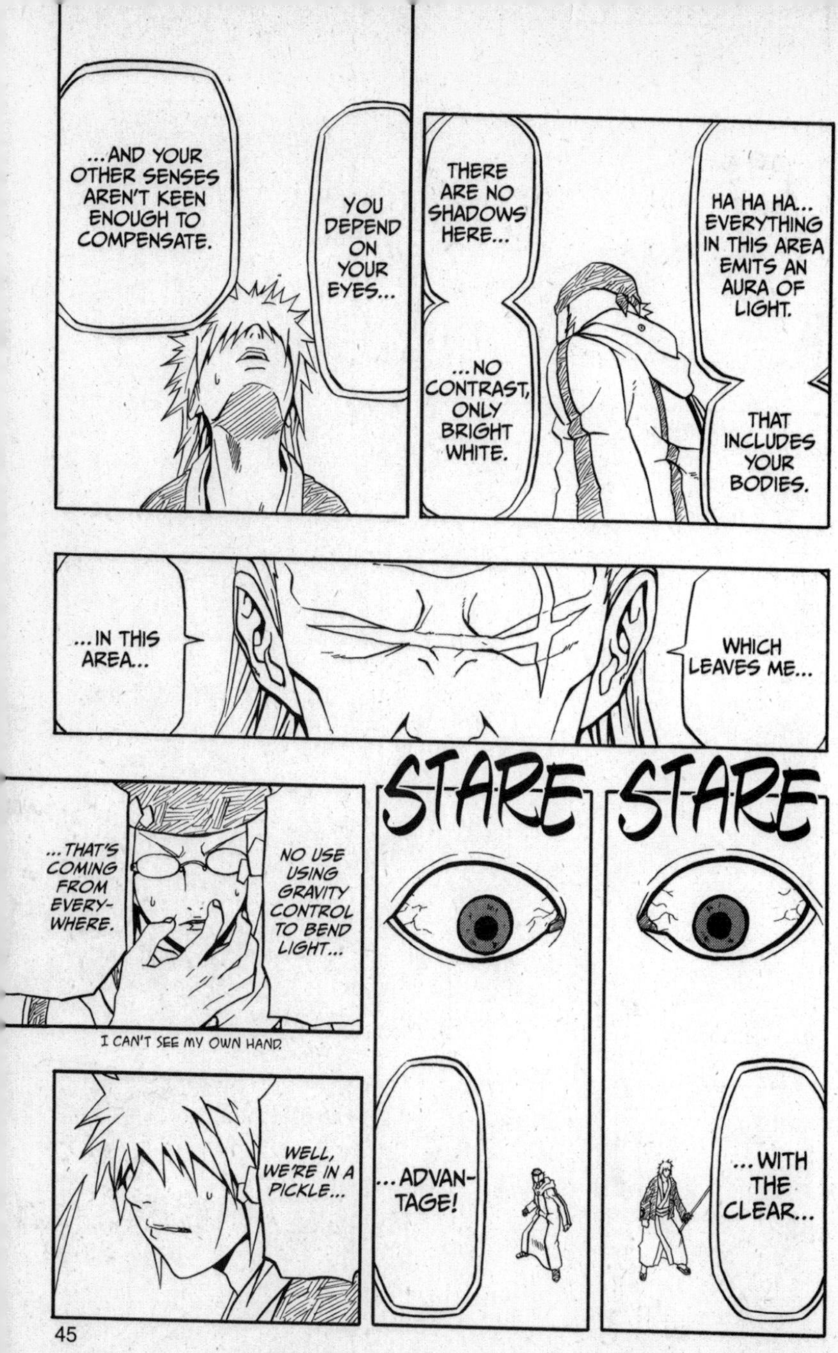
HA HA HA... EVERYTHING IN THIS AREA EMITS AN AURA OF LIGHT.
THAT INCLUDES YOUR BODIES.
THERE ARE NO SHADOWS HERE...
...NO CONTRAST, ONLY BRIGHT WHITE.
YOU DEPEND ON YOUR EYES...
...AND YOUR OTHER SENSES AREN'T KEEN ENOUGH TO COMPENSATE.
WHICH LEAVES ME...
...IN THIS AREA...
STARE
...WITH THE CLEAR...
STARE
...ADVAN-TAGE!
NO USE USING GRAVITY CONTROL TO BEND LIGHT...
...THAT'S COMING FROM EVERY-WHERE.
I CAN'T SEE MY OWN HAND.
WELL, WE'RE IN A PICKLE...

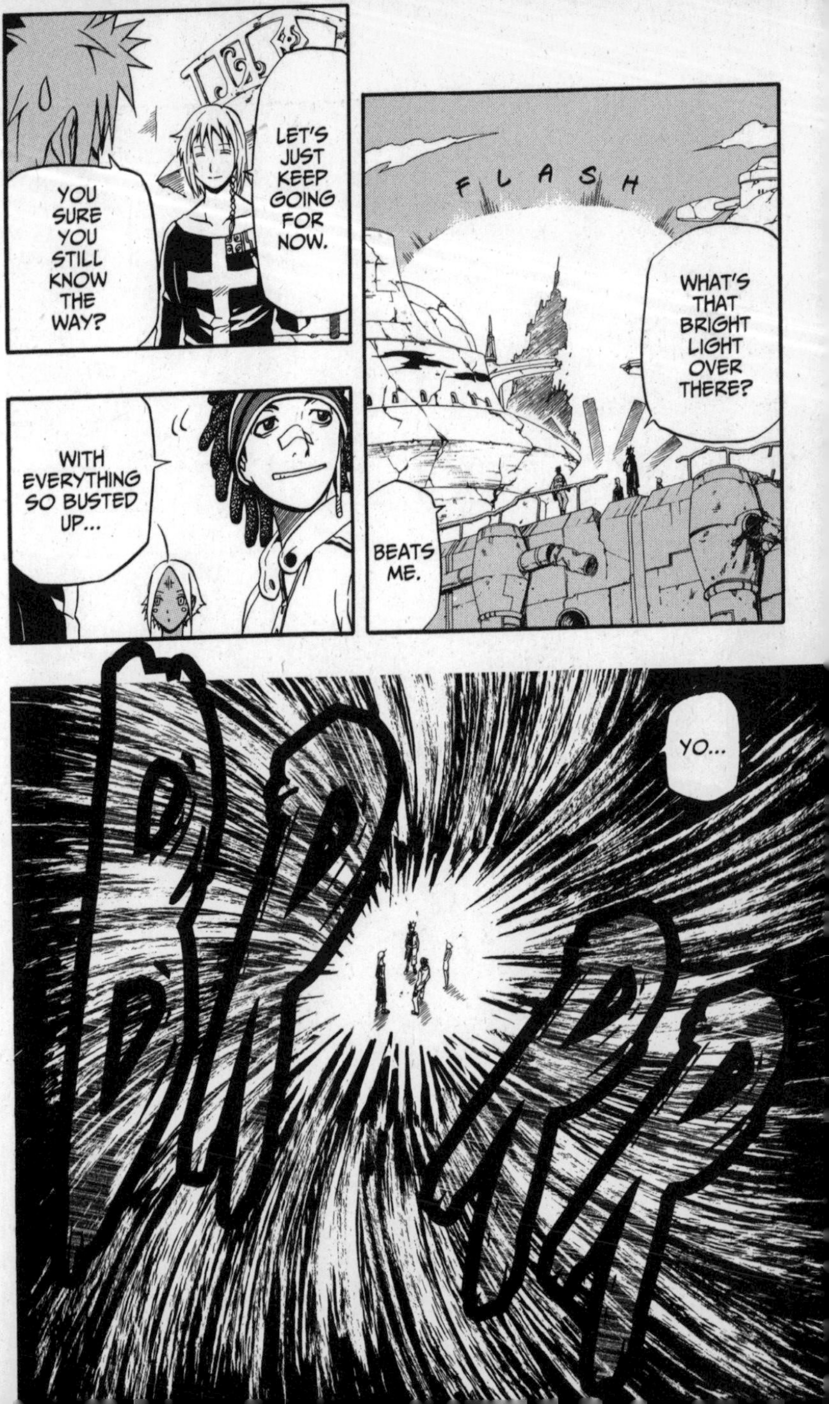

F L A S H
WHAT'S THAT BRIGHT LIGHT OVER THERE?
BEATS ME.
LET'S JUST KEEP GOING FOR NOW.
YOU SURE YOU STILL KNOW THE WAY?
WITH EVERYTHING SO BUSTED UP...
YO...

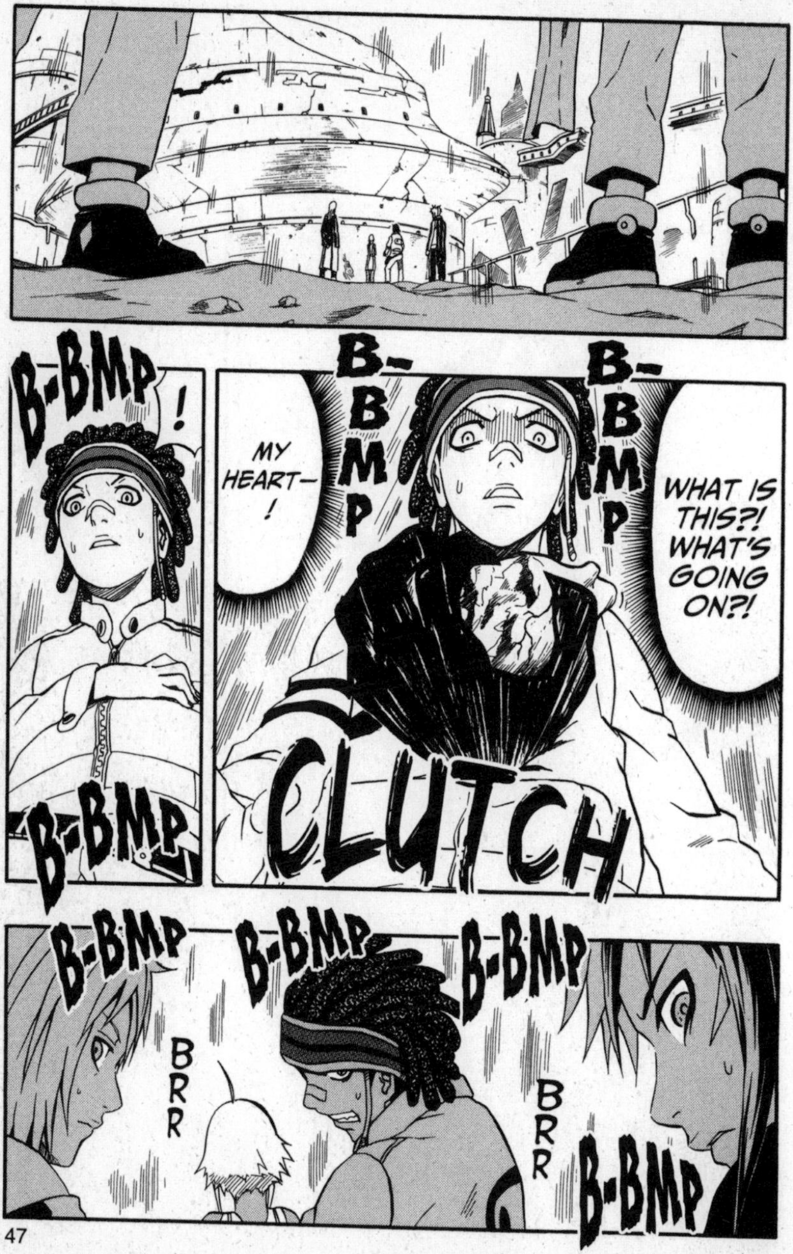
B-BMP
WHAT IS THIS?! WHAT'S GOING ON?!
B-BMP
MY HEART—!
CLUTCH
B-BMP
!
B-BMP
B-BMP
B-BMP
BRR
B-BMP
BRR
B-BMP

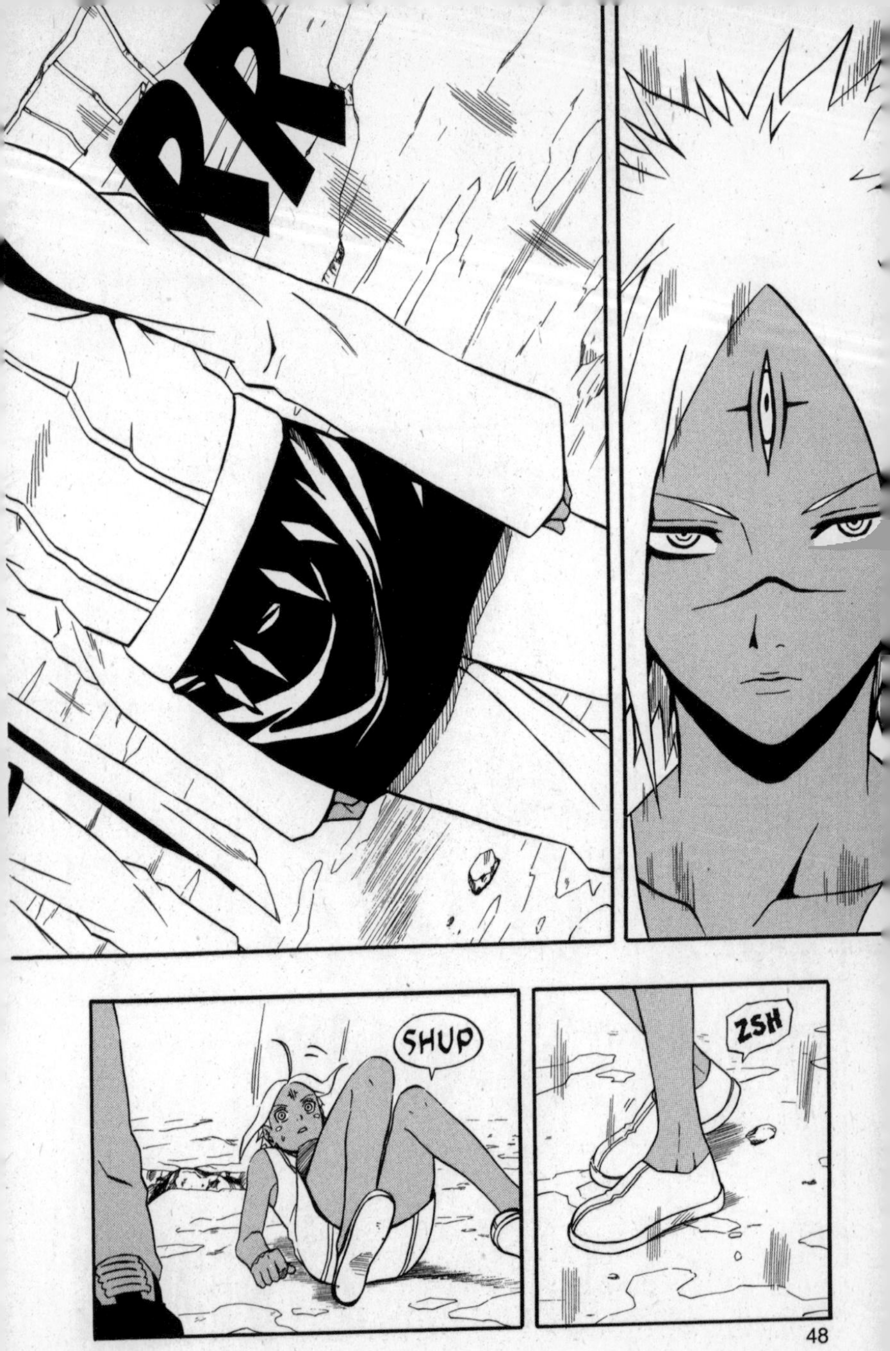
RR
ZSH
SHUP

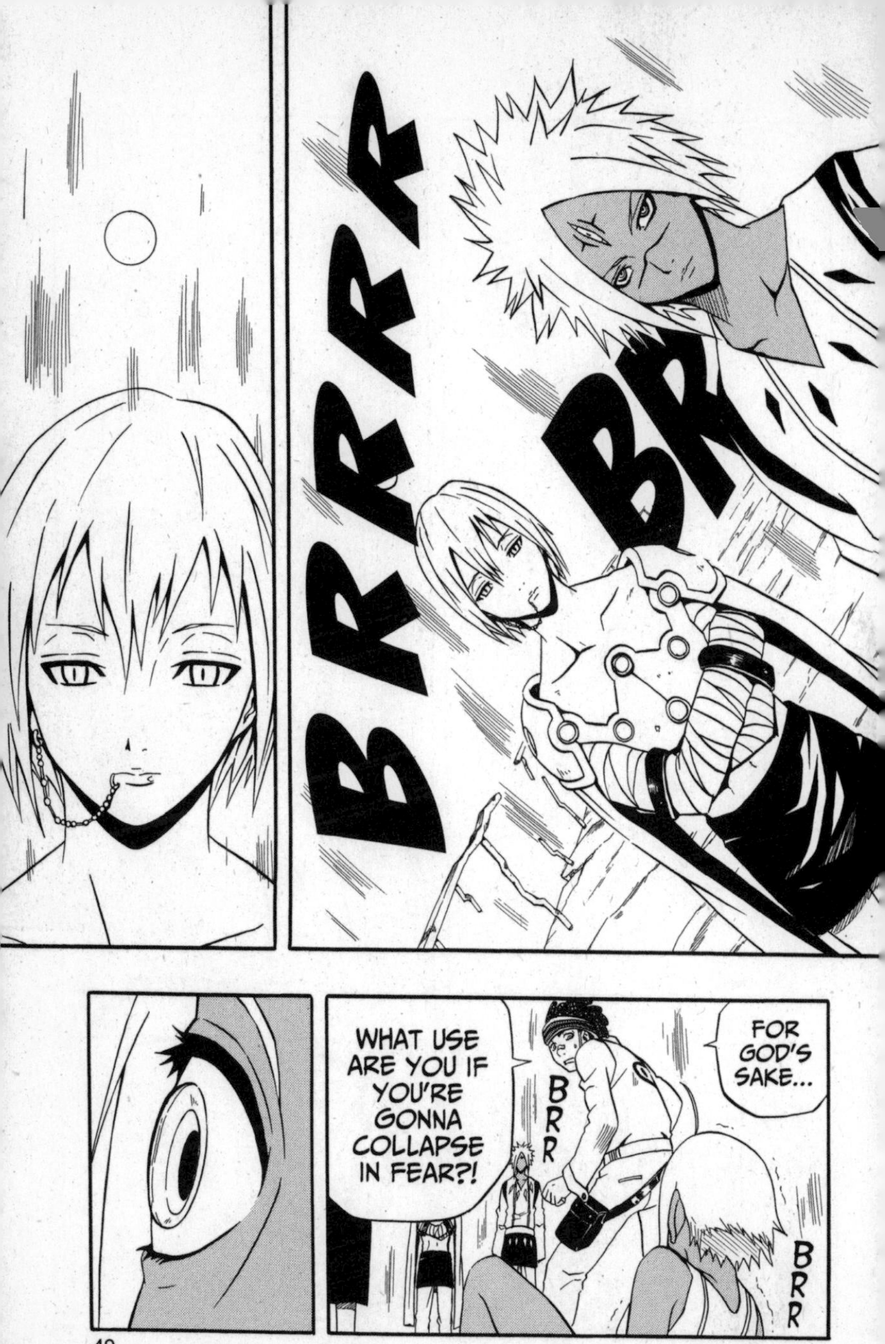
BRRRR
BR
FOR GOD'S SAKE...
WHAT USE ARE YOU IF YOU'RE GONNA COLLAPSE IN FEAR?!
BRR
BRR

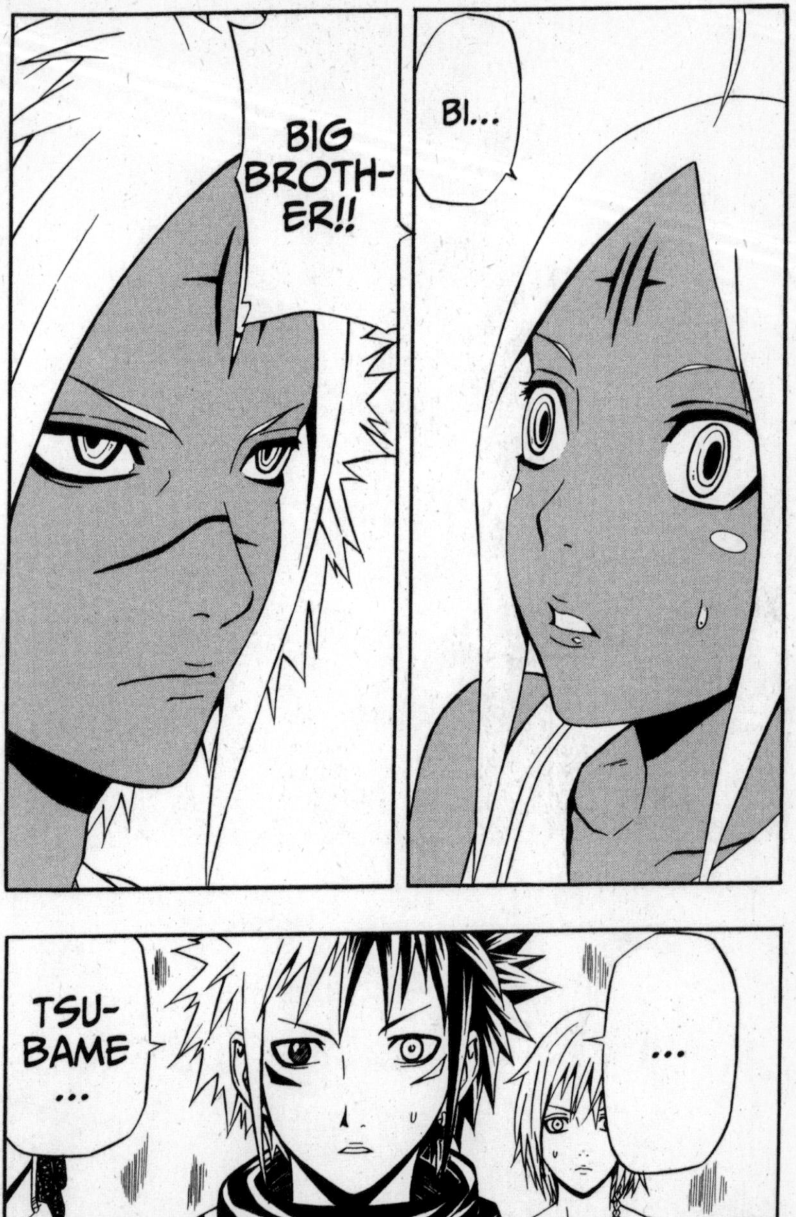
BI...
BIG BROTH-ER!!
...
TSU-BAME ...

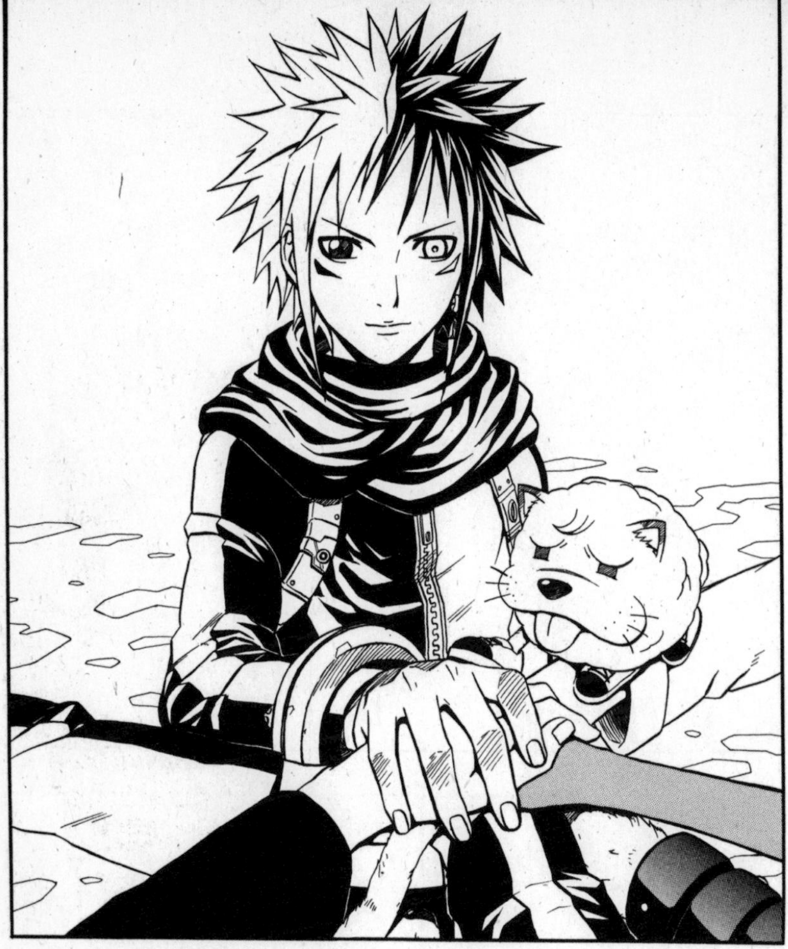

CHAPTER 58
PERSONAL BATTLES

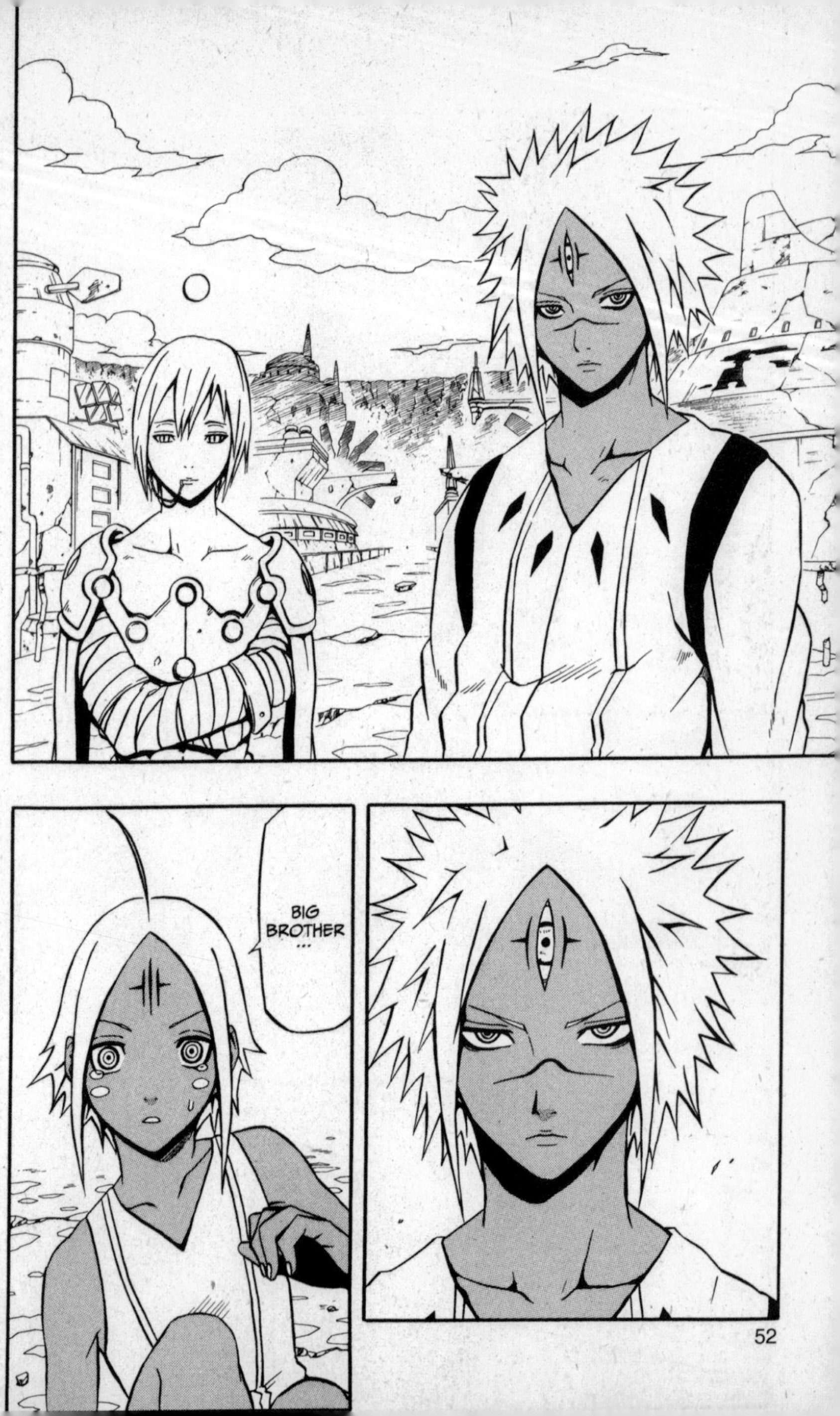
BIG BROTHER ...

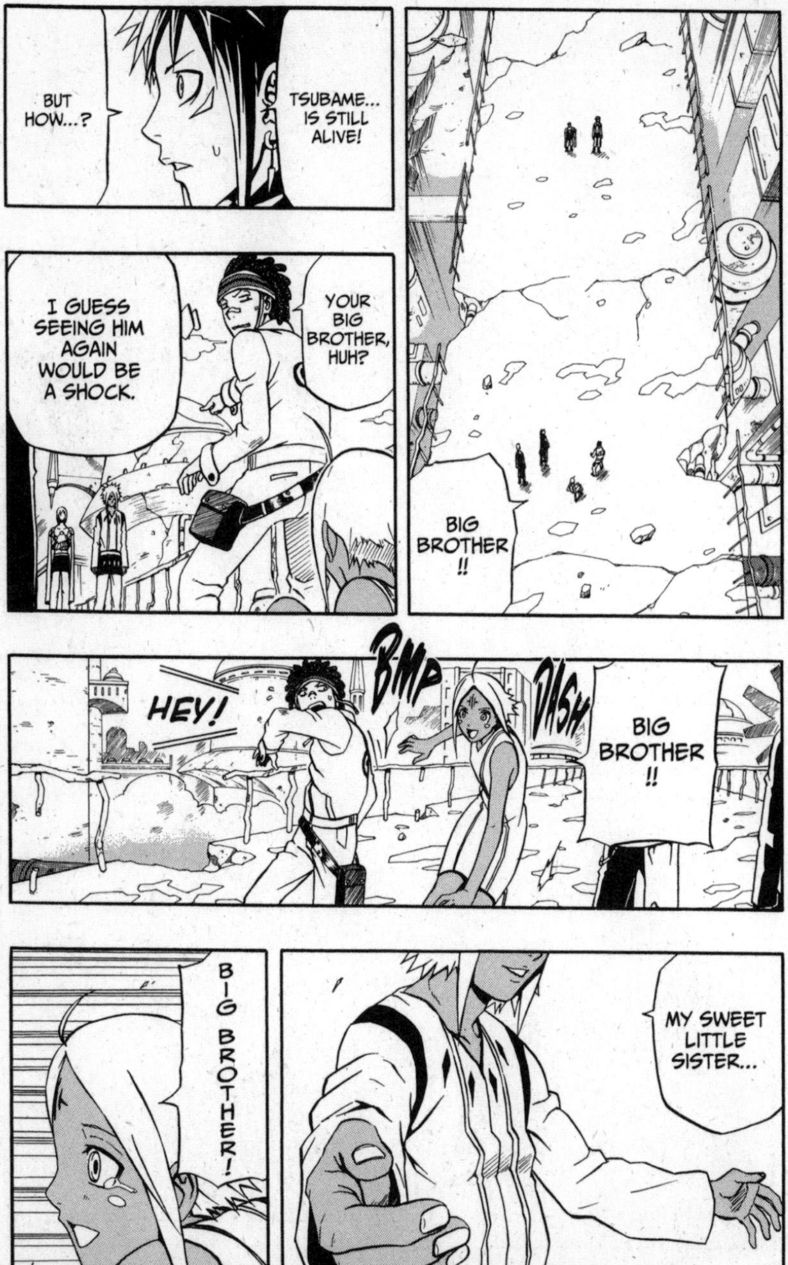
BIG BROTHER!!
TSUBAME... IS STILL ALIVE!
BUT HOW...?
YOUR BIG BROTHER, HUH?
I GUESS SEEING HIM AGAIN WOULD BE A SHOCK.
BIG BROTHER!!
DASH
B-MP
HEY!
MY SWEET LITTLE SISTER...
BIG BROTHER!

GRAB

!!

BOOM

...

ZSHH

SLP

YOU'RE FAST.

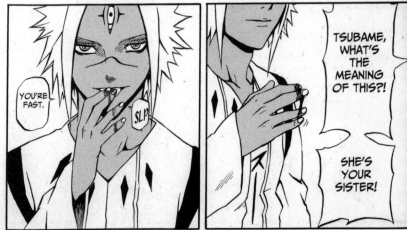

TSUBAME, WHAT'S THE MEANING OF THIS?!

SHE'S YOUR SISTER!

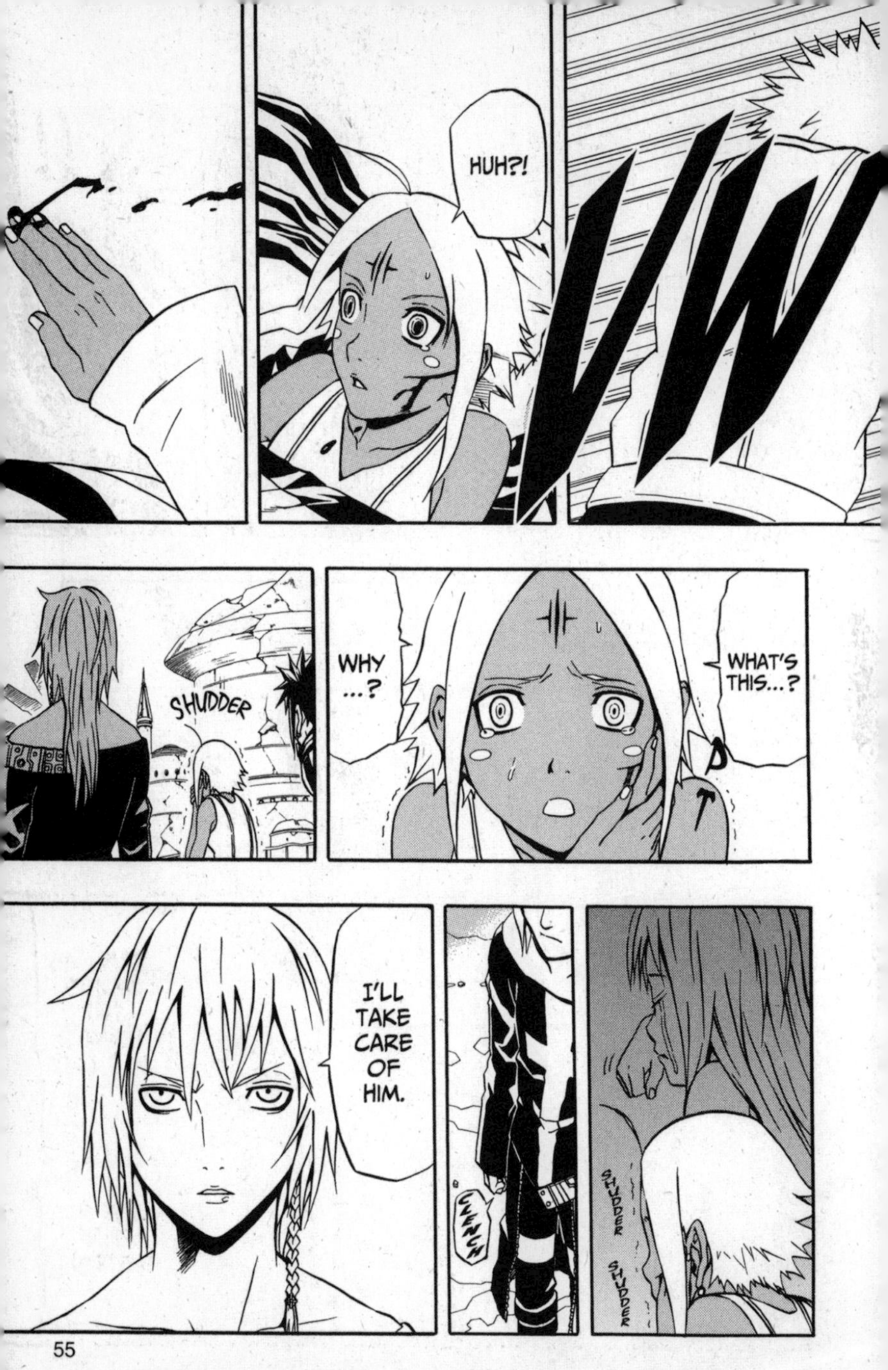
HUH?!
WHAT'S THIS...?
WHY ...?
SHUDDER
SHUDDER SHUDDER
CLENCH
I'LL TAKE CARE OF HIM.

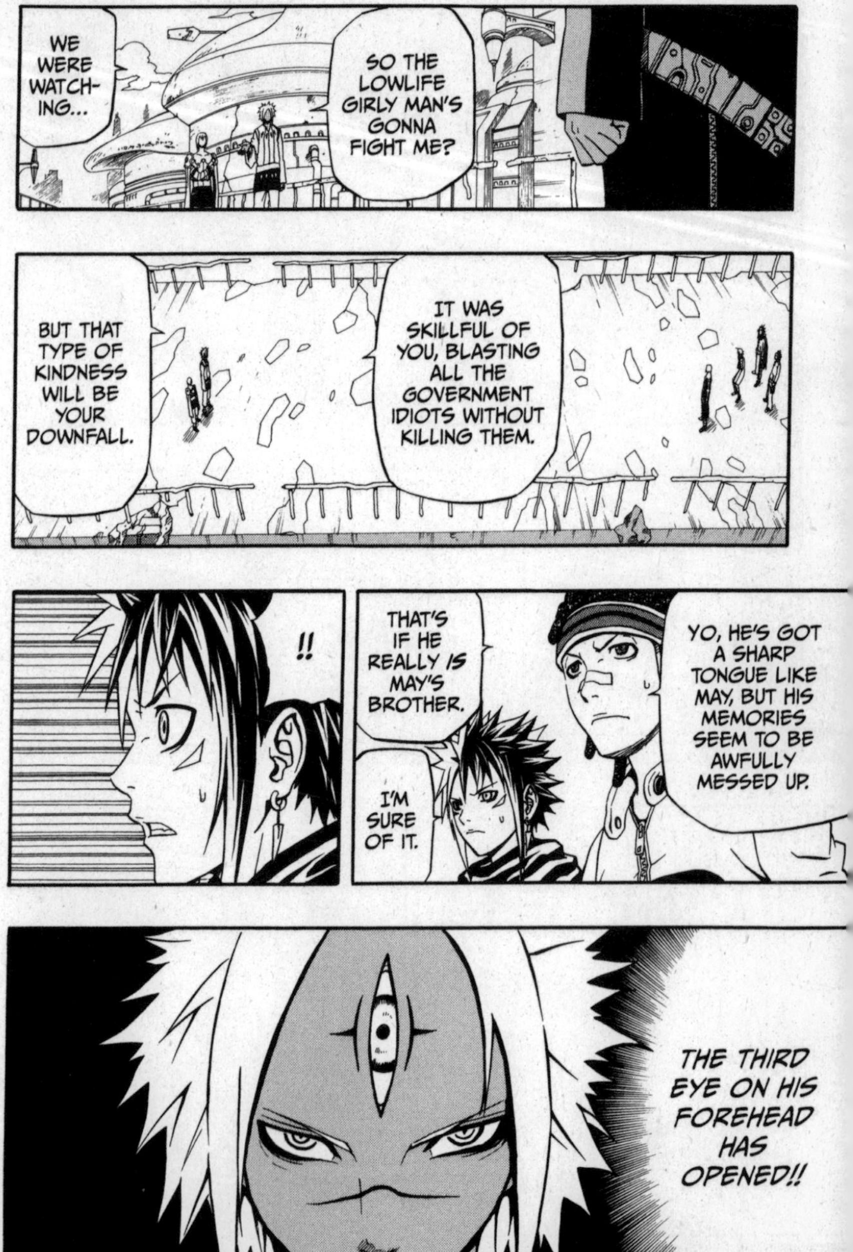
SO THE LOWLIFE GIRLY MAN'S GONNA FIGHT ME?
WE WERE WATCHING...
IT WAS SKILLFUL OF YOU, BLASTING ALL THE GOVERNMENT IDIOTS WITHOUT KILLING THEM.
BUT THAT TYPE OF KINDNESS WILL BE YOUR DOWNFALL.
YO, HE'S GOT A SHARP TONGUE LIKE MAY, BUT HIS MEMORIES SEEM TO BE AWFULLY MESSED UP.
THAT'S IF HE REALLY *IS* MAY'S BROTHER.
I'M SURE OF IT.
!!
THE THIRD EYE ON HIS FOREHEAD HAS OPENED!!

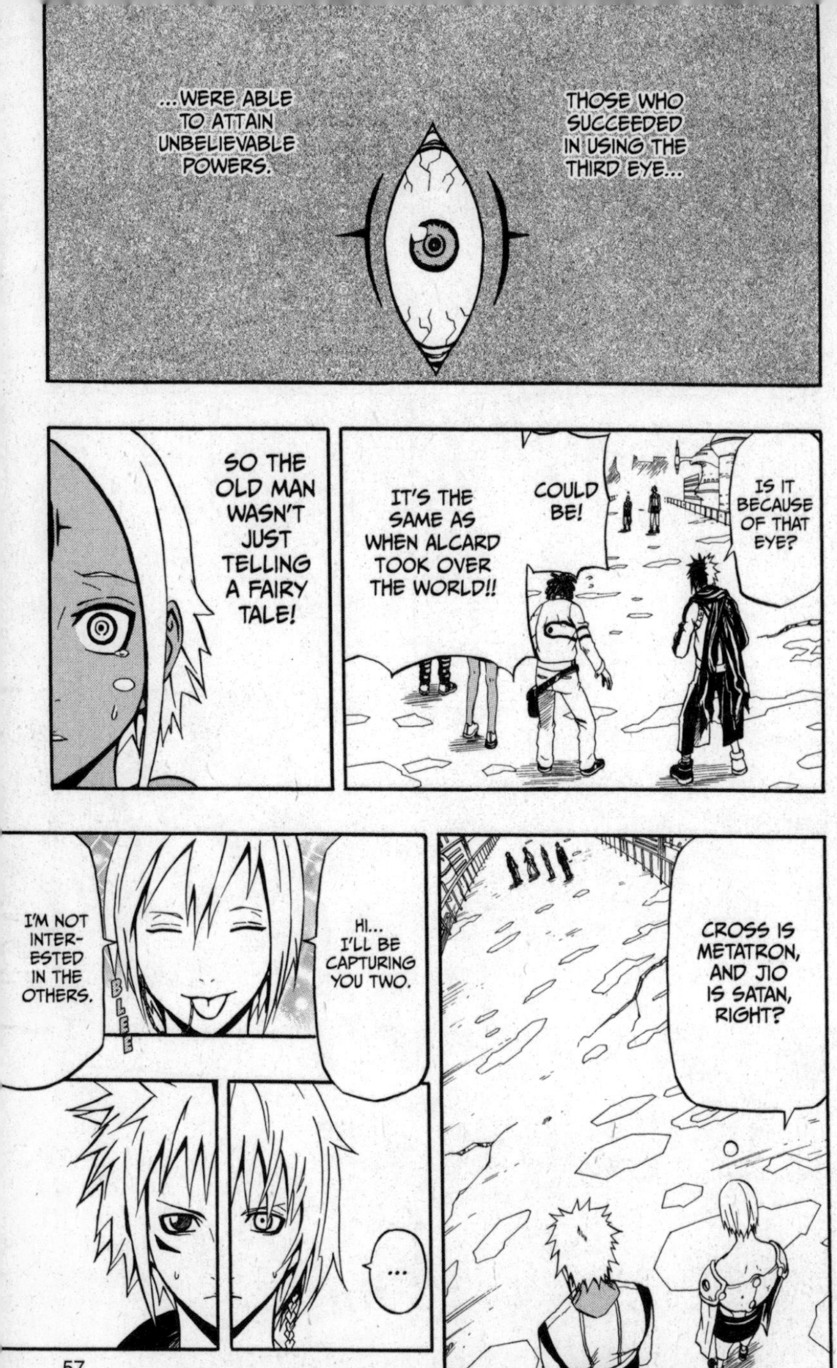
THOSE WHO SUCCEEDED IN USING THE THIRD EYE...
...WERE ABLE TO ATTAIN UNBELIEVABLE POWERS.
IS IT BECAUSE OF THAT EYE?
COULD BE!
IT'S THE SAME AS WHEN ALCARD TOOK OVER THE WORLD!!
SO THE OLD MAN WASN'T JUST TELLING A FAIRY TALE!
CROSS IS METATRON, AND JIO IS SATAN, RIGHT?
HI... I'LL BE CAPTURING YOU TWO.
BLEE
I'M NOT INTER-ESTED IN THE OTHERS.
...

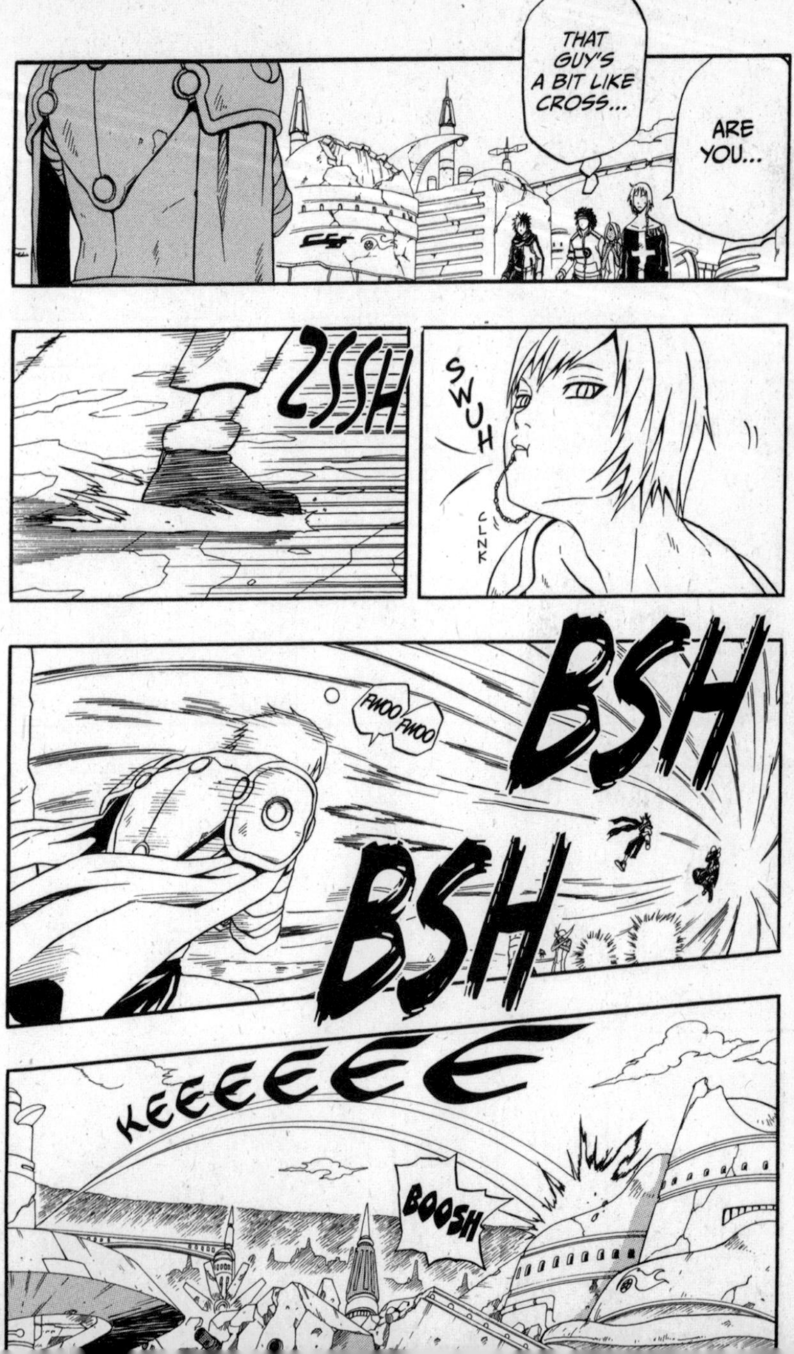
ARE YOU...
THAT GUY'S A BIT LIKE CROSS...
SWUH
CLNK
ZSSH
BSH
FWOO FWOO
BSH
KEEEEEEE
BOOSH

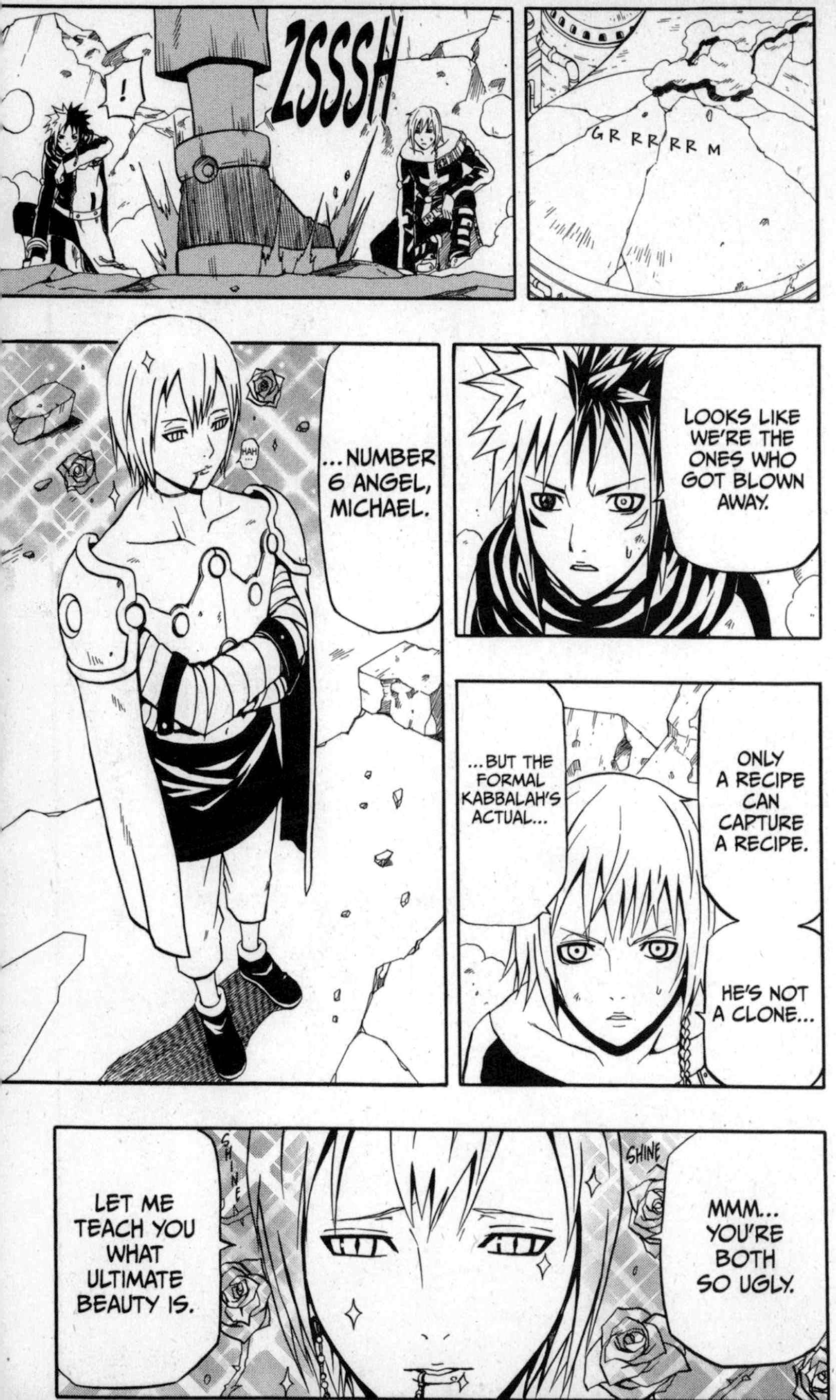
GR RR RRR M
ZSSSH
!
LOOKS LIKE WE'RE THE ONES WHO GOT BLOWN AWAY.
ONLY A RECIPE CAN CAPTURE A RECIPE.
HE'S NOT A CLONE...
...BUT THE FORMAL KABBALAH'S ACTUAL...
HAH
...NUMBER 6 ANGEL, MICHAEL.
SHINE
MMM... YOU'RE BOTH SO UGLY.
SHINE
LET ME TEACH YOU WHAT ULTIMATE BEAUTY IS.

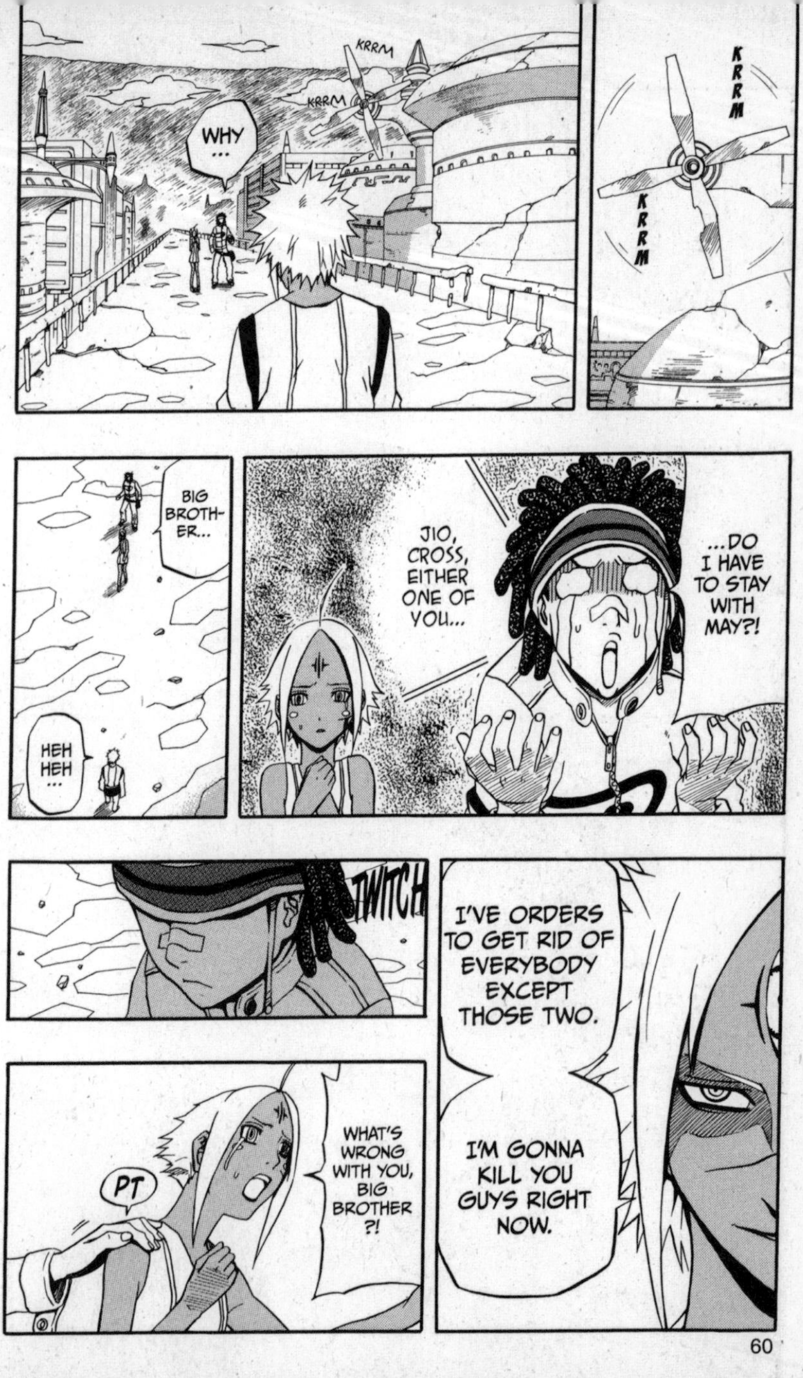
KRRM
KRRM
KRRM
KRRM
WHY...
JIO, CROSS, EITHER ONE OF YOU...
...DO I HAVE TO STAY WITH MAY?!
BIG BROTHER-ER...
HEH HEH...
I'VE ORDERS TO GET RID OF EVERYBODY EXCEPT THOSE TWO.
I'M GONNA KILL YOU GUYS RIGHT NOW.
TWITCH
PT
WHAT'S WRONG WITH YOU, BIG BROTHER?!

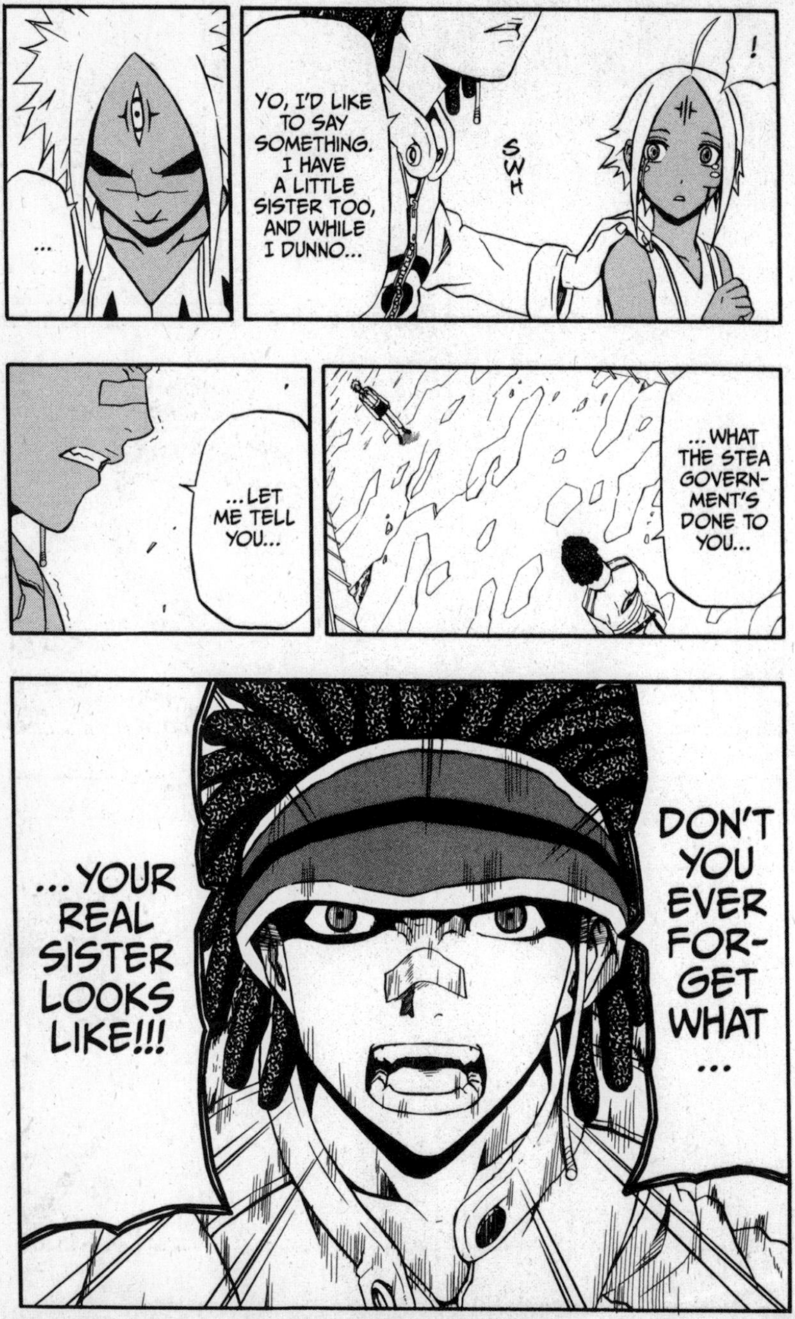
!
YO, I'D LIKE TO SAY SOMETHING. I HAVE A LITTLE SISTER TOO, AND WHILE I DUNNO...
SWH
...
...WHAT THE STEA GOVERNMENT'S DONE TO YOU...
...LET ME TELL YOU...
DON'T YOU EVER FORGET WHAT ...
...YOUR REAL SISTER LOOKS LIKE!!!

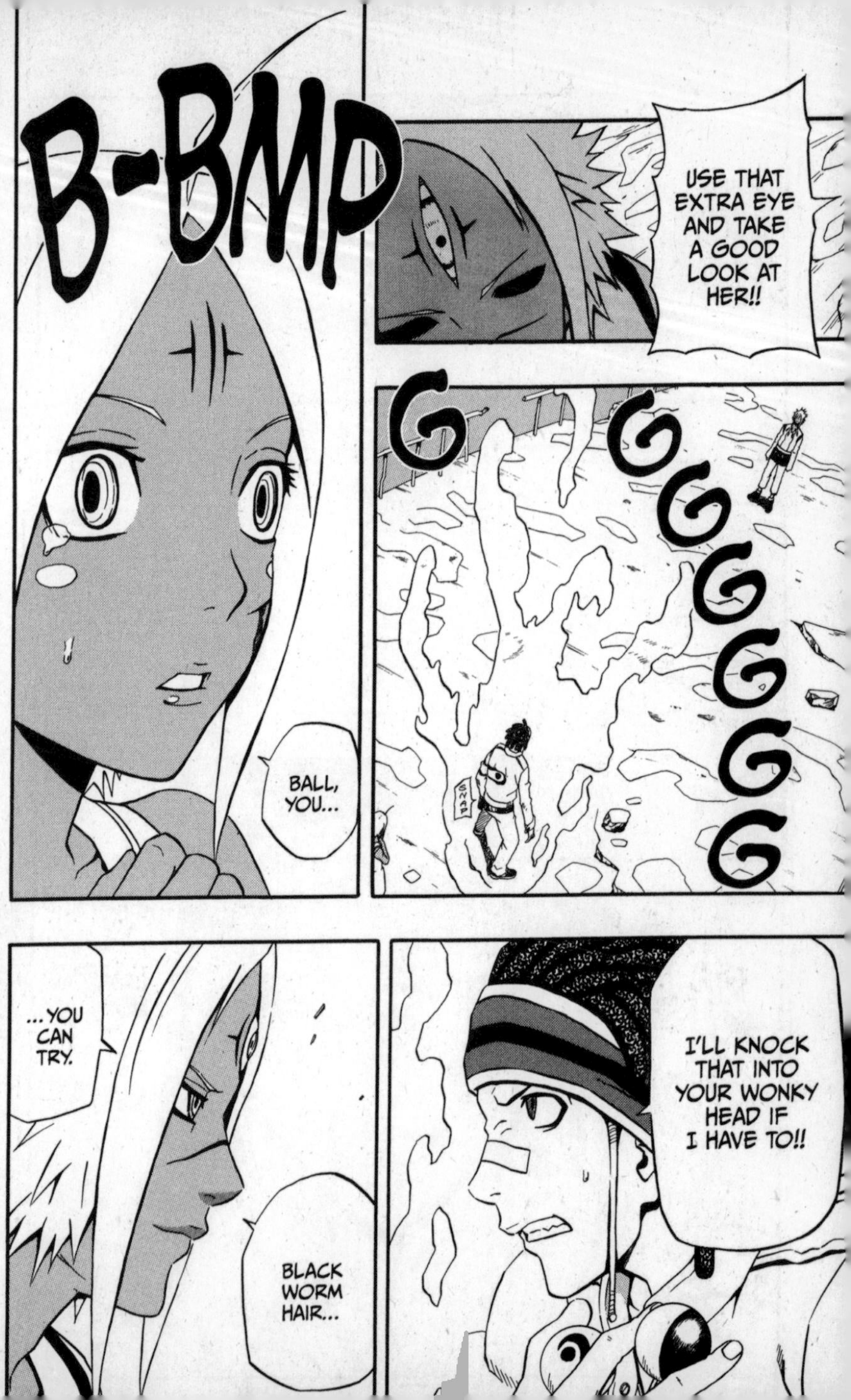
USE THAT EXTRA EYE AND TAKE A GOOD LOOK AT HER!!
GGGGGGG
SNAP
B-BMP
BALL, YOU...
I'LL KNOCK THAT INTO YOUR WONKY HEAD IF I HAVE TO!!
...YOU CAN TRY.
BLACK WORM HAIR...

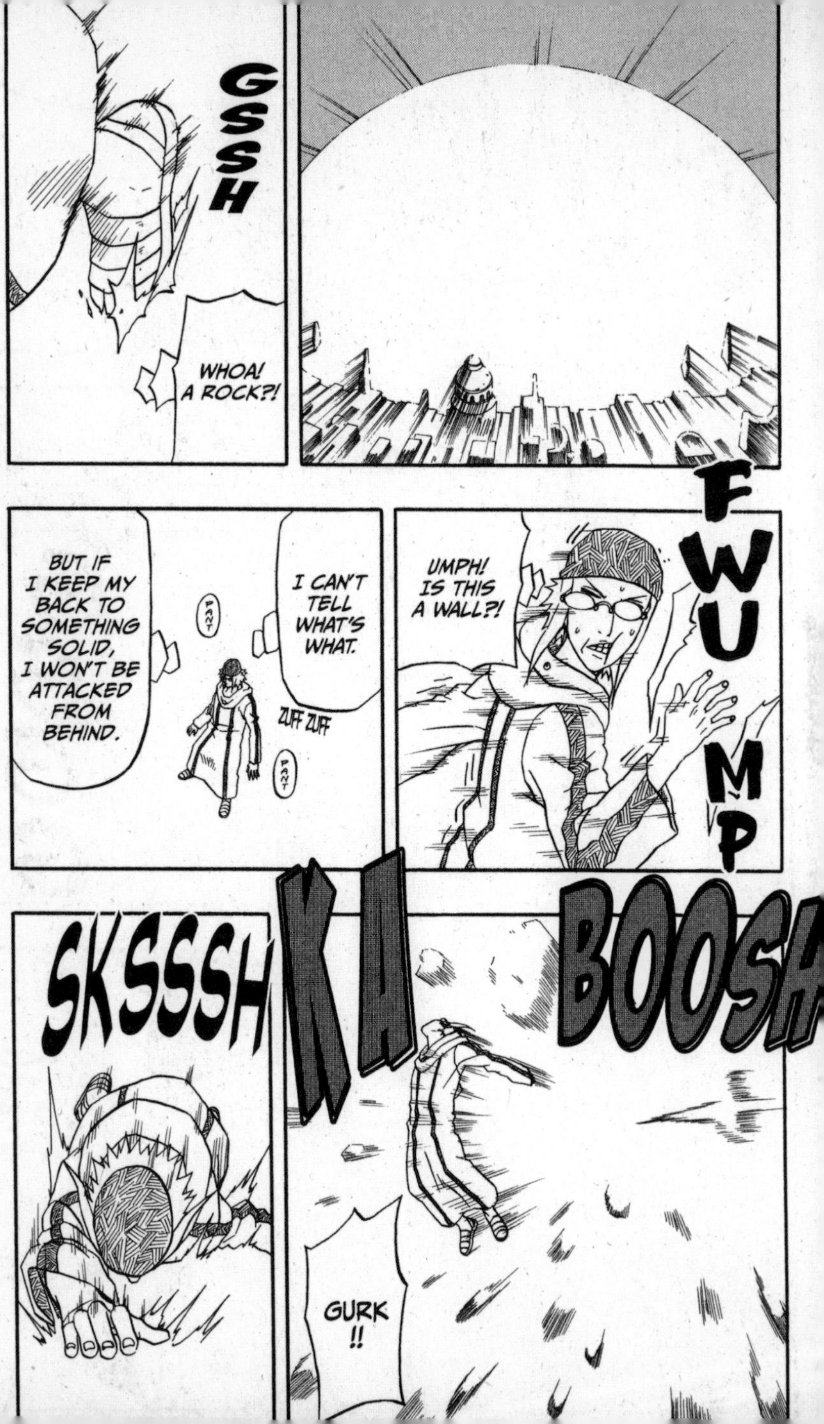
GSSH
WHOA! A ROCK?!
FWUMP
UMPH! IS THIS A WALL?!
I CAN'T TELL WHAT'S WHAT.
PANT
ZUFF ZUFF
PANT
BUT IF I KEEP MY BACK TO SOMETHING SOLID, I WON'T BE ATTACKED FROM BEHIND.
KA
BOOSH
SKSSSH
GURK !!

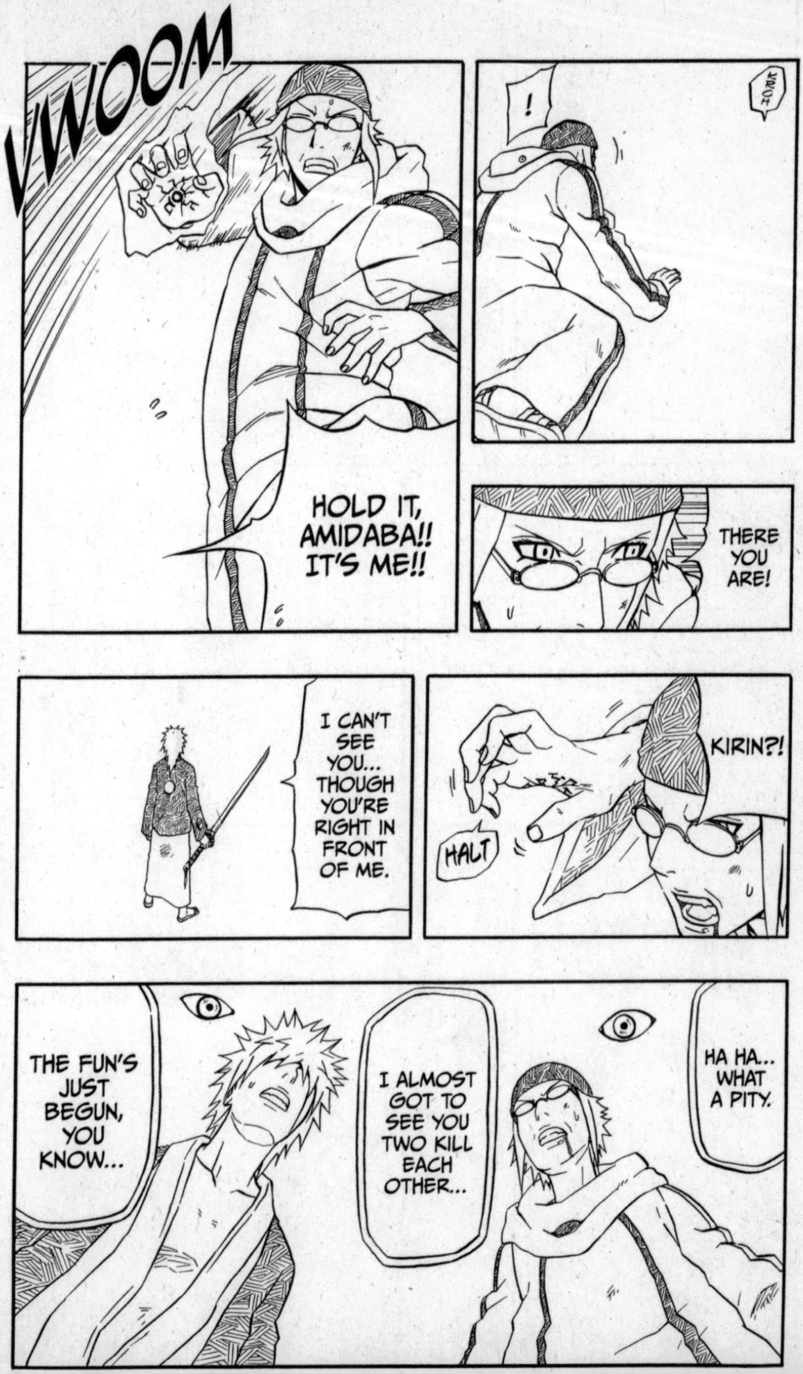
KRCH
!
THERE YOU ARE!
VWOOM
HOLD IT, AMIDABA!! IT'S ME!!
KIRIN?!
HALT
I CAN'T SEE YOU... THOUGH YOU'RE RIGHT IN FRONT OF ME.
HA HA... WHAT A PITY.
I ALMOST GOT TO SEE YOU TWO KILL EACH OTHER...
THE FUN'S JUST BEGUN, YOU KNOW...

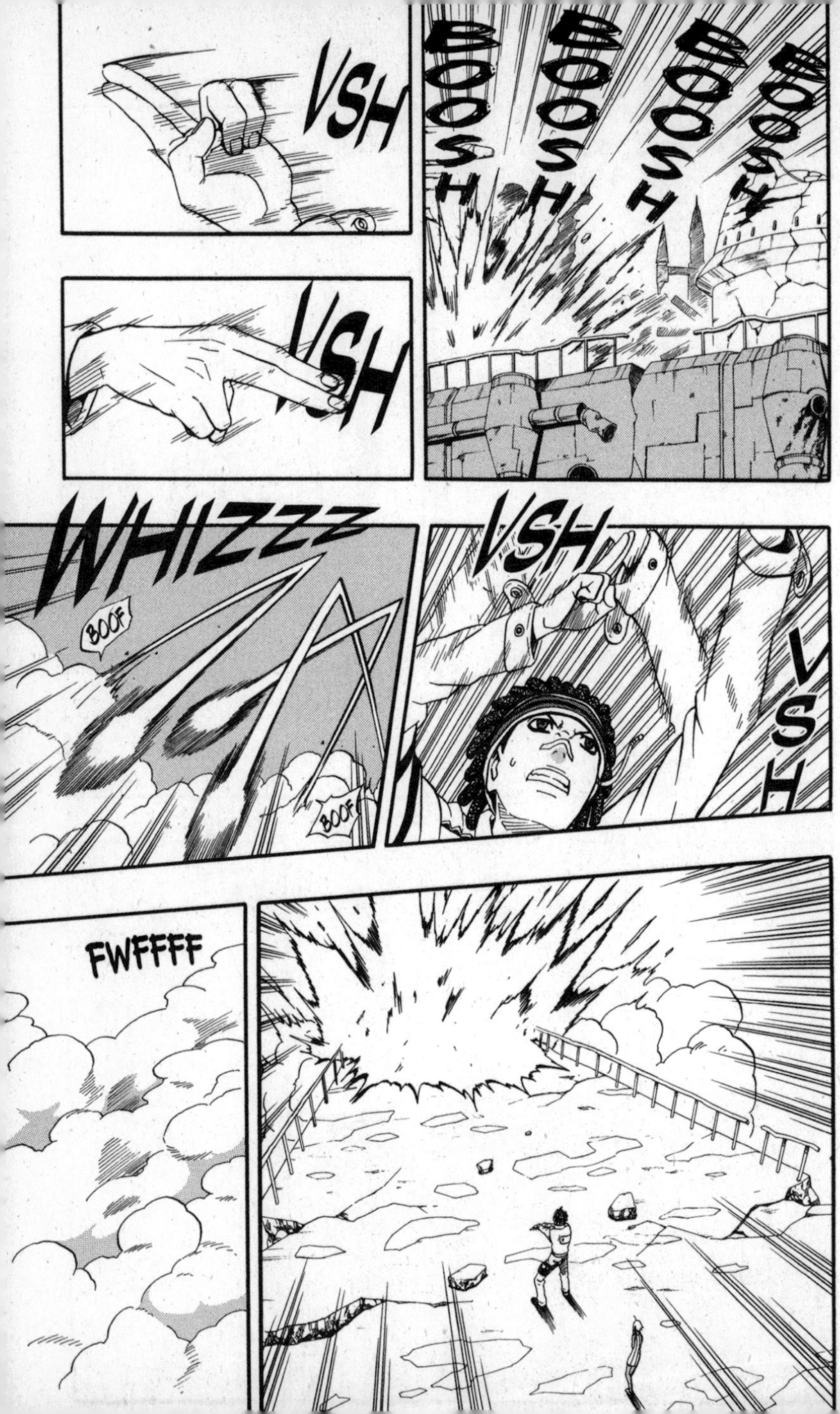
BOOSH
BOOSH
BOOSH
BOOSH
VSH
VSH
VSH
VSH
WHIZZZ
BOOF
BOOF
FWFFFF

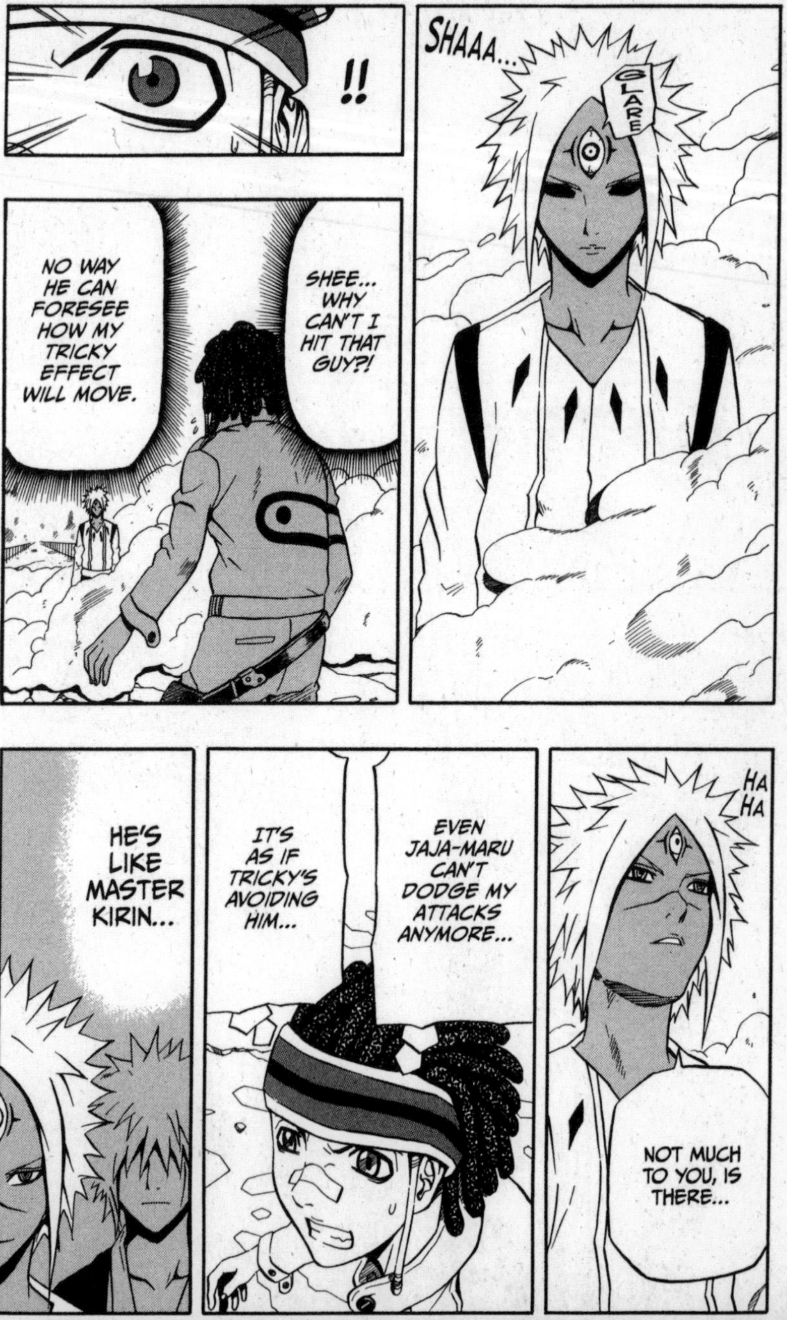
SHAAA...
GLARE
!!
SHEE... WHY CAN'T I HIT THAT GUY?!
NO WAY HE CAN FORESEE HOW MY TRICKY EFFECT WILL MOVE.
HA HA
NOT MUCH TO YOU, IS THERE...
EVEN JAJA-MARU CAN'T DODGE MY ATTACKS ANYMORE...
IT'S AS IF TRICKY'S AVOIDING HIM...
HE'S LIKE MASTER KIRIN...

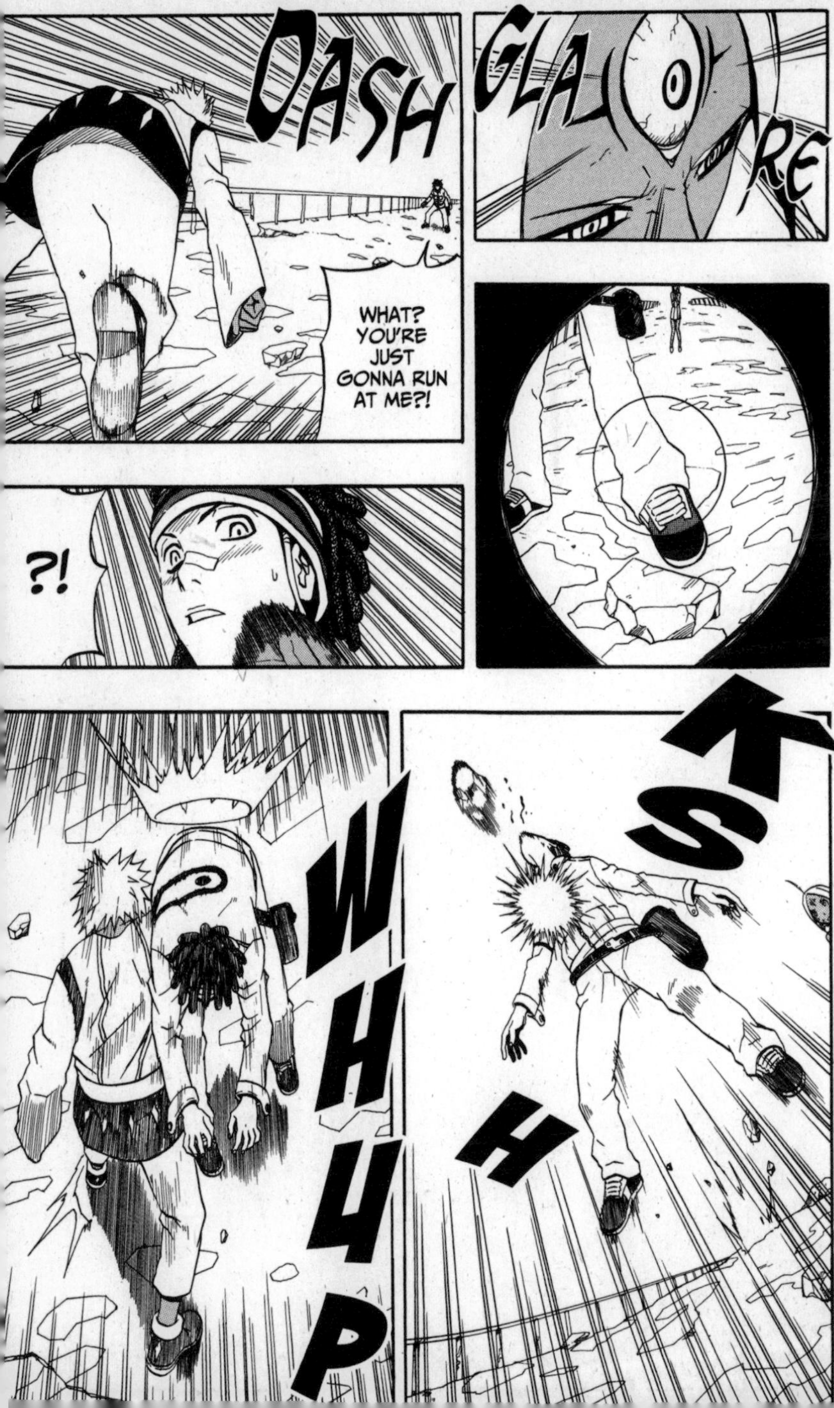
GLARE
DASH
WHAT? YOU'RE JUST GONNA RUN AT ME?!
?!
KSH
WHUP

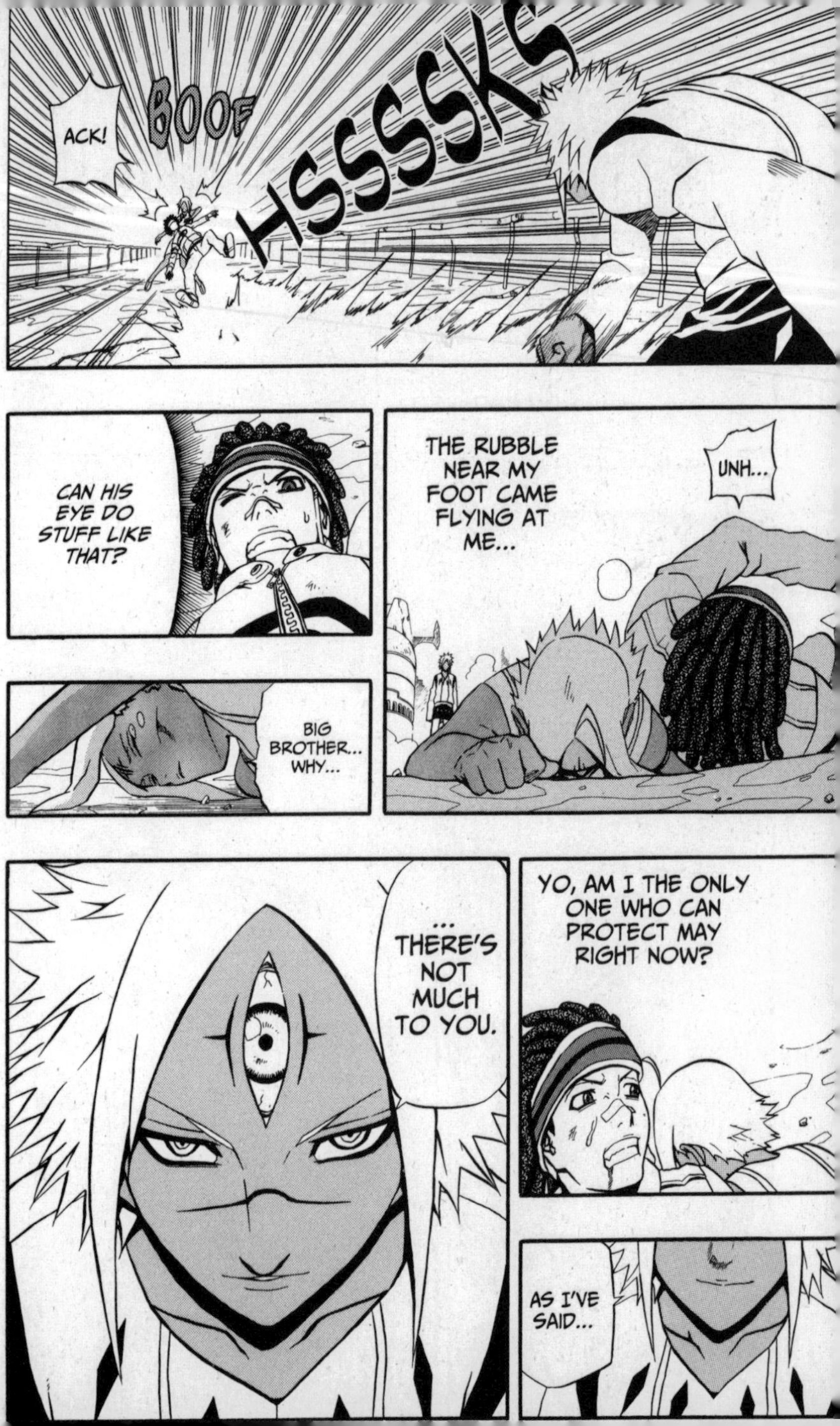
HSSSSKS
BOOF
ACK!
UNH...
THE RUBBLE NEAR MY FOOT CAME FLYING AT ME...
CAN HIS EYE DO STUFF LIKE THAT?
BIG BROTHER... WHY...
YO, AM I THE ONLY ONE WHO CAN PROTECT MAY RIGHT NOW?
AS I'VE SAID...
... THERE'S NOT MUCH TO YOU.

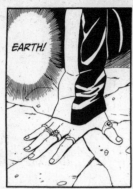

EARTH!

PM

CRASH

KADOOON

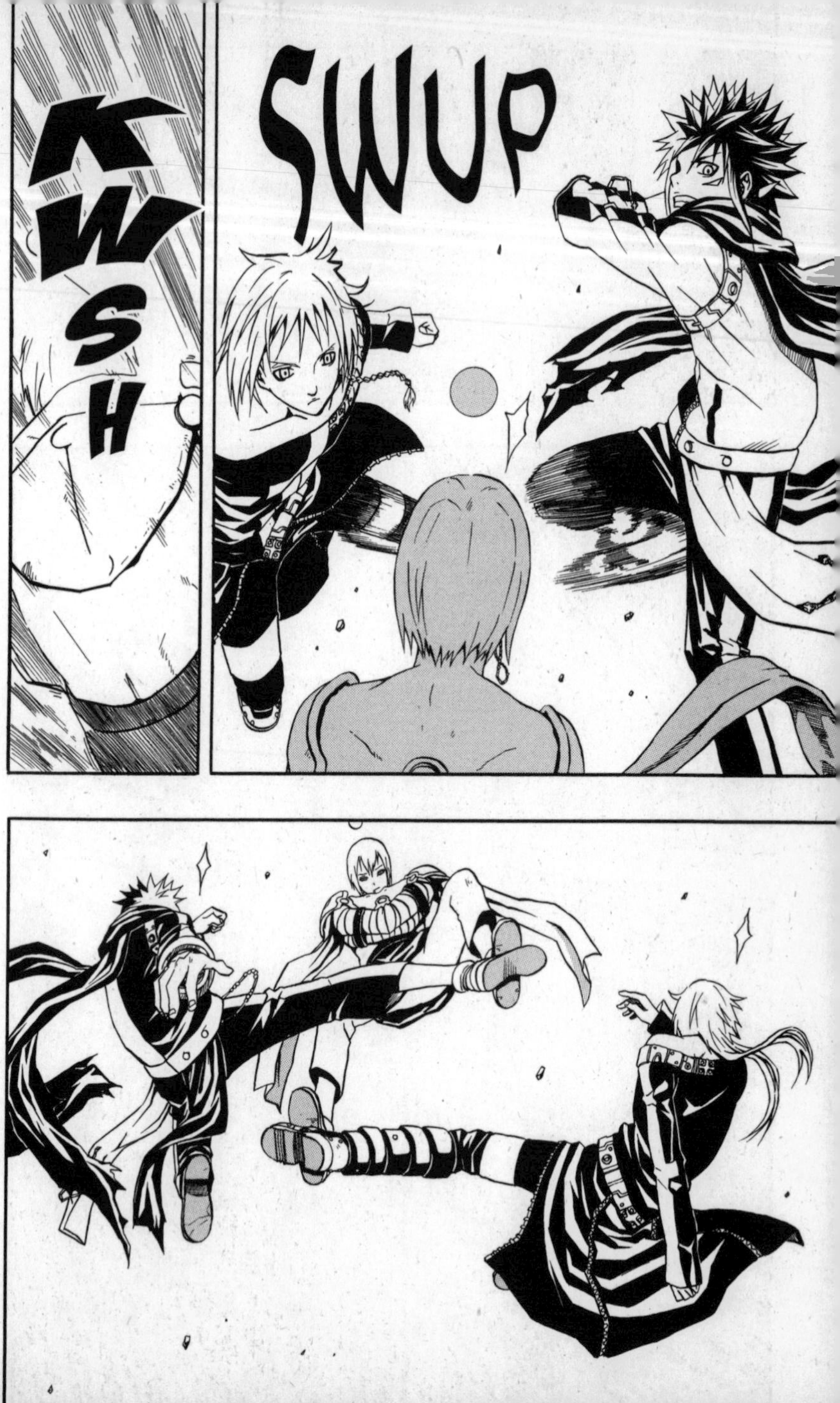
SWUP
KWSH

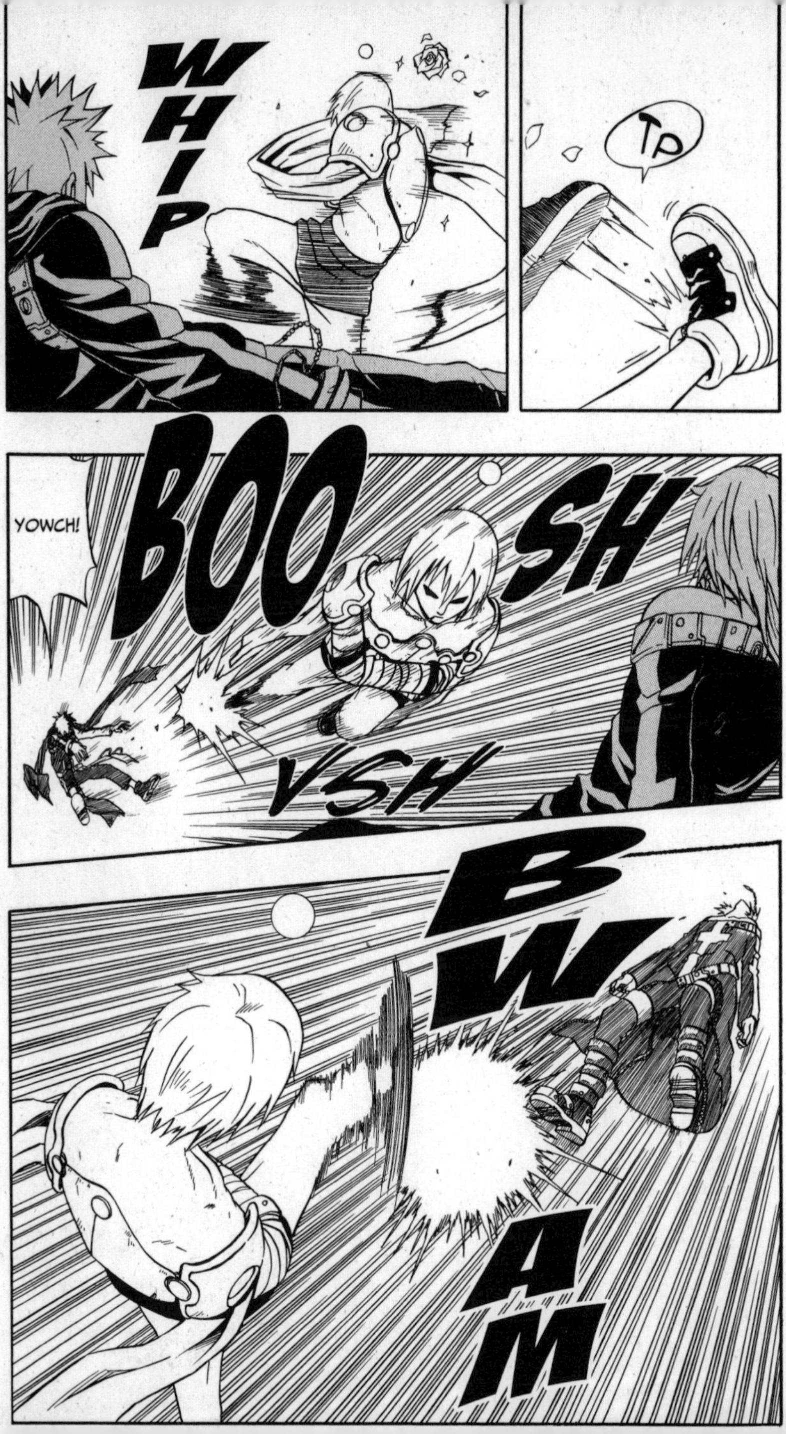
TP
WHIP
BOOSH
YOWCH!
VSH
BWAM

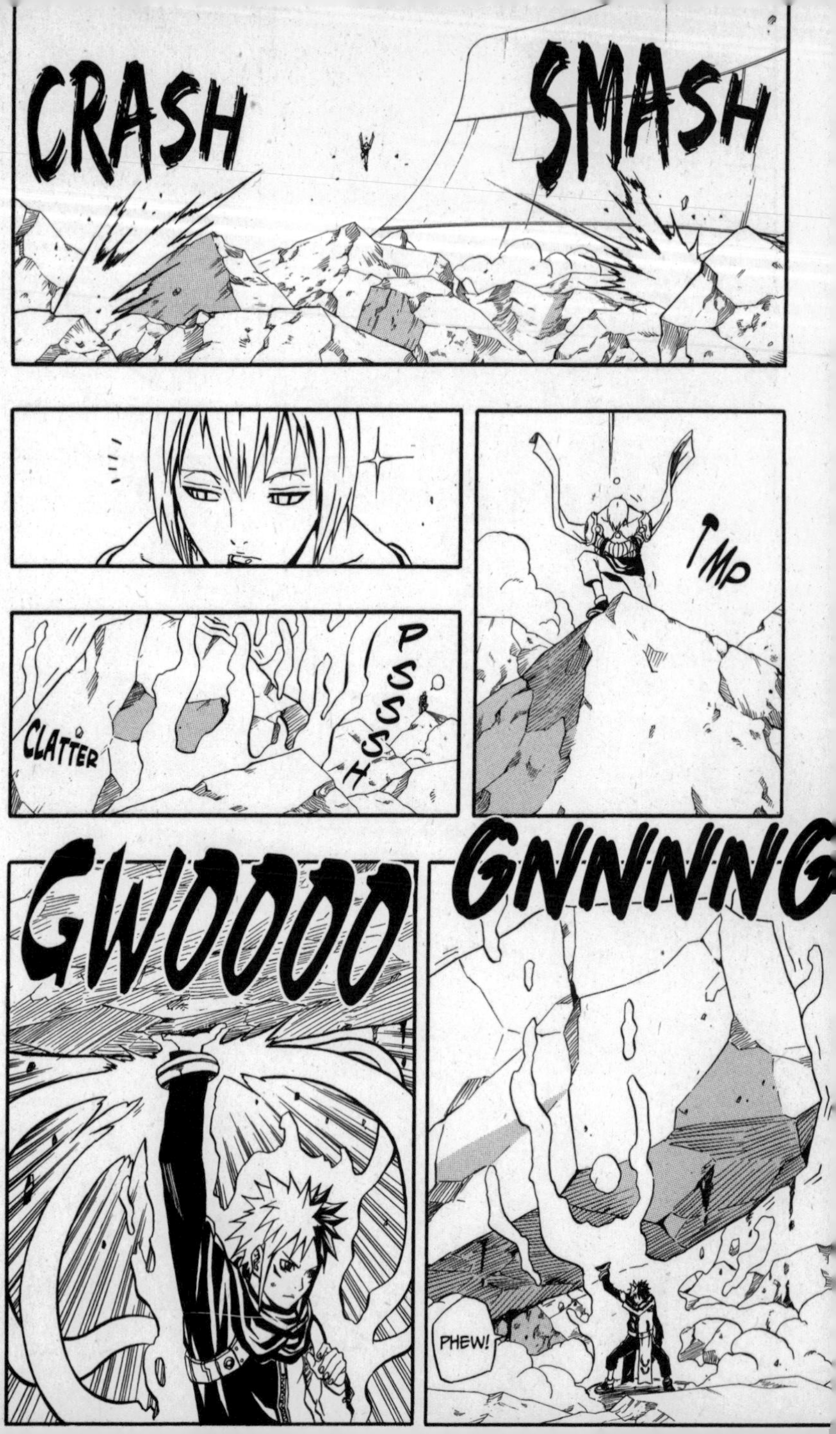
SMASH
CRASH
TMP
PSSSSH
CLATTER
GNNNNG
PHEW!
GWOOOO

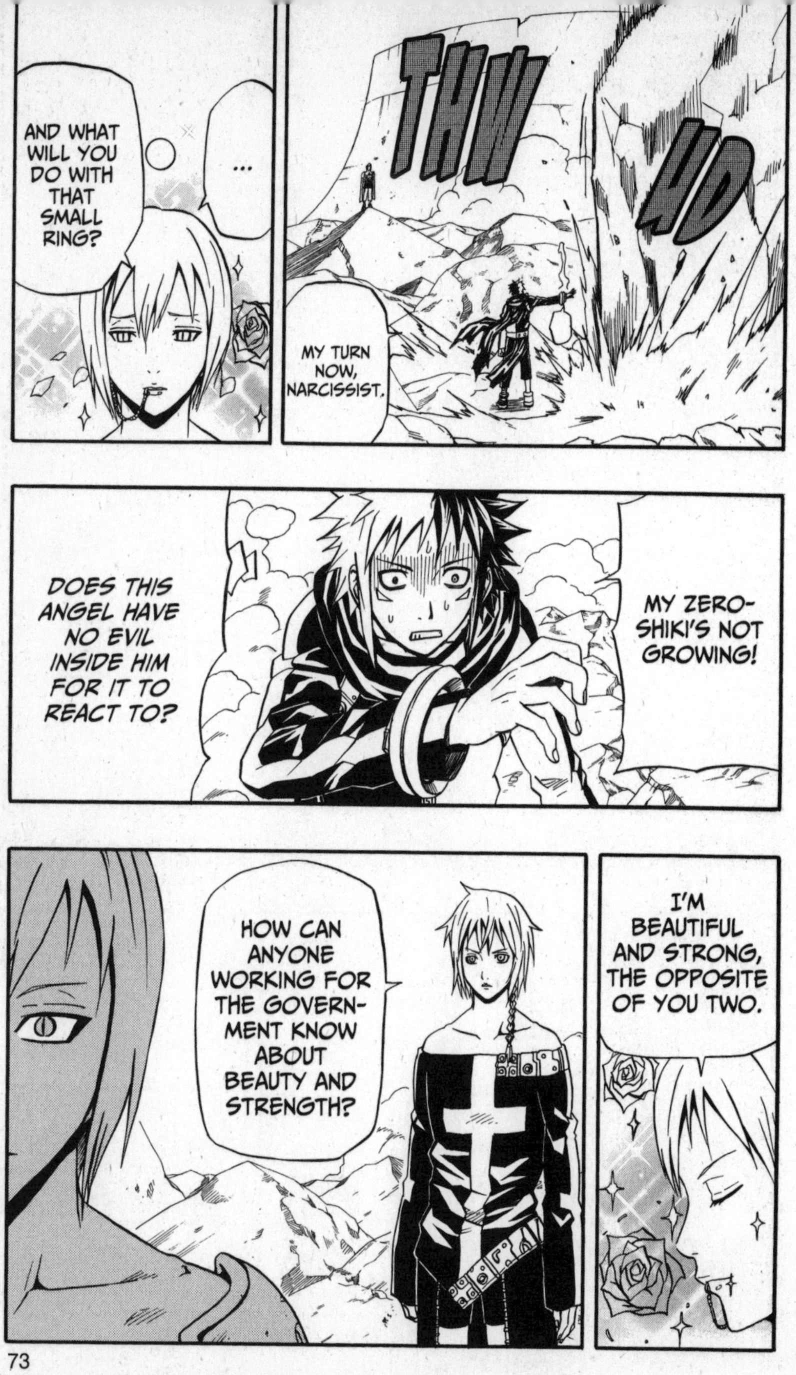
THUD
MY TURN NOW, NARCISSIST.
AND WHAT WILL YOU DO WITH THAT SMALL RING?
...
MY ZERO-SHIKI'S NOT GROWING!
DOES THIS ANGEL HAVE NO EVIL INSIDE HIM FOR IT TO REACT TO?
I'M BEAUTIFUL AND STRONG, THE OPPOSITE OF YOU TWO.
HOW CAN ANYONE WORKING FOR THE GOVERN-MENT KNOW ABOUT BEAUTY AND STRENGTH?

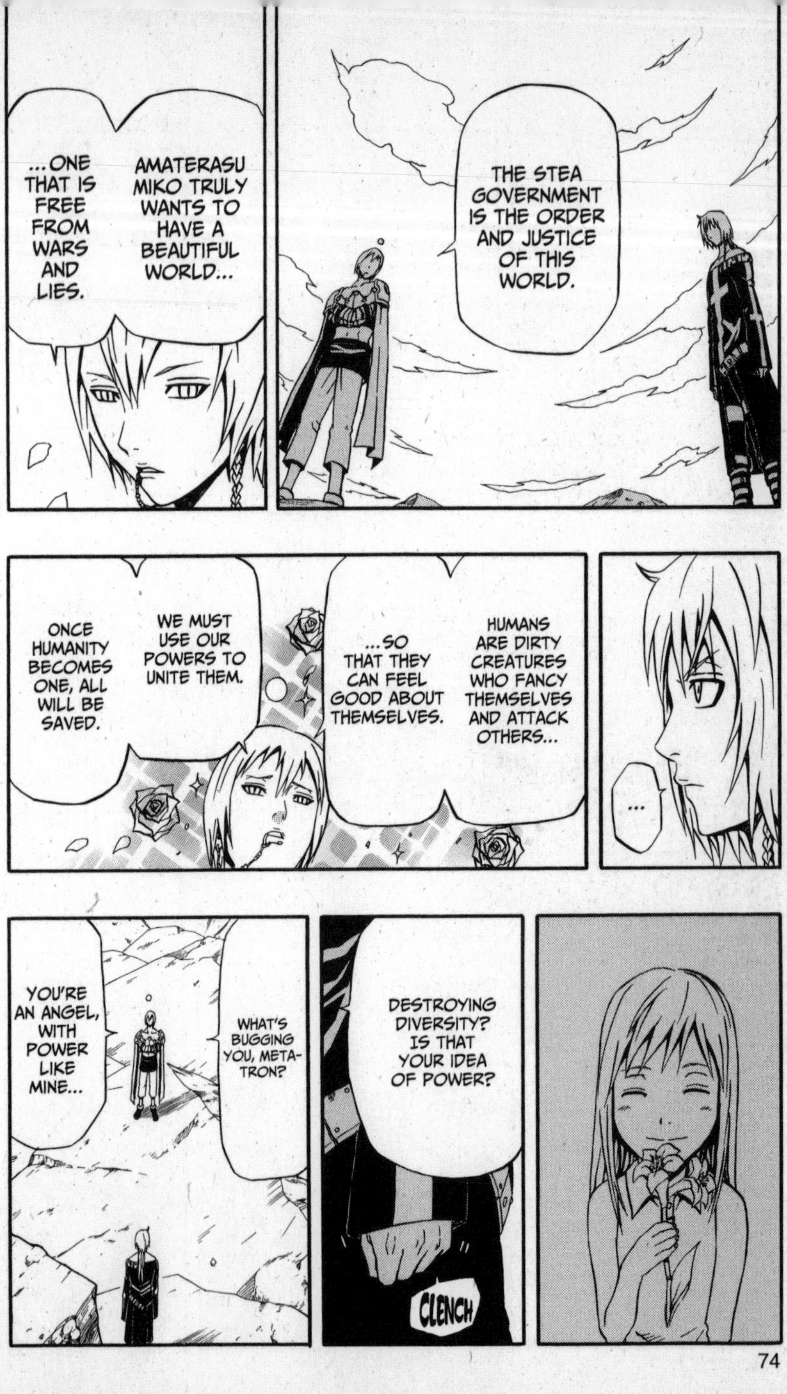
THE STEA GOVERNMENT IS THE ORDER AND JUSTICE OF THIS WORLD.
AMATERASU MIKO TRULY WANTS TO HAVE A BEAUTIFUL WORLD...
...ONE THAT IS FREE FROM WARS AND LIES.
...
HUMANS ARE DIRTY CREATURES WHO FANCY THEMSELVES AND ATTACK OTHERS...
...SO THAT THEY CAN FEEL GOOD ABOUT THEMSELVES.
WE MUST USE OUR POWERS TO UNITE THEM.
ONCE HUMANITY BECOMES ONE, ALL WILL BE SAVED.
DESTROYING DIVERSITY? IS THAT YOUR IDEA OF POWER?
CLENCH
WHAT'S BUGGING YOU, META-TRON?
YOU'RE AN ANGEL, WITH POWER LIKE MINE...

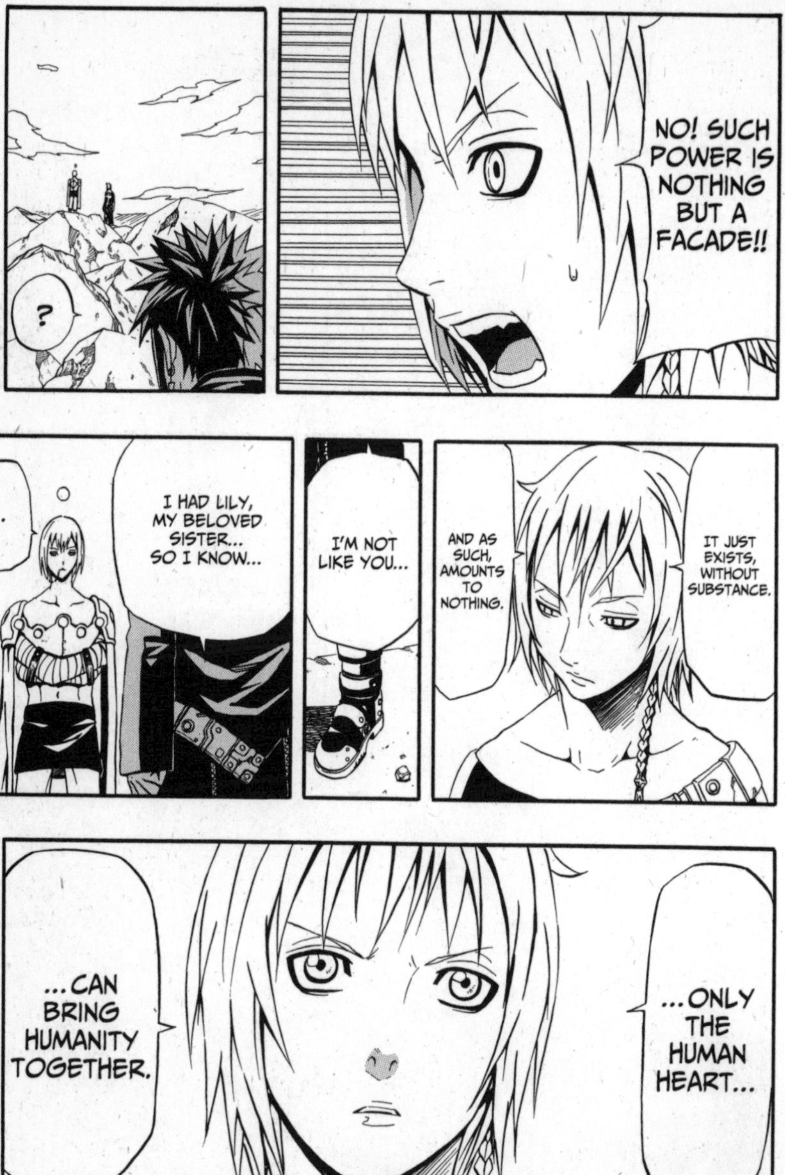
NO! SUCH POWER IS NOTHING BUT A FACADE!!
?
IT JUST EXISTS, WITHOUT SUBSTANCE.
AND AS SUCH, AMOUNTS TO NOTHING.
I'M NOT LIKE YOU...
I HAD LILY, MY BELOVED SISTER... SO I KNOW...
...
...ONLY THE HUMAN HEART...
...CAN BRING HUMANITY TOGETHER.

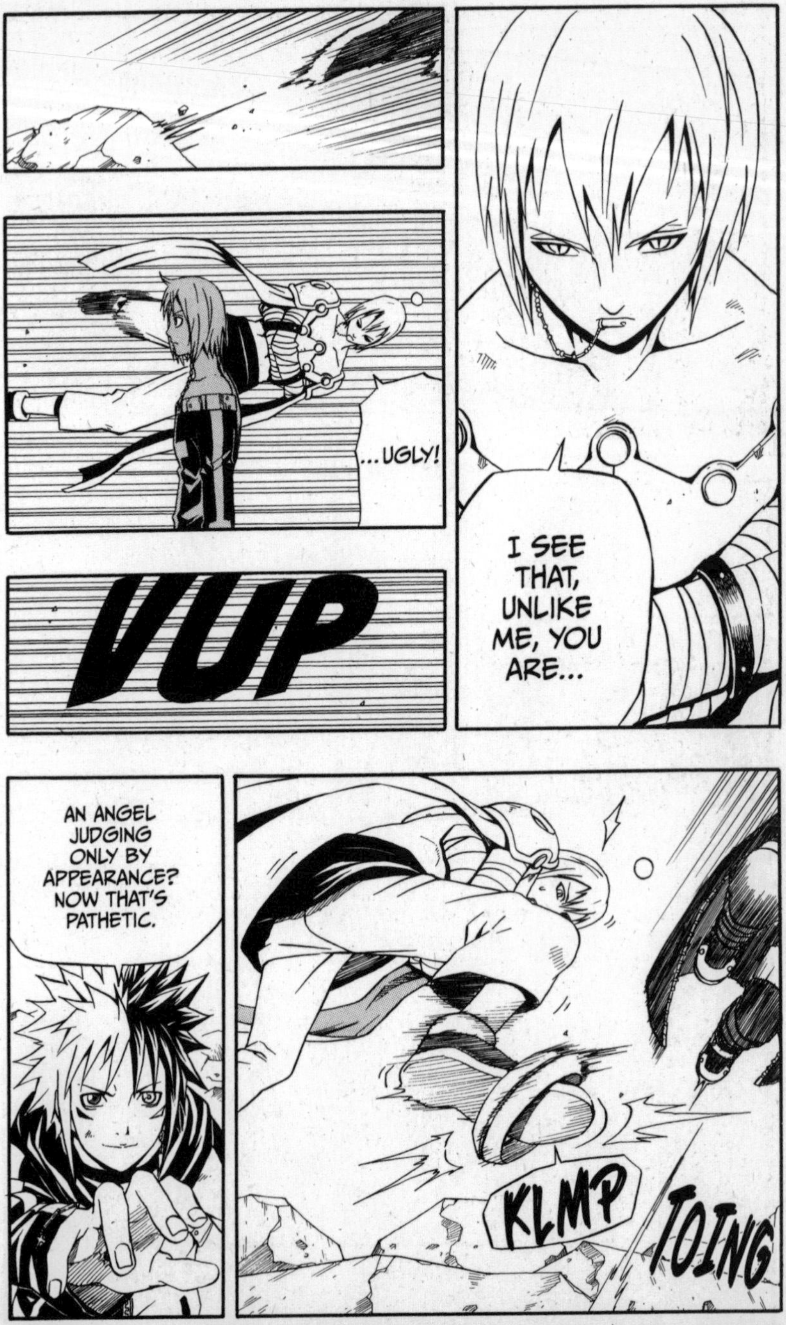
I SEE THAT, UNLIKE ME, YOU ARE...
...UGLY!
VUP
TOING
KLMP
AN ANGEL JUDGING ONLY BY APPEARANCE? NOW THAT'S PATHETIC.

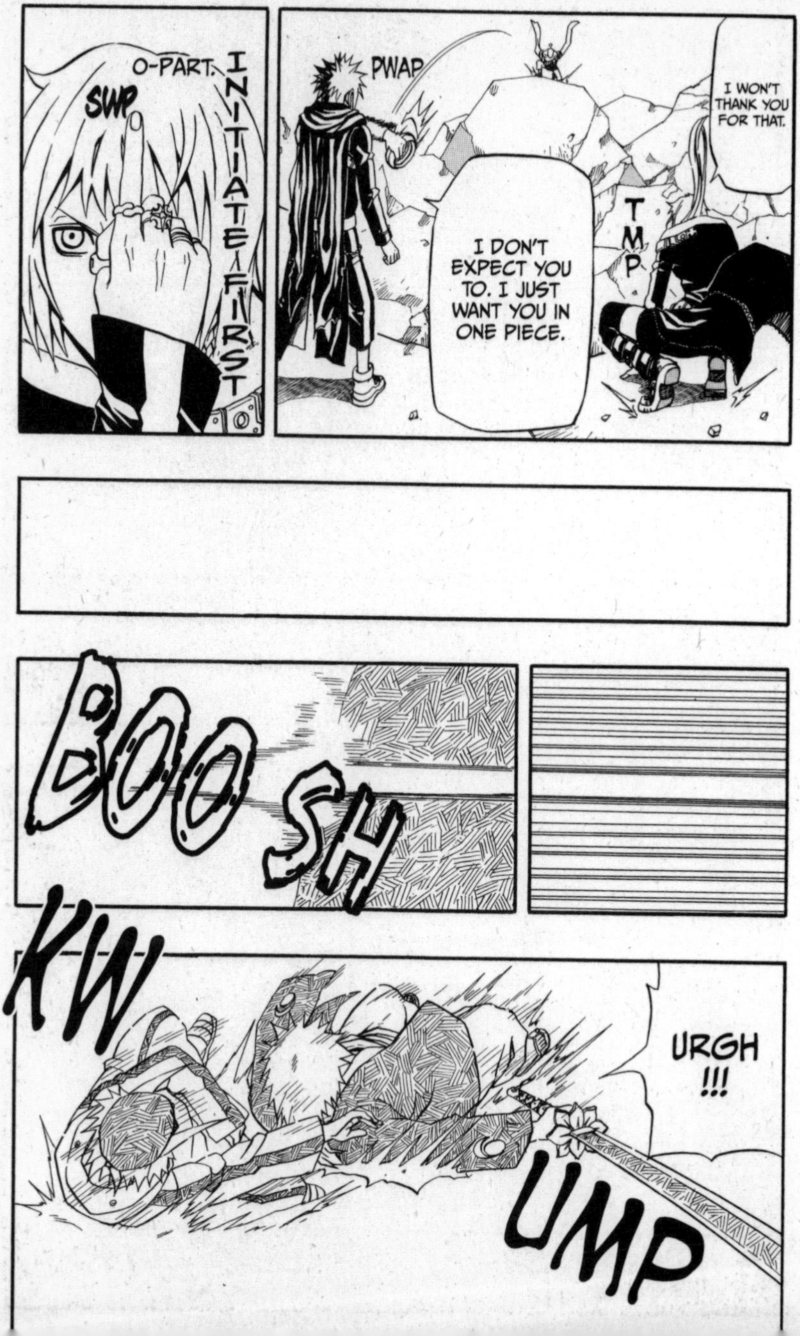
I WON'T THANK YOU FOR THAT.
TMP
I DON'T EXPECT YOU TO. I JUST WANT YOU IN ONE PIECE.
PWAP
INITIATE FIRST
O-PART.
SWP
BOOSH
KWUMP
URGH !!!

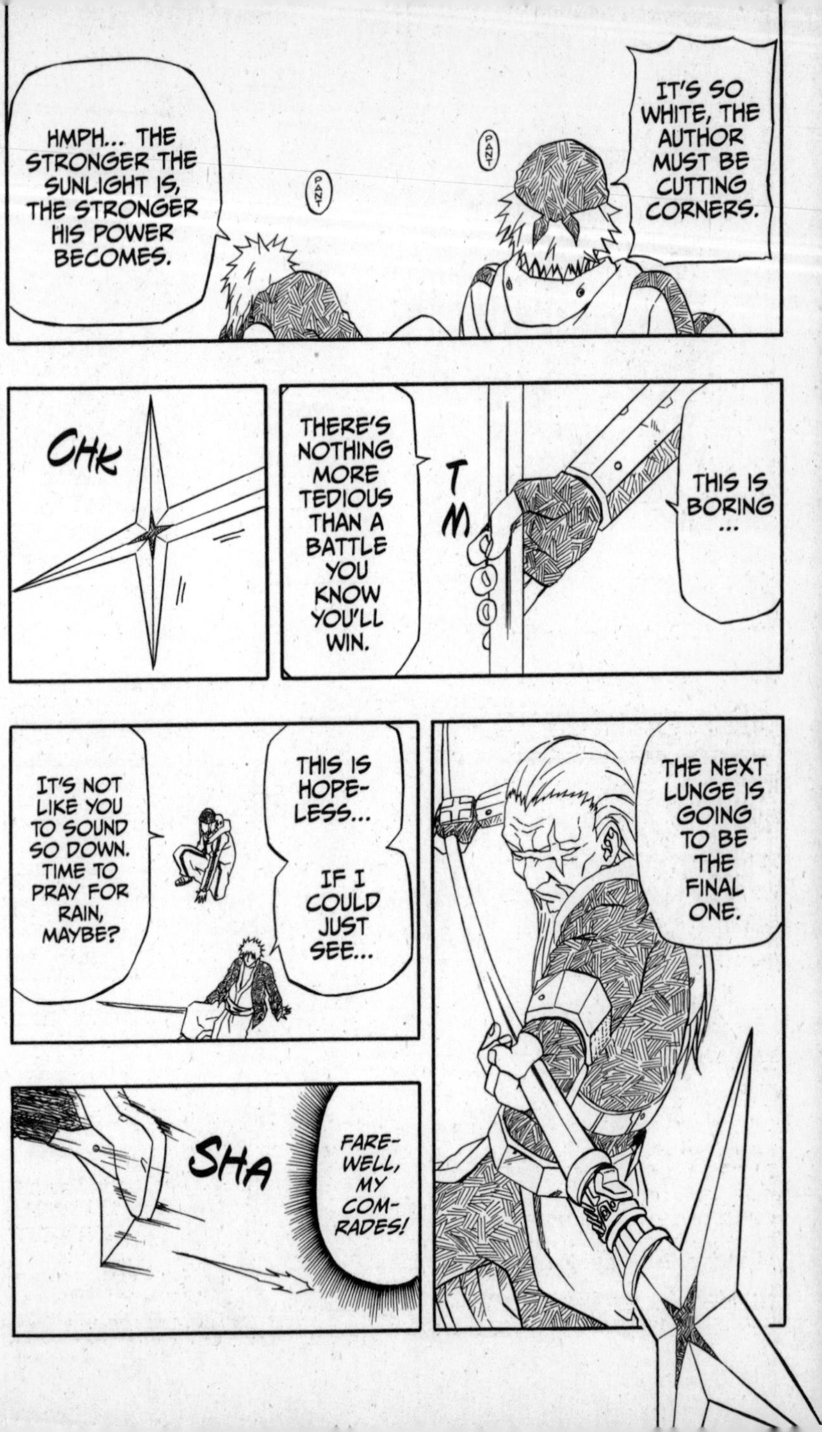
IT'S SO WHITE, THE AUTHOR MUST BE CUTTING CORNERS.
PANT
PANT
HMPH... THE STRONGER THE SUNLIGHT IS, THE STRONGER HIS POWER BECOMES.
THIS IS BORING ...
TM
THERE'S NOTHING MORE TEDIOUS THAN A BATTLE YOU KNOW YOU'LL WIN.
CHK
THE NEXT LUNGE IS GOING TO BE THE FINAL ONE.
THIS IS HOPE-LESS...
IF I COULD JUST SEE...
IT'S NOT LIKE YOU TO SOUND SO DOWN. TIME TO PRAY FOR RAIN, MAYBE?
FARE-WELL, MY COM-RADES!
SHA

WHERE'S HE ATTACKING FROM ?!

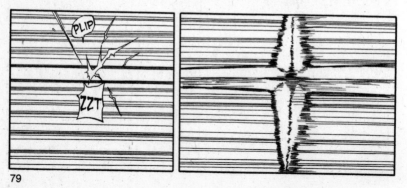

PLIP

ZZT

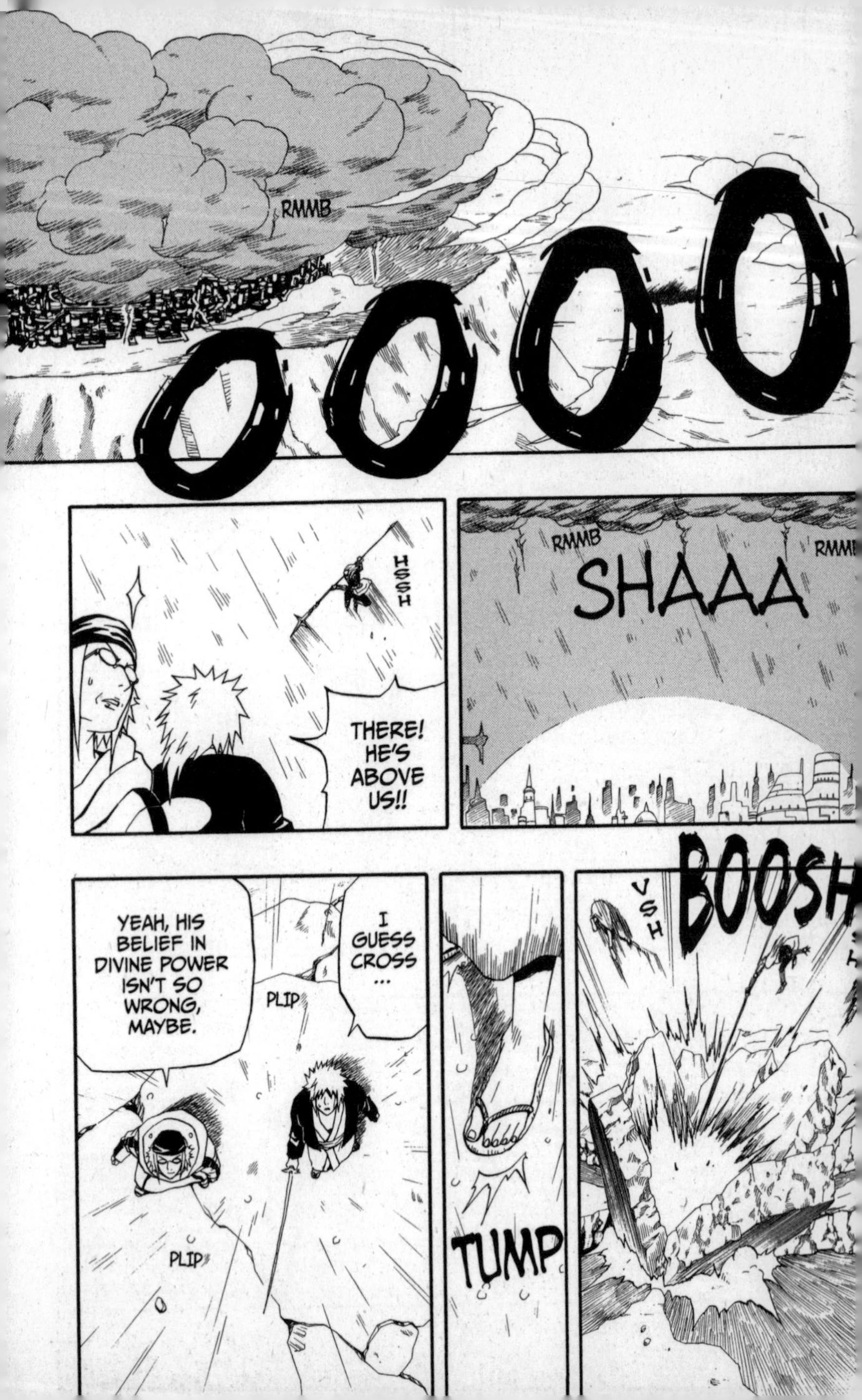
RMMB
OOOO
RMMB
RMM
SHAAA
HSSH
THERE! HE'S ABOVE US!!
VSH
BOOSH
TUMP
I GUESS CROSS ...
YEAH, HIS BELIEF IN DIVINE POWER ISN'T SO WRONG, MAYBE.
PLIP
PLIP

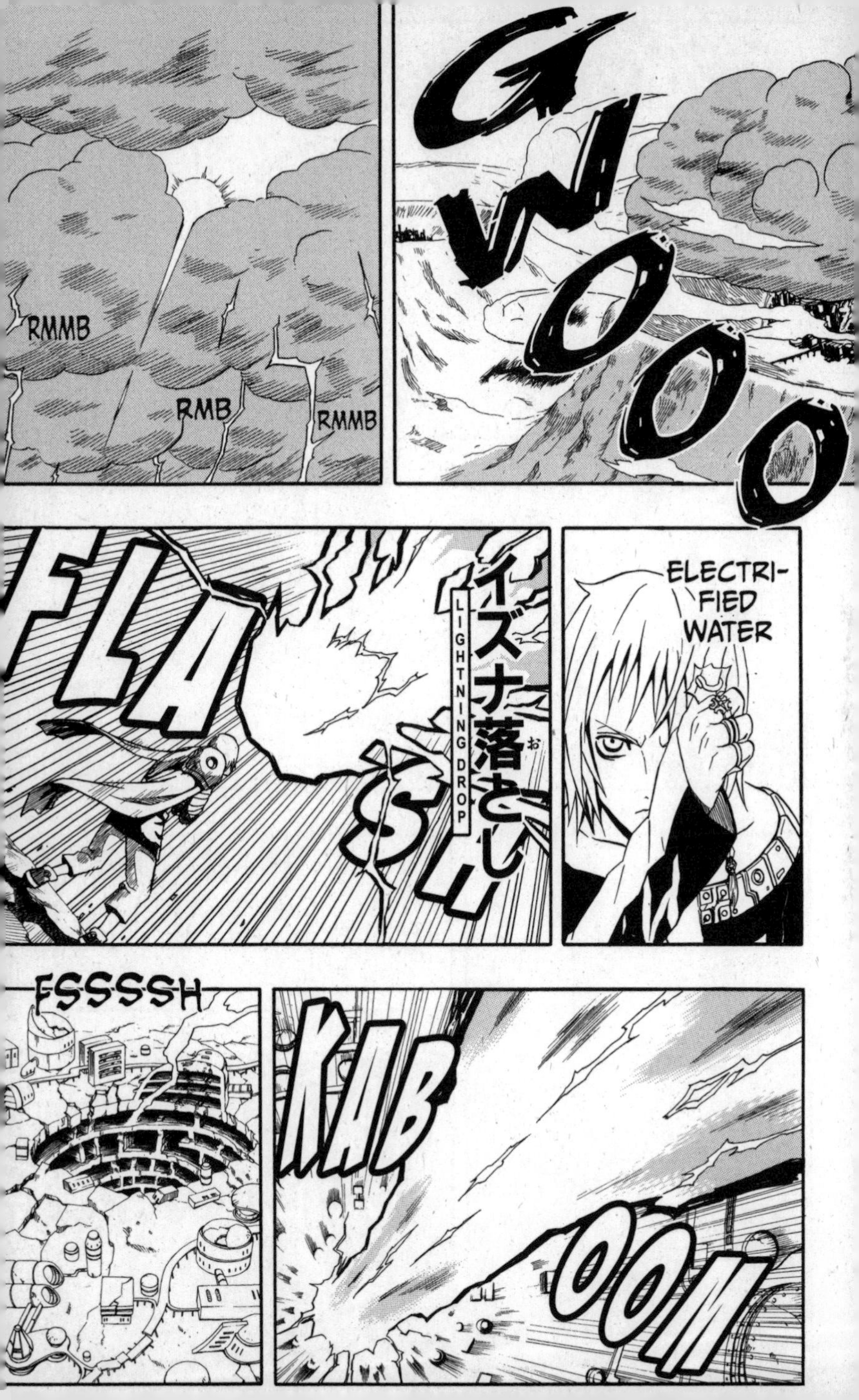
GWOOOO
RMMB
RMB
RMMB
ELECTRI-
FIED
WATER
FLA
SH
イズナ落とし
LIGHTNING DROP
KAB
OOOM
FSSSSH

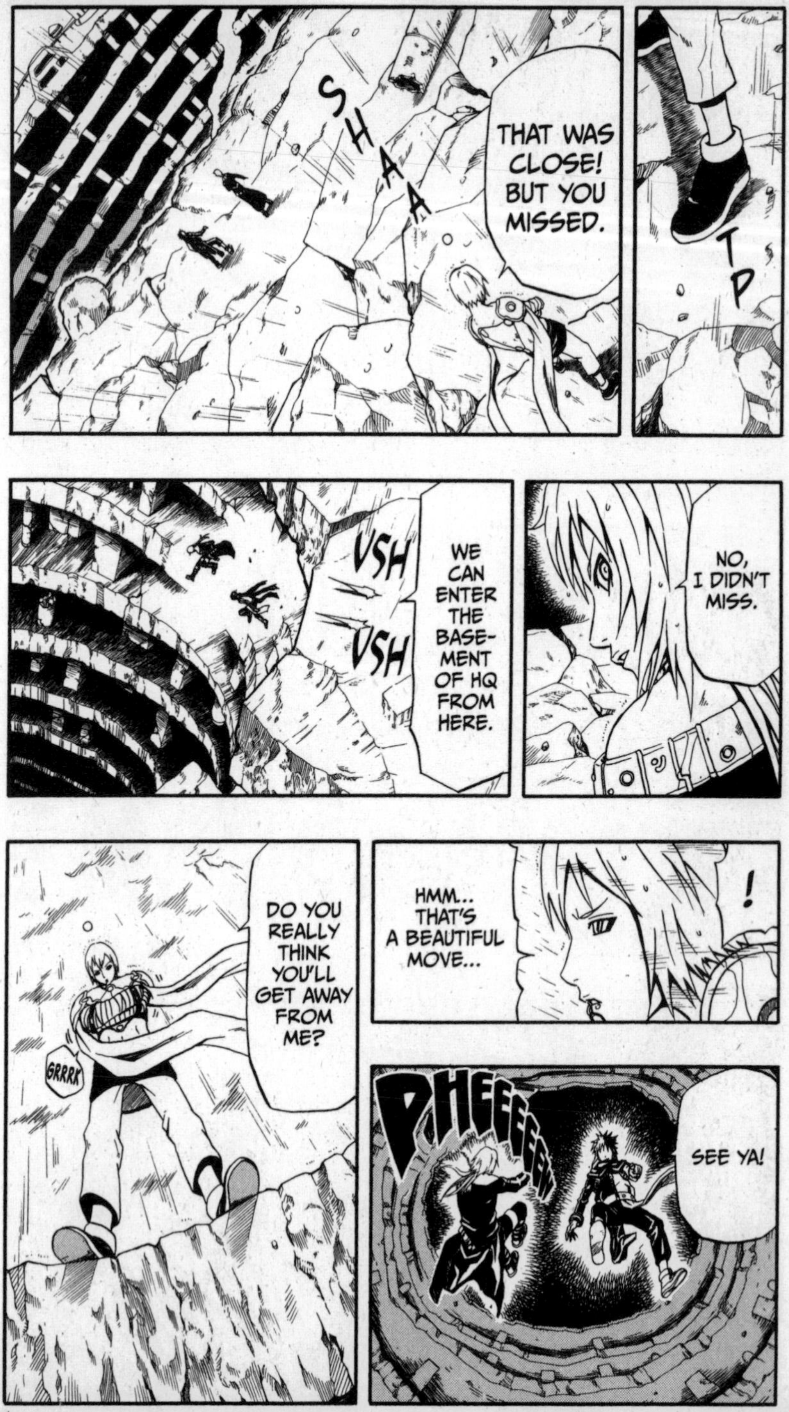
TP
SHAAA
THAT WAS CLOSE! BUT YOU MISSED.
NO, I DIDN'T MISS.
VSH
VSH
WE CAN ENTER THE BASEMENT OF HQ FROM HERE.
!
HMM... THAT'S A BEAUTIFUL MOVE...
DHEEEEEW
SEE YA!
DO YOU REALLY THINK YOU'LL GET AWAY FROM ME?
GRRRK

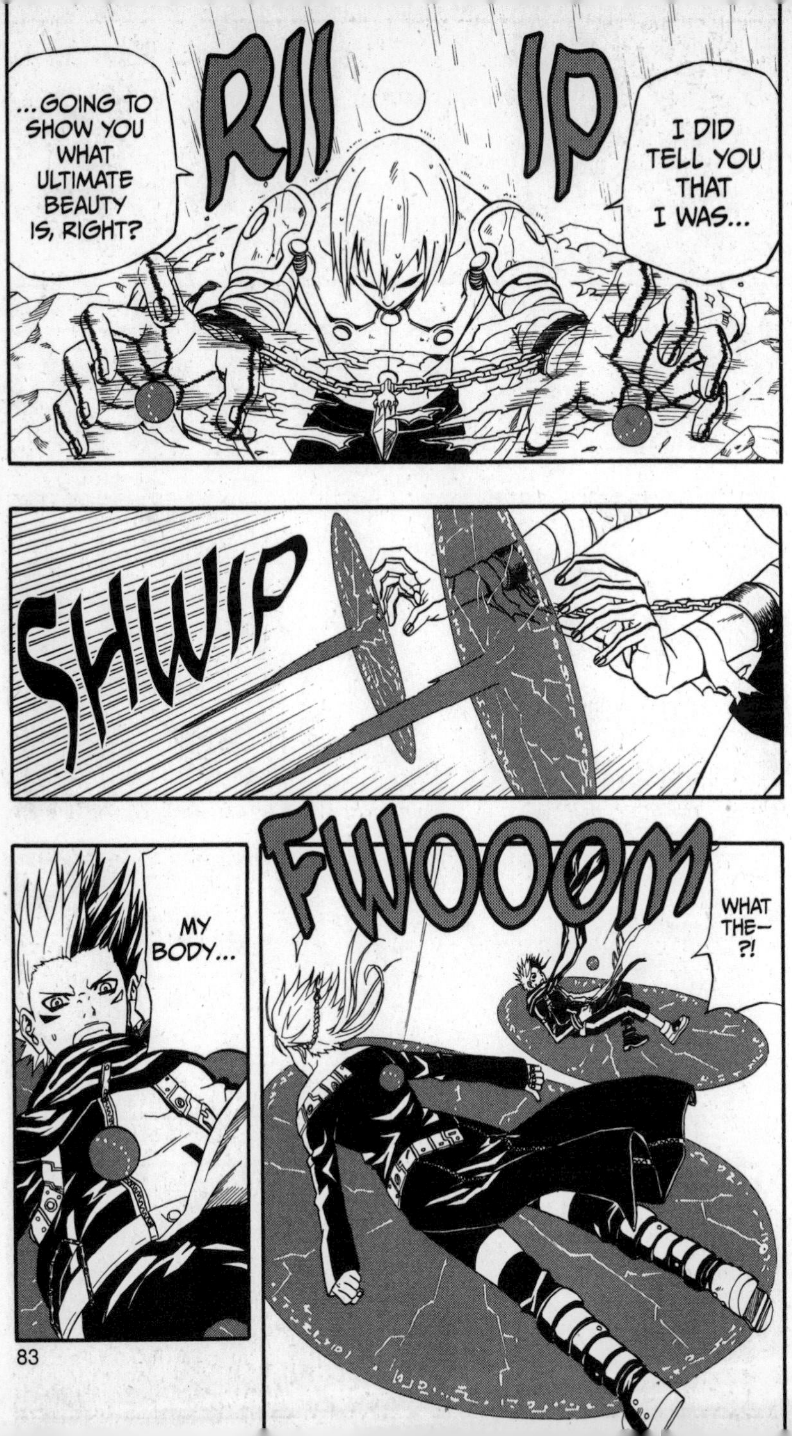
I DID TELL YOU THAT I WAS...
RII IP
...GOING TO SHOW YOU WHAT ULTIMATE BEAUTY IS, RIGHT?
SHWIP
FWOOOM
WHAT THE—?!
MY BODY...

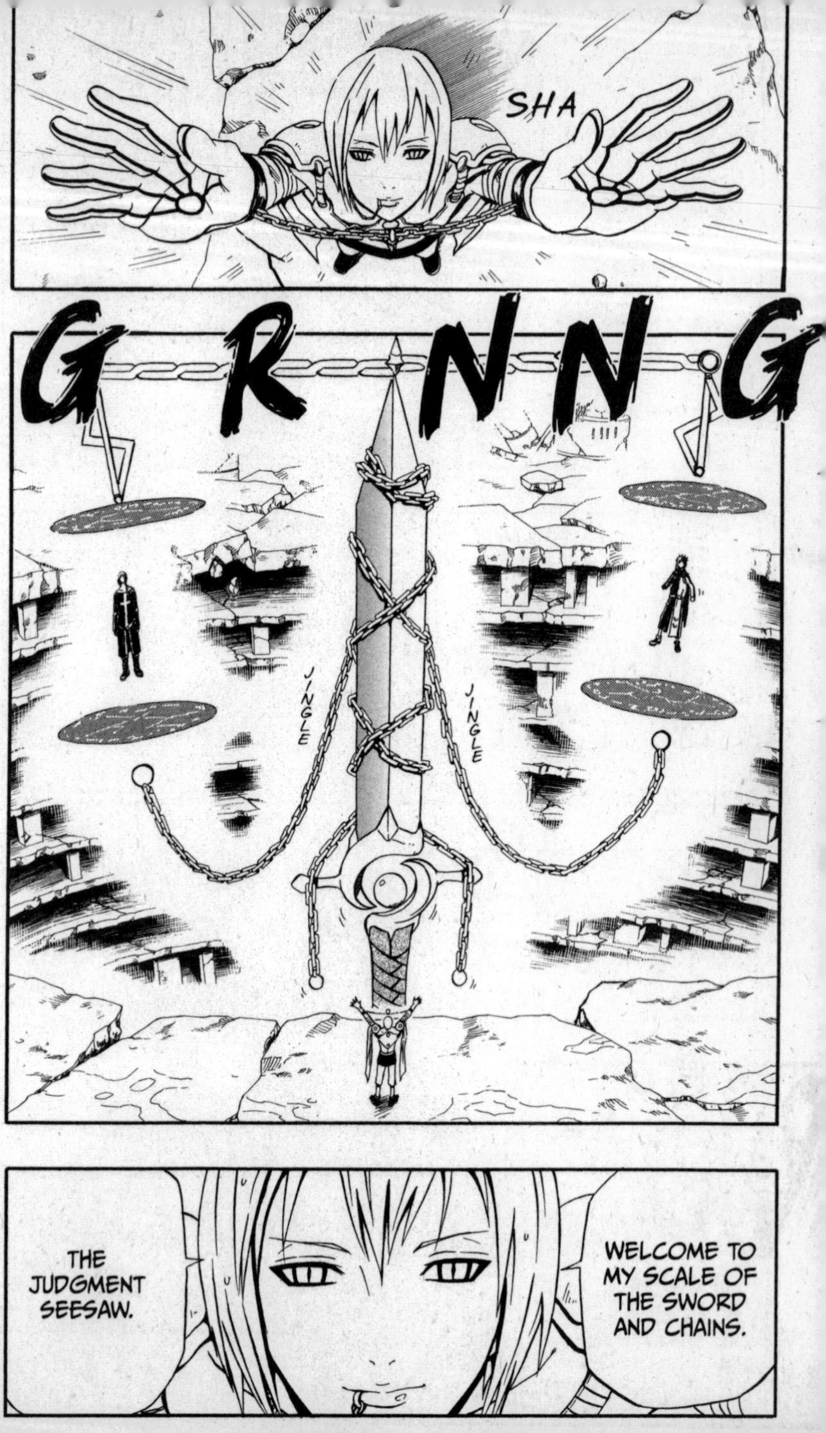
SHA
GRNNG
JINGLE
JINGLE
WELCOME TO MY SCALE OF THE SWORD AND CHAINS.
THE JUDGMENT SEESAW.

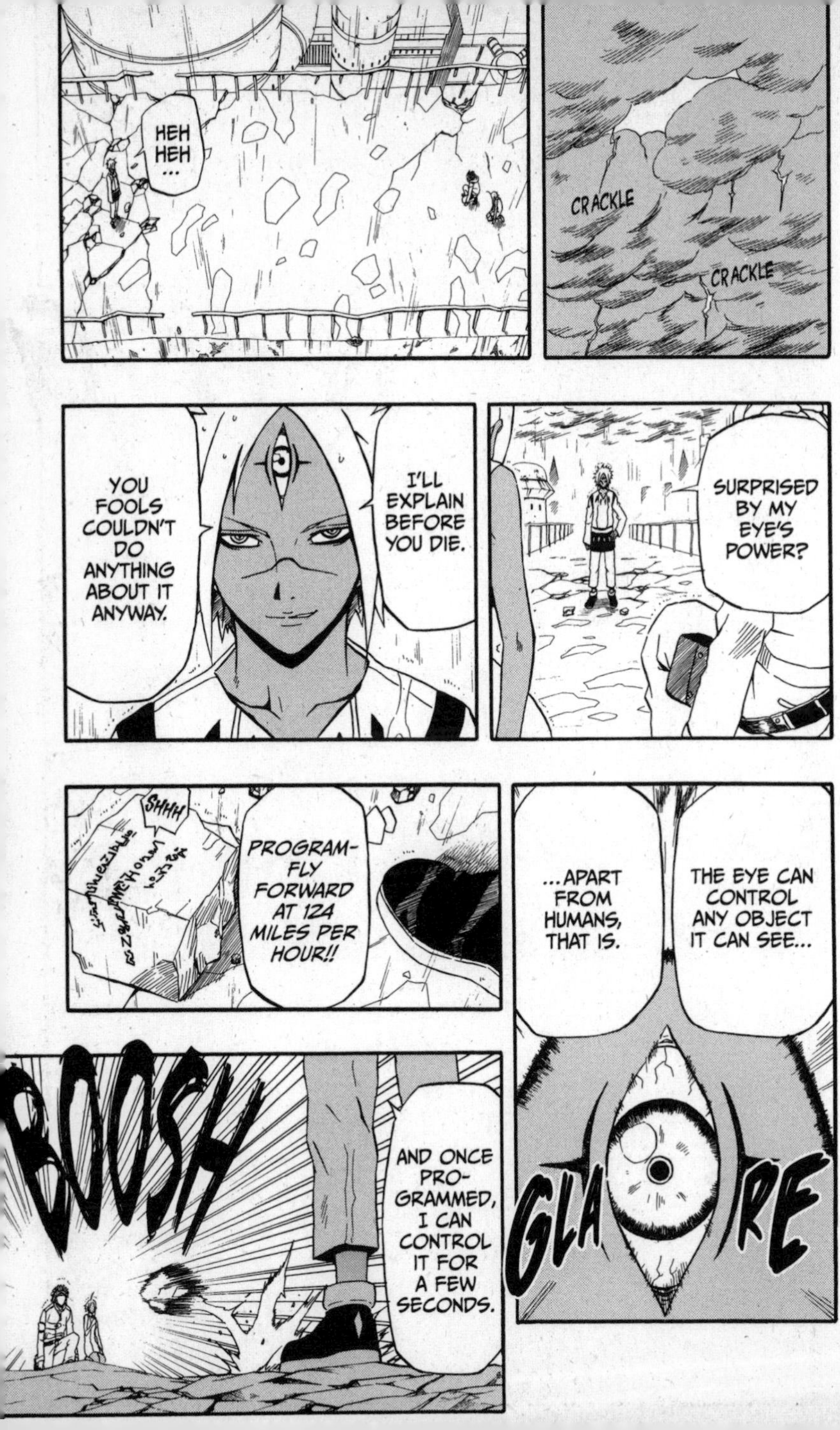
CRACKLE
CRACKLE
HEH HEH ...
SURPRISED BY MY EYE'S POWER?
I'LL EXPLAIN BEFORE YOU DIE.
YOU FOOLS COULDN'T DO ANYTHING ABOUT IT ANYWAY.
THE EYE CAN CONTROL ANY OBJECT IT CAN SEE...
...APART FROM HUMANS, THAT IS.
GLARE
SHHH
PROGRAM-FLY FORWARD AT 124 MILES PER HOUR!!
AND ONCE PRO-GRAMMED, I CAN CONTROL IT FOR A FEW SECONDS.
BOOSH

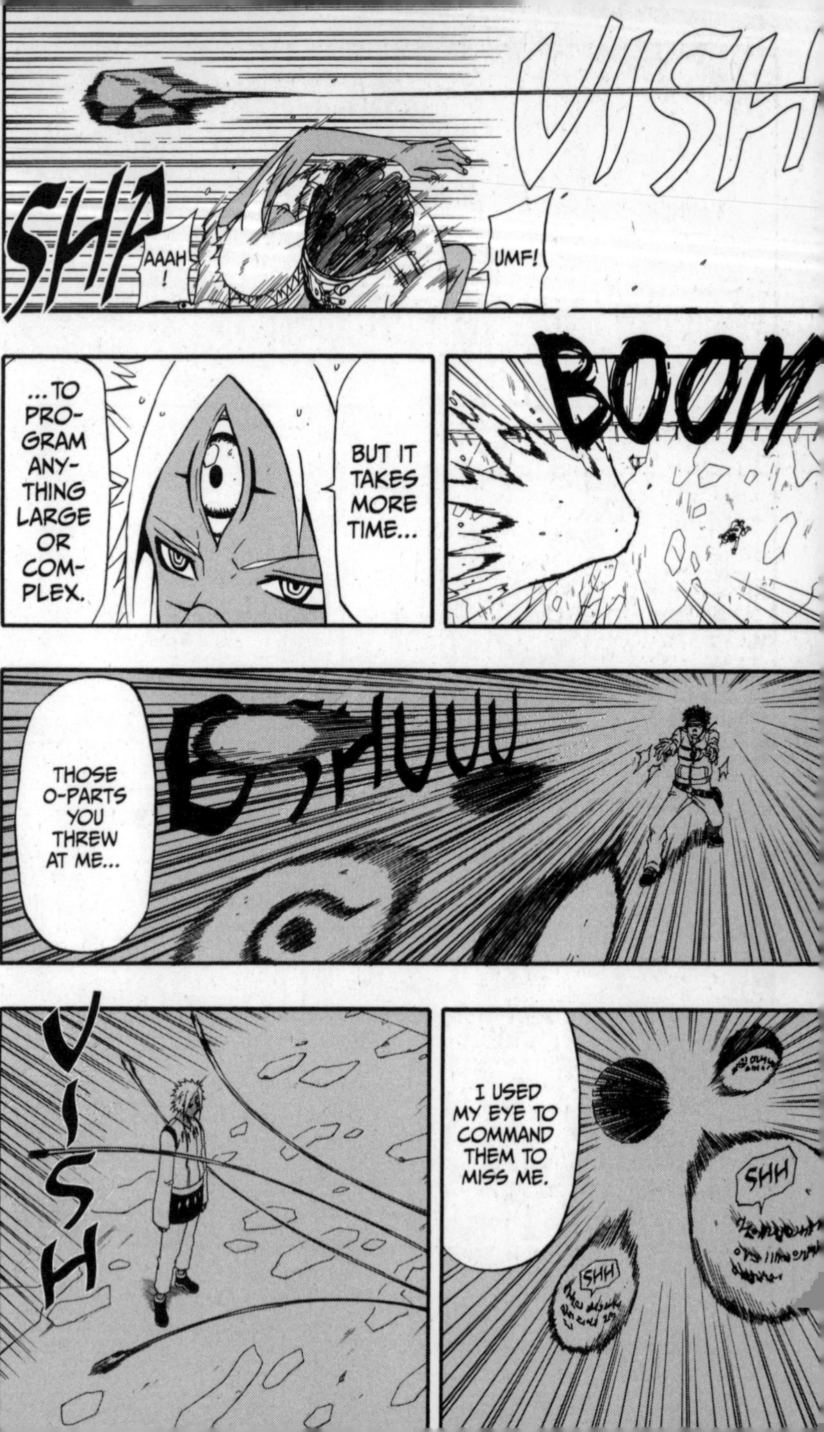
VISH
UMF!
AAAH!
SHP
BOOM
BUT IT TAKES MORE TIME...
...TO PROGRAM ANYTHING LARGE OR COMPLEX.
SHUUU
THOSE O-PARTS YOU THREW AT ME...
I USED MY EYE TO COMMAND THEM TO MISS ME.
SHH
SHH
VISH

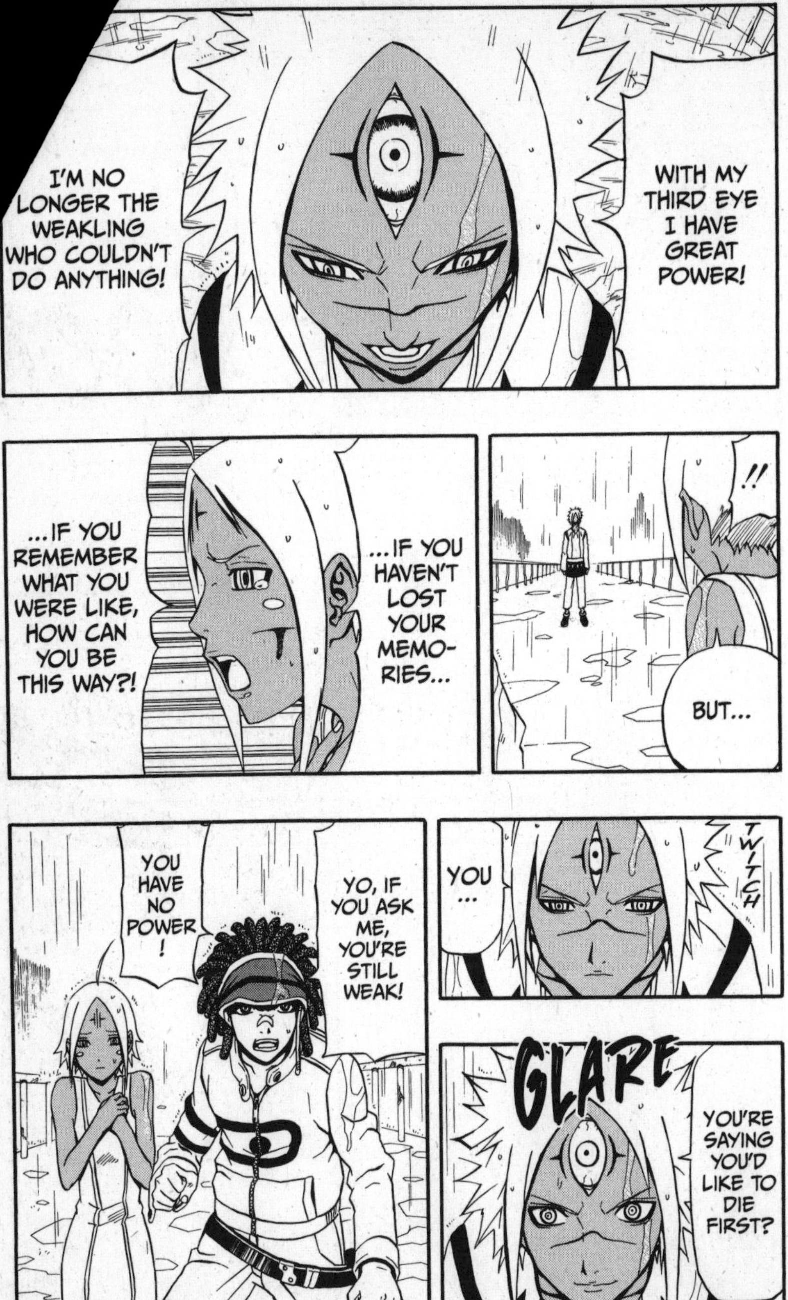
WITH MY THIRD EYE I HAVE GREAT POWER!
I'M NO LONGER THE WEAKLING WHO COULDN'T DO ANYTHING!
!!
BUT...
...IF YOU HAVEN'T LOST YOUR MEMO-RIES...
...IF YOU REMEMBER WHAT YOU WERE LIKE, HOW CAN YOU BE THIS WAY?!
TWITCH
YOU ...
GLARE
YOU'RE SAYING YOU'D LIKE TO DIE FIRST?
YO, IF YOU ASK ME, YOU'RE STILL WEAK!
YOU HAVE NO POWER!

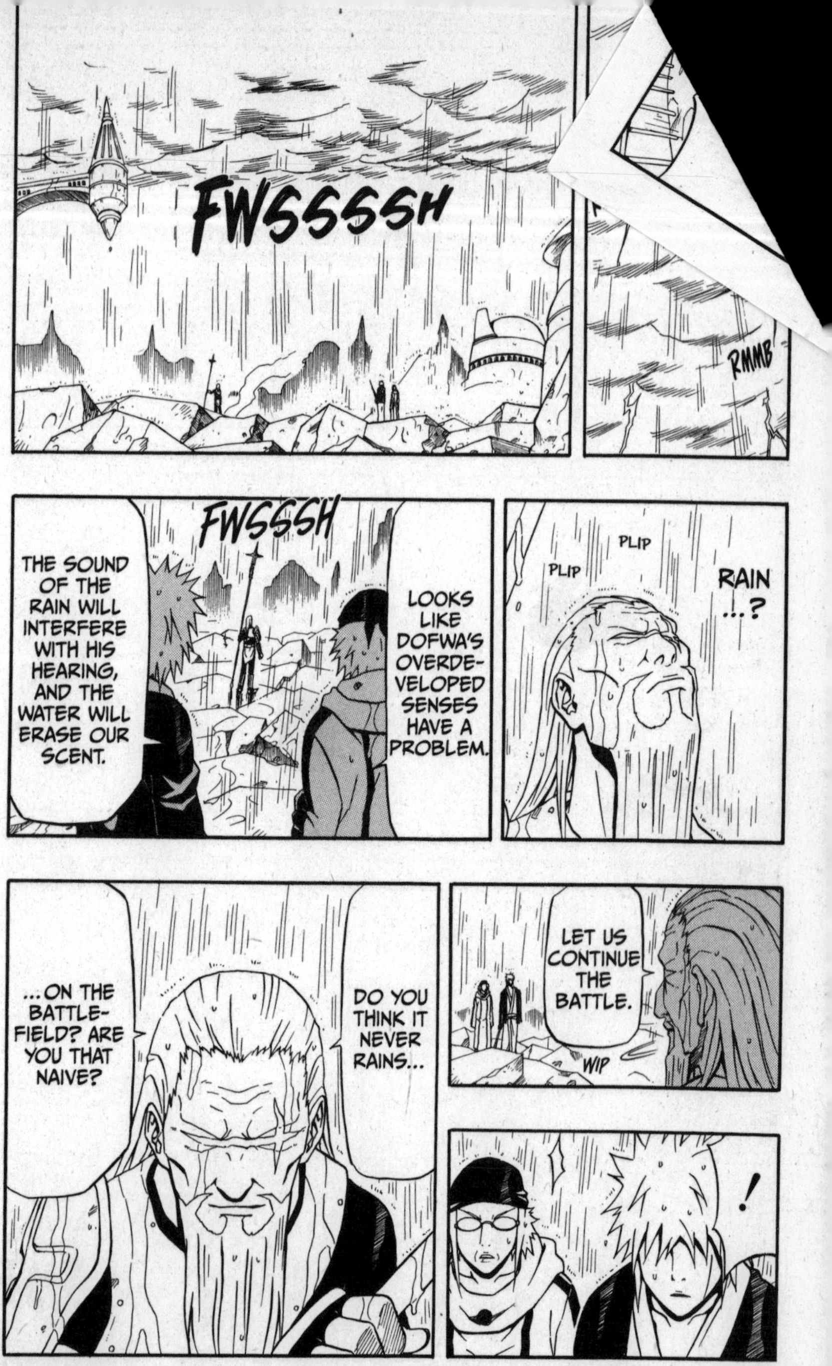
RMMB
FWSSSSH
PLIP
PLIP
RAIN ...?
FWSSSH
LOOKS LIKE DOFWA'S OVERDEVELOPED SENSES HAVE A PROBLEM.
THE SOUND OF THE RAIN WILL INTERFERE WITH HIS HEARING, AND THE WATER WILL ERASE OUR SCENT.
LET US CONTINUE THE BATTLE.
WIP
!
DO YOU THINK IT NEVER RAINS...
...ON THE BATTLEFIELD? ARE YOU THAT NAIVE?

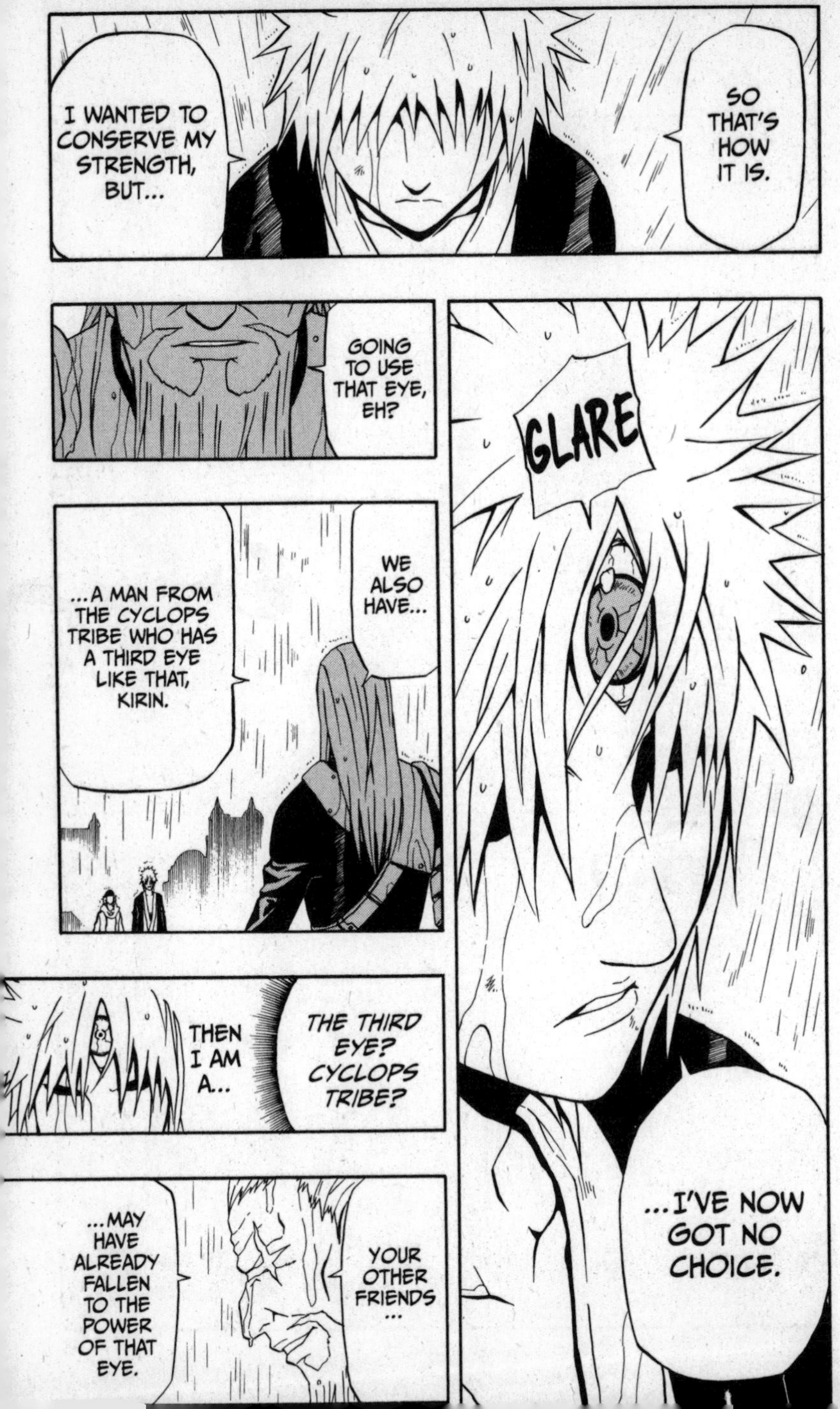
SO THAT'S HOW IT IS.
I WANTED TO CONSERVE MY STRENGTH, BUT...
GLARE
...I'VE NOW GOT NO CHOICE.
GOING TO USE THAT EYE, EH?
WE ALSO HAVE...
...A MAN FROM THE CYCLOPS TRIBE WHO HAS A THIRD EYE LIKE THAT, KIRIN.
THE THIRD EYE? CYCLOPS TRIBE?
THEN I AM A...
YOUR OTHER FRIENDS...
...MAY HAVE ALREADY FALLEN TO THE POWER OF THAT EYE.

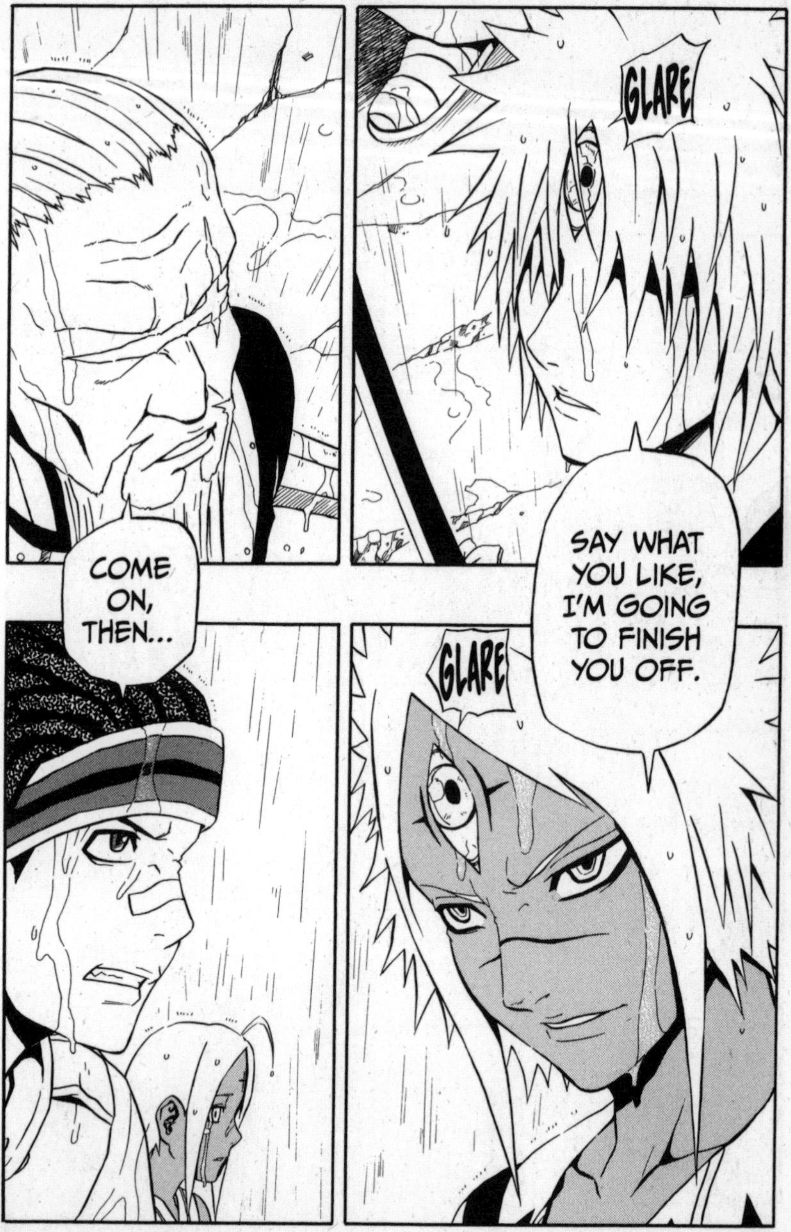
GLARE
SAY WHAT YOU LIKE, I'M GOING TO FINISH YOU OFF.
COME ON, THEN...
GLARE

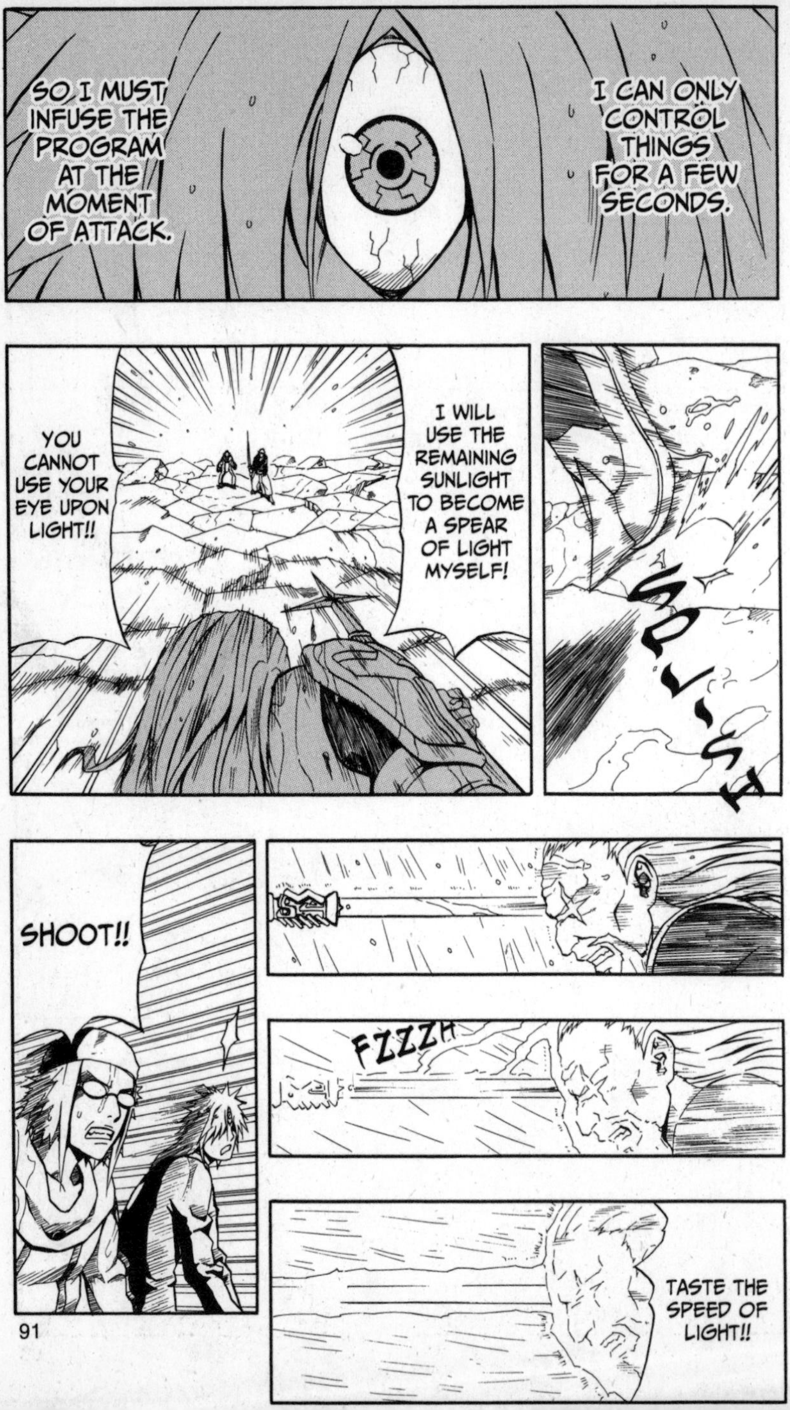
I CAN ONLY CONTROL THINGS FOR A FEW SECONDS.
SO I MUST INFUSE THE PROGRAM AT THE MOMENT OF ATTACK.
SQUISH
I WILL USE THE REMAINING SUNLIGHT TO BECOME A SPEAR OF LIGHT MYSELF!
YOU CANNOT USE YOUR EYE UPON LIGHT!!
FZZZH
TASTE THE SPEED OF LIGHT!!
SHOOT!!

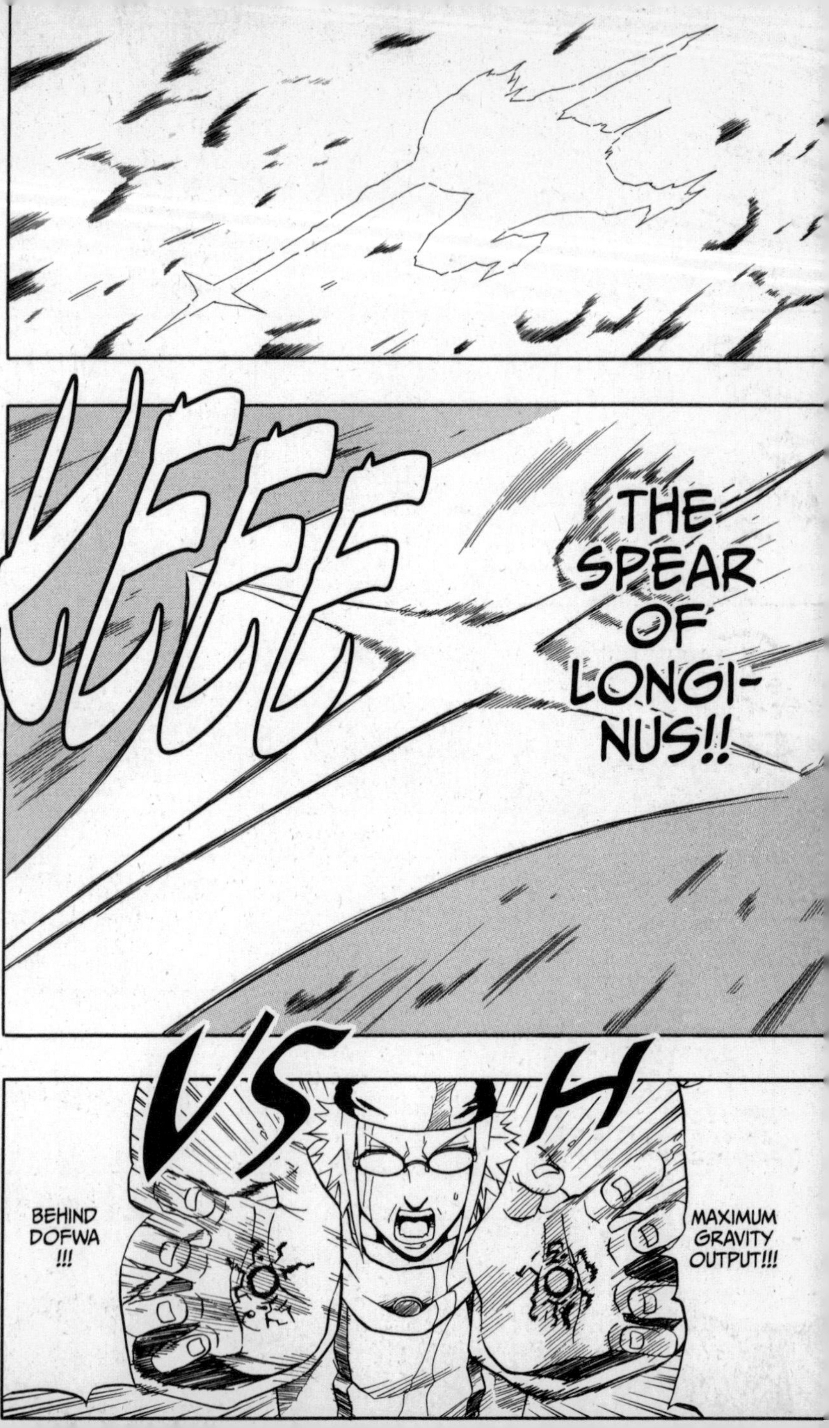
KEEE
THE SPEAR OF LONGI-NUS!!
VSSH
MAXIMUM GRAVITY OUTPUT!!!
BEHIND DOFWA!!!

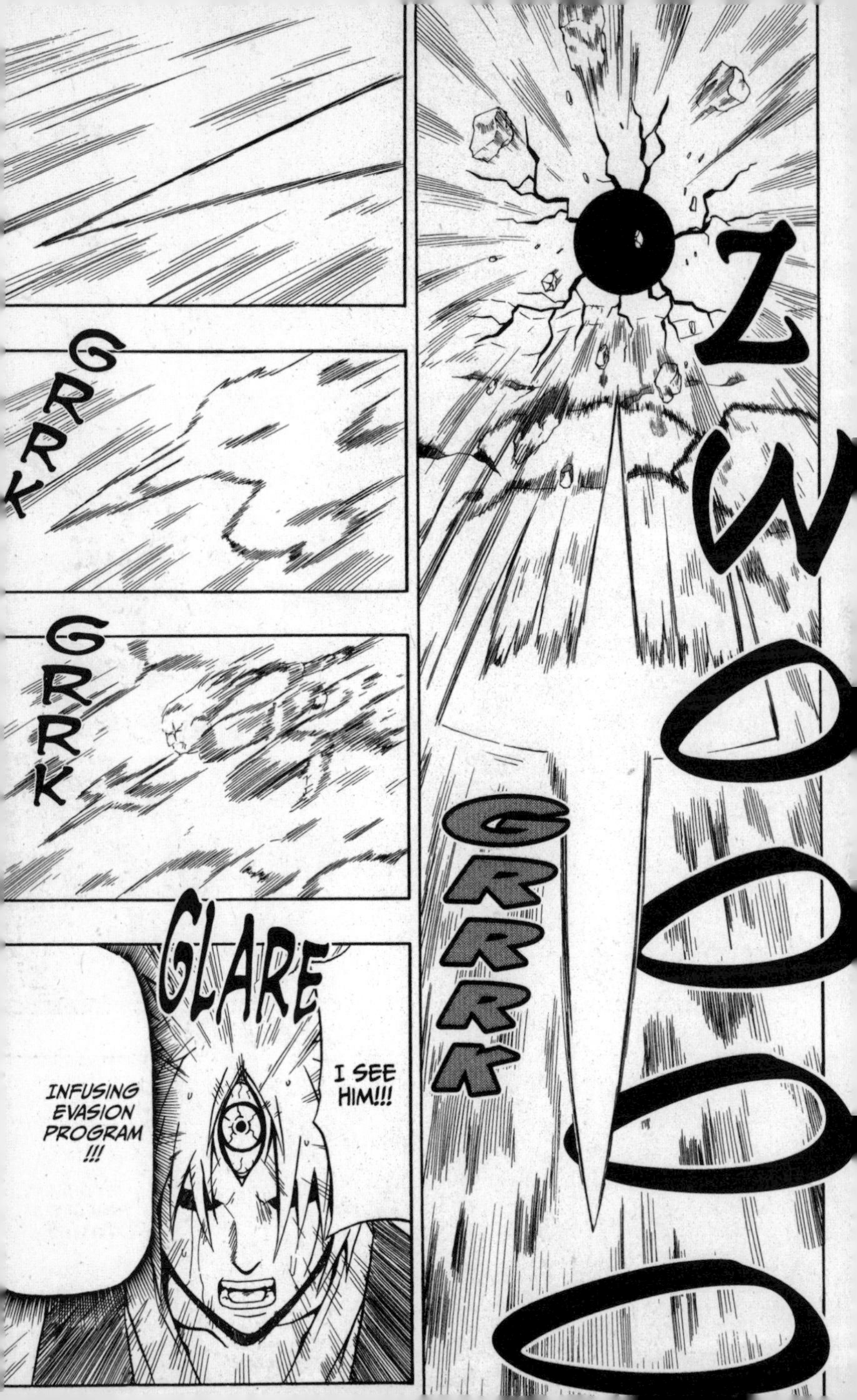
ZWOOOO
GRRRK
GRRK
GRRK
GLARE
I SEE HIM!!!
INFUSING EVASION PROGRAM!!!

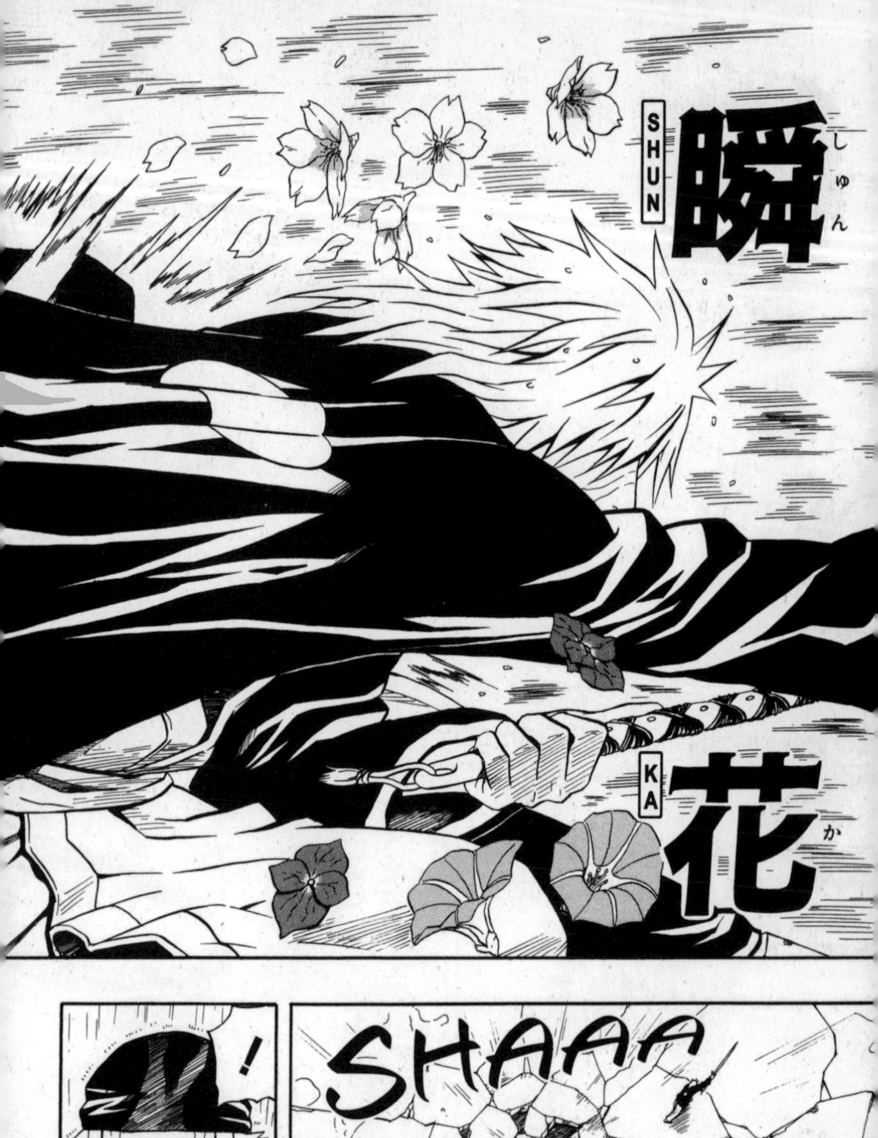
瞬 しゅん
SHUN
花 か
KA

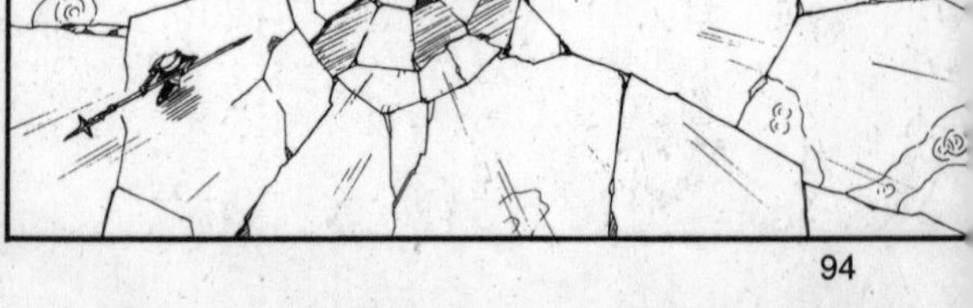
SHAAA

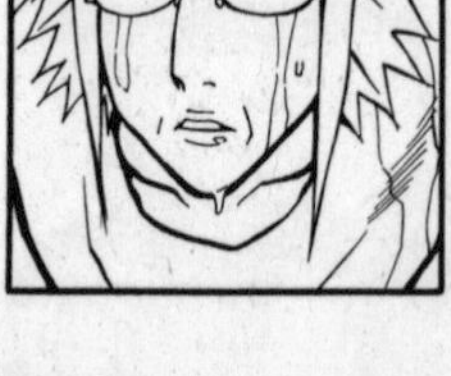
!

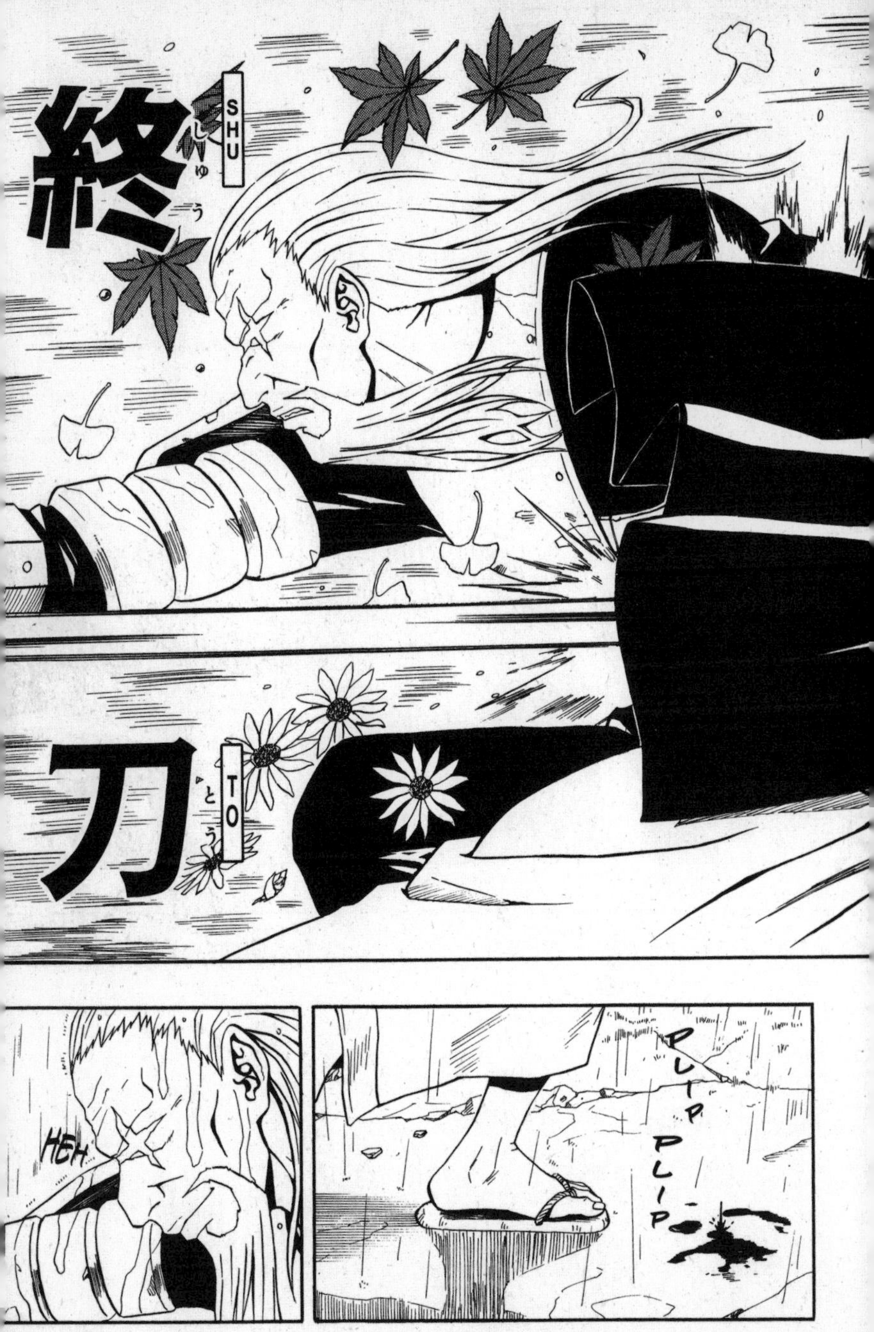
終 しゅう SHU
刀 とう TO
PLIP PLIP
HEH...

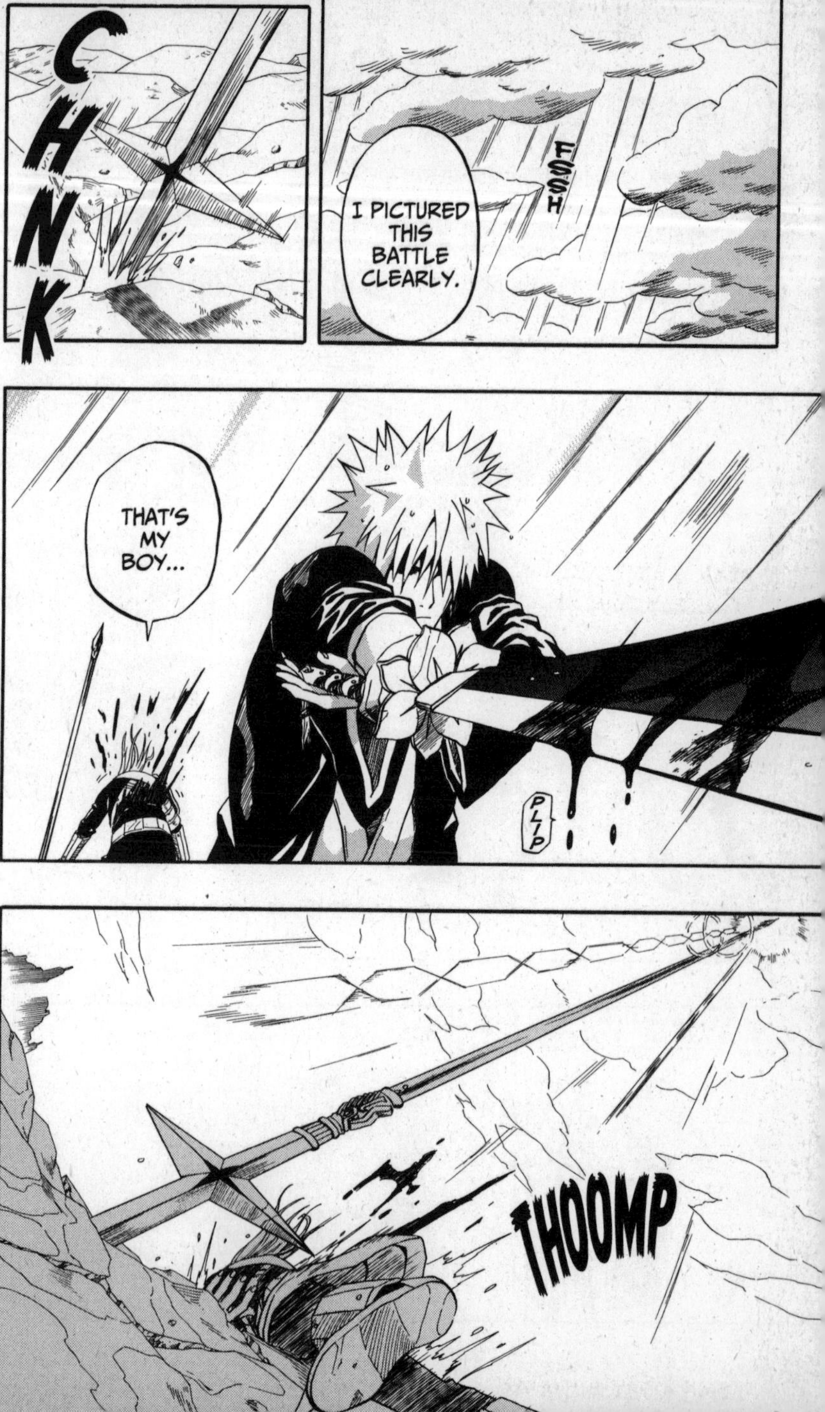
I PICTURED THIS BATTLE CLEARLY.
FSSH
CHNK
THAT'S MY BOY...
PLIP
THOOMP

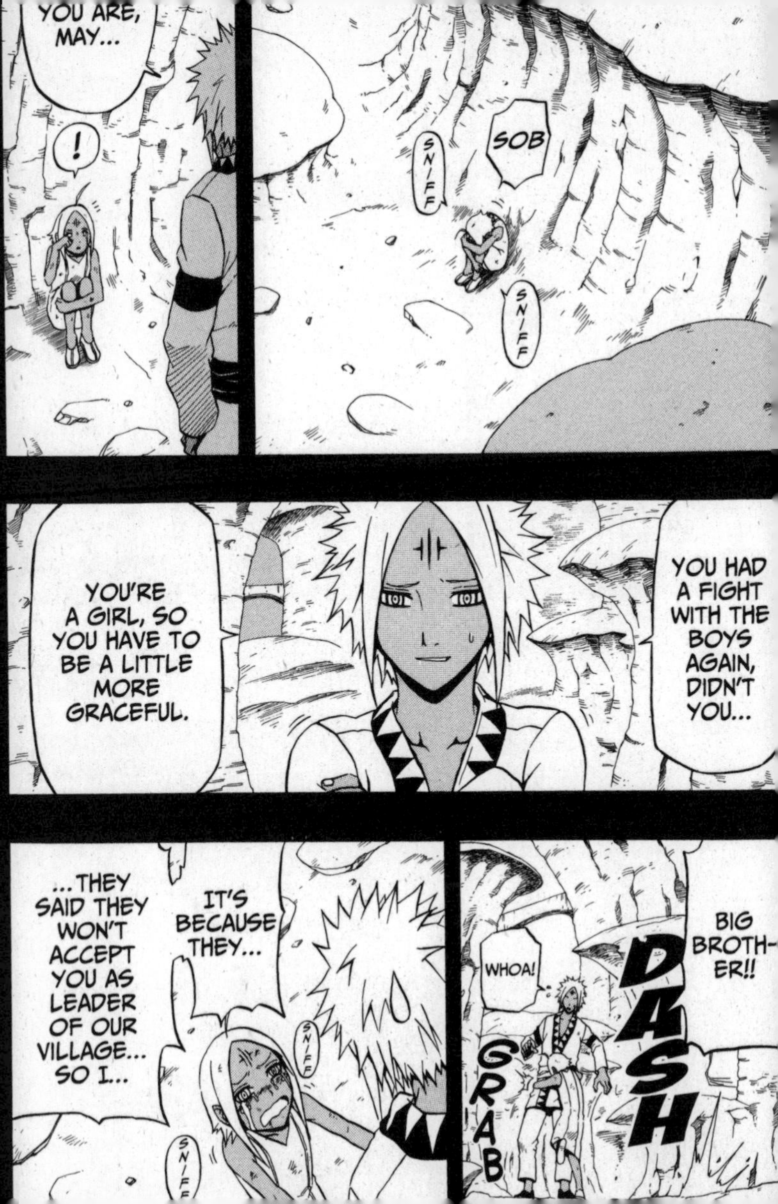
SOB
SNIFF
SNIFF
YOU ARE, MAY...
!
YOU HAD A FIGHT WITH THE BOYS AGAIN, DIDN'T YOU...
YOU'RE A GIRL, SO YOU HAVE TO BE A LITTLE MORE GRACEFUL.
BIG BROTH-ER!!
DASH
WHOA!
GRAB
IT'S BECAUSE THEY...
...THEY SAID THEY WON'T ACCEPT YOU AS LEADER OF OUR VILLAGE... SO I...
SNIFF
SNIFF

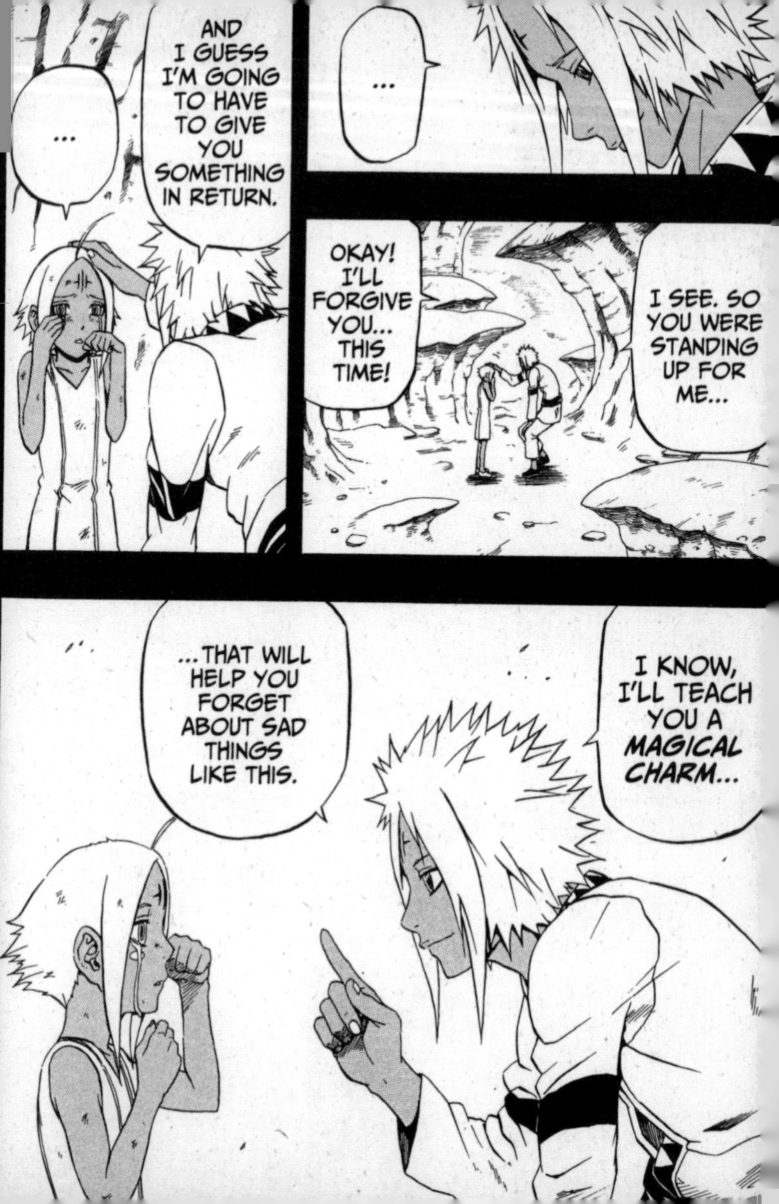
...
I SEE. SO YOU WERE STANDING UP FOR ME...
OKAY! I'LL FORGIVE YOU... THIS TIME!
AND I GUESS I'M GOING TO HAVE TO GIVE YOU SOMETHING IN RETURN.
...
I KNOW, I'LL TEACH YOU A *MAGICAL CHARM*...
...THAT WILL HELP YOU FORGET ABOUT SAD THINGS LIKE THIS.

CHAPTER 59
THE MAGICAL CHARM

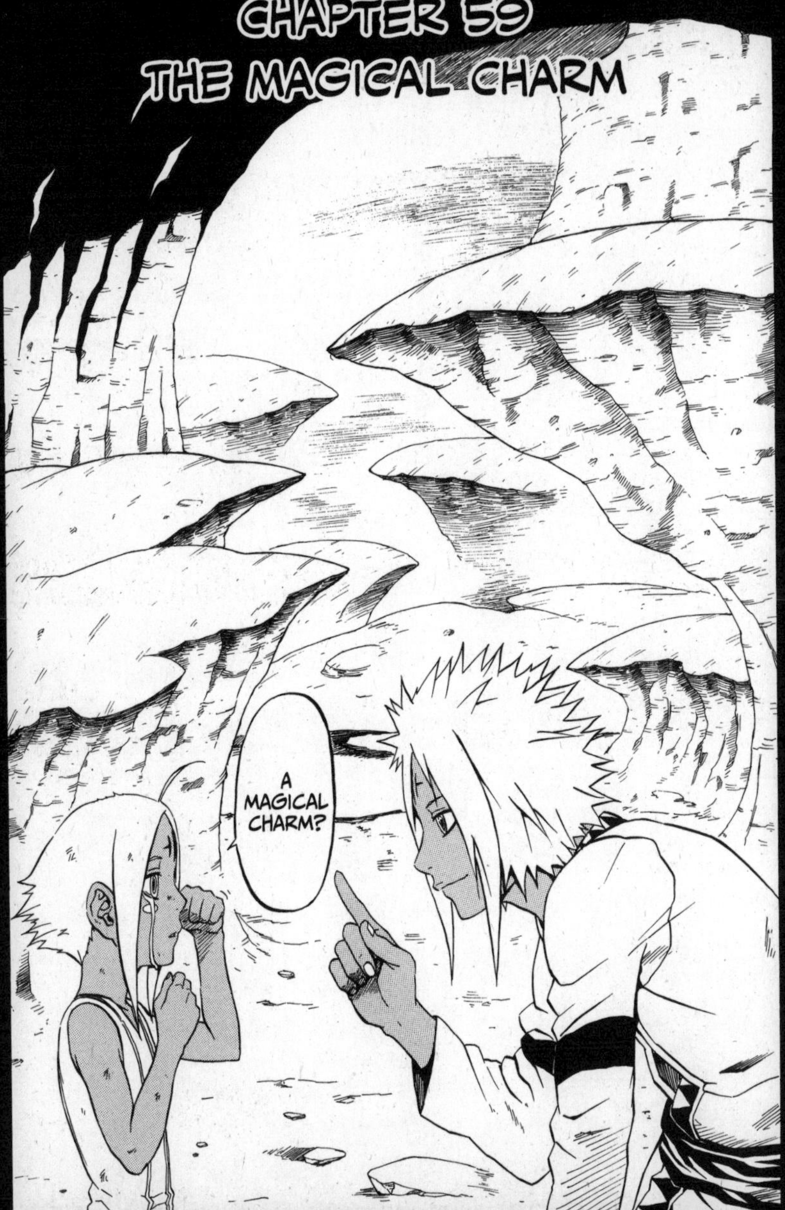
A MAGICAL CHARM?

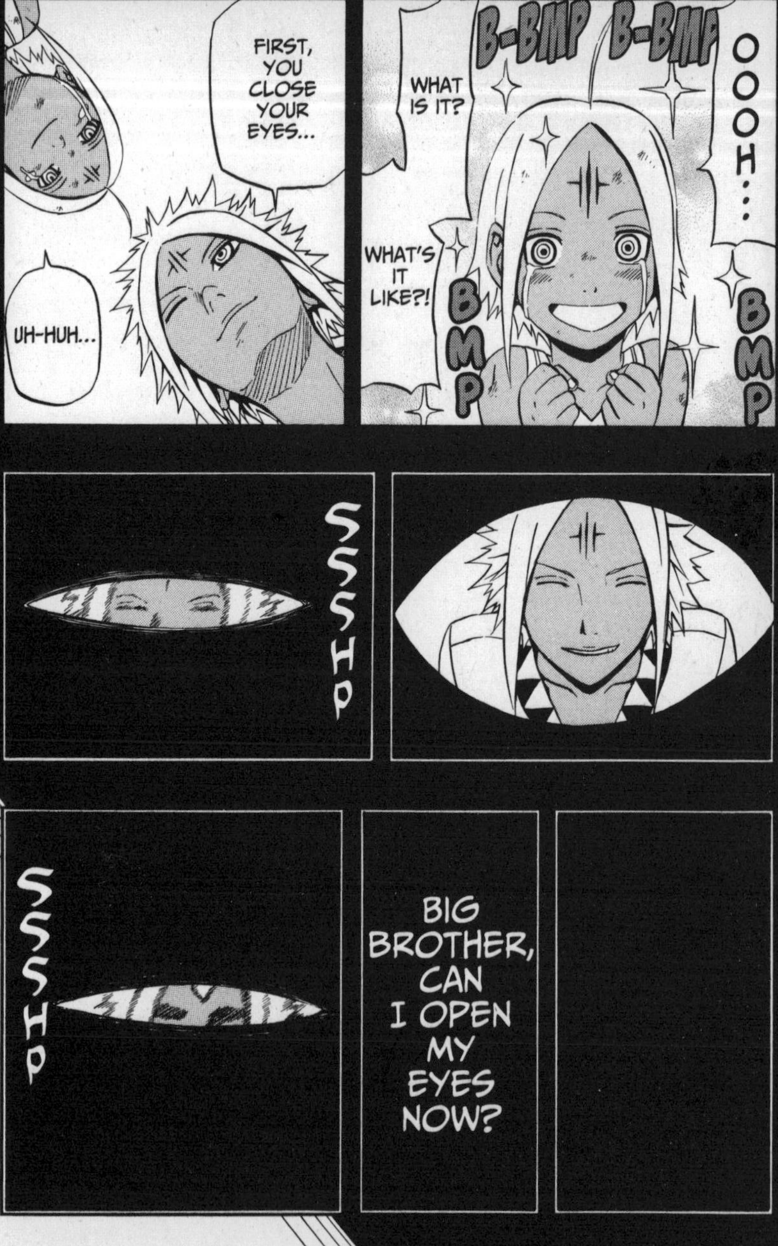
B-BMP B-BMP
OOOH...
WHAT IS IT?
WHAT'S IT LIKE?!
BMP
BMP
FIRST, YOU CLOSE YOUR EYES...
UH-HUH...
SSSHP
BIG BROTHER, CAN I OPEN MY EYES NOW?
SSSHP

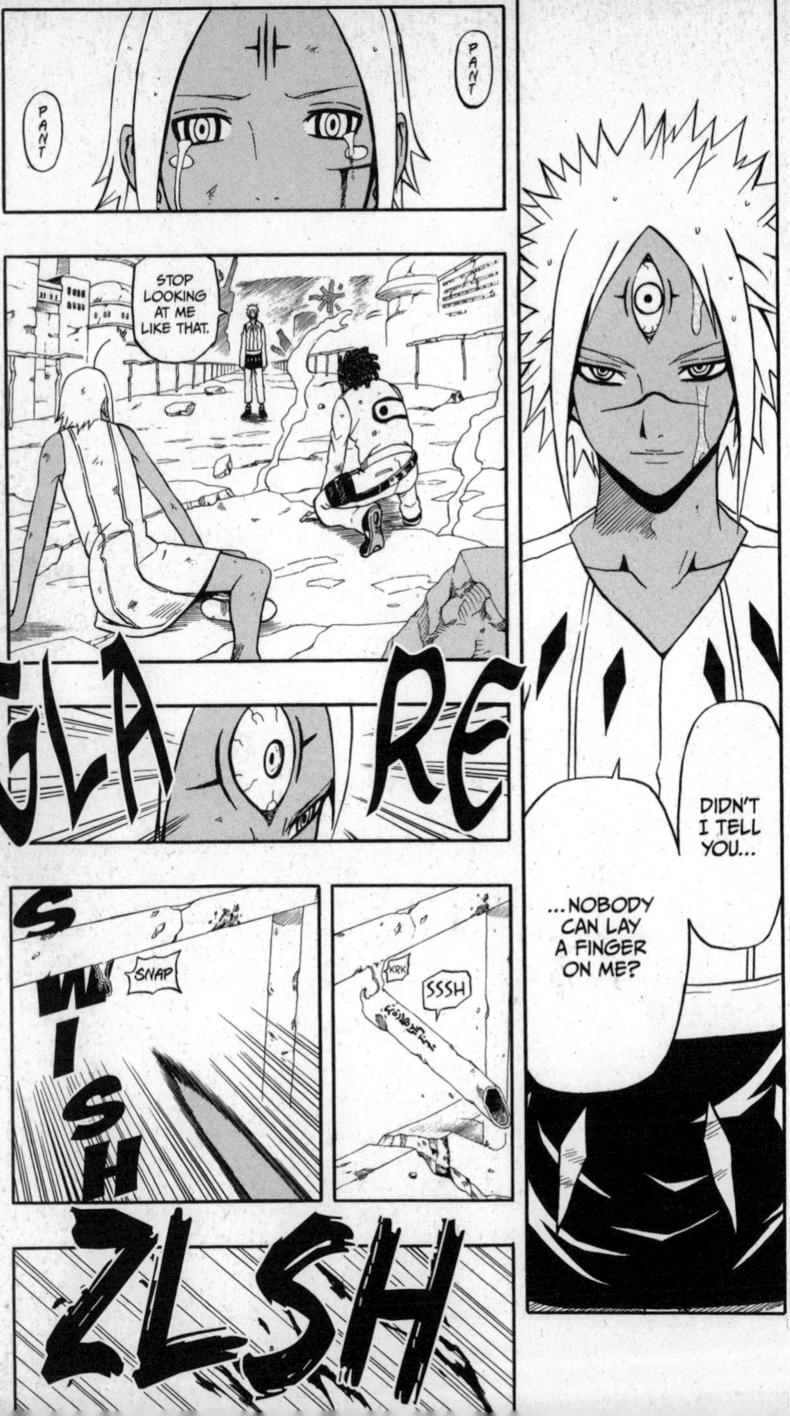
DIDN'T I TELL YOU...
...NOBODY CAN LAY A FINGER ON ME?
PANT
PANT
STOP LOOKING AT ME LIKE THAT.
GLARE
KRK
SSSH
SWISH
SNAP
ZLSH

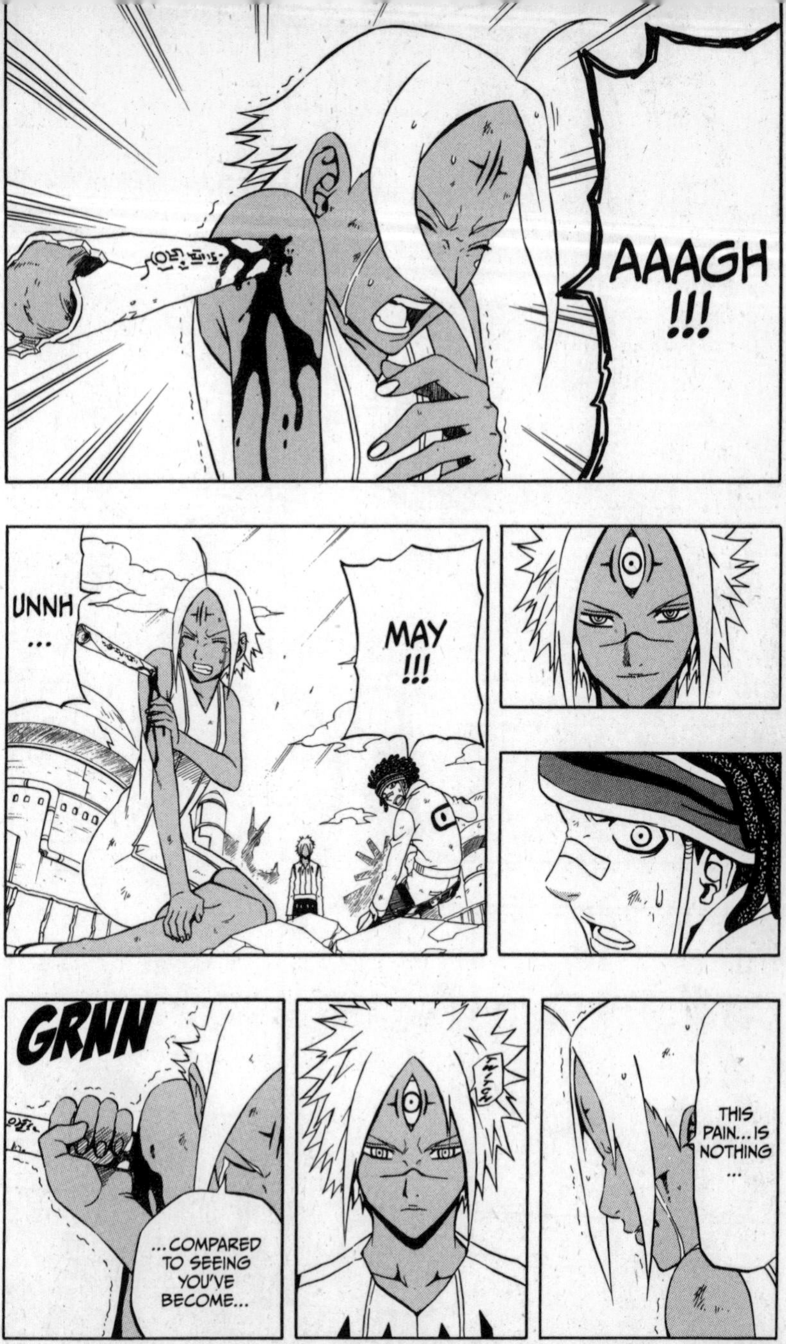
AAAGH!!!
MAY!!!
UNNH...
THIS PAIN... IS NOTHING...
GRNN
...COMPARED TO SEEING YOU'VE BECOME...

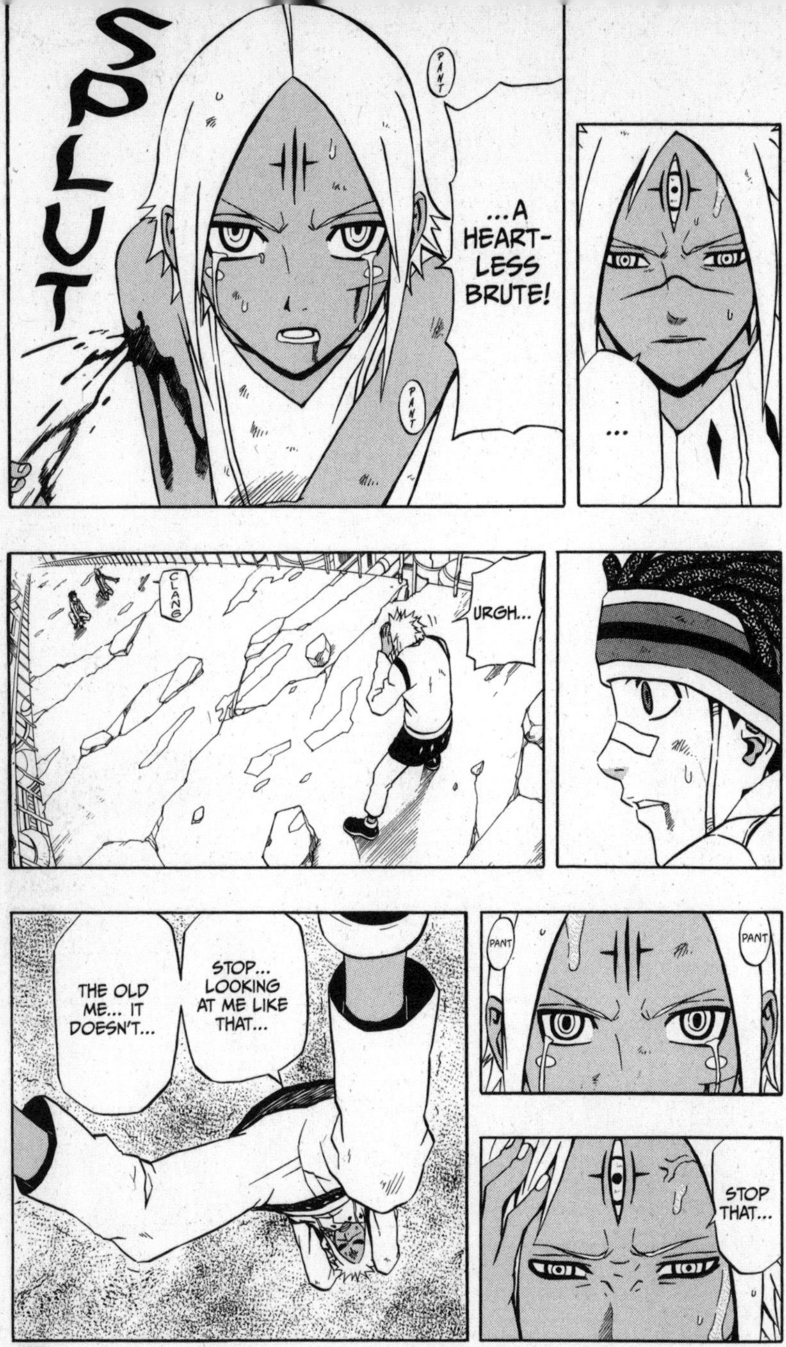
...
PANT
...A HEART-LESS BRUTE!
PANT
SPLUT
URGH...
CLANG
PANT
PANT
STOP THAT...
STOP... LOOKING AT ME LIKE THAT...
THE OLD ME... IT DOESN'T...

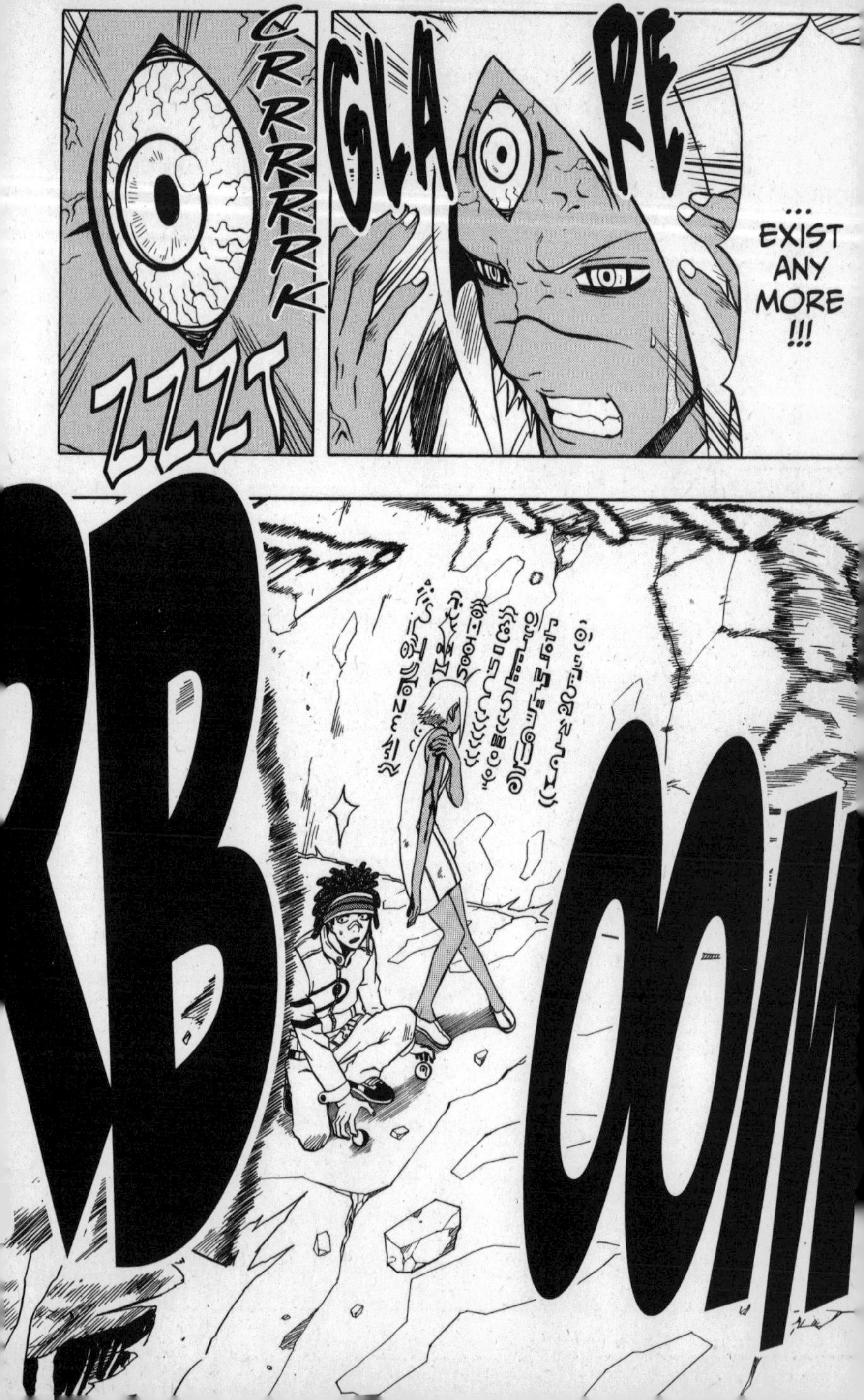
GLA RE
... EXIST ANY MORE !!!
CRRRRRRK
ZZZT
OOM

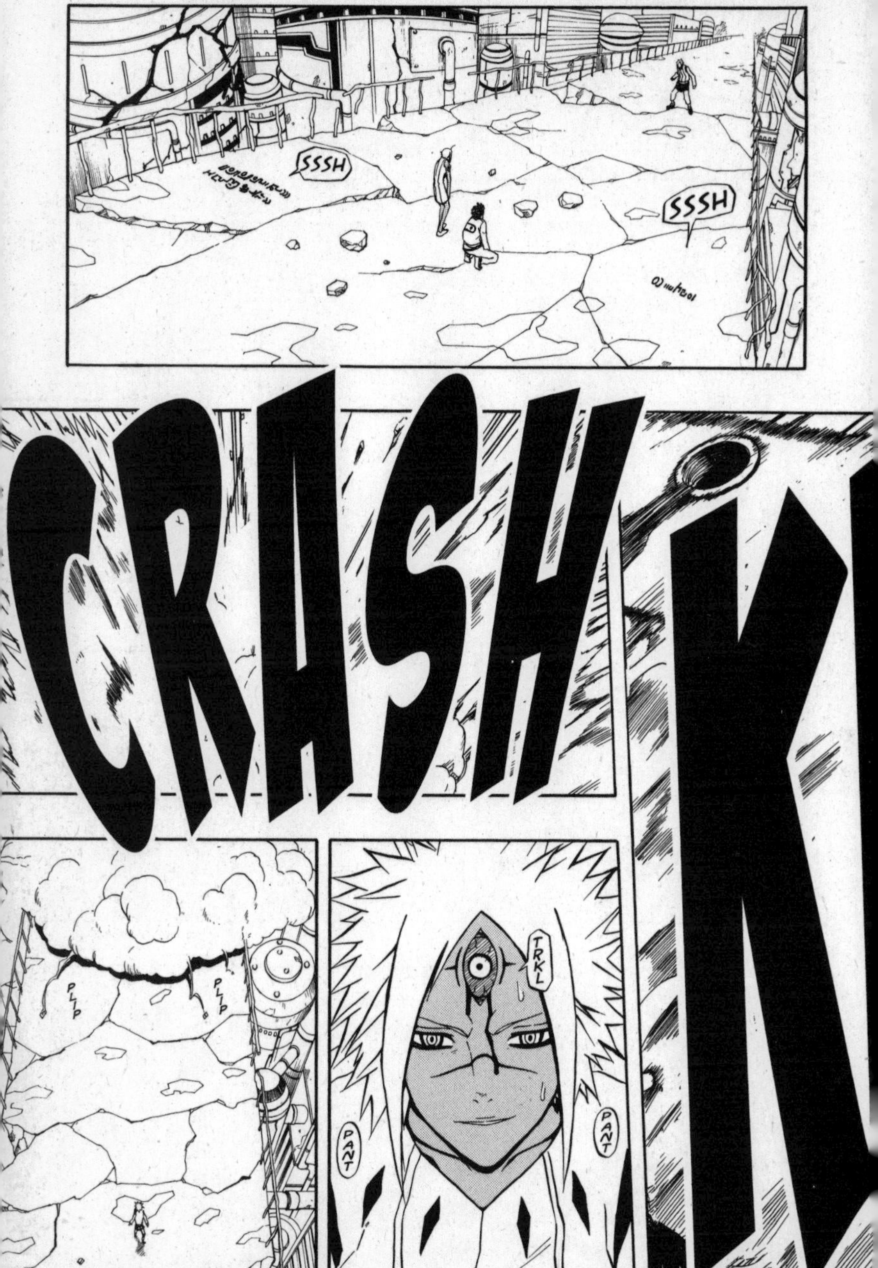
SSSH
SSSH
CRASH
TRKL
PANT
PANT
PLIP
PLIP

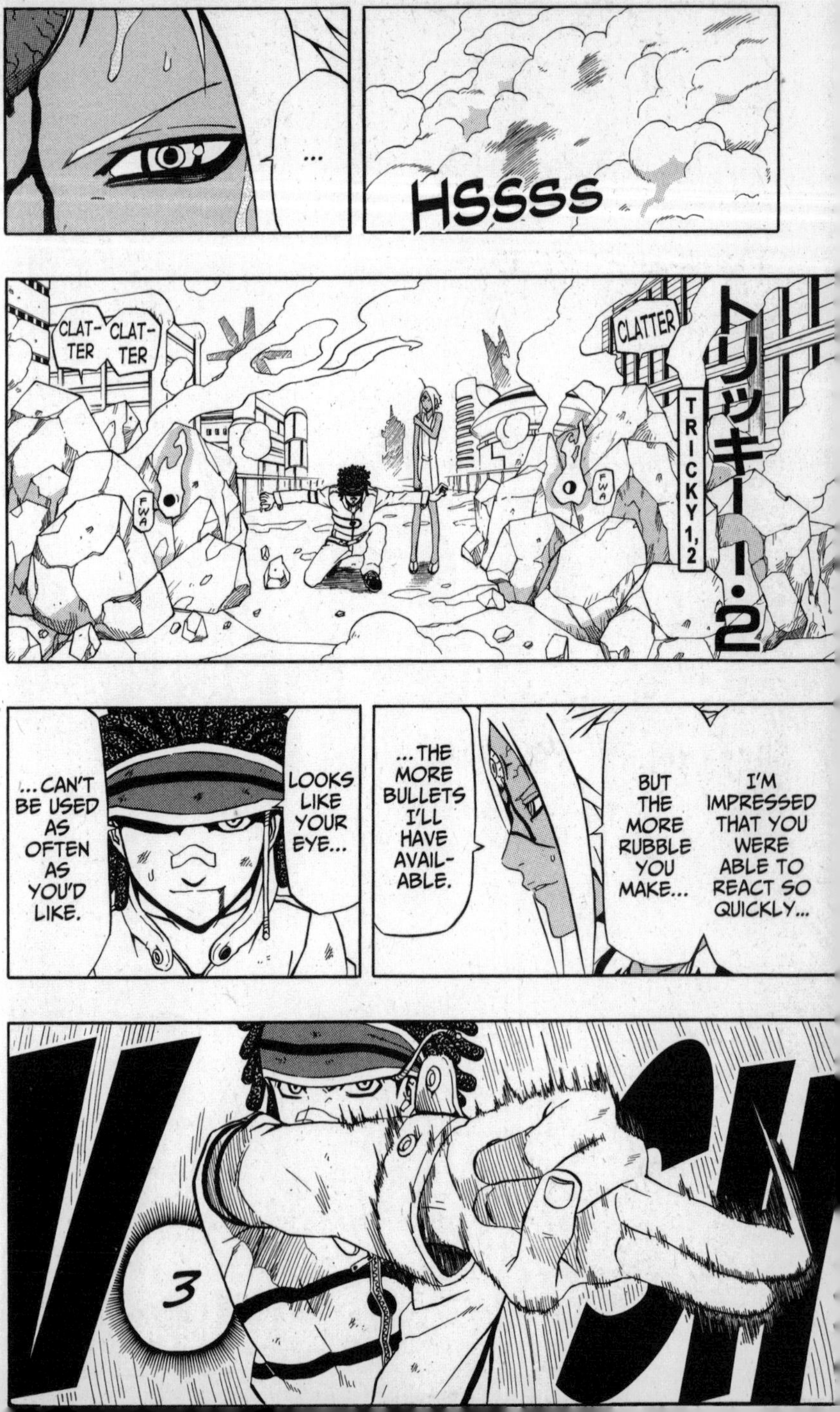
HSSSS
...
トリッキー・2
TRICKY 1, 2
CLATTER
FWA
CLAT-TER
CLAT-TER
FWA
I'M IMPRESSED THAT YOU WERE ABLE TO REACT SO QUICKLY...
BUT THE MORE RUBBLE YOU MAKE...
...THE MORE BULLETS I'LL HAVE AVAIL-ABLE.
LOOKS LIKE YOUR EYE...
...CAN'T BE USED AS OFTEN AS YOU'D LIKE.
3

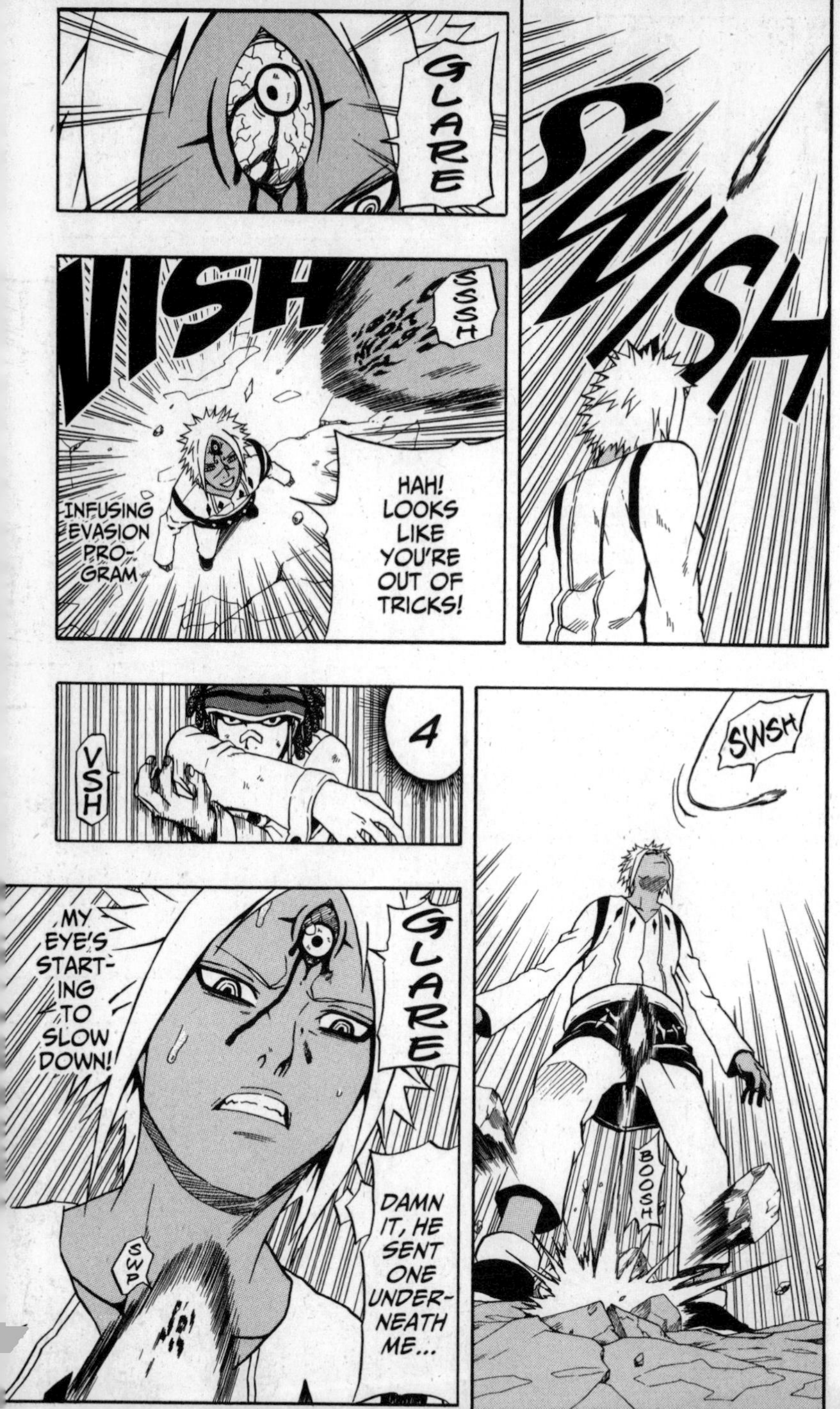
SWISH
GLARE
VISH
SSSH
HAH! LOOKS LIKE YOU'RE OUT OF TRICKS!
INFUSING EVASION PRO-GRAM
SWSH
BOOSH
4
VSH
GLARE
MY EYE'S START-ING TO SLOW DOWN!
DAMN IT, HE SENT ONE UNDER-NEATH ME...
SWP

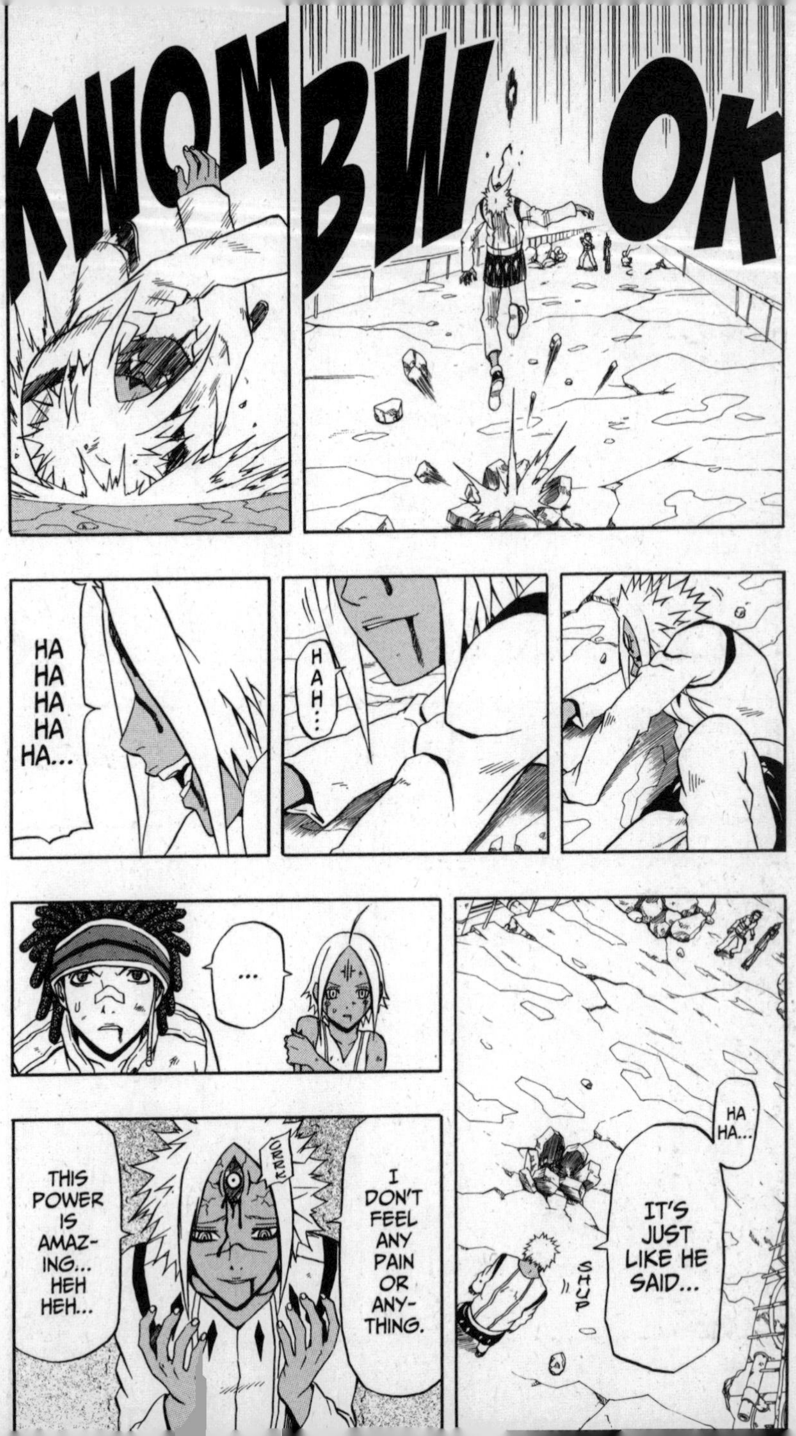
KWOMBWOK
HAH...
HA HA HA HA HA...
HA HA...
IT'S JUST LIKE HE SAID...
SHUP
...
CREEK
I DON'T FEEL ANY PAIN OR ANYTHING.
THIS POWER IS AMAZING... HEH HEH...

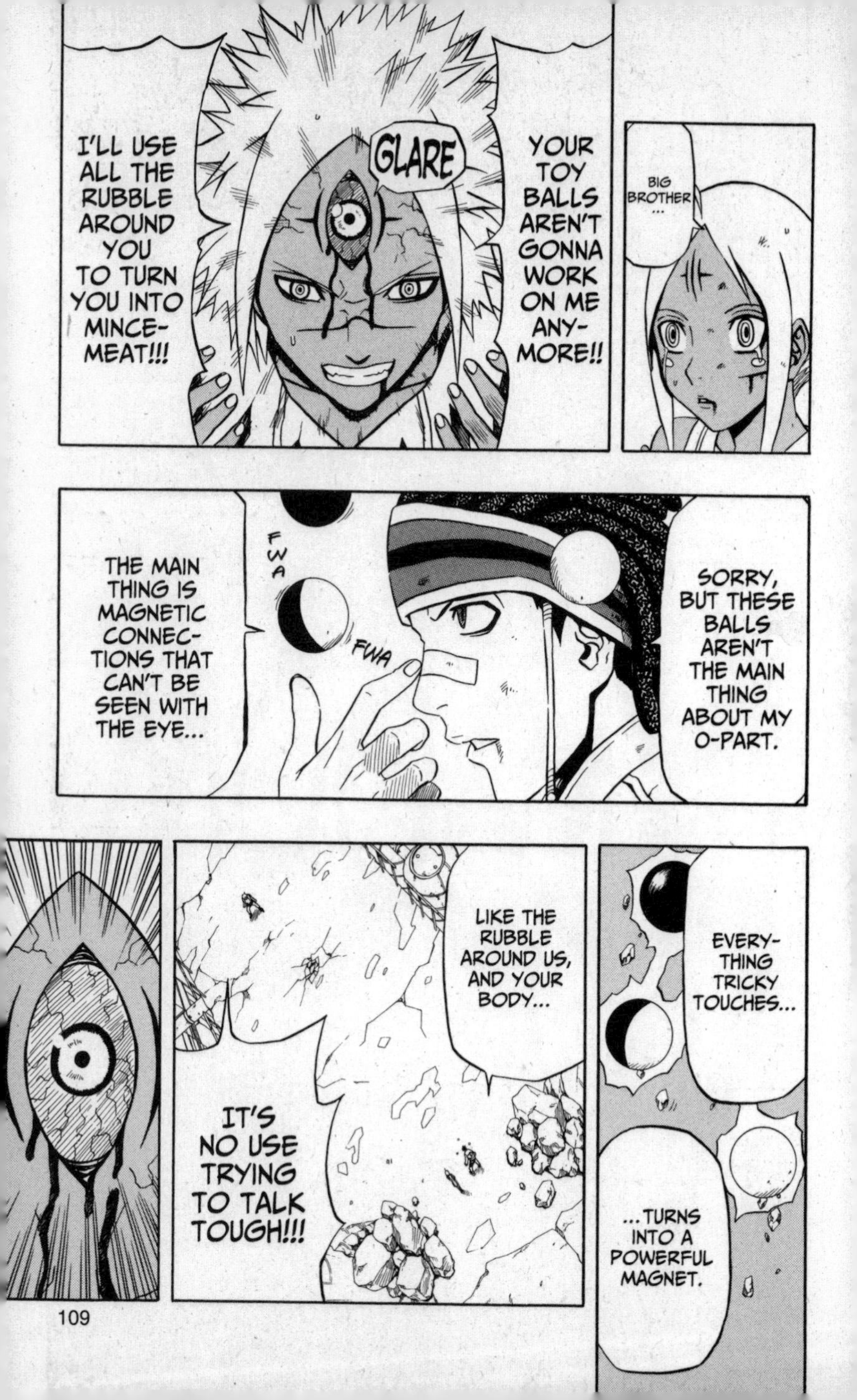
BIG BROTHER...
GLARE
YOUR TOY BALLS AREN'T GONNA WORK ON ME ANY-MORE!!
I'LL USE ALL THE RUBBLE AROUND YOU TO TURN YOU INTO MINCE-MEAT!!!
SORRY, BUT THESE BALLS AREN'T THE MAIN THING ABOUT MY O-PART.
FWA
FWA
THE MAIN THING IS MAGNETIC CONNEC-TIONS THAT CAN'T BE SEEN WITH THE EYE...
EVERY-THING TRICKY TOUCHES...
...TURNS INTO A POWERFUL MAGNET.
LIKE THE RUBBLE AROUND US, AND YOUR BODY...
IT'S NO USE TRYING TO TALK TOUGH!!!

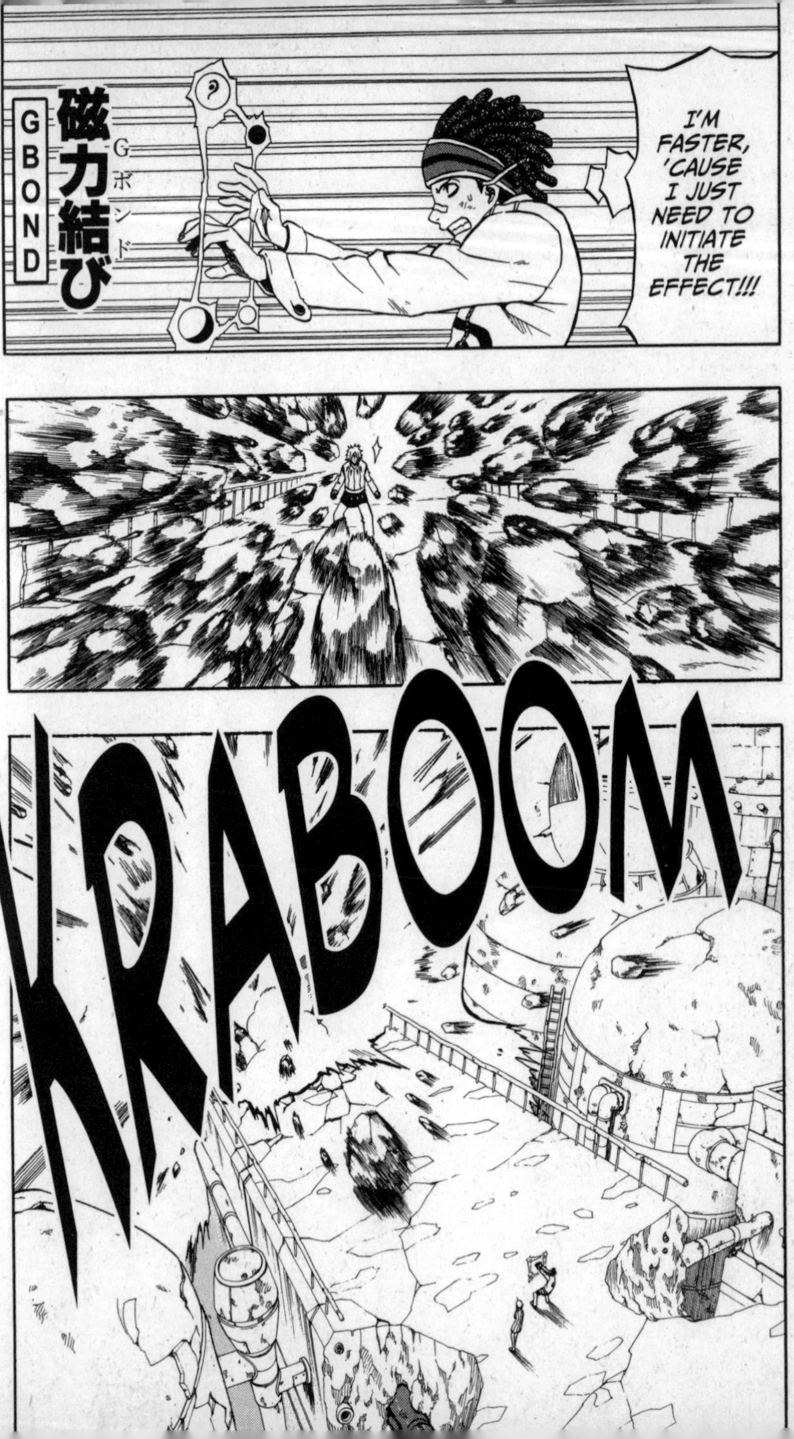
I'M FASTER, 'CAUSE I JUST NEED TO INITIATE THE EFFECT!!!
磁力結び
Gボンド
G BOND
KRABOOM

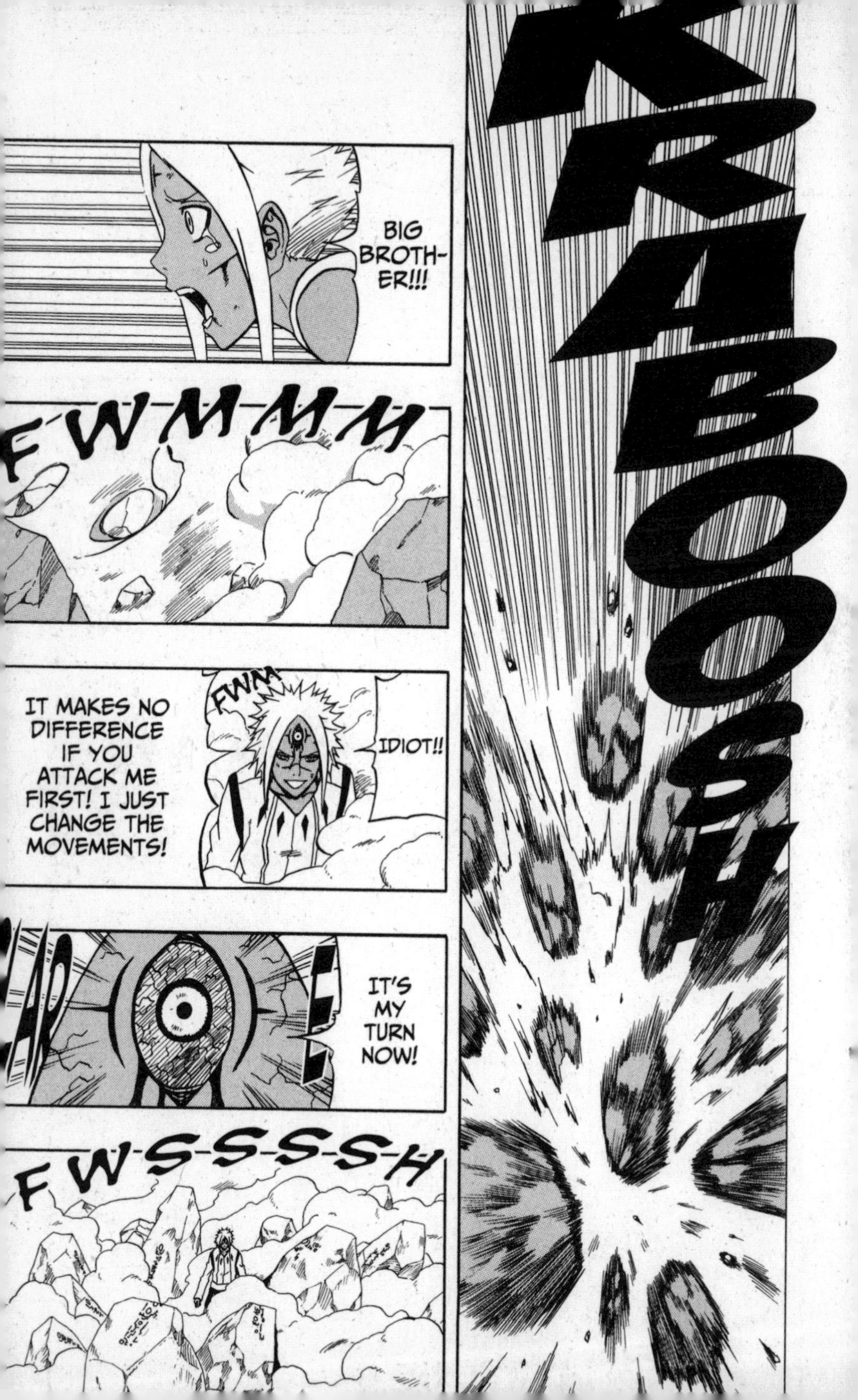
KRABOOOSH
BIG BROTHER!!!
FWMMMM
IDIOT!!
FWM
IT MAKES NO DIFFERENCE IF YOU ATTACK ME FIRST! I JUST CHANGE THE MOVEMENTS!
IT'S MY TURN NOW!
FWSSSSH

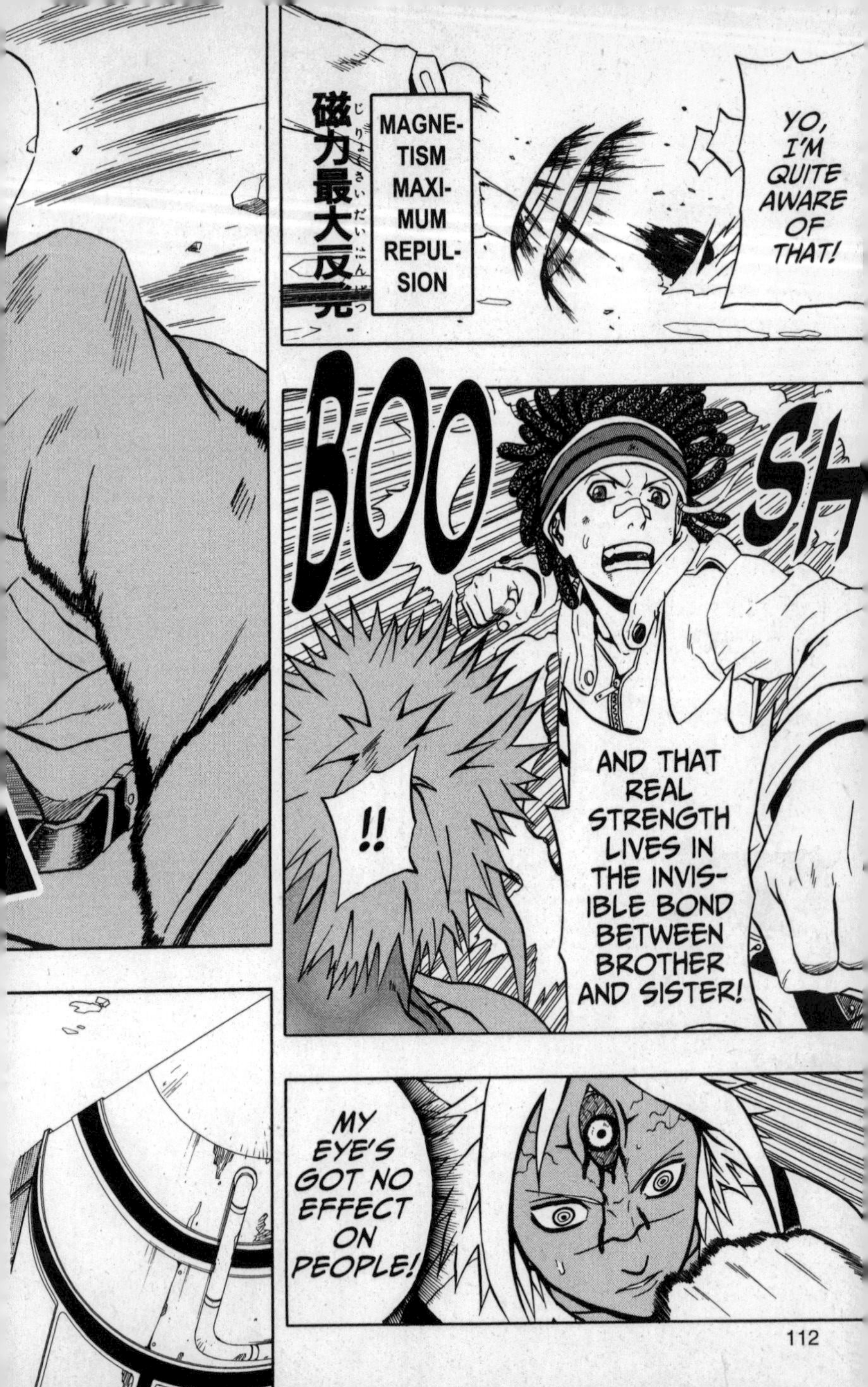
YO, I'M QUITE AWARE OF THAT!
MAGNETISM MAXIMUM REPULSION
磁力最大反発
BOOSH
AND THAT REAL STRENGTH LIVES IN THE INVISIBLE BOND BETWEEN BROTHER AND SISTER!
!!
MY EYE'S GOT NO EFFECT ON PEOPLE!

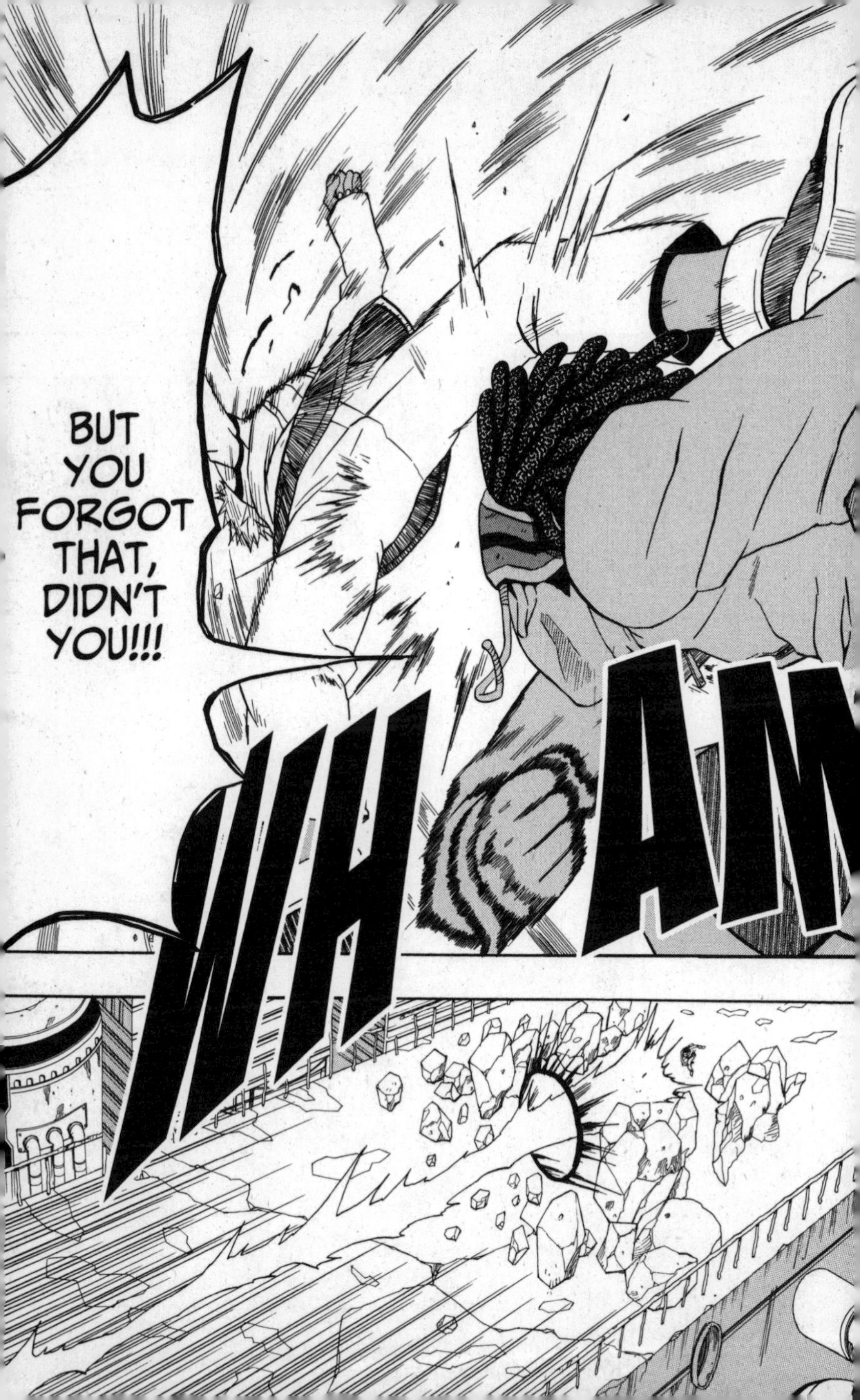
BUT YOU FORGOT THAT, DIDN'T YOU!!!
WHAM

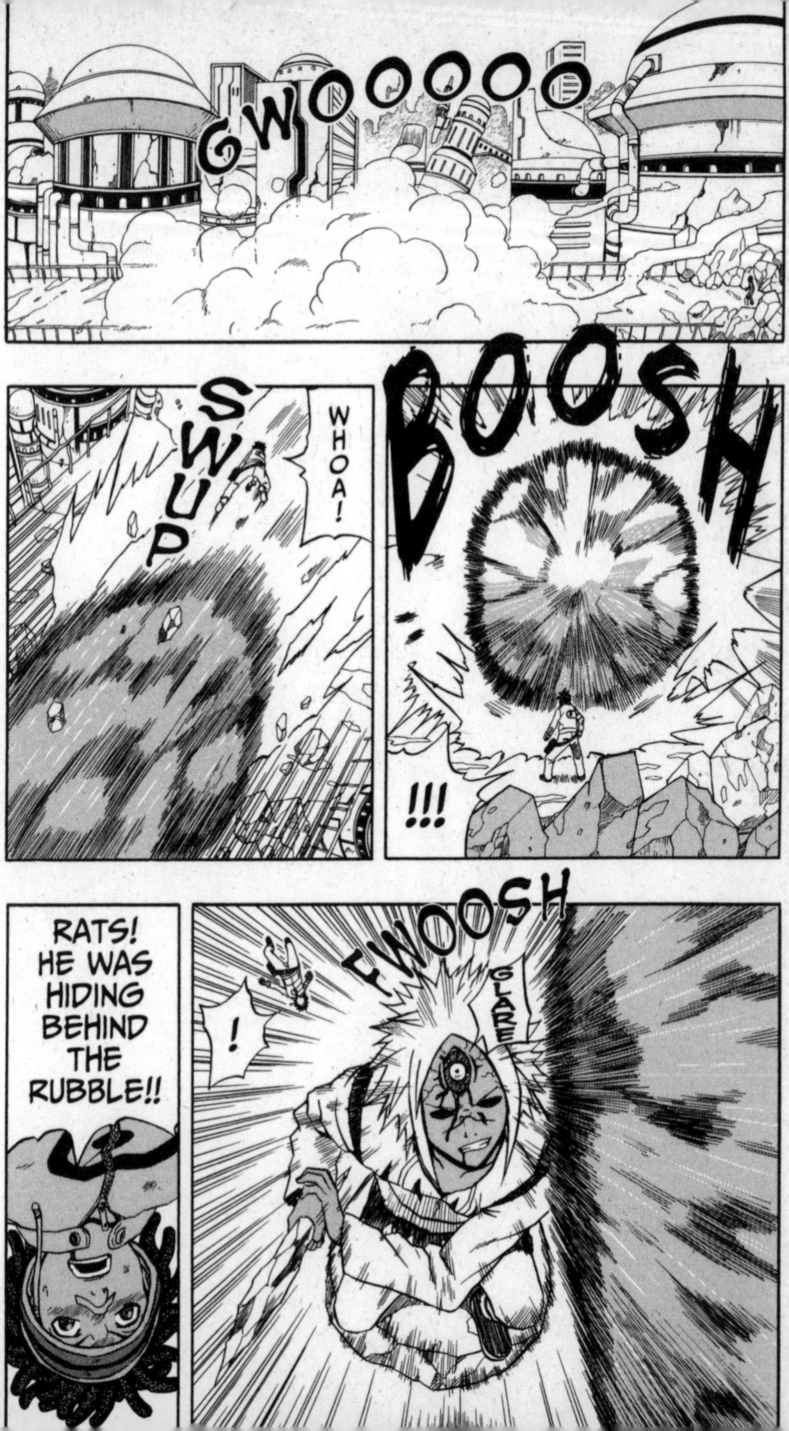
GWOOOOO
BOOSH
!!!
SWUP
WHOA!
FWOOSH
GLARE
!
RATS! HE WAS HIDING BEHIND THE RUBBLE!!

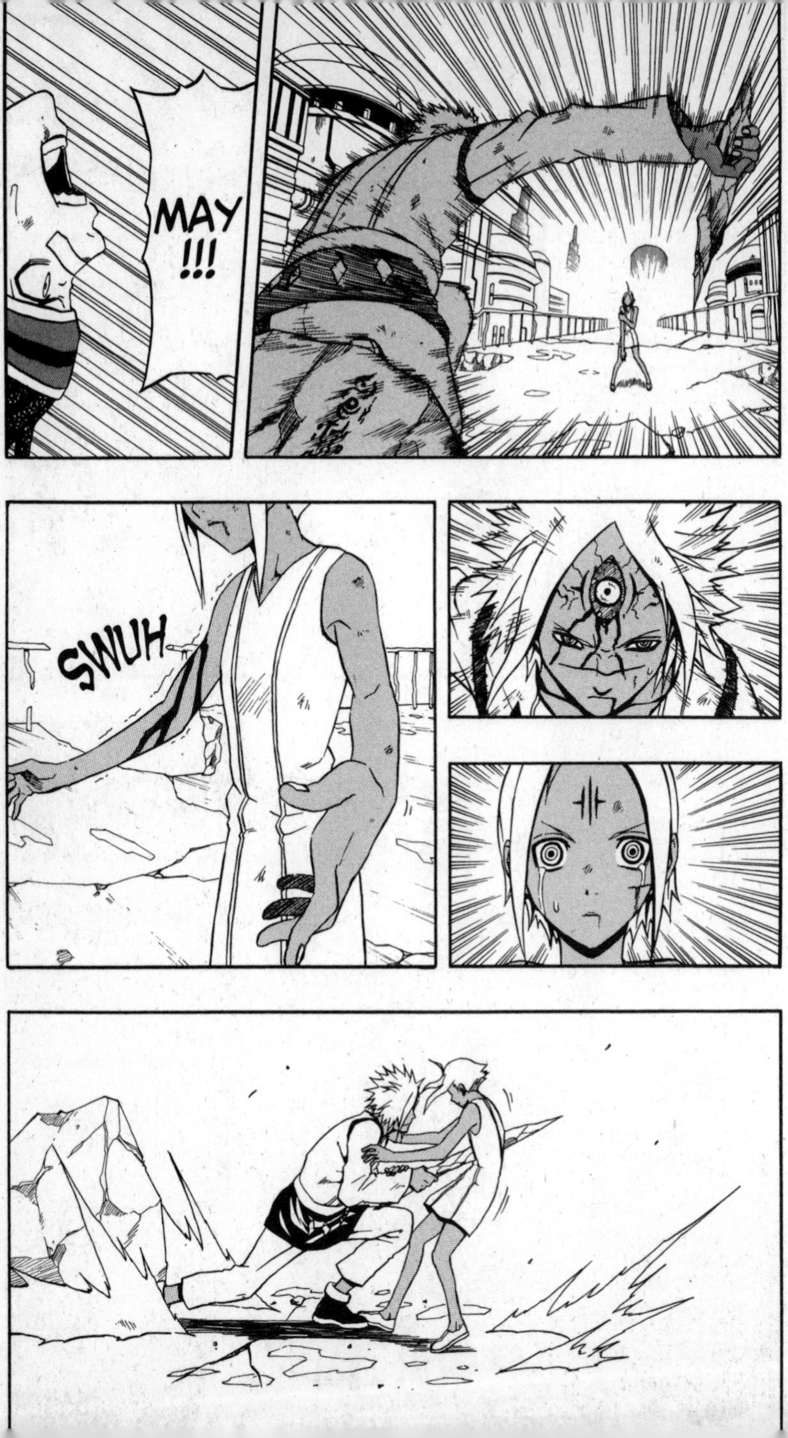
MAY !!!
SWUH

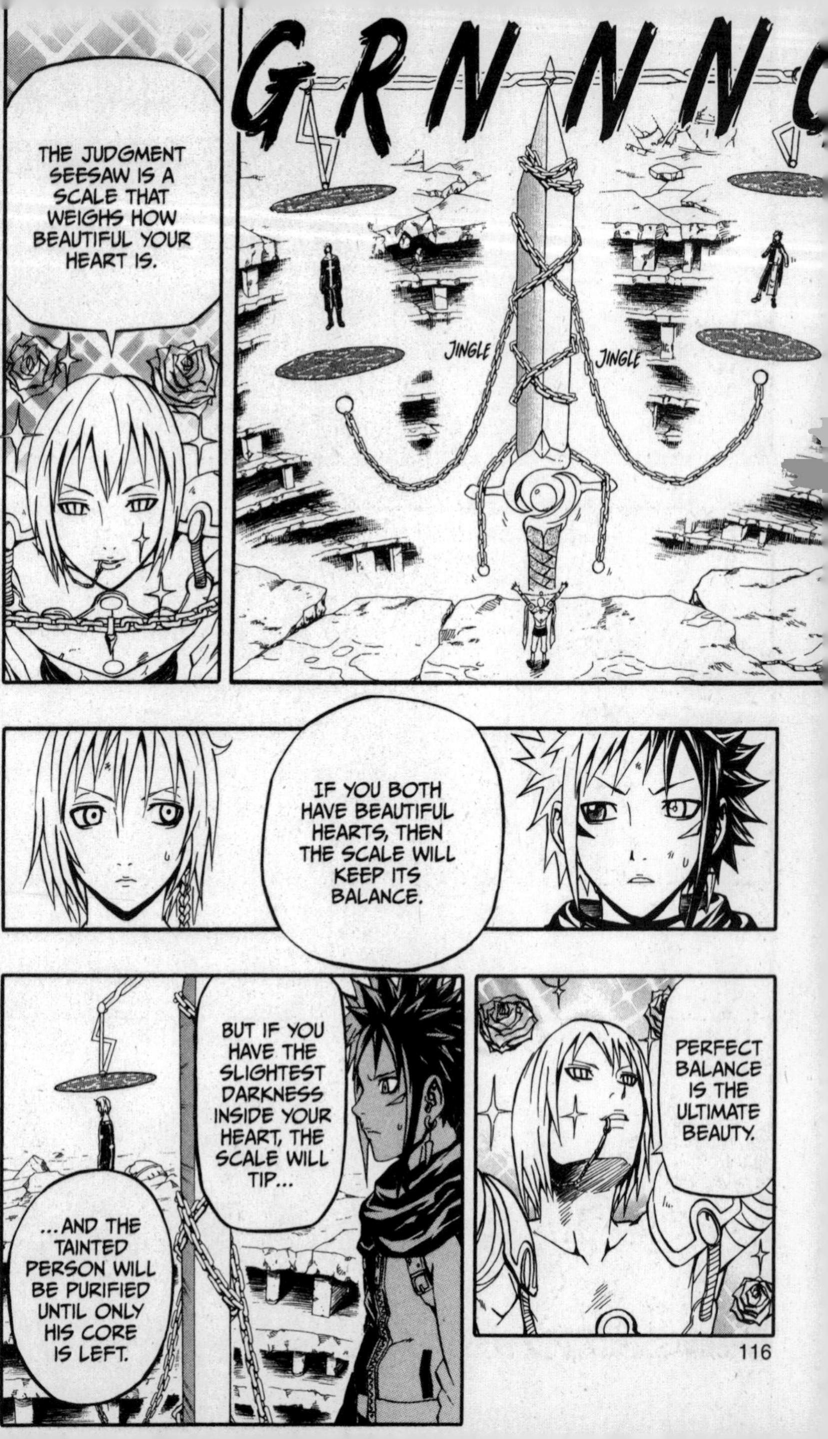
GRNNN
JINGLE
JINGLE
THE JUDGMENT SEESAW IS A SCALE THAT WEIGHS HOW BEAUTIFUL YOUR HEART IS.
IF YOU BOTH HAVE BEAUTIFUL HEARTS, THEN THE SCALE WILL KEEP ITS BALANCE.
PERFECT BALANCE IS THE ULTIMATE BEAUTY.
BUT IF YOU HAVE THE SLIGHTEST DARKNESS INSIDE YOUR HEART, THE SCALE WILL TIP...
...AND THE TAINTED PERSON WILL BE PURIFIED UNTIL ONLY HIS CORE IS LEFT.

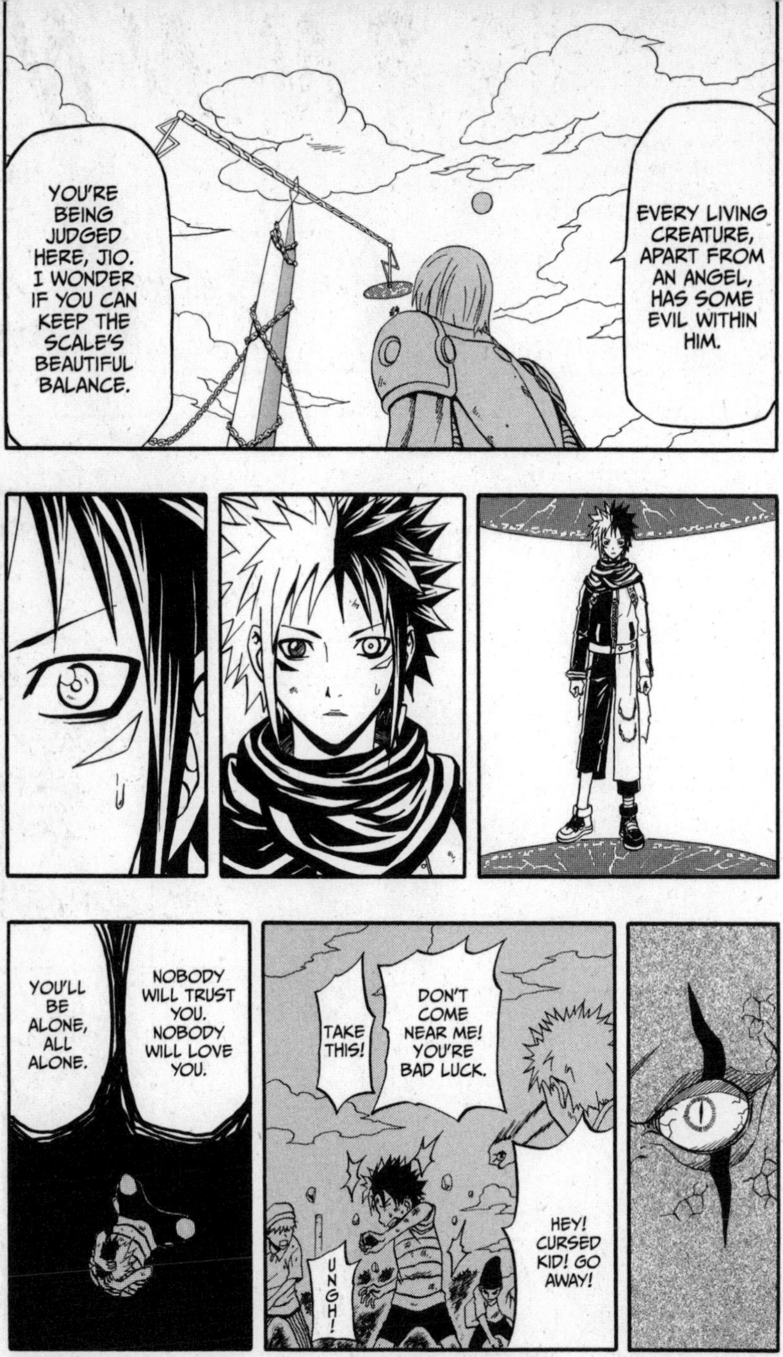
EVERY LIVING CREATURE, APART FROM AN ANGEL, HAS SOME EVIL WITHIN HIM.
YOU'RE BEING JUDGED HERE, JIO. I WONDER IF YOU CAN KEEP THE SCALE'S BEAUTIFUL BALANCE.
DON'T COME NEAR ME! YOU'RE BAD LUCK.
TAKE THIS!
HEY! CURSED KID! GO AWAY!
UNGH!
NOBODY WILL TRUST YOU. NOBODY WILL LOVE YOU.
YOU'LL BE ALONE, ALL ALONE.

PLIP PLIP

SHUDDER SHUDDER

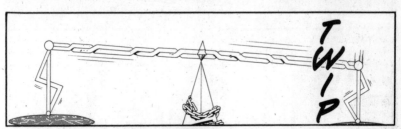

TWIP

MY SIDE IS DIPPING!

NOT TOO SUR- PRISING...

WOOOSH

KRK

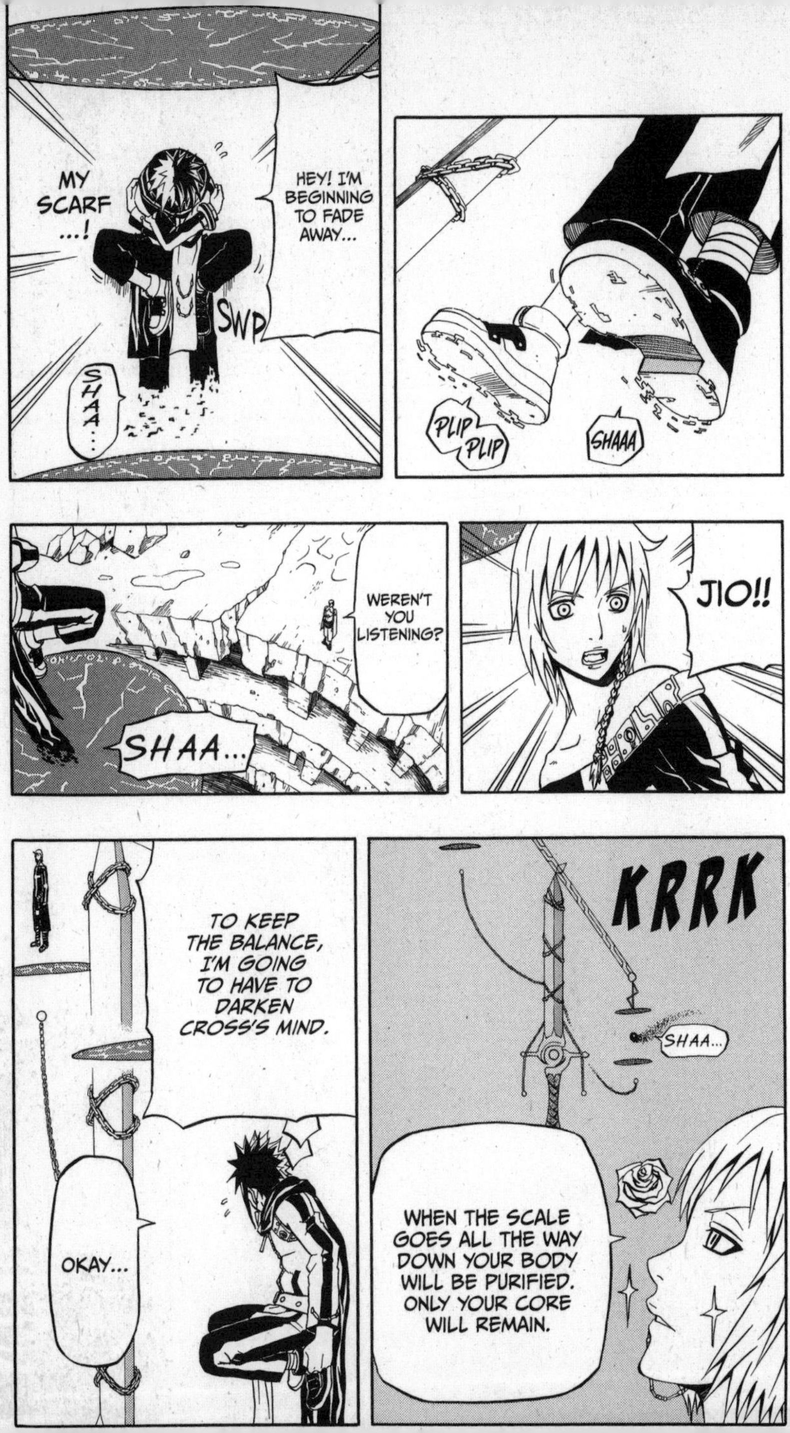
PLIP PLIP
SHAAA
HEY! I'M BEGINNING TO FADE AWAY...
MY SCARF ...!
SWP
SHAA...
JIO!!
WEREN'T YOU LISTENING?
SHAA...
KRRK
SHAA...
WHEN THE SCALE GOES ALL THE WAY DOWN YOUR BODY WILL BE PURIFIED. ONLY YOUR CORE WILL REMAIN.
TO KEEP THE BALANCE, I'M GOING TO HAVE TO DARKEN CROSS'S MIND.
OKAY...

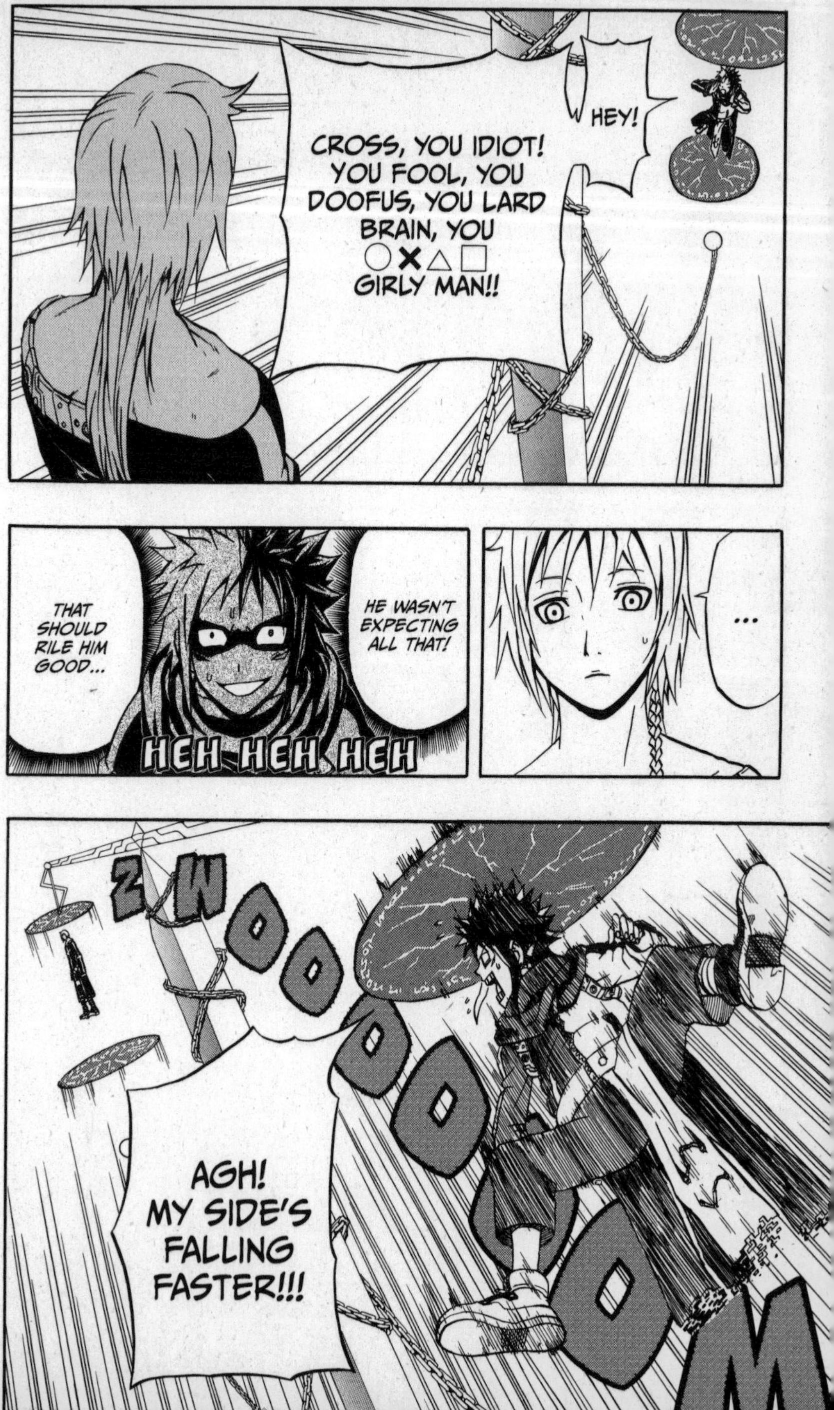
HEY!
CROSS, YOU IDIOT! YOU FOOL, YOU DOOFUS, YOU LARD BRAIN, YOU ○✕△□ GIRLY MAN!!
...
HE WASN'T EXPECTING ALL THAT!
THAT SHOULD RILE HIM GOOD...
HEH HEH HEH
ZWOOOOOOOM
AGH! MY SIDE'S FALLING FASTER!!!

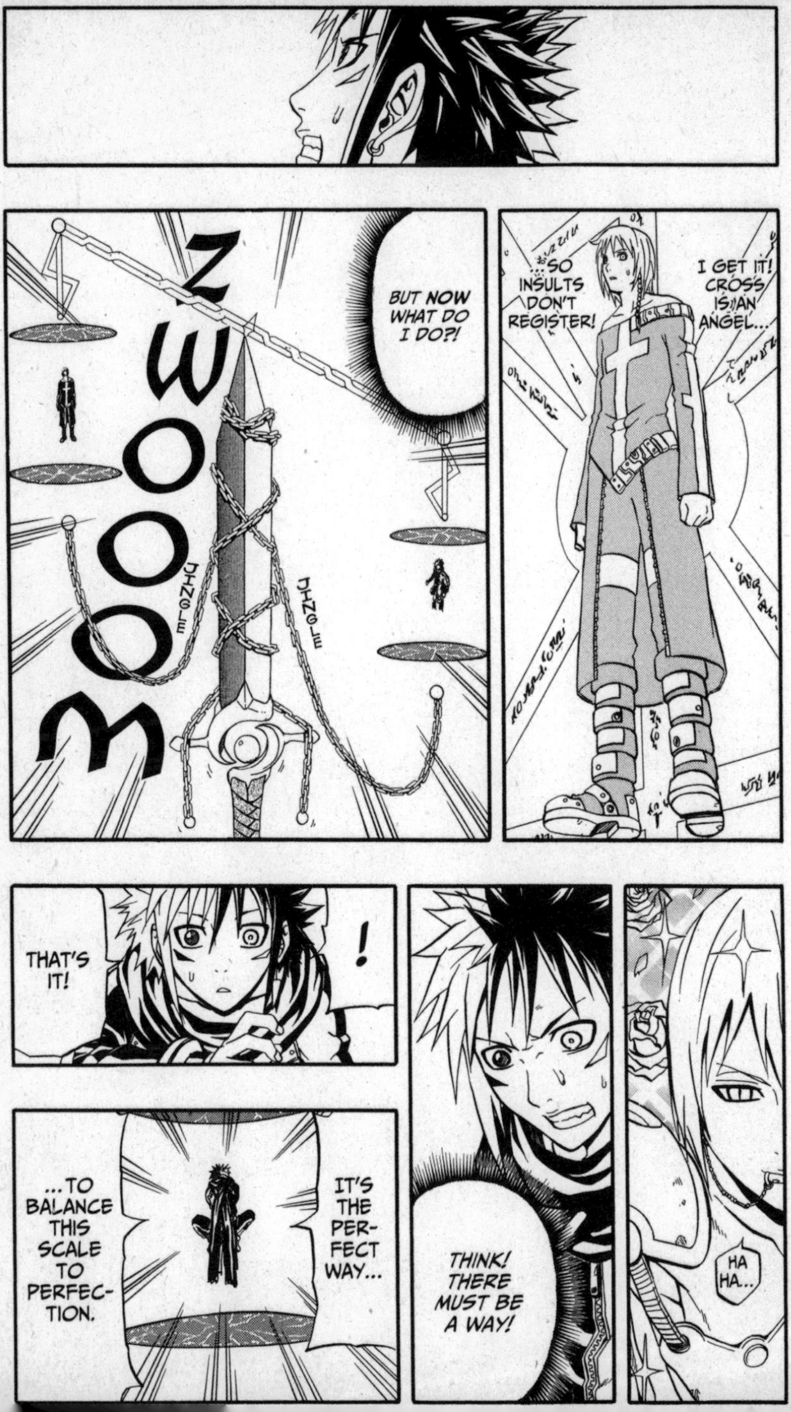
I GET IT! CROSS IS AN ANGEL...
...SO INSULTS DON'T REGISTER!
BUT NOW WHAT DO I DO?!
ZWOOOM
JINGLE
JINGLE
HA HA...
THINK! THERE MUST BE A WAY!
!
THAT'S IT!
IT'S THE PERFECT WAY...
...TO BALANCE THIS SCALE TO PERFECTION.

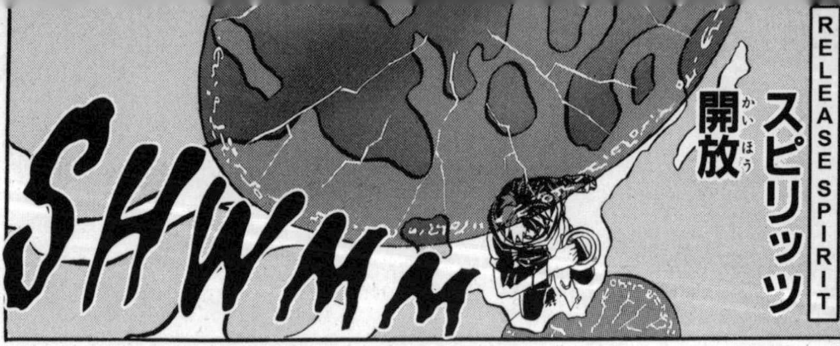
RELEASE SPIRIT
スピリッツ
開放(かいほう)
SHWMM
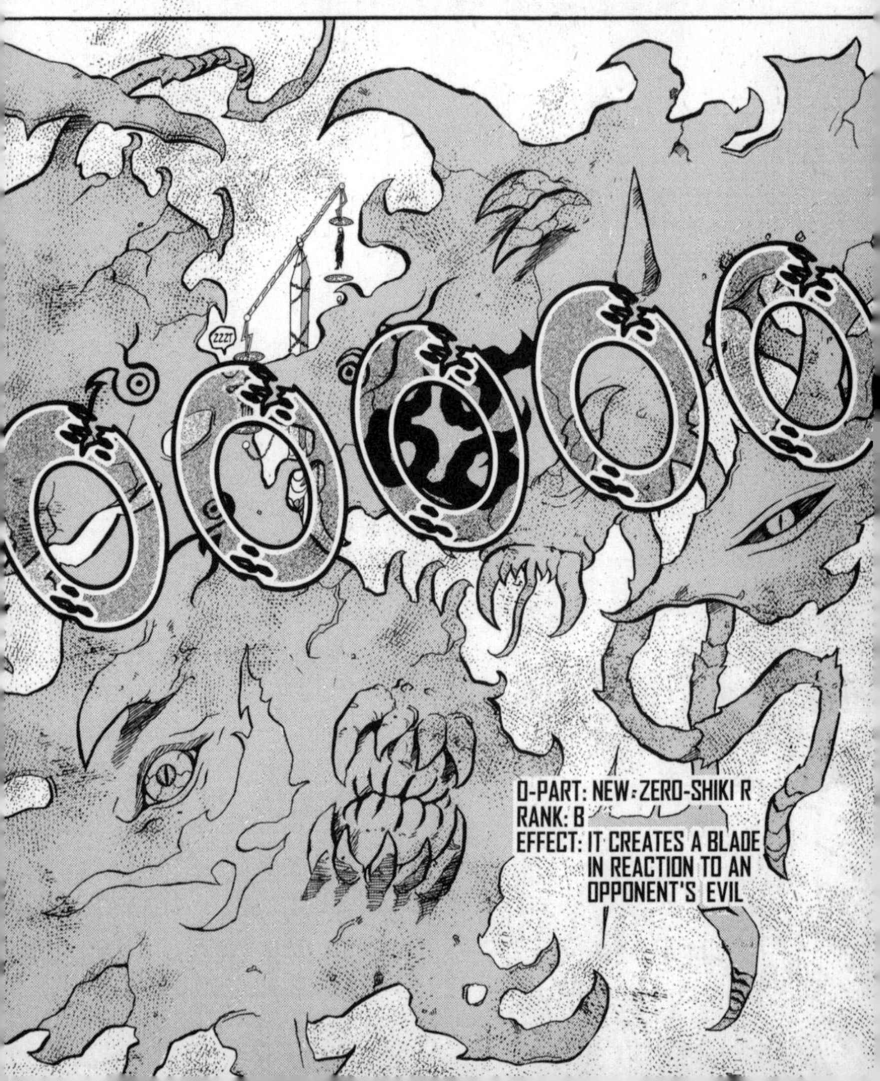
ZZZT
O-PART: NEW: ZERO-SHIKI R
RANK: B
EFFECT: IT CREATES A BLADE IN REACTION TO AN OPPONENT'S EVIL

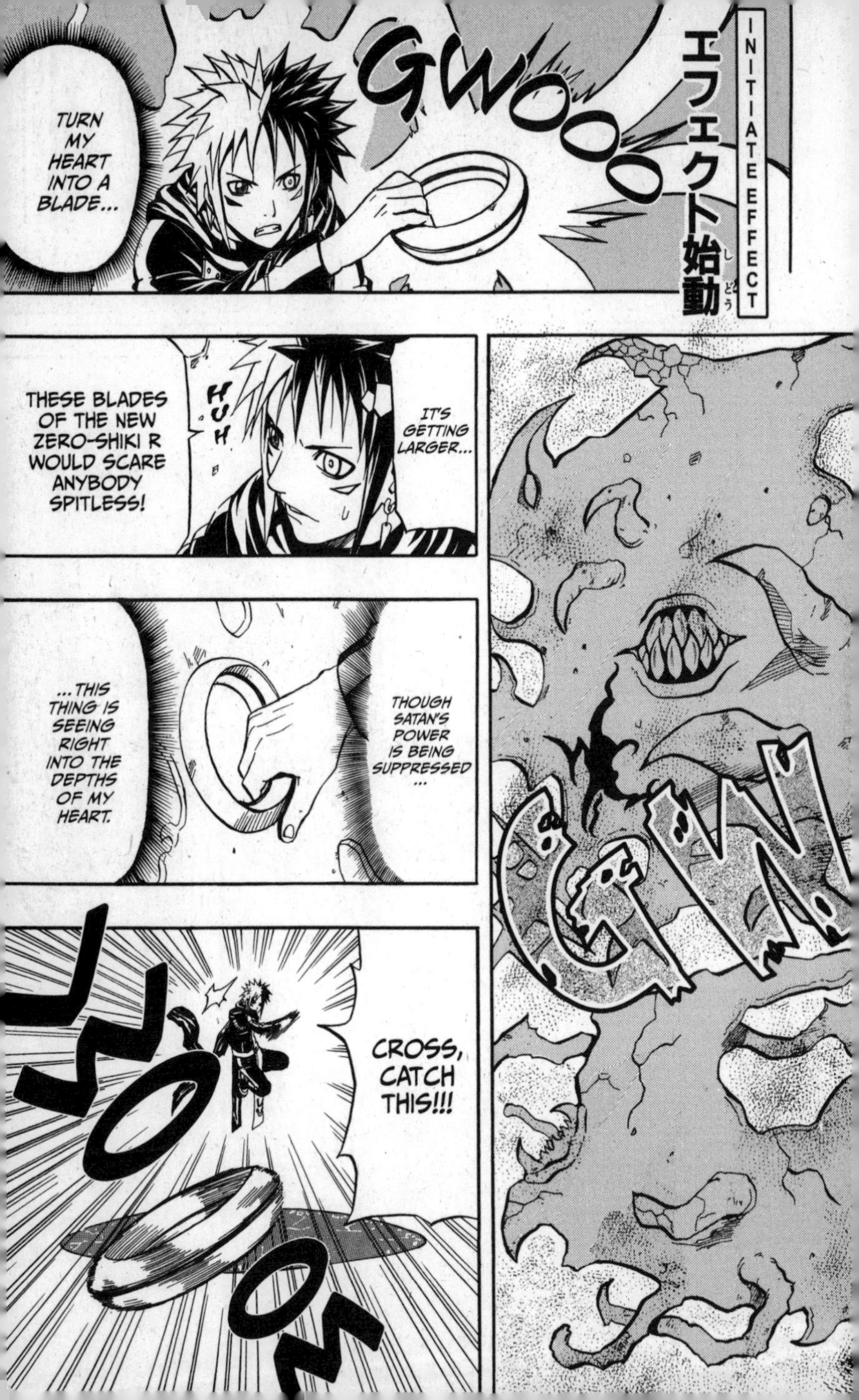
INITIATE EFFECT
エフェクト始動
GWOOOO
TURN MY HEART INTO A BLADE...
GW
IT'S GETTING LARGER...
HUH
THESE BLADES OF THE NEW ZERO-SHIKI R WOULD SCARE ANYBODY SPITLESS!
THOUGH SATAN'S POWER IS BEING SUPPRESSED...
...THIS THING IS SEEING RIGHT INTO THE DEPTHS OF MY HEART.
CROSS, CATCH THIS!!!

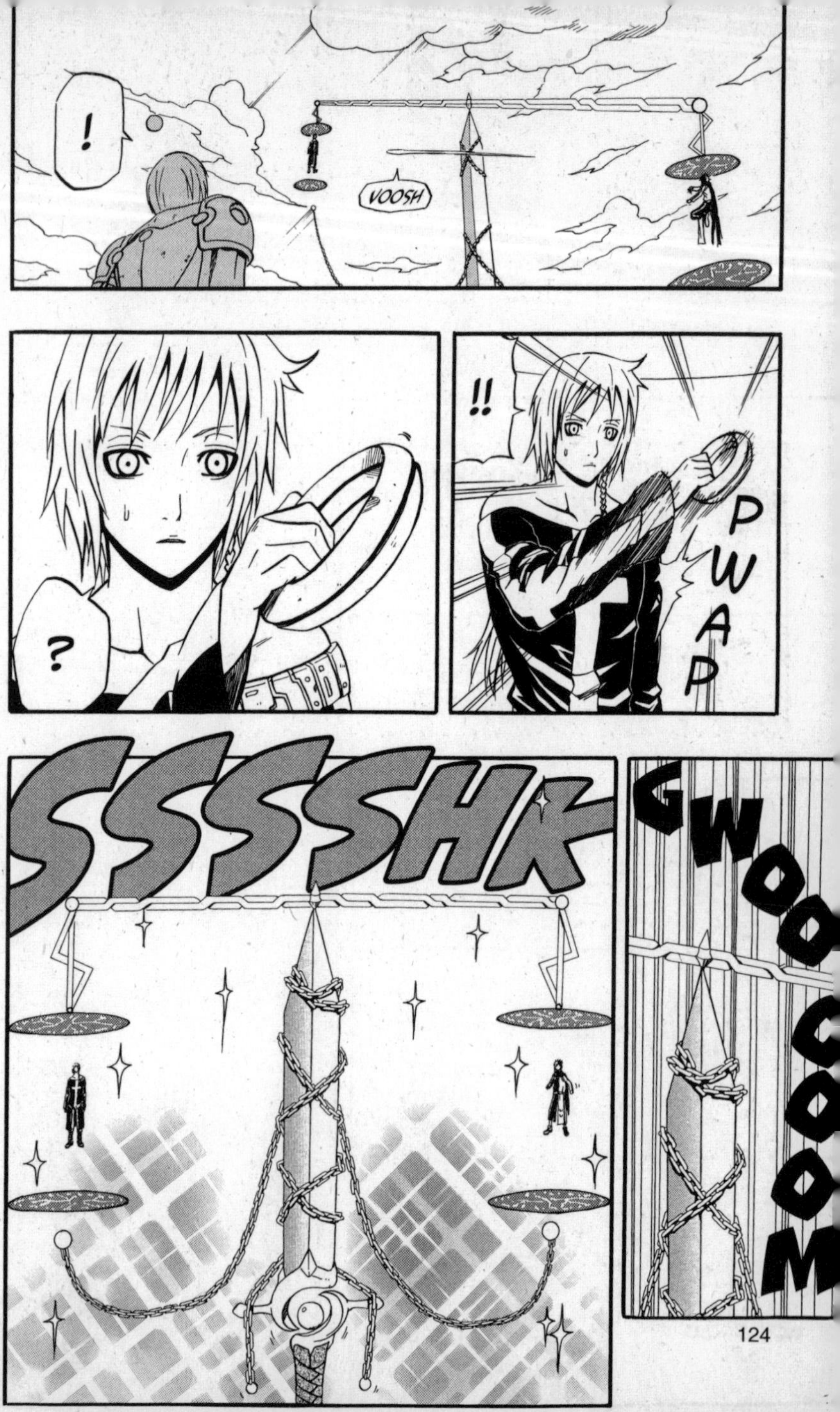
VOOSH
!
!!
PWAP
?
GWOOOOOOOM
SSSSHK

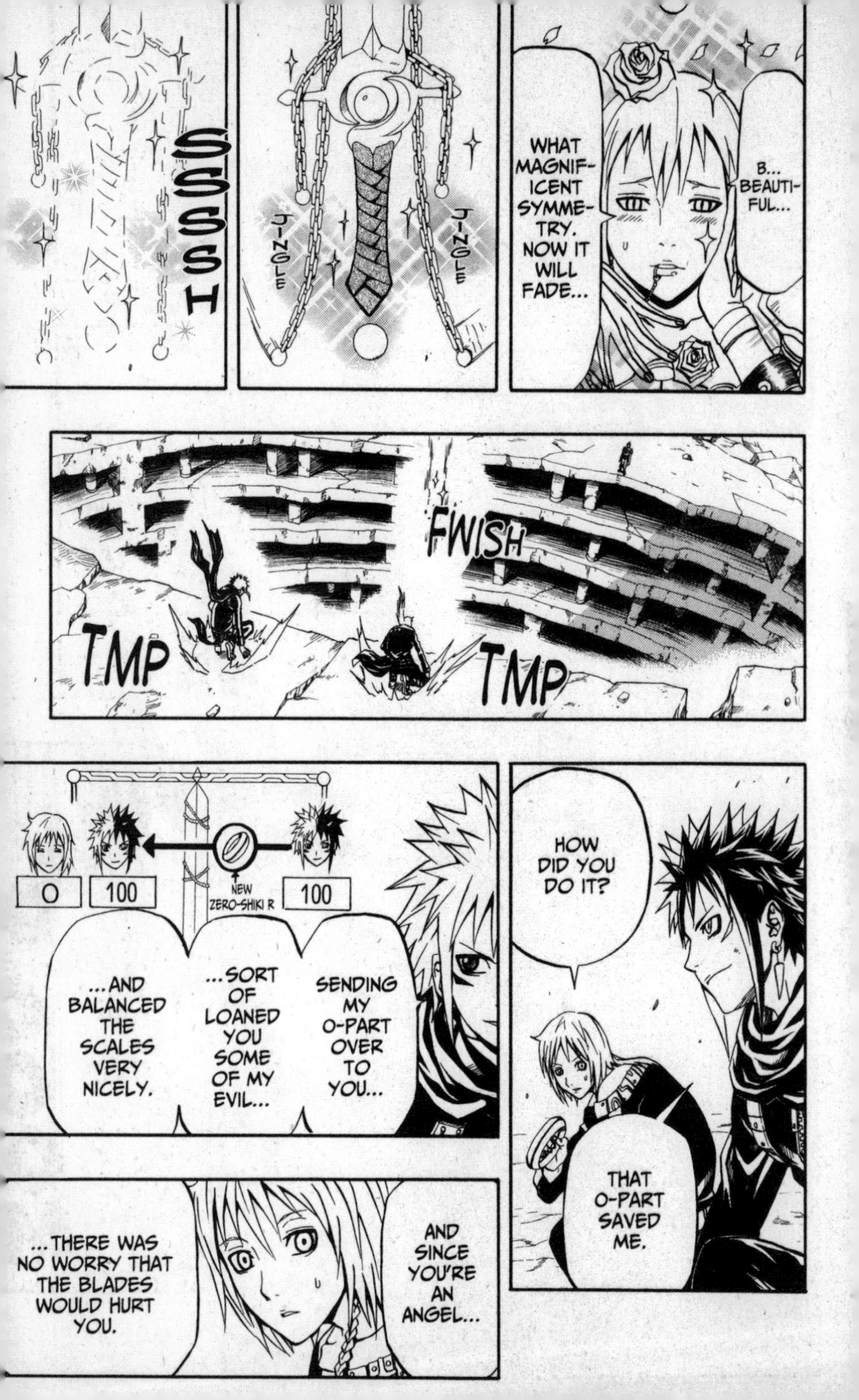
B... BEAUTIFUL...
WHAT MAGNIFICENT SYMMETRY. NOW IT WILL FADE...
JINGLE
JINGLE
SSSSH
FWISH
TMP
TMP
HOW DID YOU DO IT?
THAT O-PART SAVED ME.
100
NEW ZERO-SHIKI R
100
0
SENDING MY O-PART OVER TO YOU...
...SORT OF LOANED YOU SOME OF MY EVIL...
...AND BALANCED THE SCALES VERY NICELY.
AND SINCE YOU'RE AN ANGEL...
...THERE WAS NO WORRY THAT THE BLADES WOULD HURT YOU.

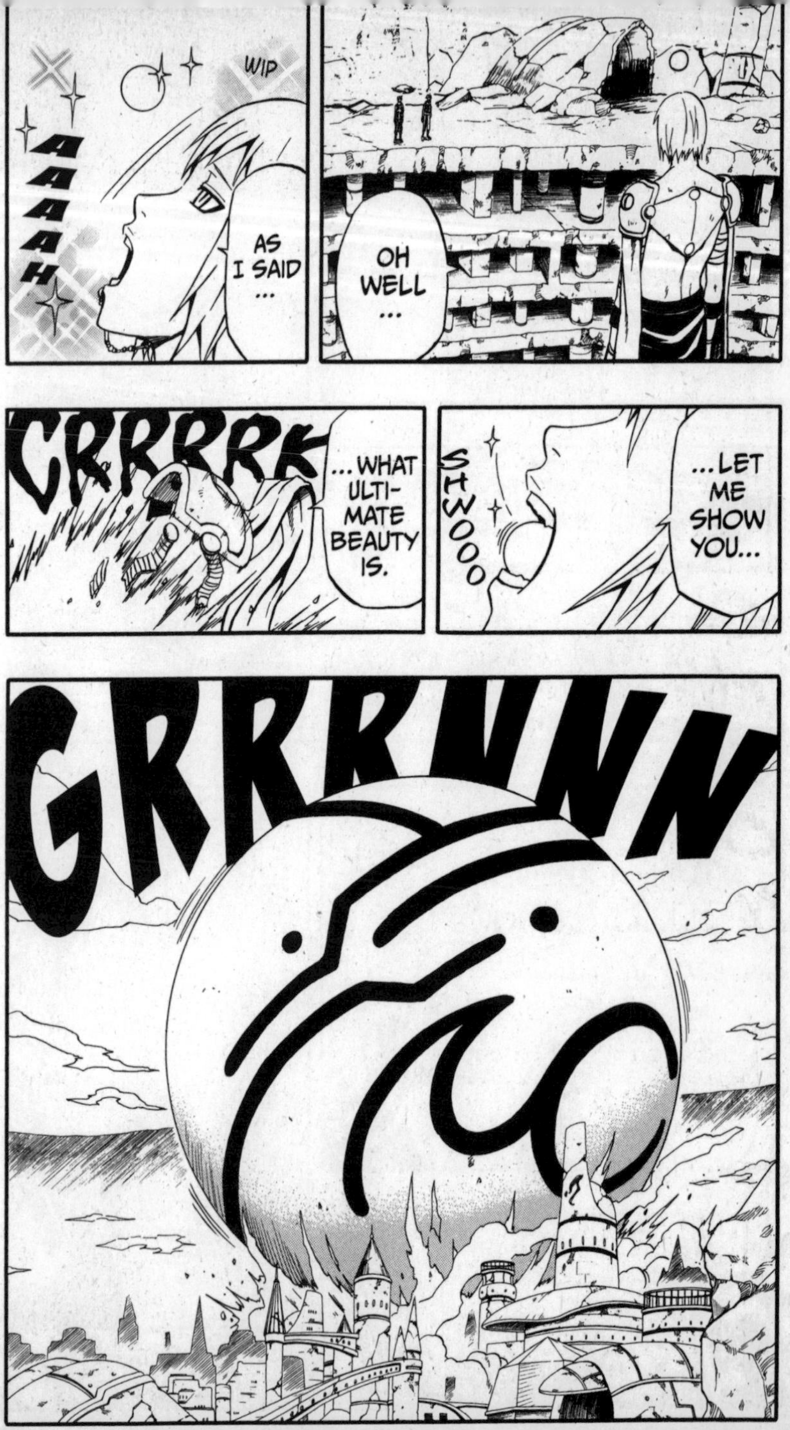
OH WELL ...
AS I SAID ...
WIP
AAAAAH
...LET ME SHOW YOU...
SHWOOO
...WHAT ULTI-MATE BEAUTY IS.
CRRRRK
GRRRNNN

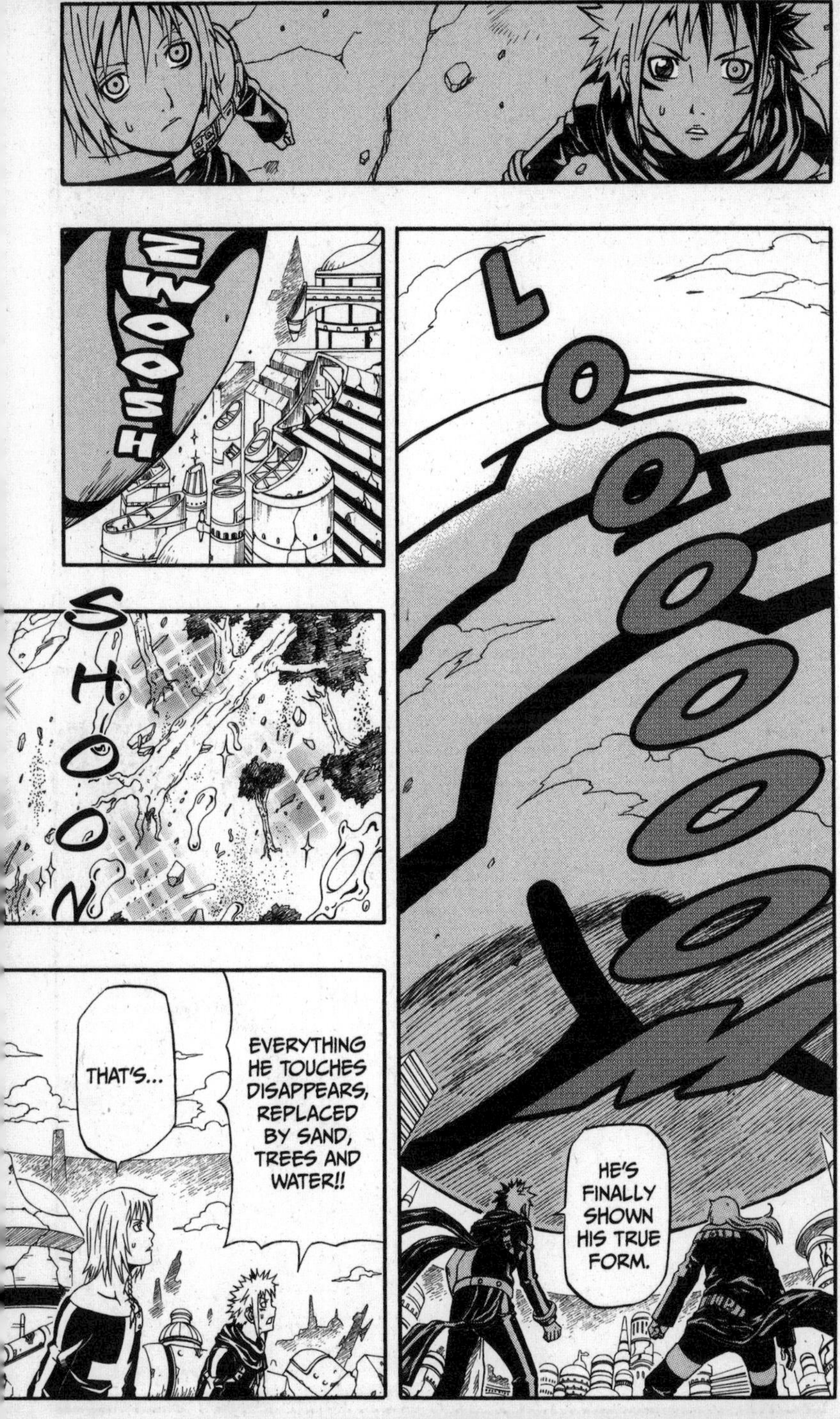
HE'S FINALLY SHOWN HIS TRUE FORM.
WHOOSH
SHOOON
THAT'S...
EVERYTHING HE TOUCHES DISAPPEARS, REPLACED BY SAND, TREES AND WATER!!

...PURIFICATION OF THE CONCRETE AND THE STEEL OF THE BUILDINGS...
...TURNING THEM BACK INTO THEIR NATURAL SOURCES.
CONCRETE
SAND
CEMENT
GRAVEL
WATER
IRON OXIDE
CLAY
LIMESTONE
WHEW! THAT'S WHAT I CALL ANGELIC JUSTICE...
...UPON HUMAN DEPREDATION OF NATURE!
AREN'T I BEAUTIFUL? THE SPHERE IS THE ESSENCE OF ALL CONCRETE FORMS...
...AND IS THE ULTIMATE SHAPE IN THREE DIMENSIONS.
...
I'M GOING TO PURIFY YOU NOW AND HAND YOUR CORES OVER TO MIKO.
I'M GLAD...
I'M GLAD...
...BALL DIDN'T WIND UP FIGHTING THIS ONE...

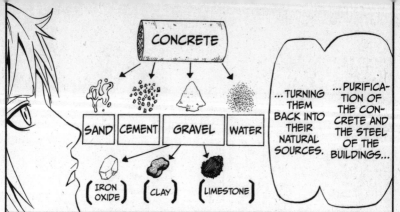

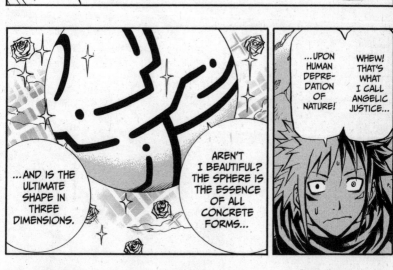

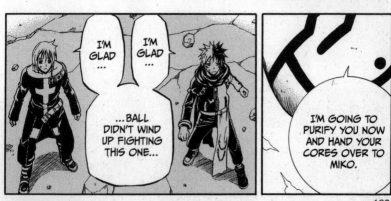

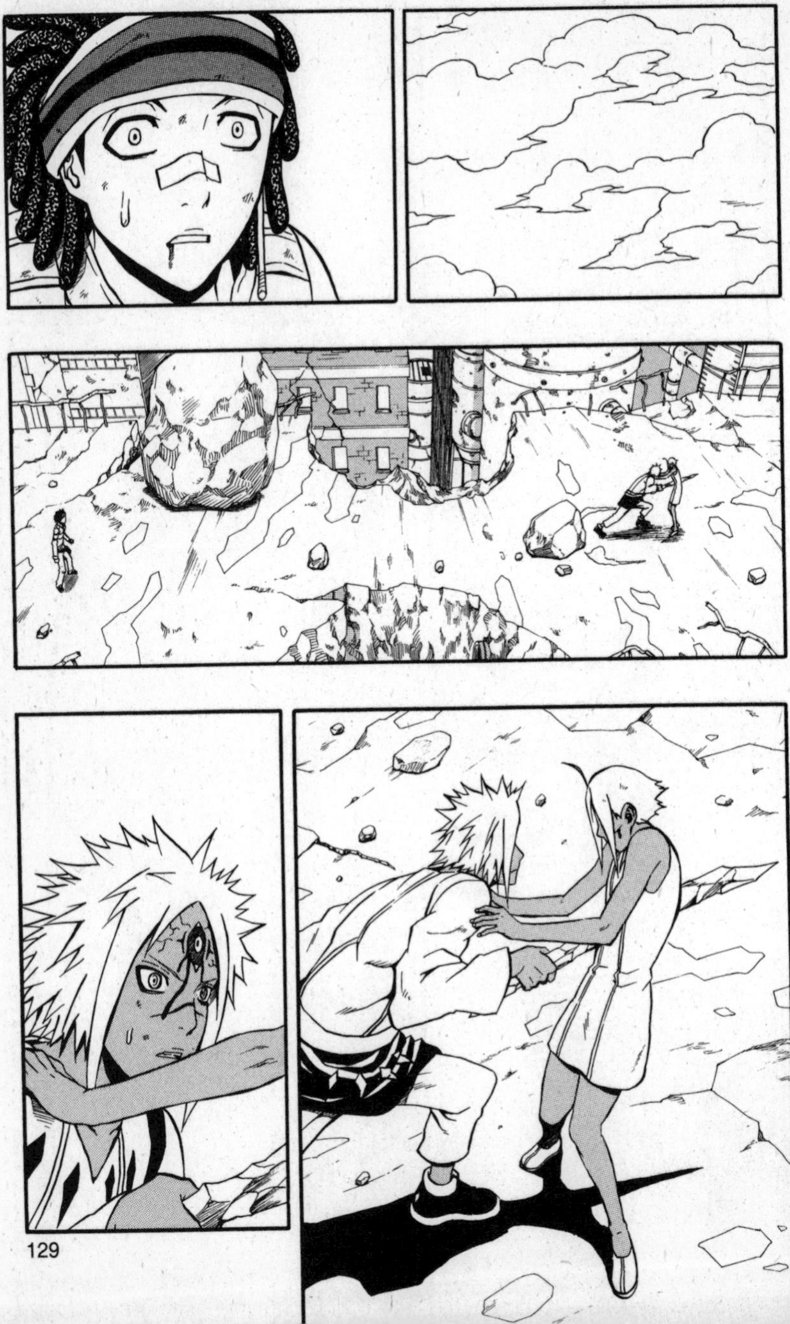

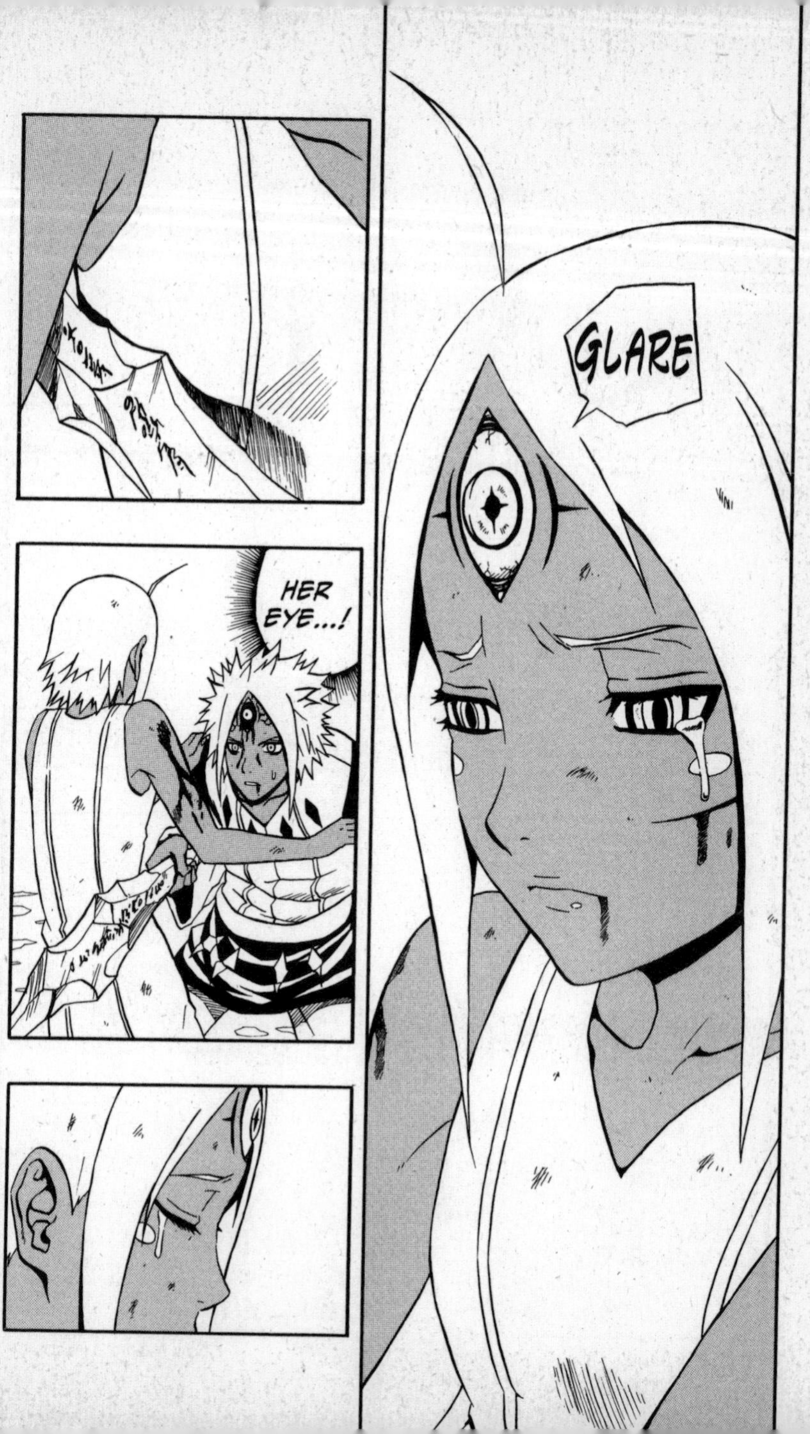
GLARE
HER EYE...!

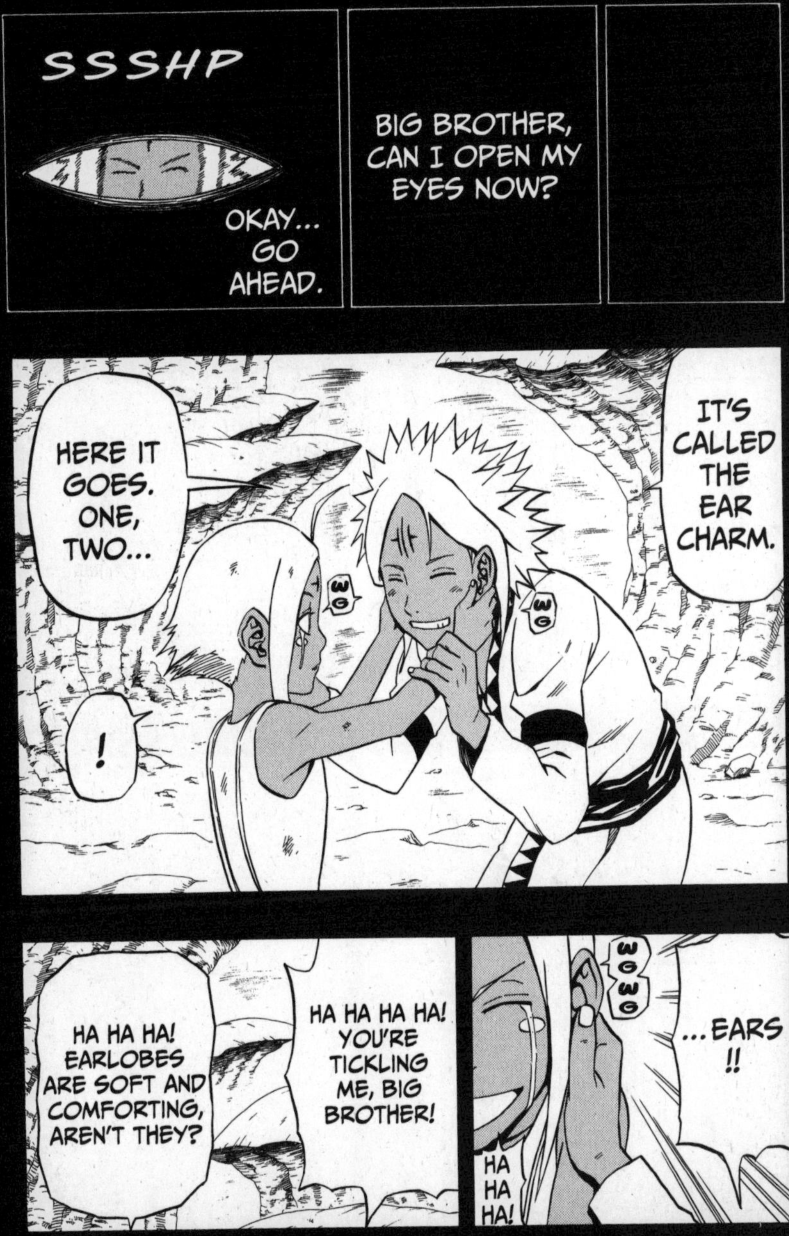
BIG BROTHER, CAN I OPEN MY EYES NOW?
SSSHP
OKAY... GO AHEAD.
IT'S CALLED THE EAR CHARM.
HERE IT GOES. ONE, TWO...
!
...EARS !!
HA HA HA!
HA HA HA HA! YOU'RE TICKLING ME, BIG BROTHER!
HA HA HA! EARLOBES ARE SOFT AND COMFORTING, AREN'T THEY?

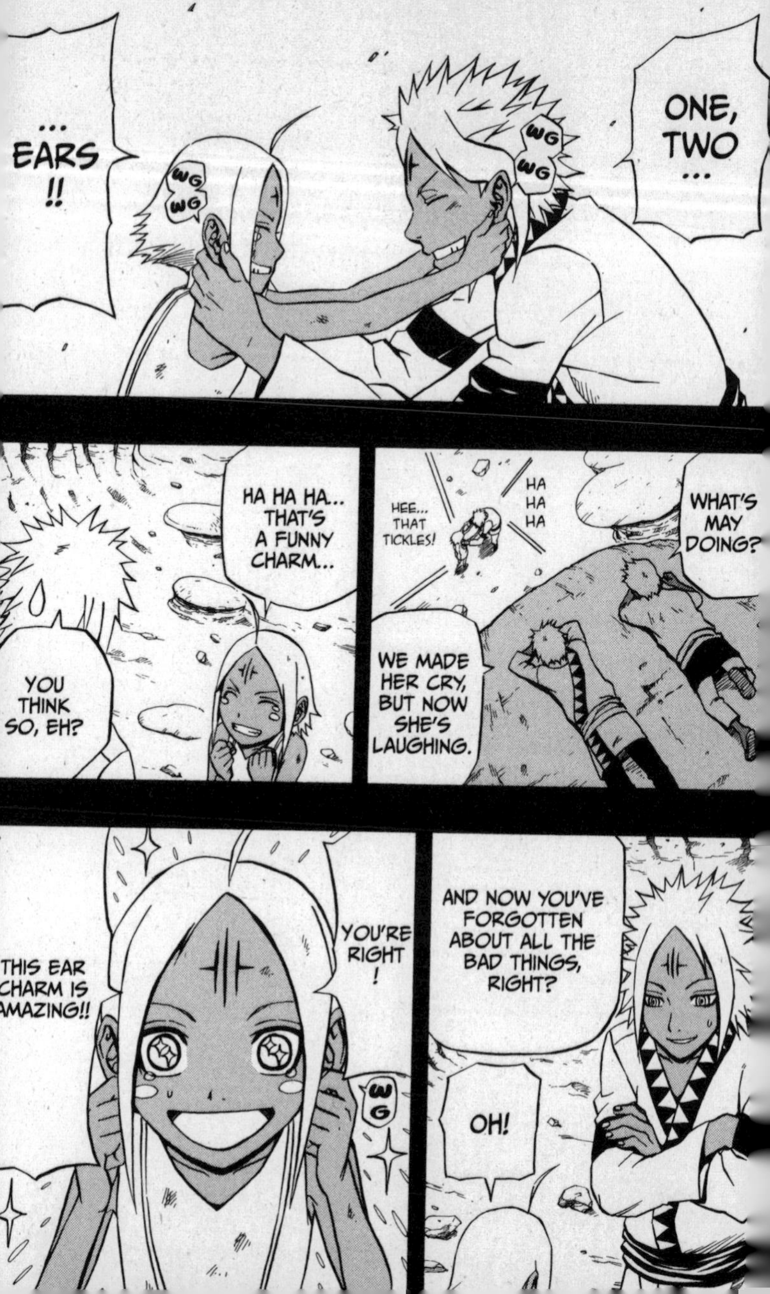
ONE, TWO...
WG WG
WG WG
...EARS!!
WHAT'S MAY DOING?
HA HA HA
HEE... THAT TICKLES!
WE MADE HER CRY, BUT NOW SHE'S LAUGHING.
HA HA HA.. THAT'S A FUNNY CHARM...
YOU THINK SO, EH?
AND NOW YOU'VE FORGOTTEN ABOUT ALL THE BAD THINGS, RIGHT?
OH!
YOU'RE RIGHT!
WG
THIS EAR CHARM IS AMAZING!!

SSSHP

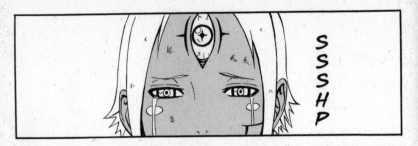

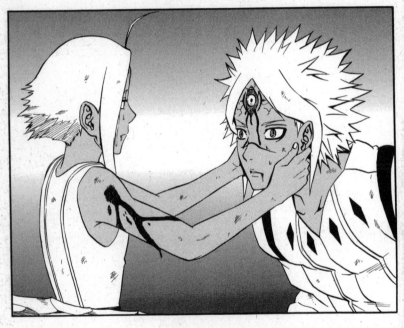

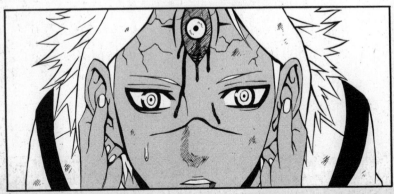

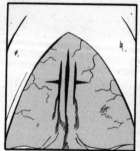

YOU'VE GROWN UP...

PLIP

CLANG

YEAH...

...MAY...

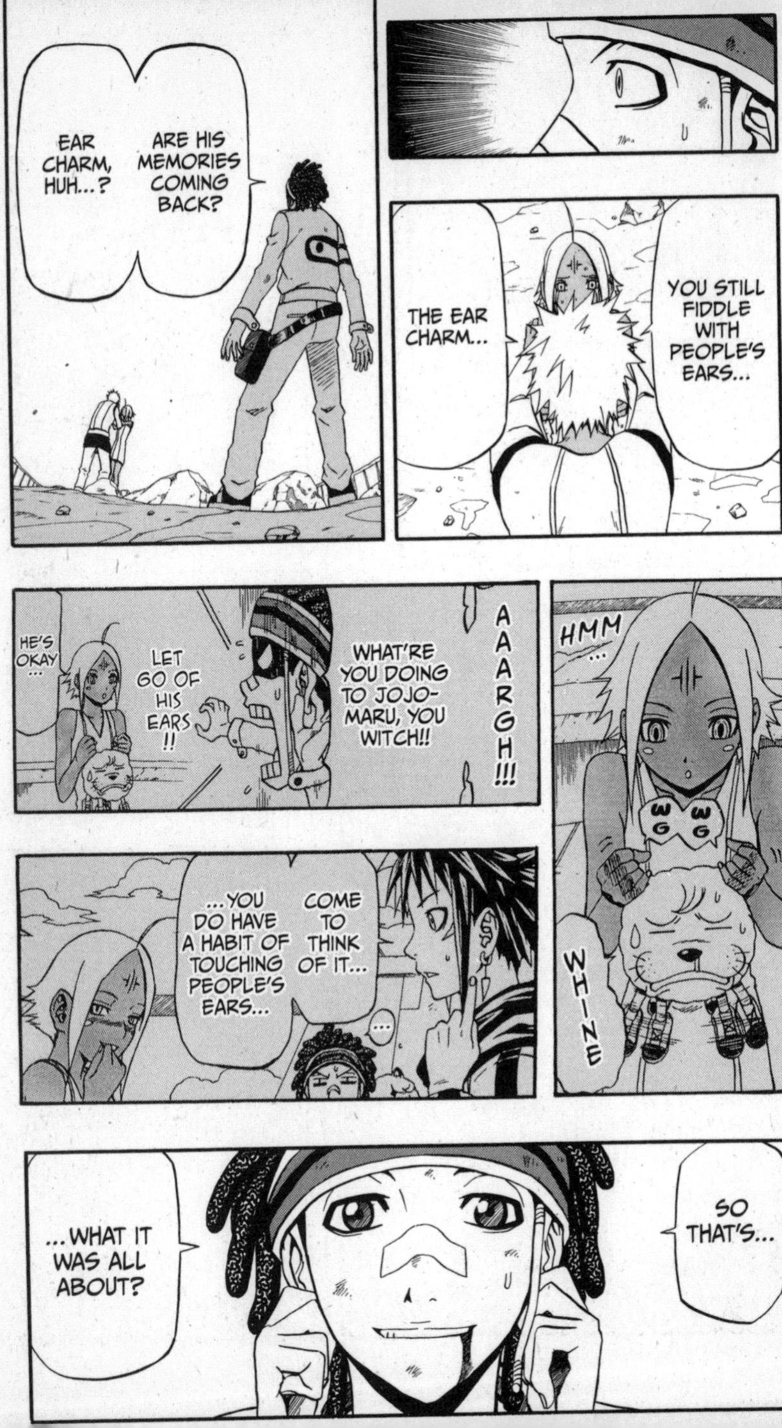
YOU STILL FIDDLE WITH PEOPLE'S EARS...
THE EAR CHARM...
ARE HIS MEMORIES COMING BACK?
EAR CHARM, HUH...?
HMM...
WG WG
WHINE
AAAARGH!!!
WHAT'RE YOU DOING TO JOJO-MARU, YOU WITCH!!
LET GO OF HIS EARS!!
HE'S OKAY...
COME TO THINK OF IT...
...YOU DO HAVE A HABIT OF TOUCHING PEOPLE'S EARS...
...
SO THAT'S...
...WHAT IT WAS ALL ABOUT?

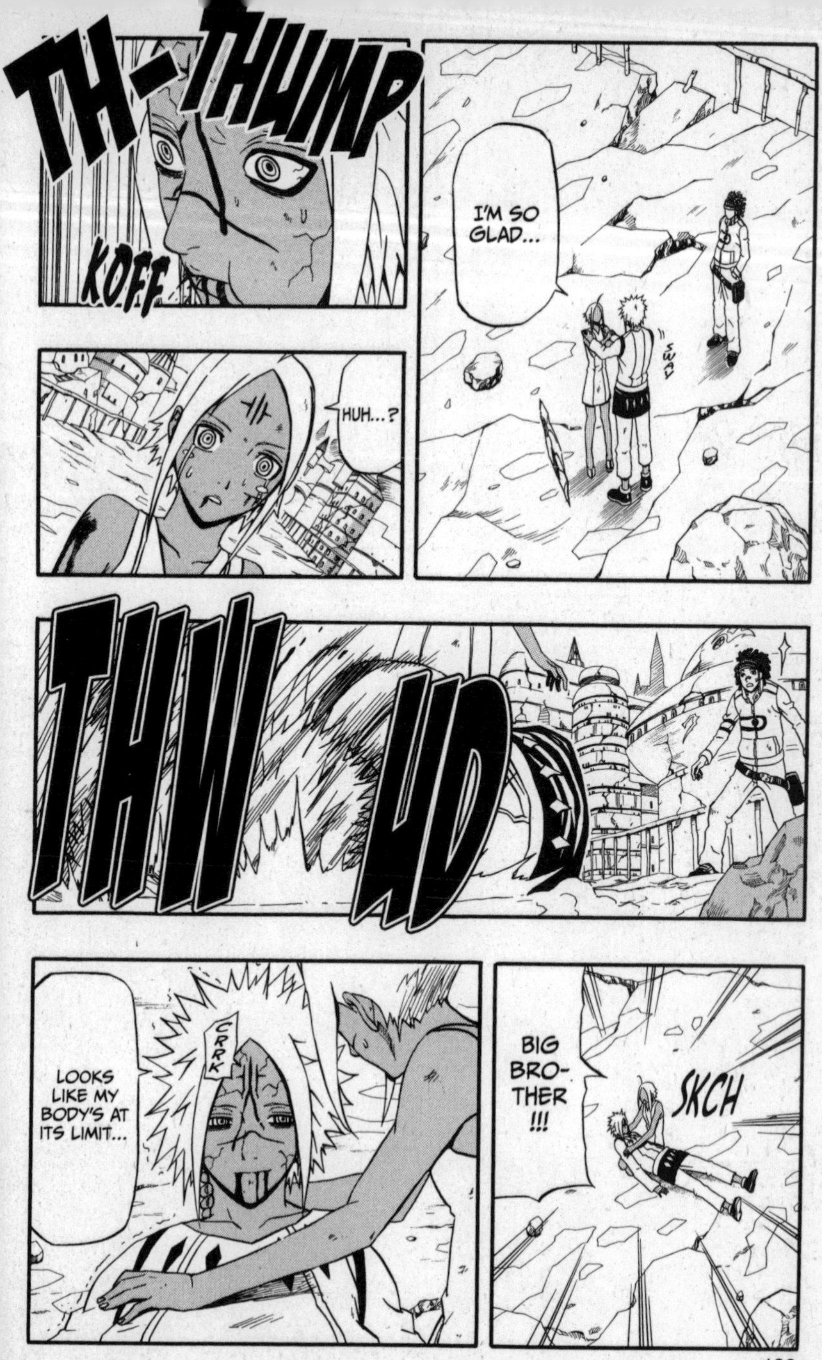
I'M SO GLAD...
SWAY
TH-THUMP
KOFF
HUH...?
THWUD
BIG BRO-THER!!!
SKCH
CRRK
LOOKS LIKE MY BODY'S AT ITS LIMIT...

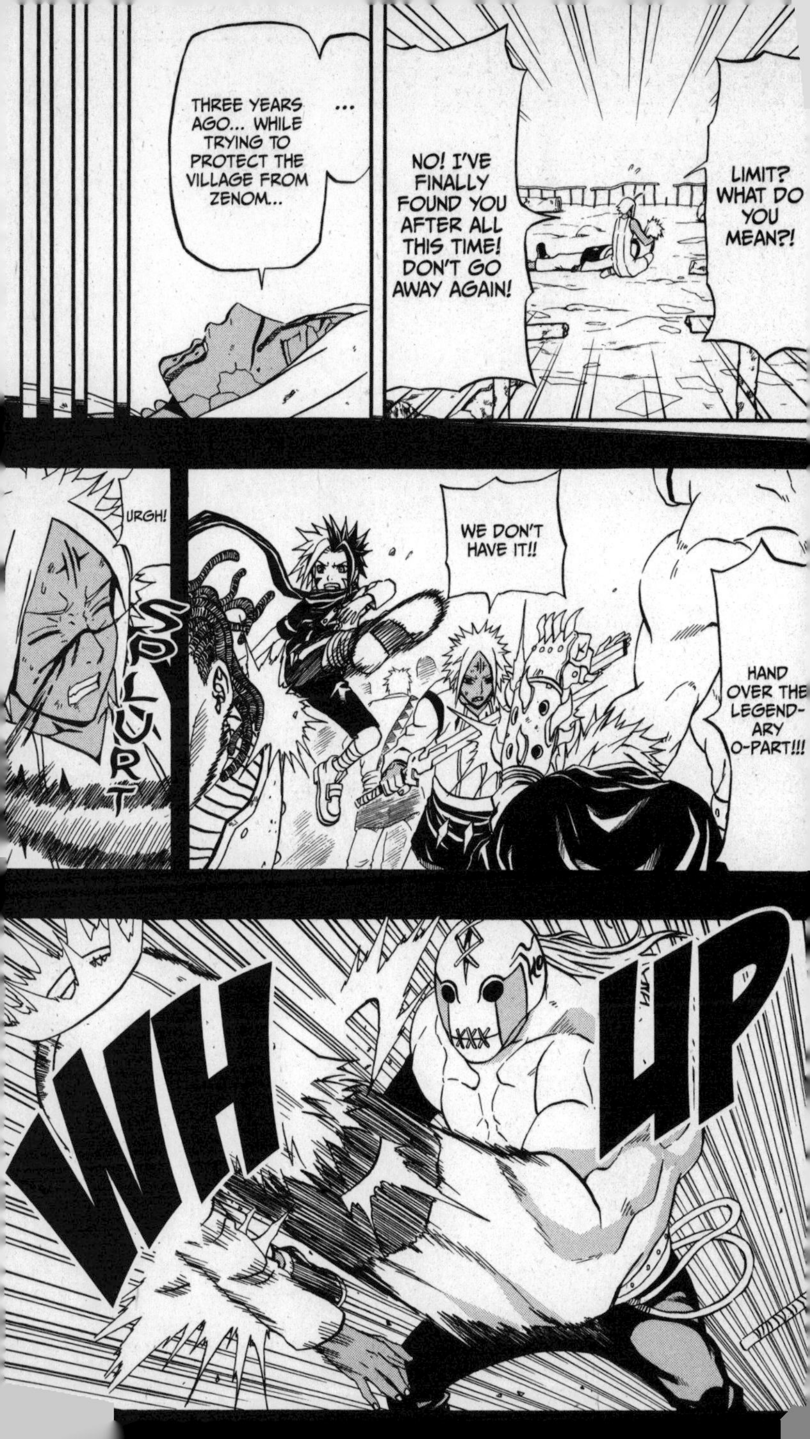
LIMIT? WHAT DO YOU MEAN?!
NO! I'VE FINALLY FOUND YOU AFTER ALL THIS TIME! DON'T GO AWAY AGAIN!
...
THREE YEARS AGO... WHILE TRYING TO PROTECT THE VILLAGE FROM ZENOM...
HAND OVER THE LEGENDARY O-PART!!!
WE DON'T HAVE IT!!
URGH!
SPLURT
WHUP

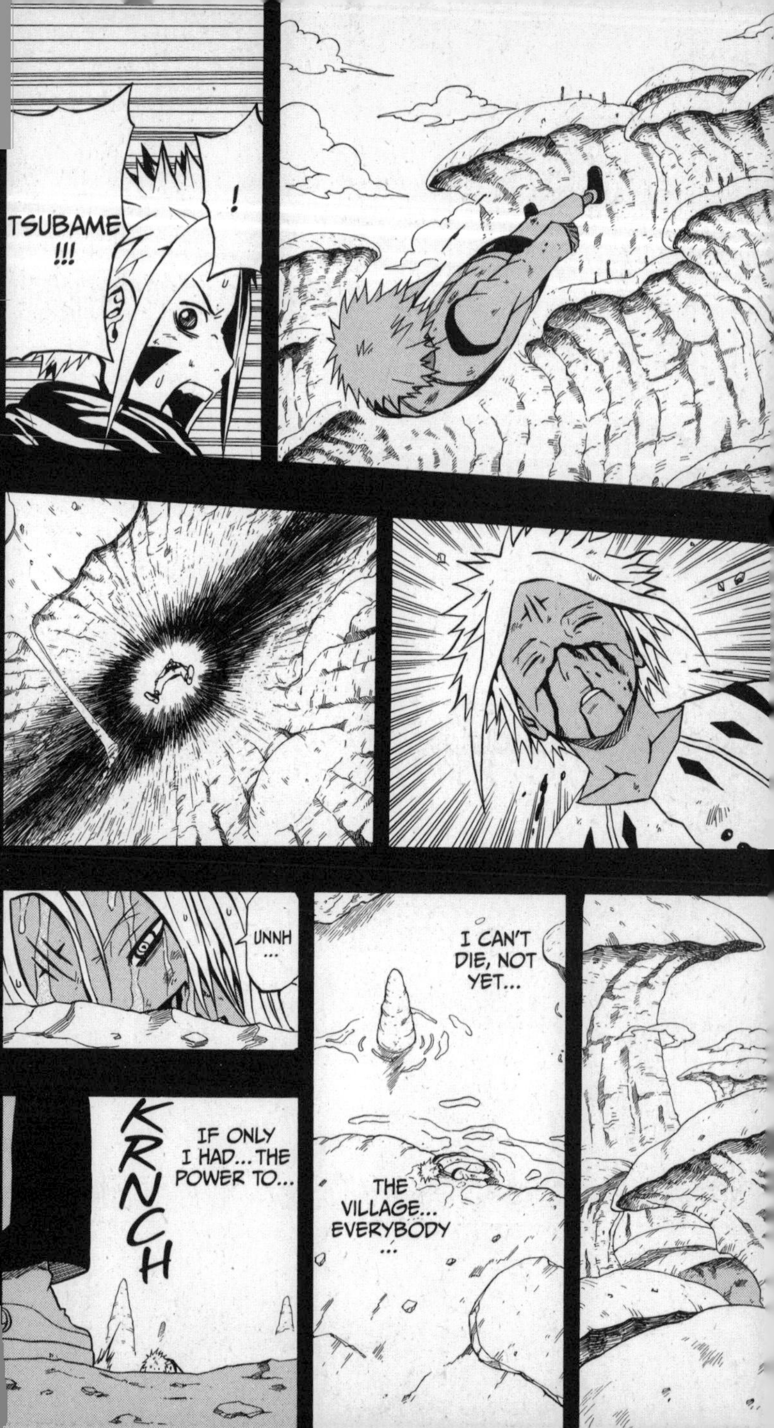
!
TSUBAME !!!
I CAN'T DIE, NOT YET...
THE VILLAGE... EVERYBODY ...
UNNH ...
IF ONLY I HAD... THE POWER TO...
KRNCH

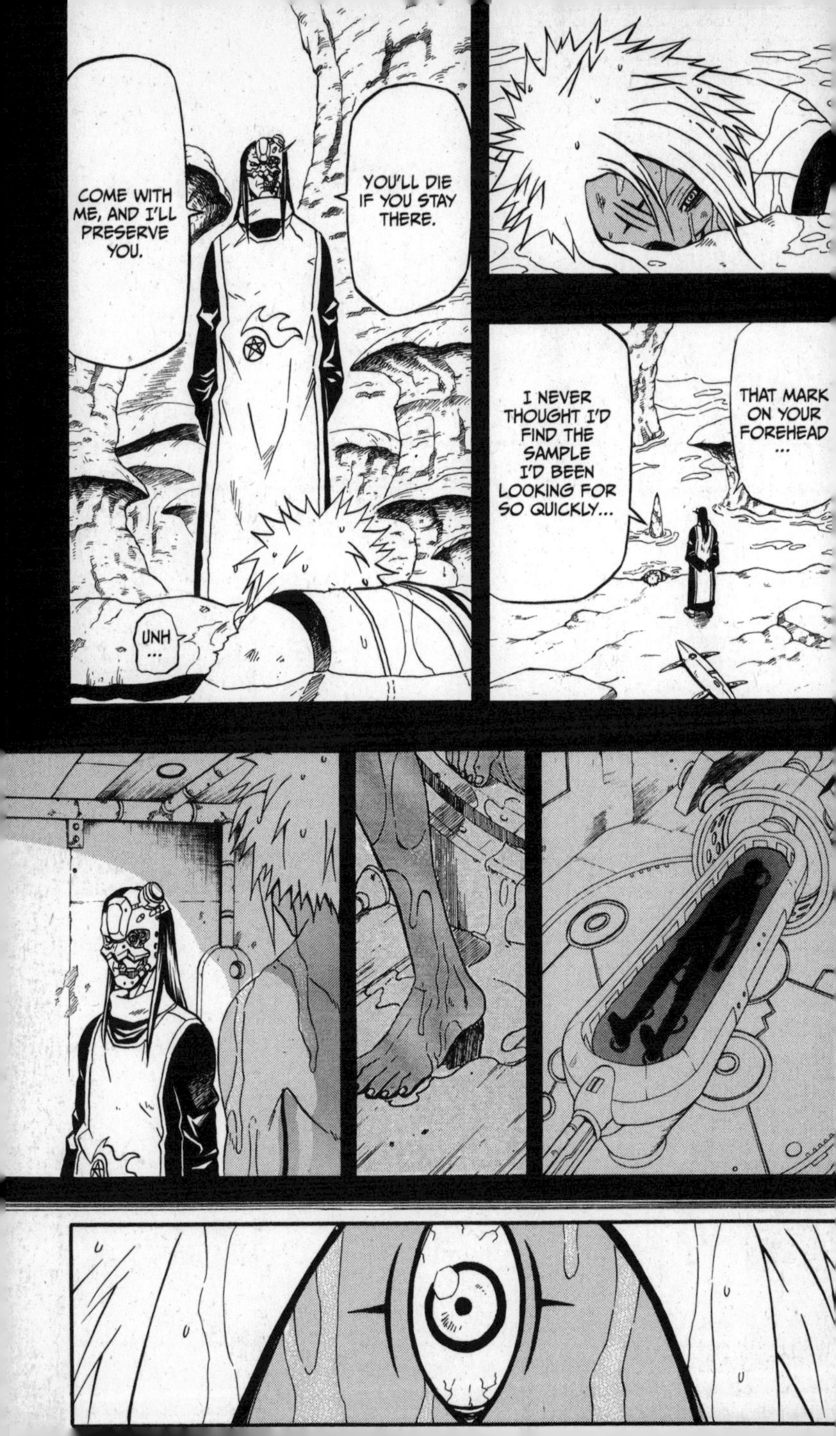
THAT MARK ON YOUR FOREHEAD ...
I NEVER THOUGHT I'D FIND THE SAMPLE I'D BEEN LOOKING FOR SO QUICKLY...
YOU'LL DIE IF YOU STAY THERE.
COME WITH ME, AND I'LL PRESERVE YOU.
UNH ...

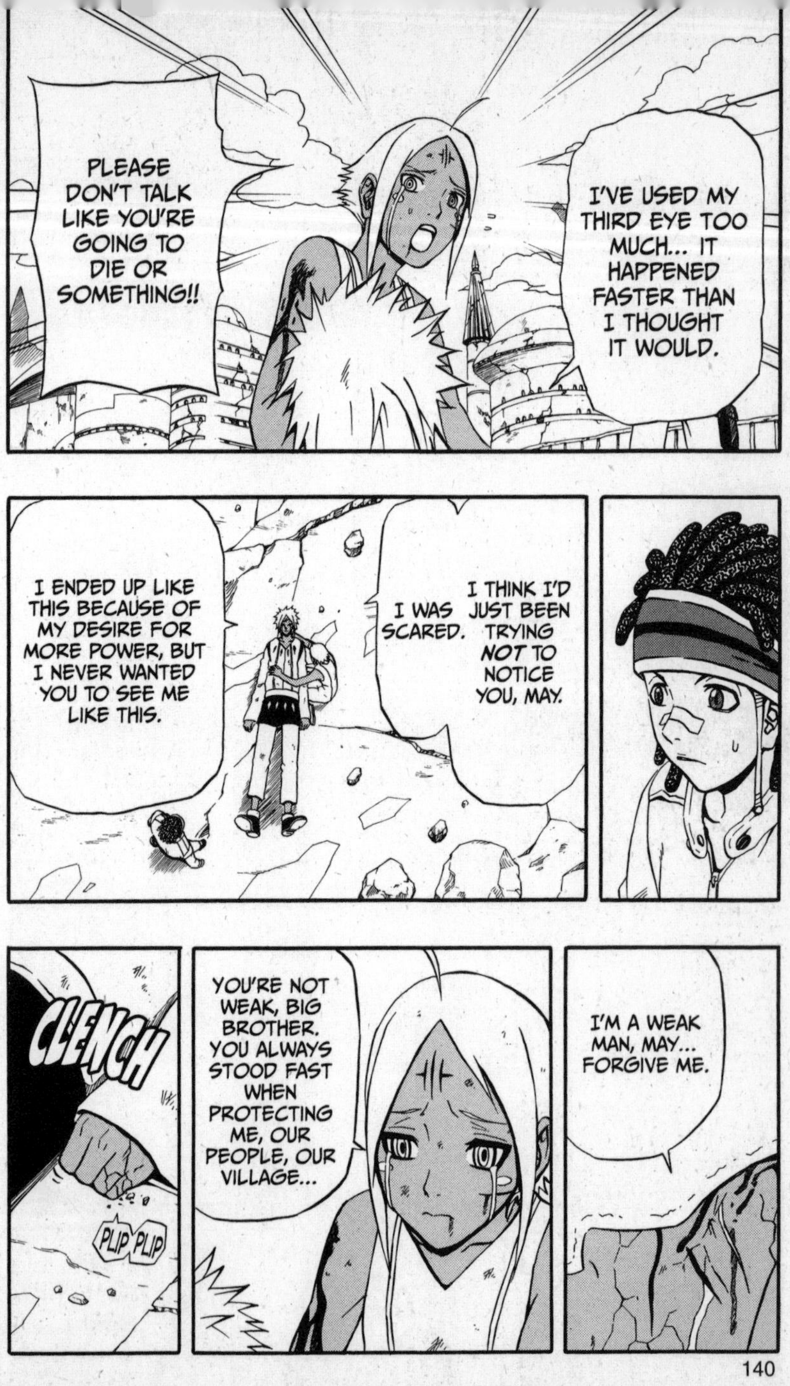
I'VE USED MY THIRD EYE TOO MUCH... IT HAPPENED FASTER THAN I THOUGHT IT WOULD.
PLEASE DON'T TALK LIKE YOU'RE GOING TO DIE OR SOMETHING!!
I THINK I'D JUST BEEN TRYING *NOT* TO NOTICE YOU, MAY.
I WAS SCARED.
I ENDED UP LIKE THIS BECAUSE OF MY DESIRE FOR MORE POWER, BUT I NEVER WANTED YOU TO SEE ME LIKE THIS.
I'M A WEAK MAN, MAY... FORGIVE ME.
YOU'RE NOT WEAK, BIG BROTHER. YOU ALWAYS STOOD FAST WHEN PROTECTING ME, OUR PEOPLE, OUR VILLAGE...
CLENCH
PLIP PLIP

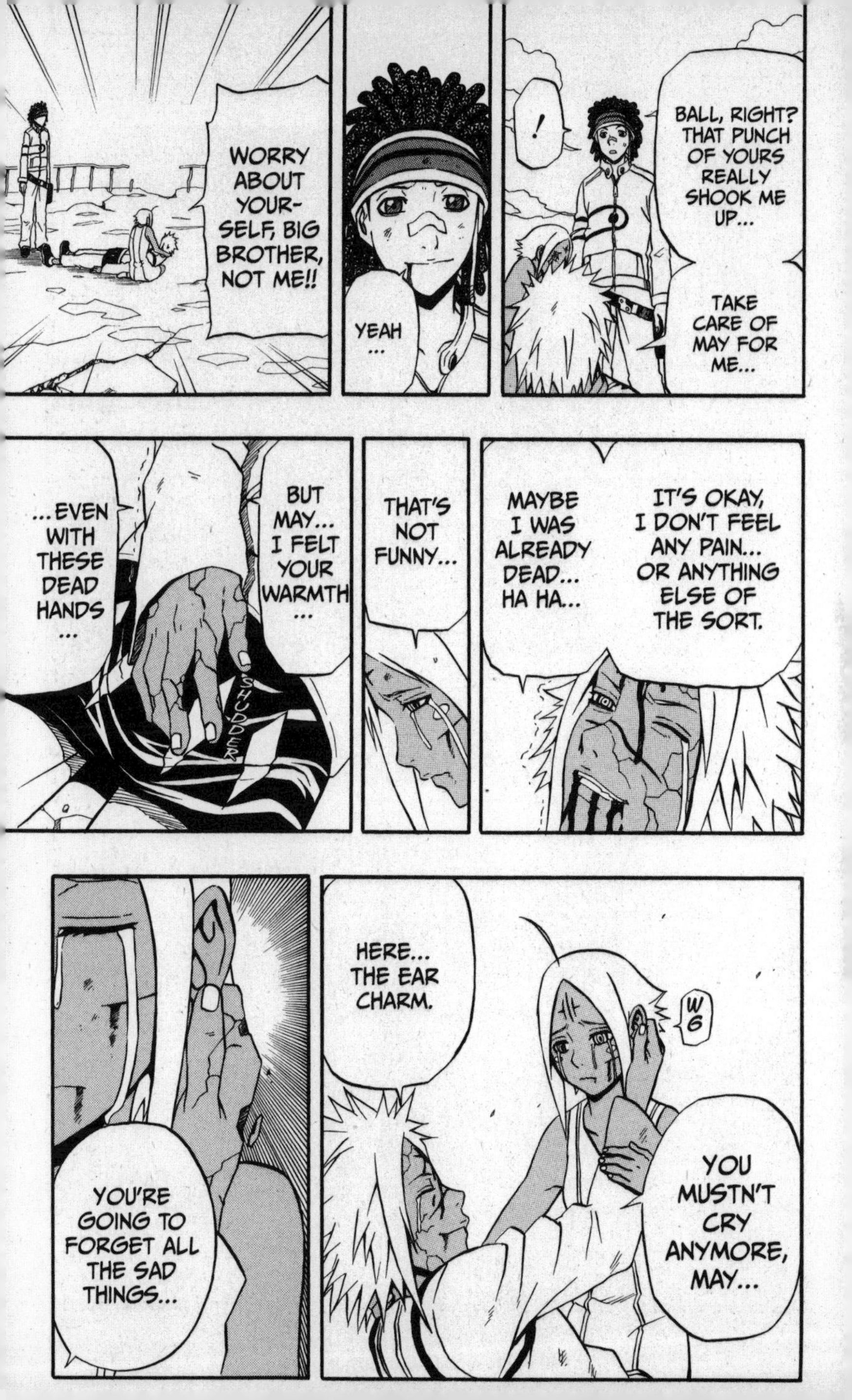
!
BALL, RIGHT? THAT PUNCH OF YOURS REALLY SHOOK ME UP...
TAKE CARE OF MAY FOR ME...
YEAH ...
WORRY ABOUT YOUR-SELF, BIG BROTHER, NOT ME!!
IT'S OKAY, I DON'T FEEL ANY PAIN... OR ANYTHING ELSE OF THE SORT.
MAYBE I WAS ALREADY DEAD... HA HA...
THAT'S NOT FUNNY...
BUT MAY... I FELT YOUR WARMTH ...
...EVEN WITH THESE DEAD HANDS ...
SHUDDER
HERE... THE EAR CHARM.
YOU MUSTN'T CRY ANYMORE, MAY...
YOU'RE GOING TO FORGET ALL THE SAD THINGS...

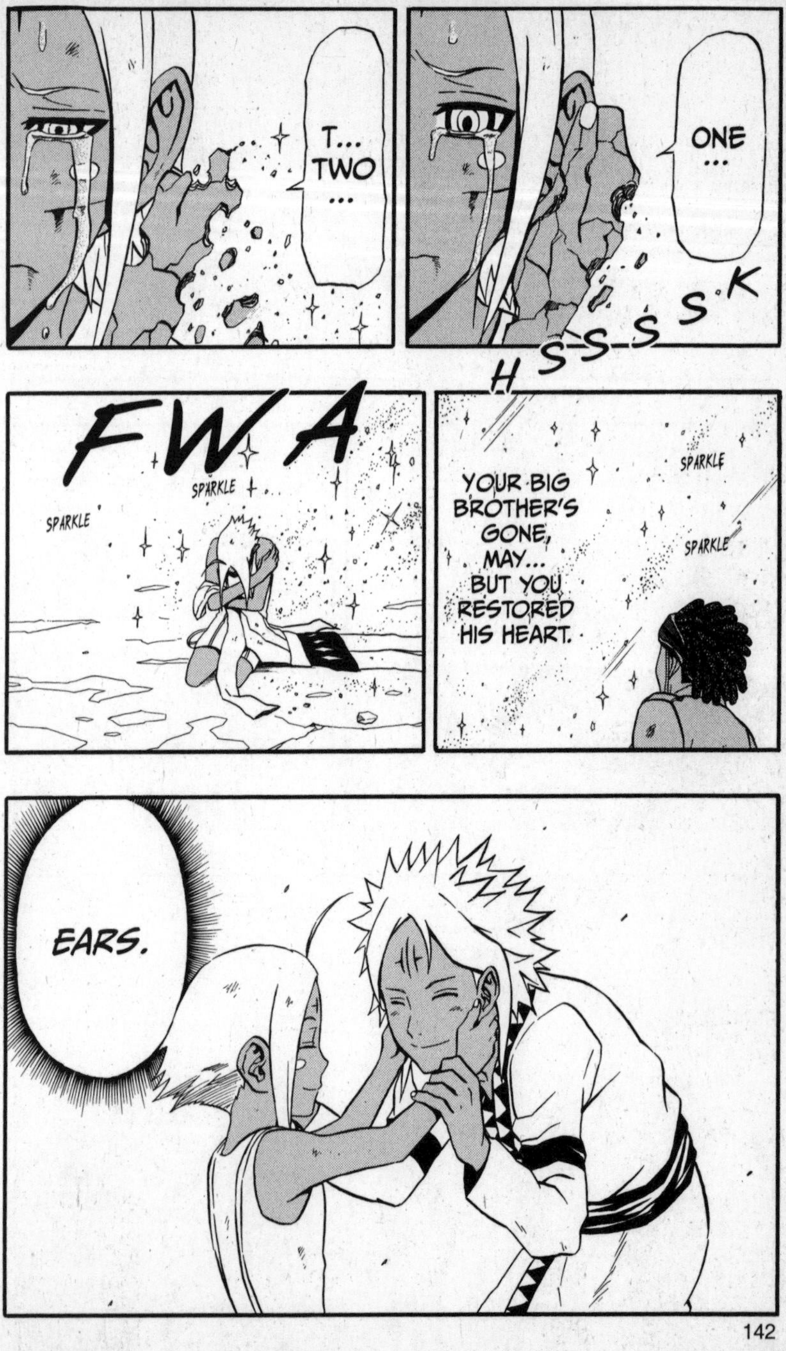
ONE ...
HSSSSK
T... TWO ...
YOUR BIG BROTHER'S GONE, MAY... BUT YOU RESTORED HIS HEART.
SPARKLE
SPARKLE
FWA
SPARKLE
SPARKLE
EARS.

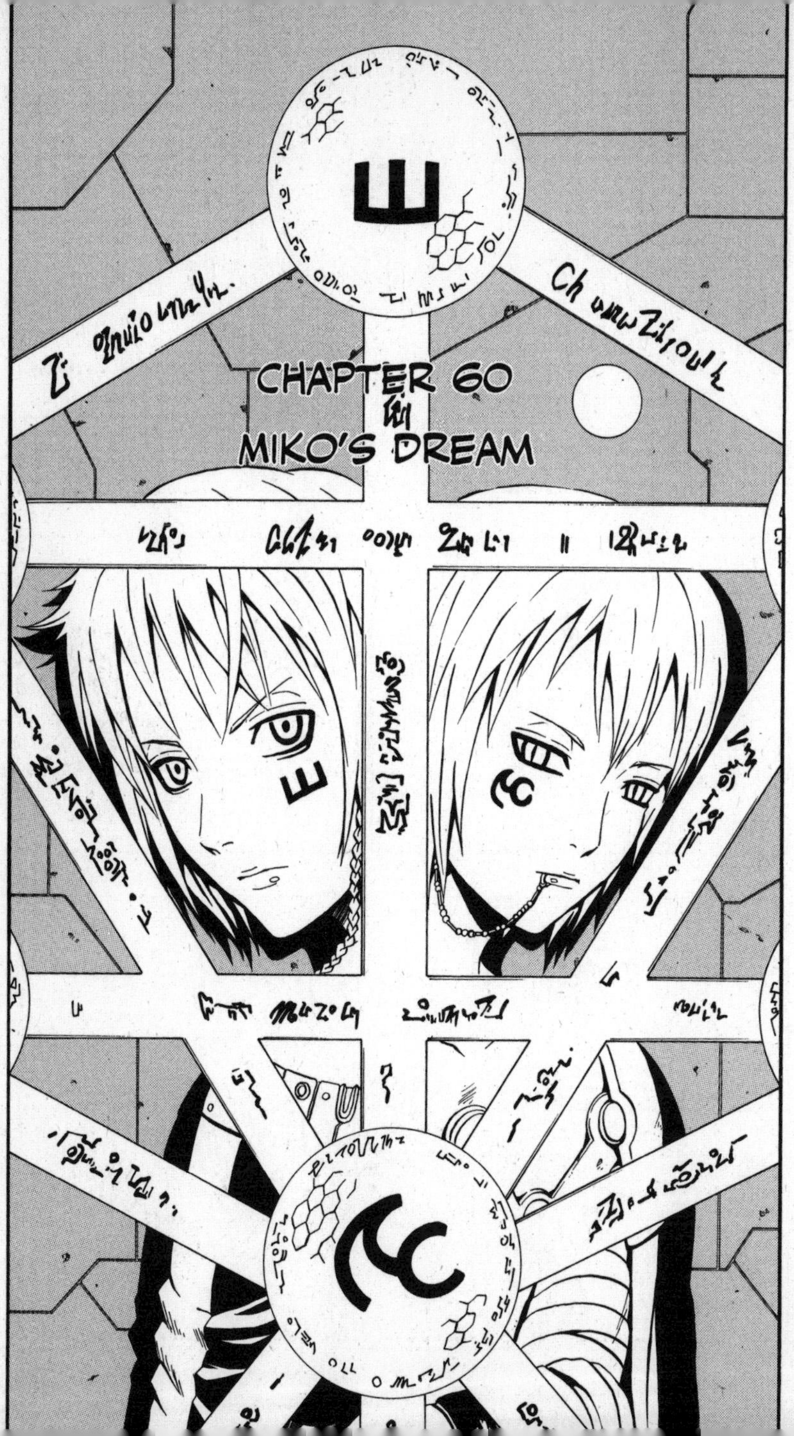
CHAPTER 60
MIKO'S DREAM

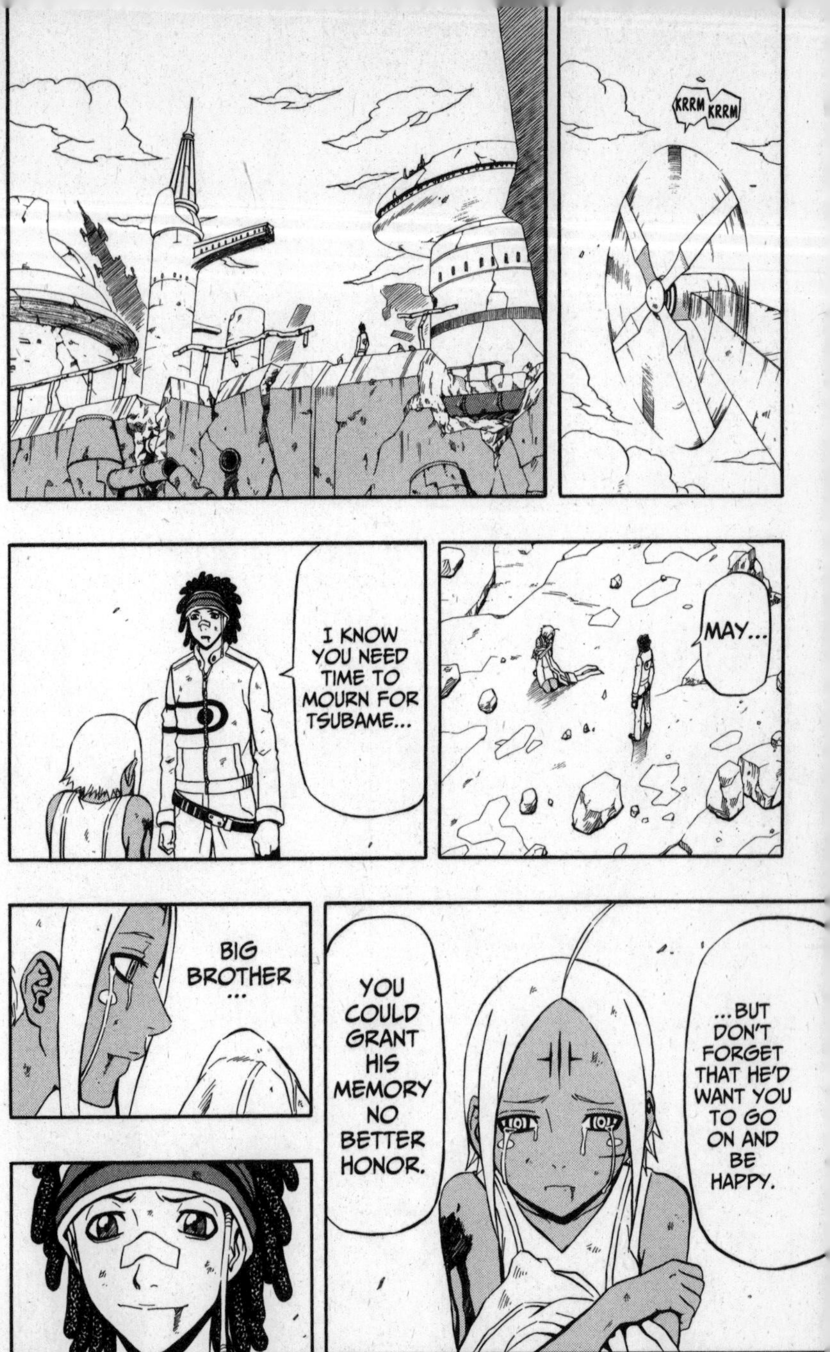
KRRM KRRM
MAY...
I KNOW YOU NEED TIME TO MOURN FOR TSUBAME...
...BUT DON'T FORGET THAT HE'D WANT YOU TO GO ON AND BE HAPPY.
YOU COULD GRANT HIS MEMORY NO BETTER HONOR.
BIG BROTHER ...

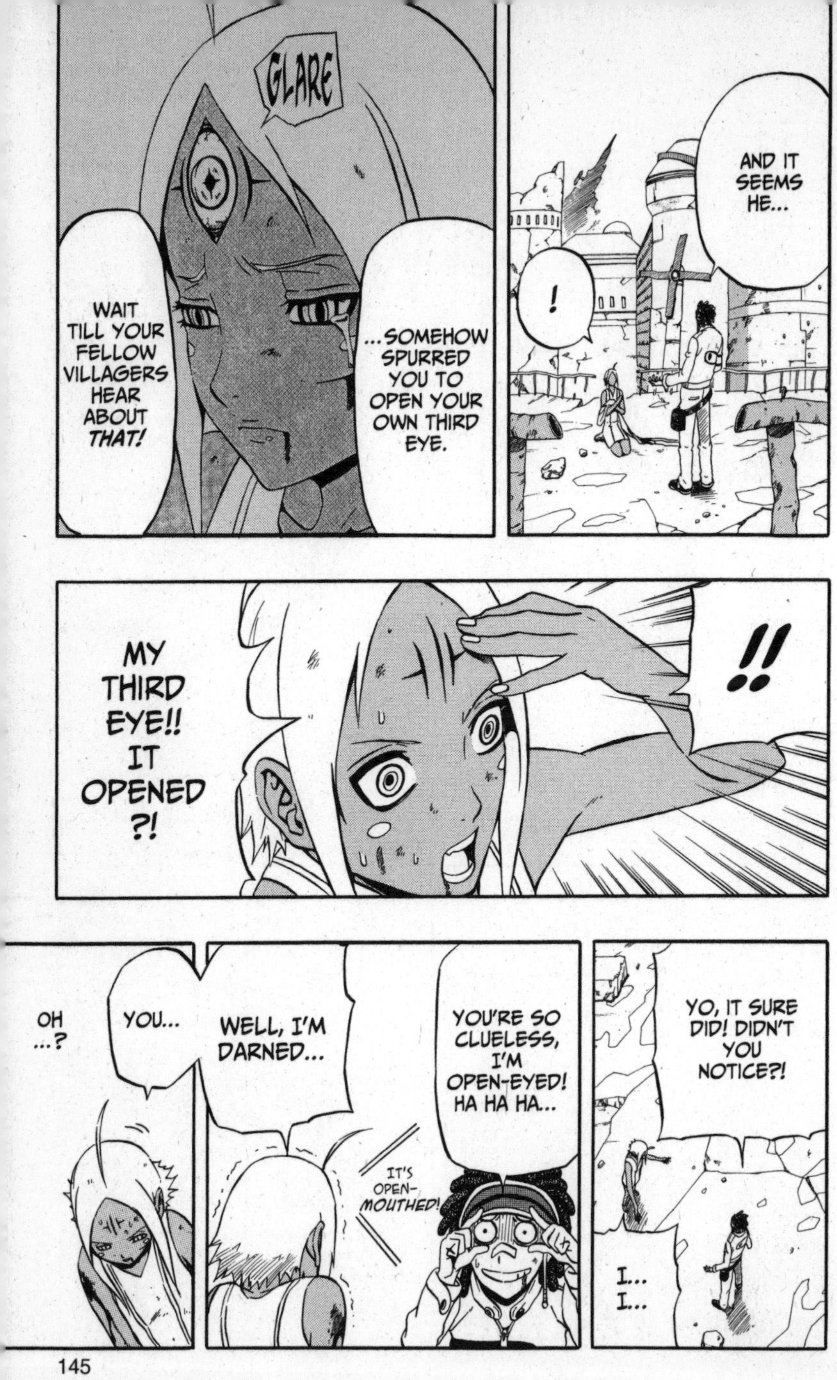
AND IT SEEMS HE...
!
GLARE
...SOMEHOW SPURRED YOU TO OPEN YOUR OWN THIRD EYE.
WAIT TILL YOUR FELLOW VILLAGERS HEAR ABOUT THAT!
!!
MY THIRD EYE!! IT OPENED ?!
YO, IT SURE DID! DIDN'T YOU NOTICE?!
I... I...
YOU'RE SO CLUELESS, I'M OPEN-EYED! HA HA HA...
IT'S OPEN-MOUTHED!
WELL, I'M DARNED...
YOU...
OH ...?

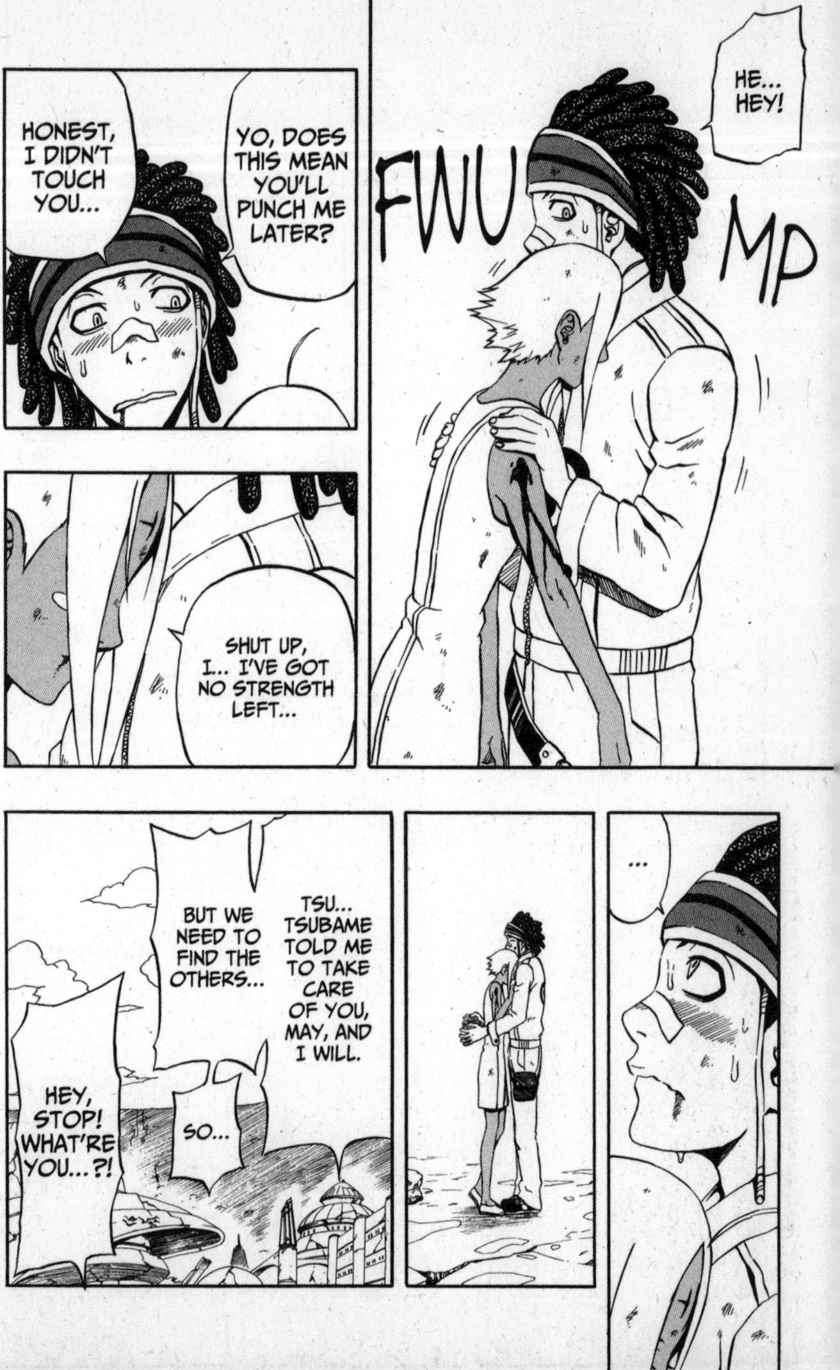
HE... HEY!
FWUMP
YO, DOES THIS MEAN YOU'LL PUNCH ME LATER?
HONEST, I DIDN'T TOUCH YOU...
SHUT UP, I... I'VE GOT NO STRENGTH LEFT...
...
TSU... TSUBAME TOLD ME TO TAKE CARE OF YOU, MAY, AND I WILL.
BUT WE NEED TO FIND THE OTHERS...
SO...
HEY, STOP! WHAT'RE YOU...?!

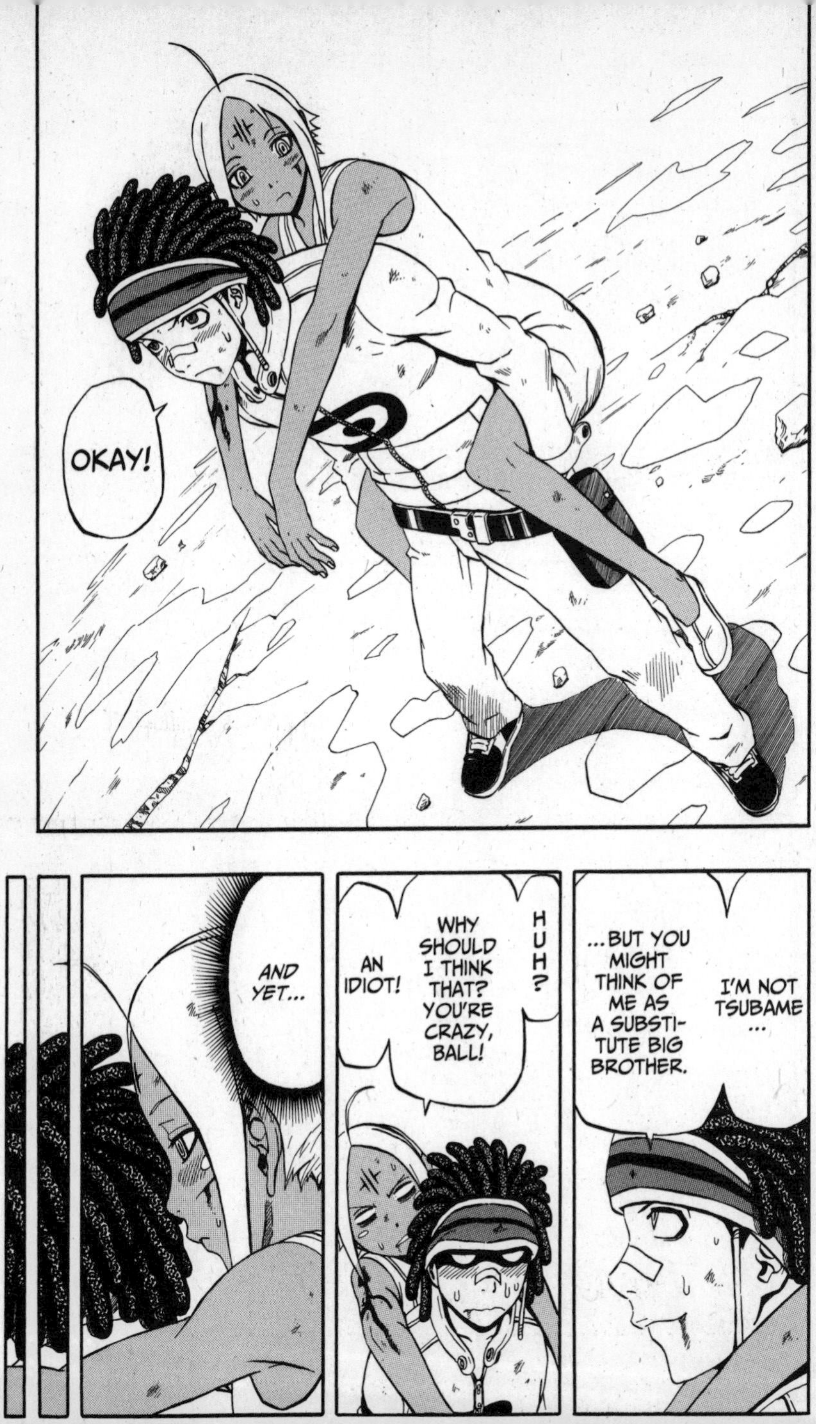
OKAY!
I'M NOT TSUBAME...
...BUT YOU MIGHT THINK OF ME AS A SUBSTITUTE BIG BROTHER.
HUH?
WHY SHOULD I THINK THAT? YOU'RE CRAZY, BALL!
AN IDIOT!
AND YET...

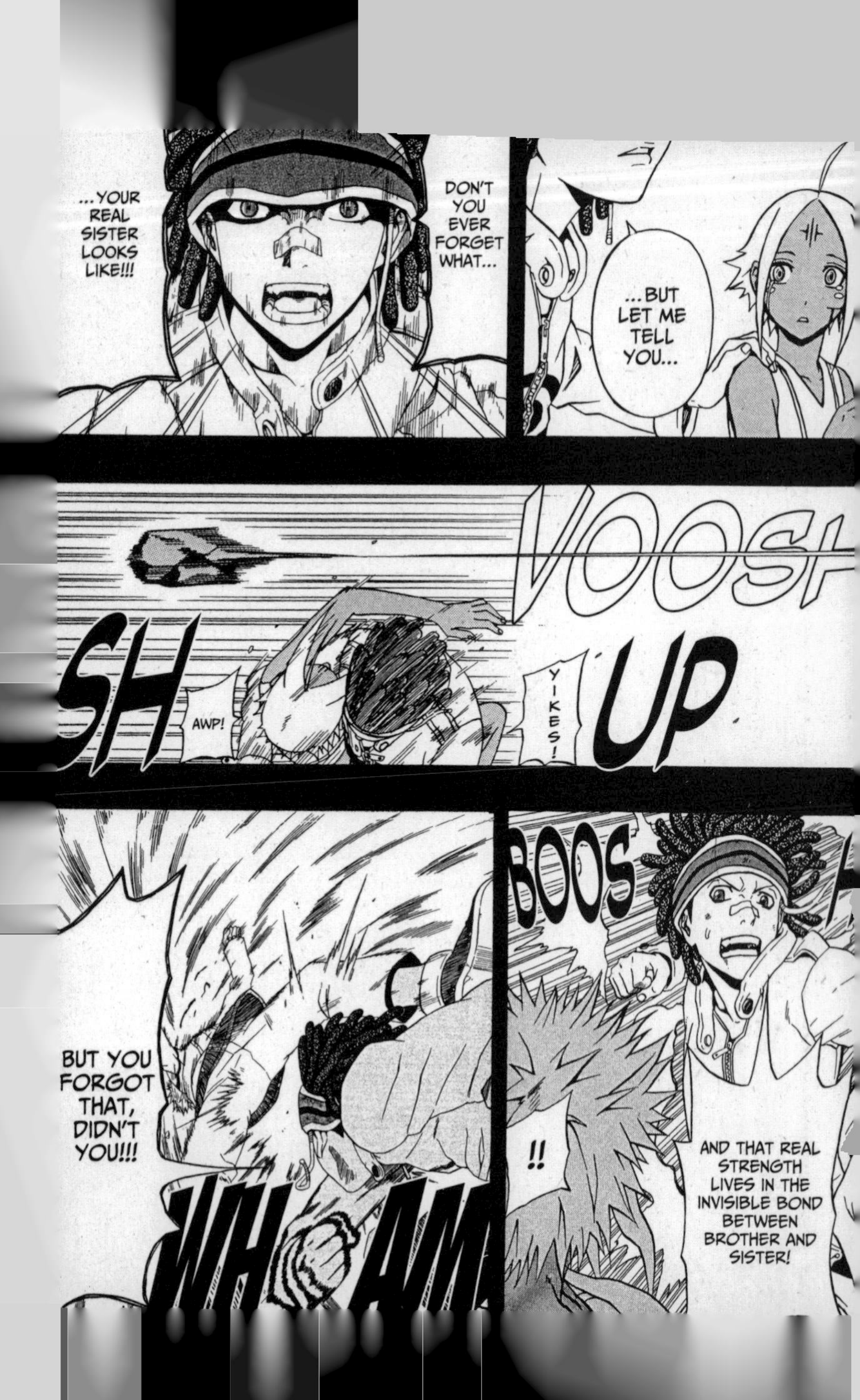
...BUT LET ME TELL YOU...
DON'T YOU EVER FORGET WHAT...
...YOUR REAL SISTER LOOKS LIKE!!!
VOOSH
UP
YIKES!
AWP!
SH
BOOS
AND THAT REAL STRENGTH LIVES IN THE INVISIBLE BOND BETWEEN BROTHER AND SISTER!
!!
BUT YOU FORGOT THAT, DIDN'T YOU!!!
WHAM

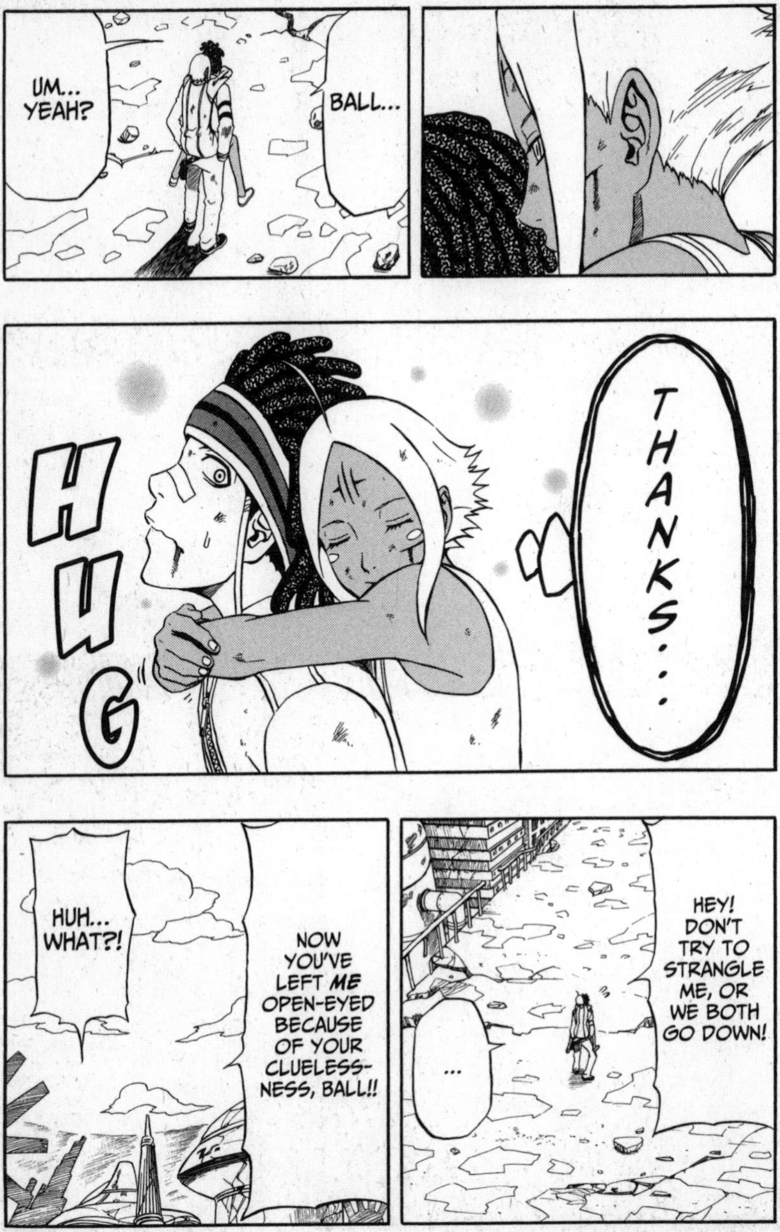
BALL...
UM... YEAH?
THANKS...
HUG
HEY! DON'T TRY TO STRANGLE ME, OR WE BOTH GO DOWN!
...
NOW YOU'VE LEFT *ME* OPEN-EYED BECAUSE OF YOUR CLUELESS-NESS, BALL!!
HUH... WHAT?!

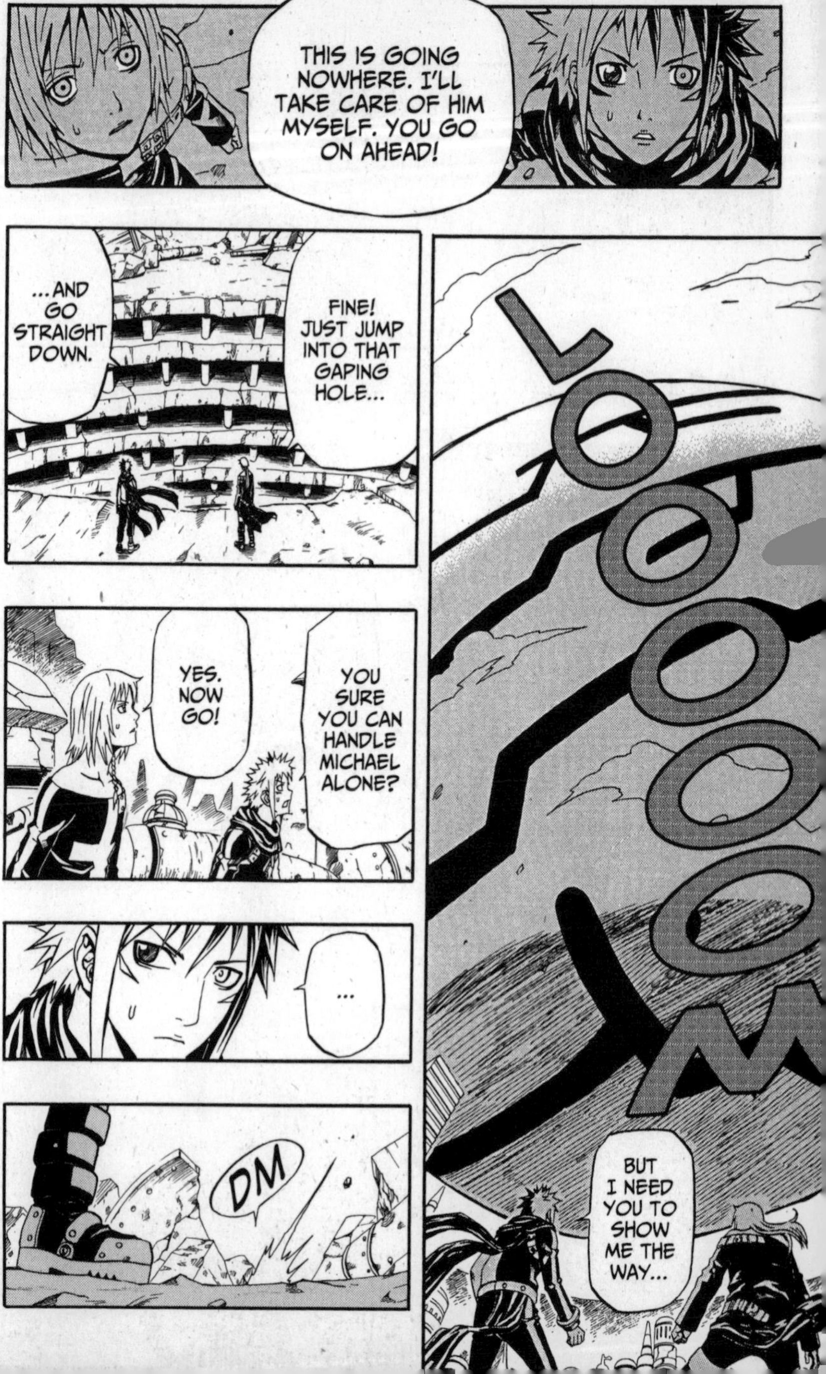
THIS IS GOING NOWHERE. I'LL TAKE CARE OF HIM MYSELF. YOU GO ON AHEAD!
LOOOOOOM
BUT I NEED YOU TO SHOW ME THE WAY...
FINE! JUST JUMP INTO THAT GAPING HOLE...
...AND GO STRAIGHT DOWN.
YOU SURE YOU CAN HANDLE MICHAEL ALONE?
YES. NOW GO!
...
DM

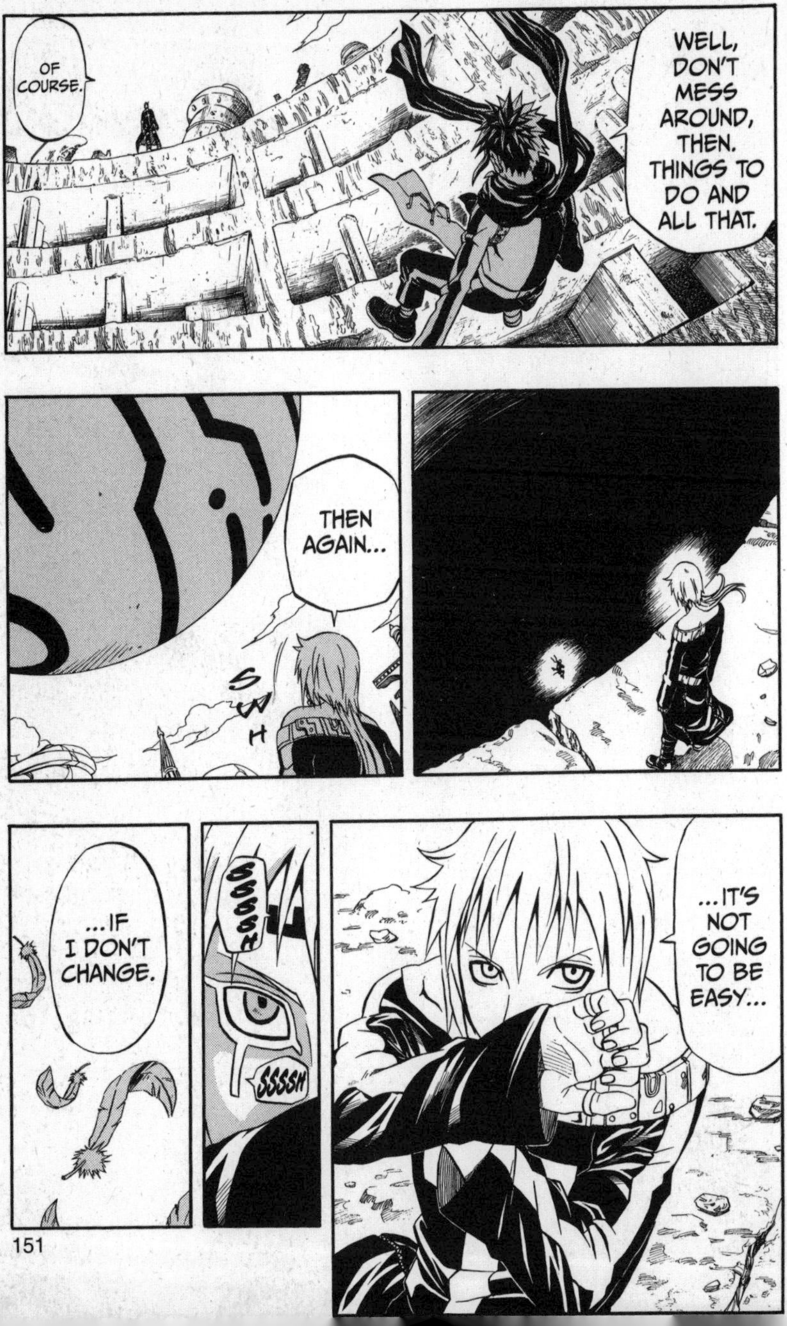
WELL, DON'T MESS AROUND, THEN. THINGS TO DO AND ALL THAT.
OF COURSE.
THEN AGAIN...
SWH
...IT'S NOT GOING TO BE EASY...
SSSSH
SSSSH
...IF I DON'T CHANGE.

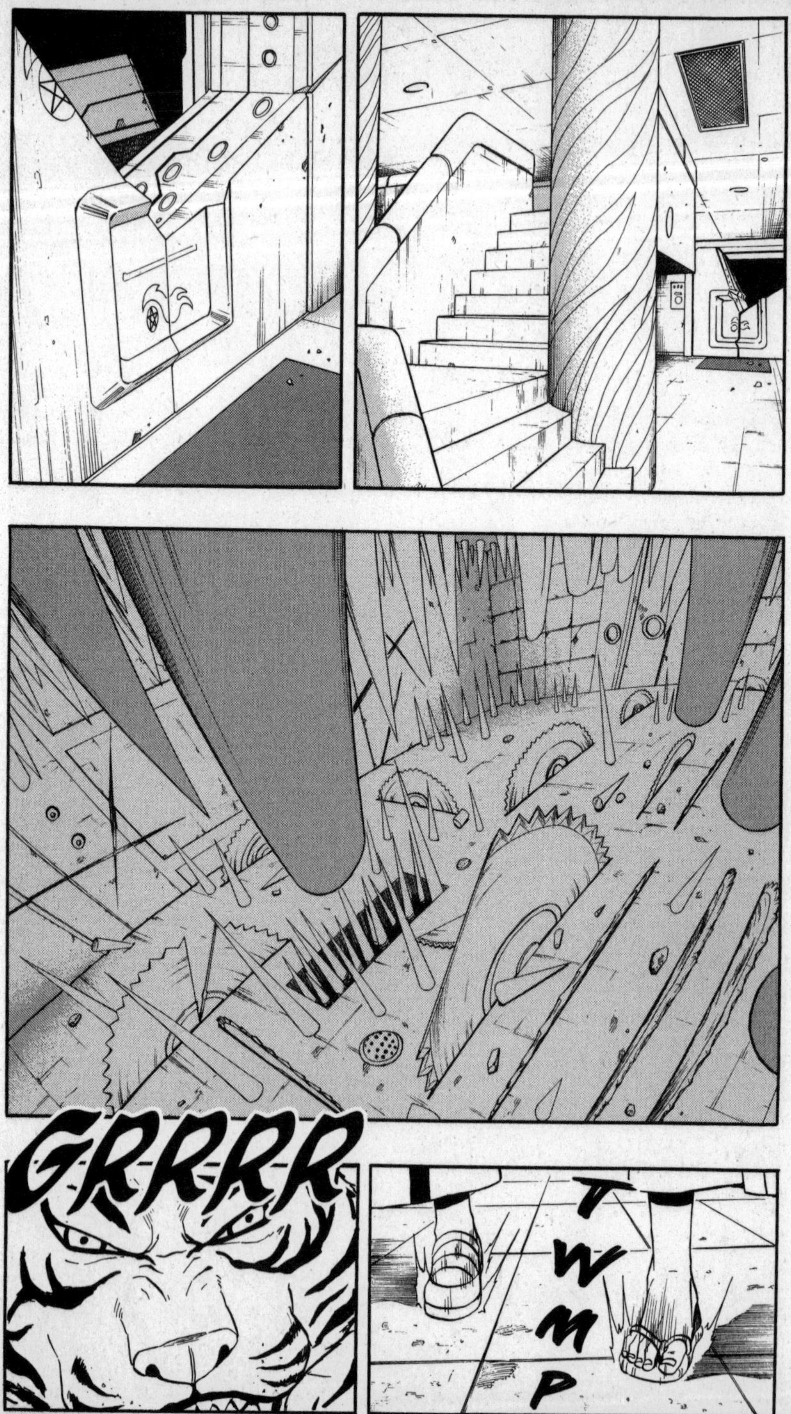
TWMP
GRRRR

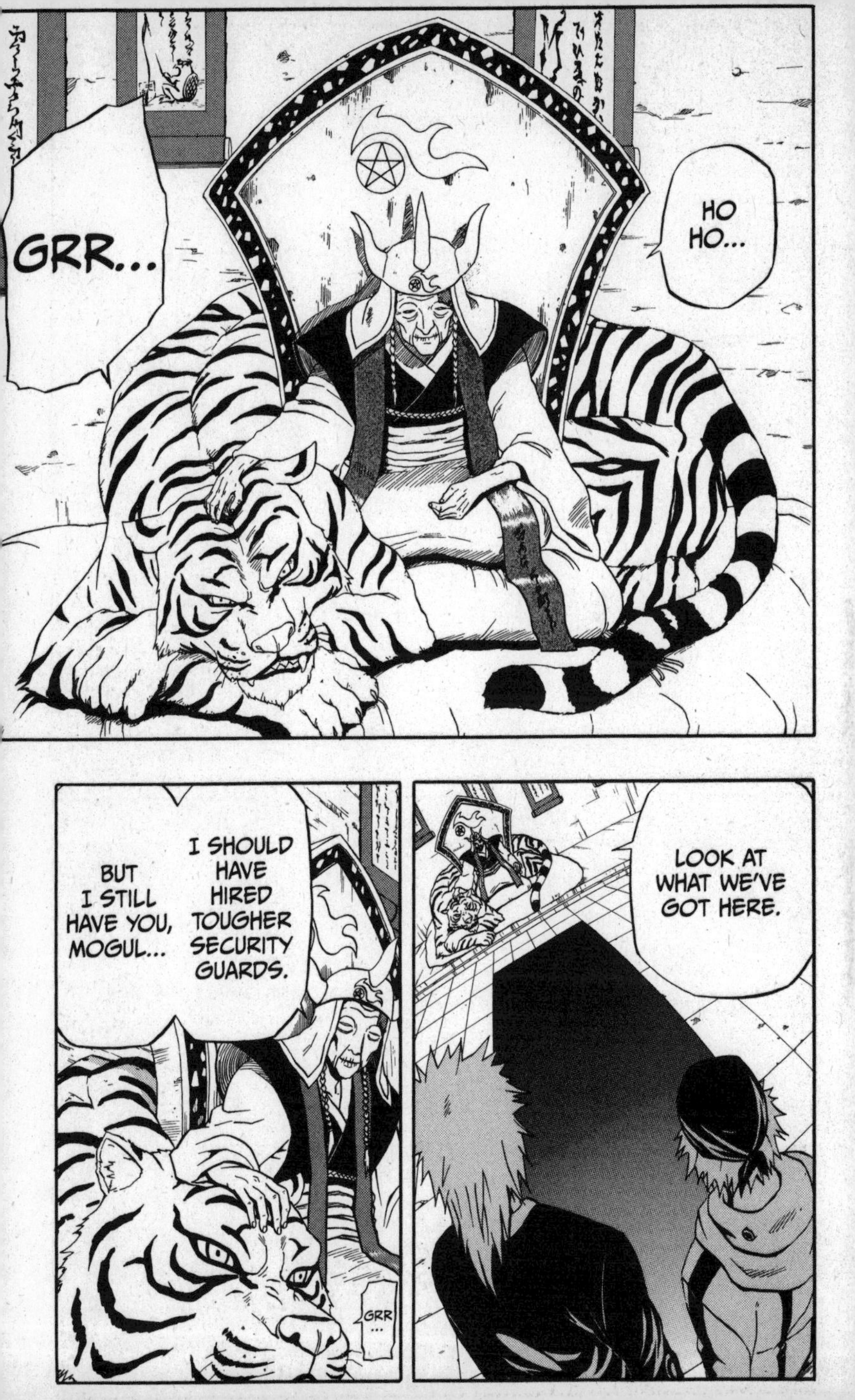
HO HO...
GRR...
LOOK AT WHAT WE'VE GOT HERE.
I SHOULD HAVE HIRED TOUGHER SECURITY GUARDS.
BUT I STILL HAVE YOU, MOGUL...
GRR ...

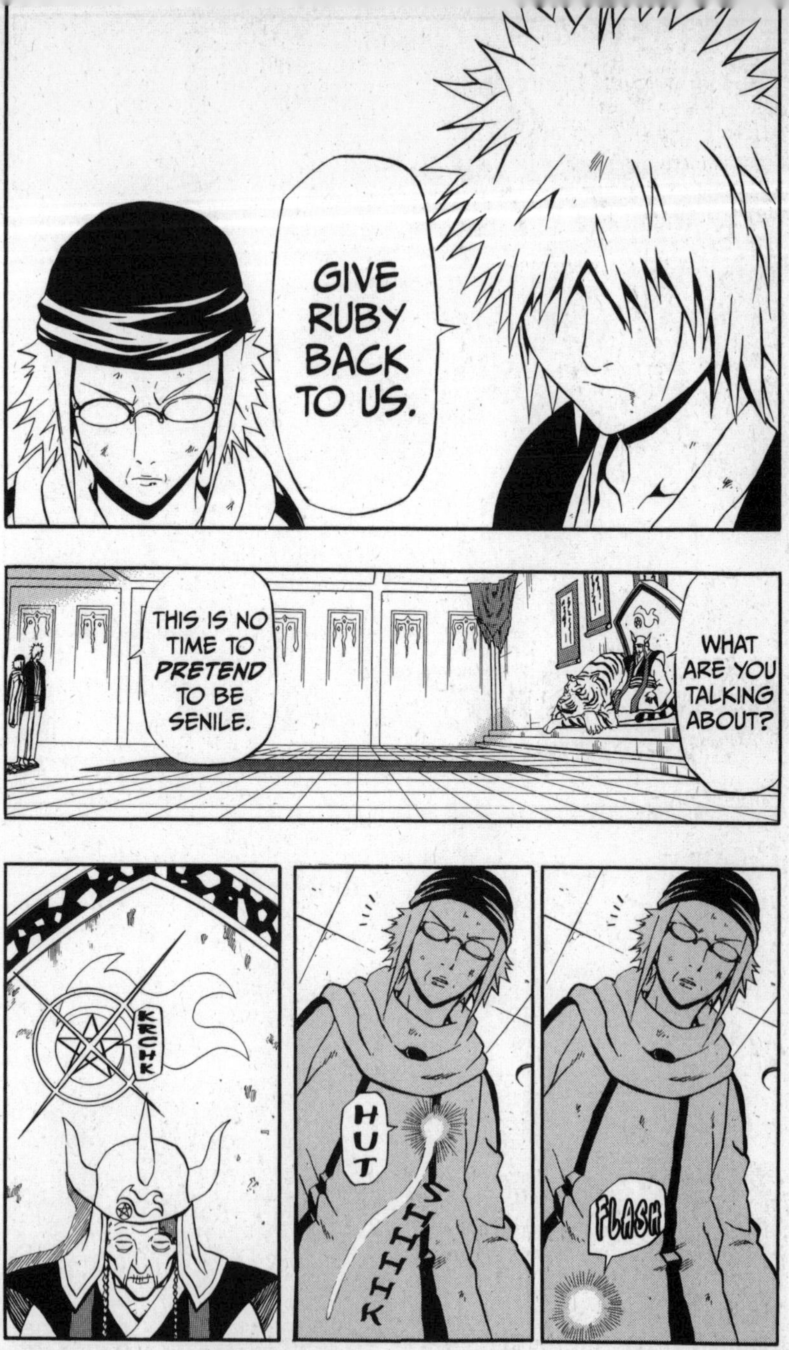
GIVE RUBY BACK TO US.
WHAT ARE YOU TALKING ABOUT?
THIS IS NO TIME TO PRETEND TO BE SENILE.
FLASH
HUT
SHHHHK
KRCHK

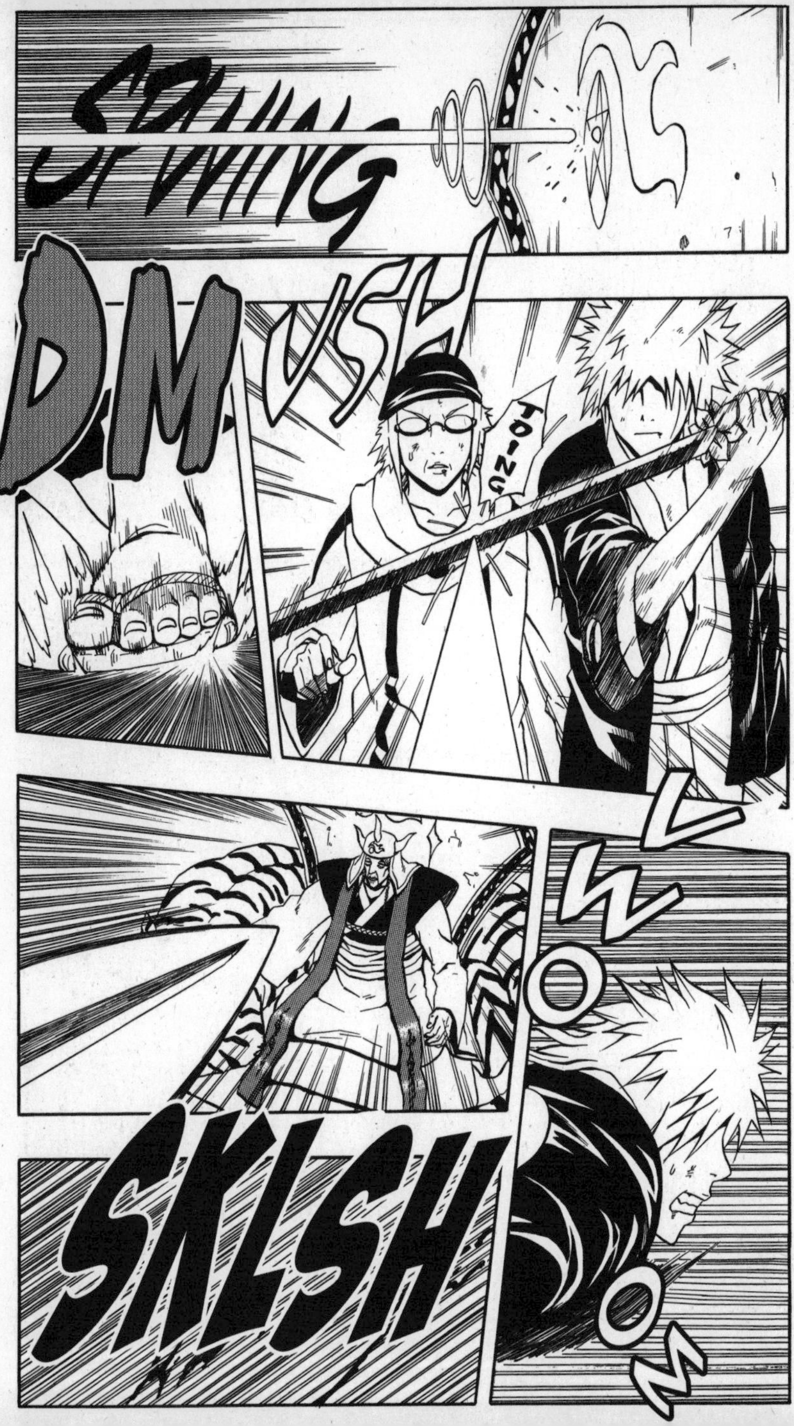
SPWING
TOING
DMUSH
VWOOM
SKLISH

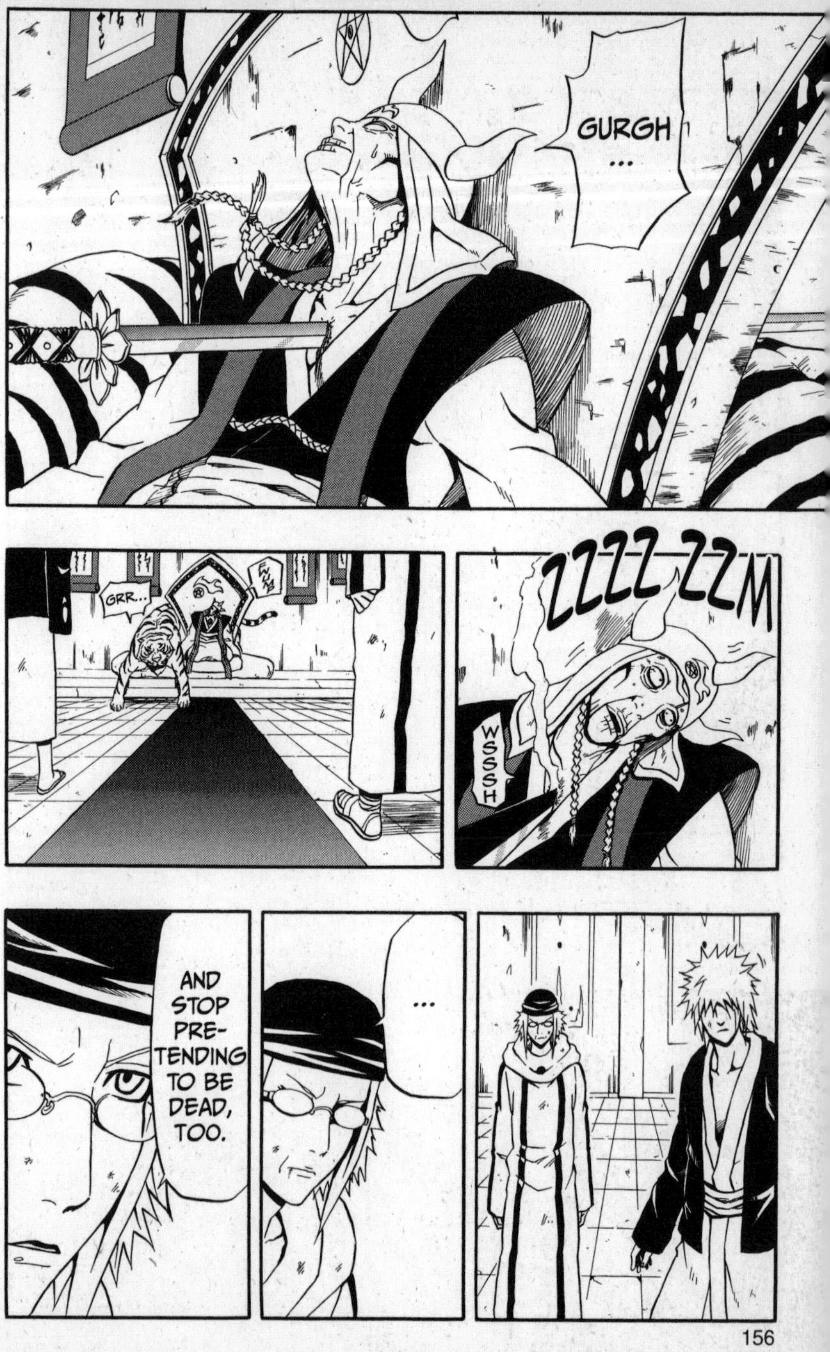
GURGH ...
ZZZZ ZZM
WSSSH
GRR...
...
AND STOP PRE-TENDING TO BE DEAD, TOO.

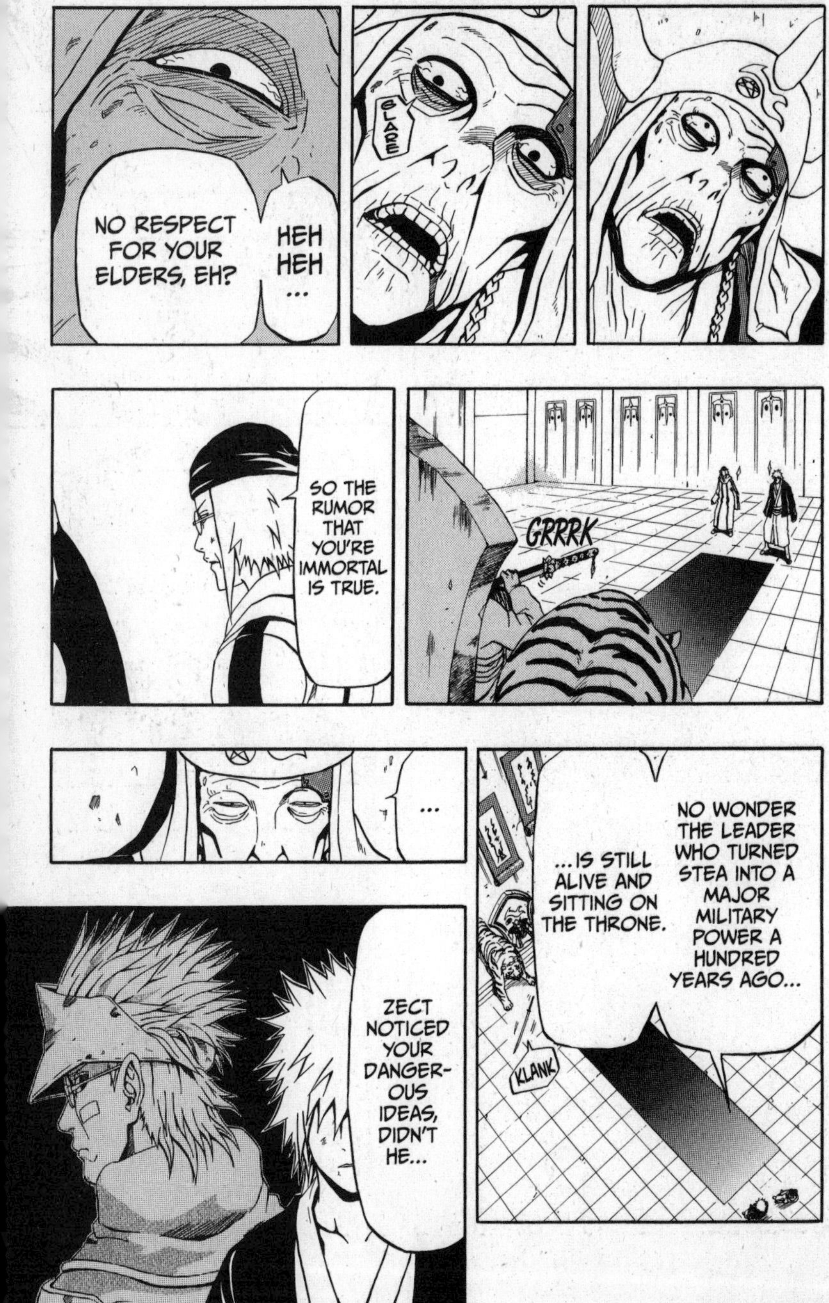
GLARE
HEH HEH ...
NO RESPECT FOR YOUR ELDERS, EH?
GRRRK
SO THE RUMOR THAT YOU'RE IMMORTAL IS TRUE.
NO WONDER THE LEADER WHO TURNED STEA INTO A MAJOR MILITARY POWER A HUNDRED YEARS AGO...
...IS STILL ALIVE AND SITTING ON THE THRONE.
KLANK
...
ZECT NOTICED YOUR DANGER-OUS IDEAS, DIDN'T HE...

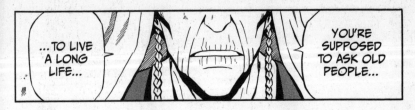

YOU'RE SUPPOSED TO ASK OLD PEOPLE...
...TO LIVE A LONG LIFE...
SPIN
...YOU KNOW!!!
!!
HER BODY!!
VRRRRM
IT'S A MACHINE!!!
KASHK

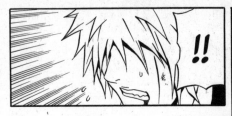

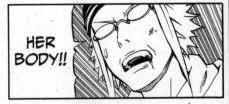

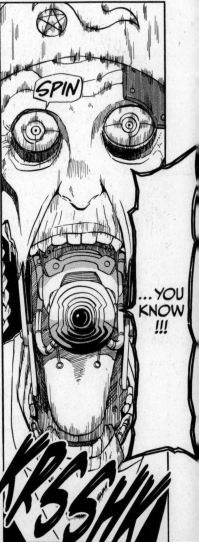

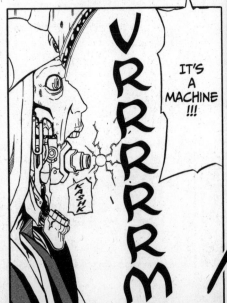

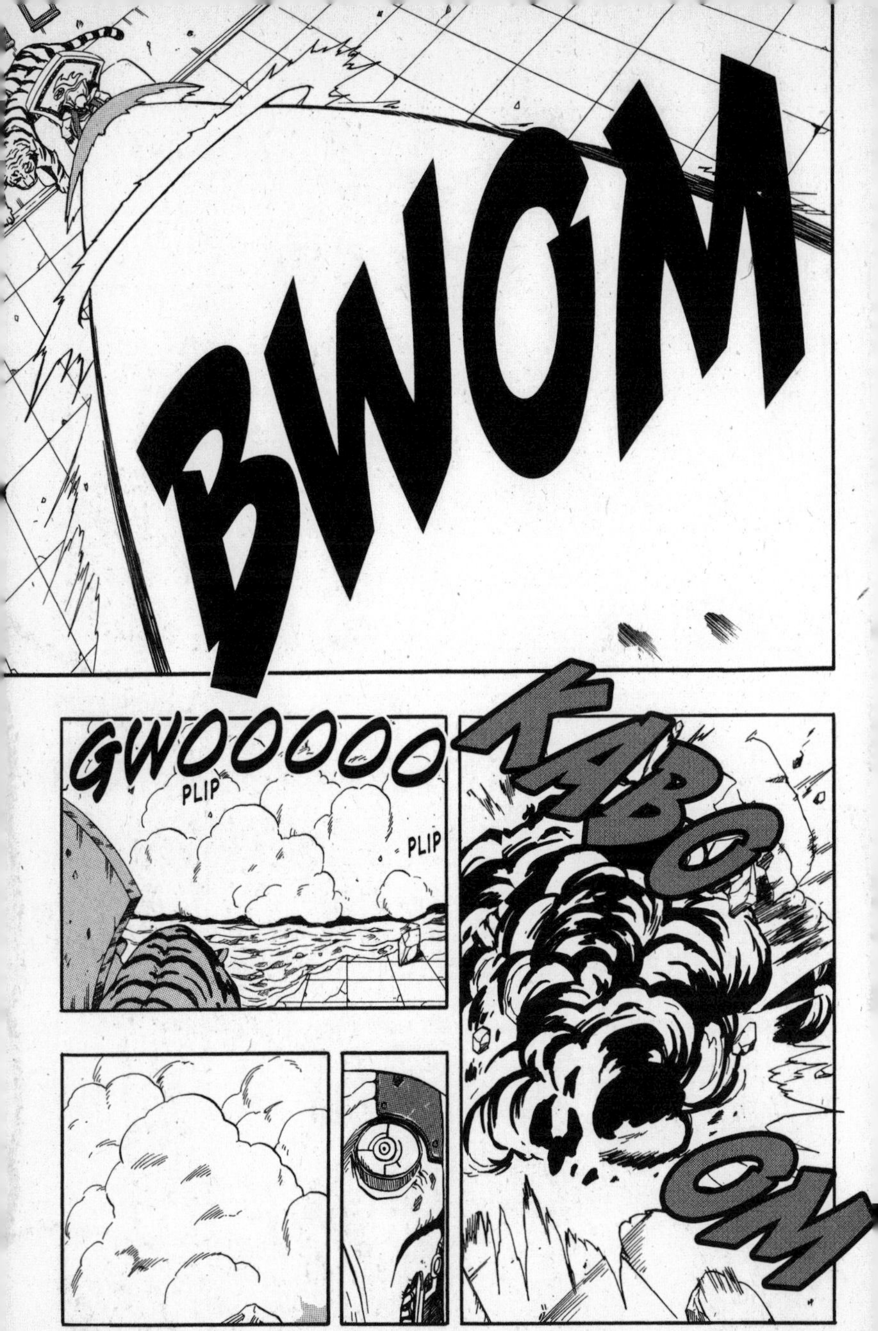
BWOM
KABOOM
GWOOOOO
PLIP
PLIP

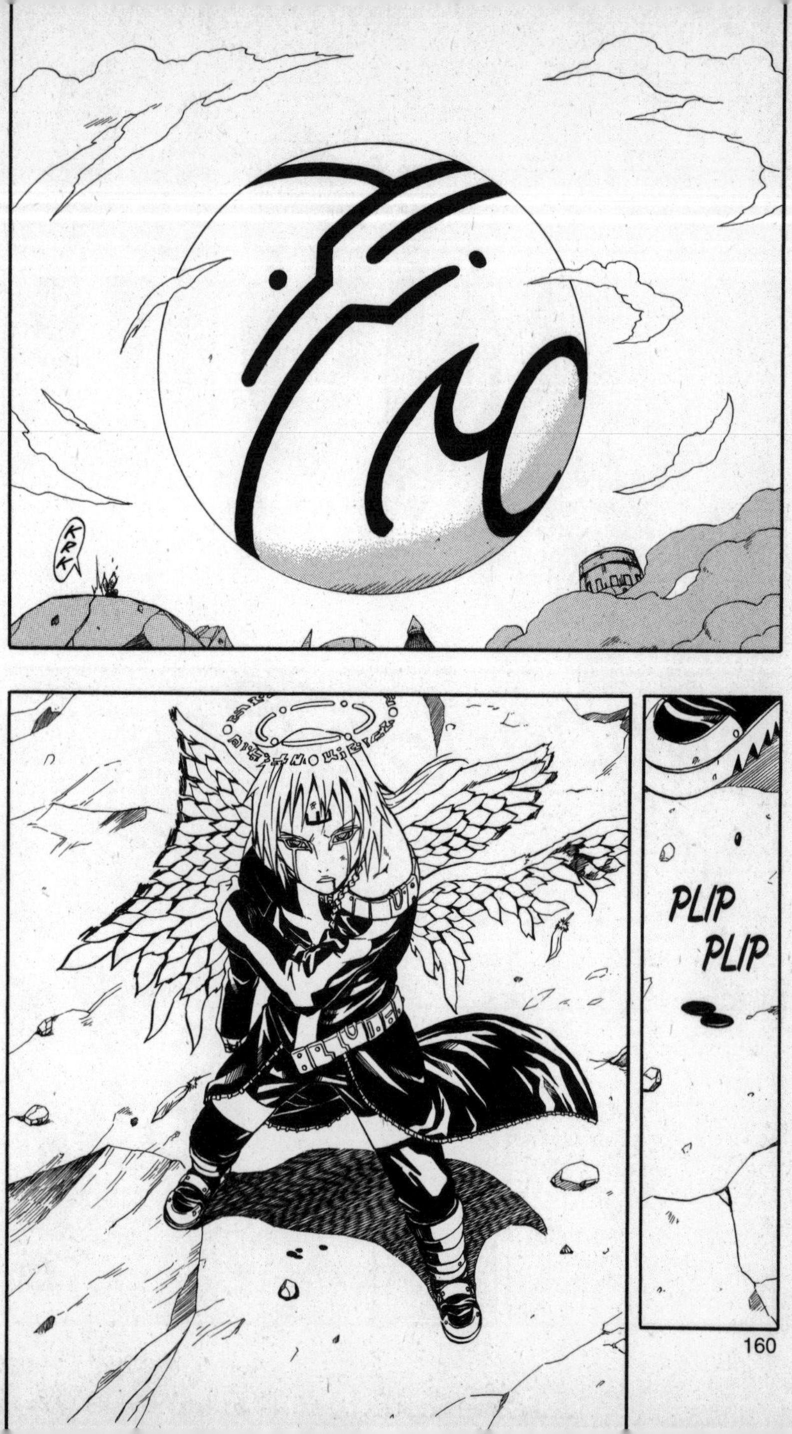
KRK
PLIP
PLIP

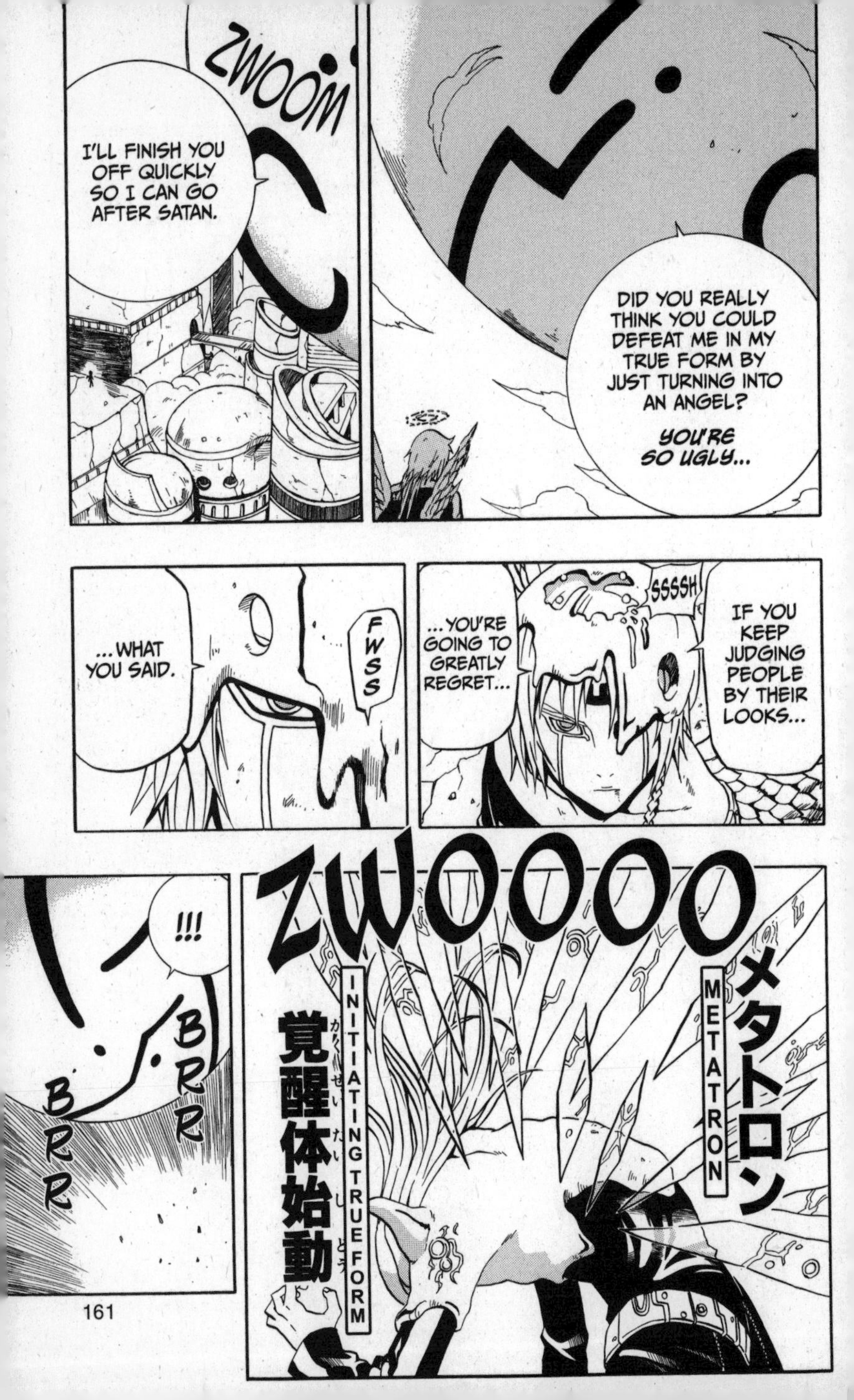
DID YOU REALLY THINK YOU COULD DEFEAT ME IN MY TRUE FORM BY JUST TURNING INTO AN ANGEL?
YOU'RE SO UGLY...
ZWOOM
I'LL FINISH YOU OFF QUICKLY SO I CAN GO AFTER SATAN.
IF YOU KEEP JUDGING PEOPLE BY THEIR LOOKS...
SSSSH
...YOU'RE GOING TO GREATLY REGRET...
FWSS
...WHAT YOU SAID.
ZWOOOO
メタトロン
METATRON
覚醒体始動
INITIATING TRUE FORM
!!!
BRR
BRR

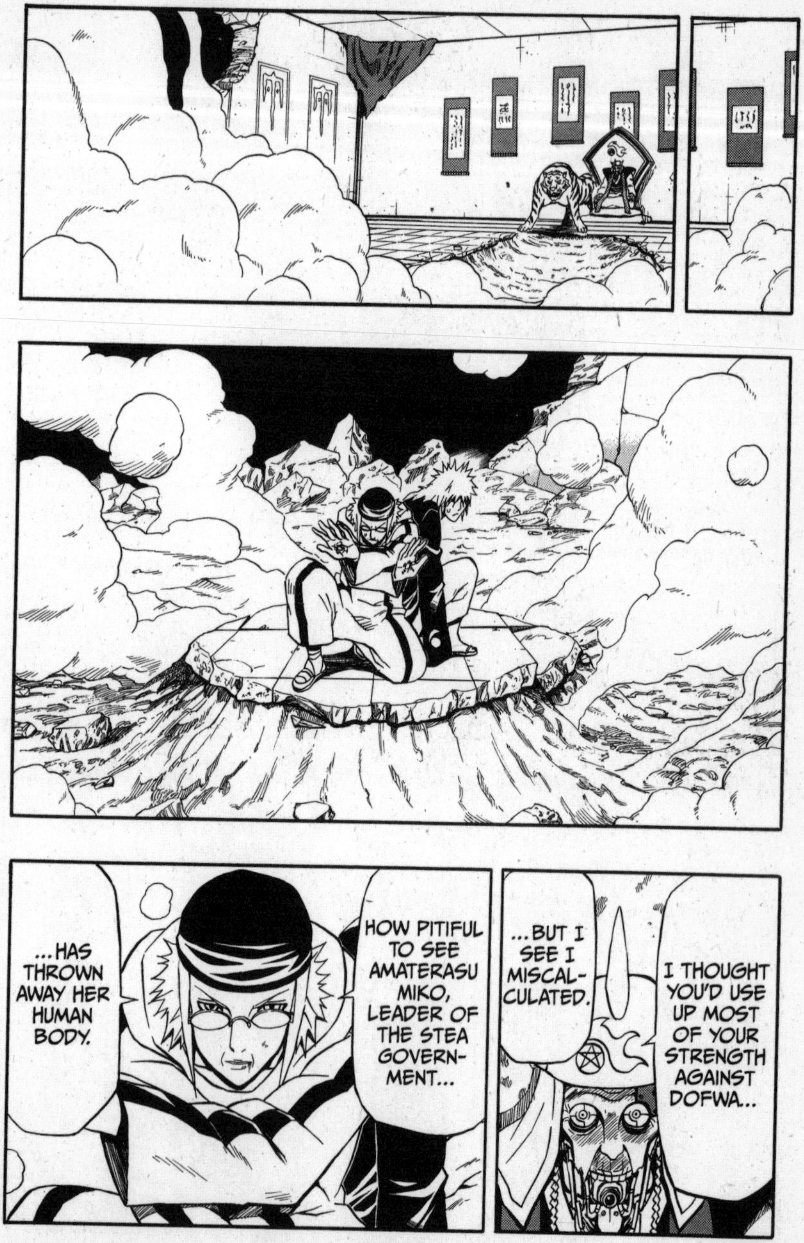
I THOUGHT YOU'D USE UP MOST OF YOUR STRENGTH AGAINST DOFWA...
...BUT I SEE I MISCALCULATED.
HOW PITIFUL TO SEE AMATERASU MIKO, LEADER OF THE STEA GOVERNMENT...
...HAS THROWN AWAY HER HUMAN BODY.

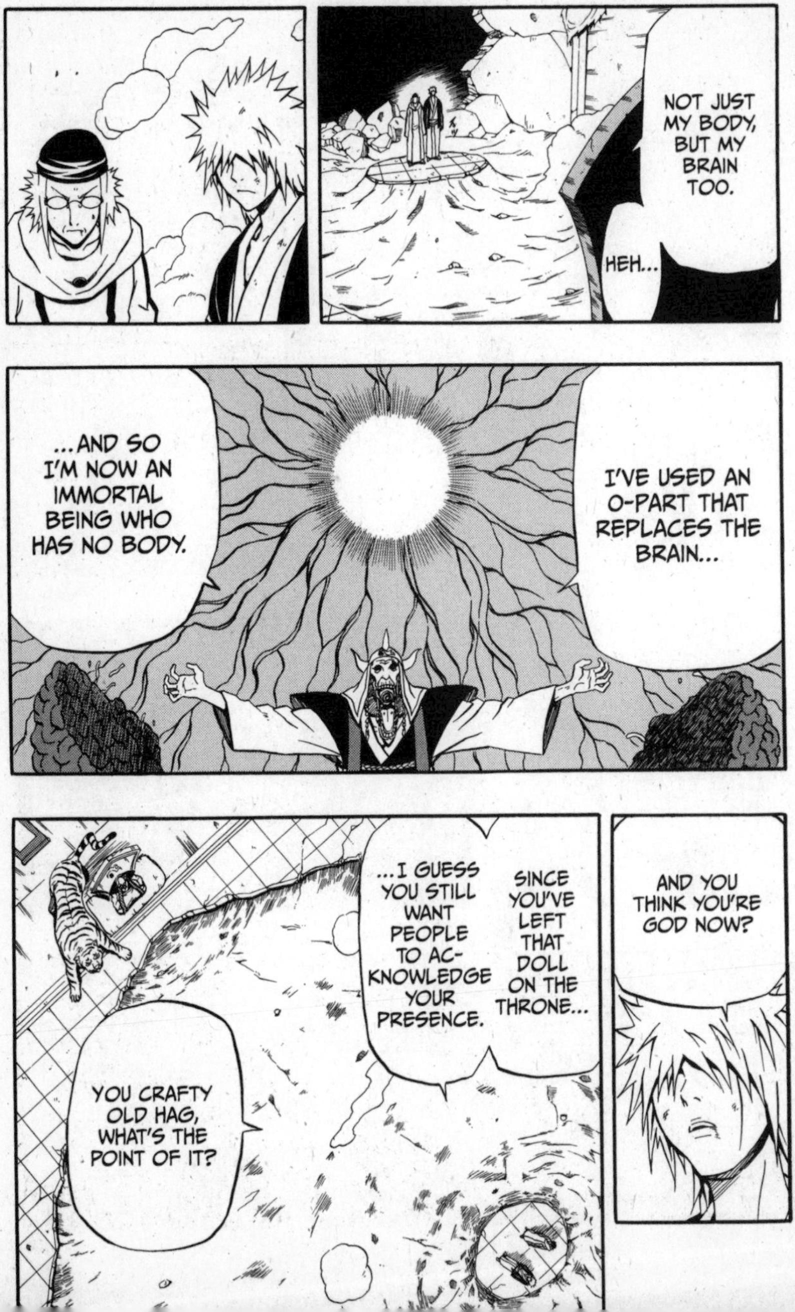
NOT JUST MY BODY, BUT MY BRAIN TOO.
HEH...
I'VE USED AN O-PART THAT REPLACES THE BRAIN...
...AND SO I'M NOW AN IMMORTAL BEING WHO HAS NO BODY.
AND YOU THINK YOU'RE GOD NOW?
SINCE YOU'VE LEFT THAT DOLL ON THE THRONE...
...I GUESS YOU STILL WANT PEOPLE TO ACKNOWLEDGE YOUR PRESENCE.
YOU CRAFTY OLD HAG, WHAT'S THE POINT OF IT?

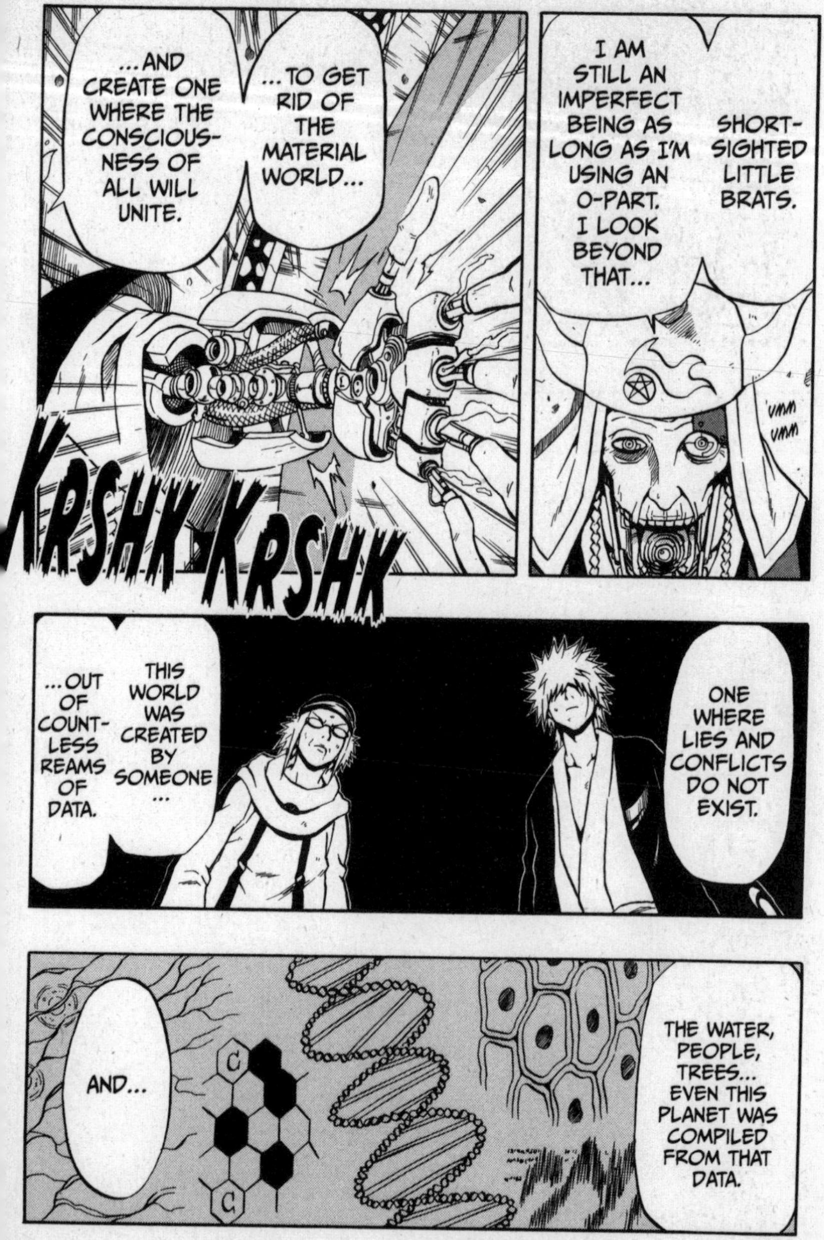
SHORT-SIGHTED LITTLE BRATS.
I AM STILL AN IMPERFECT BEING AS LONG AS I'M USING AN O-PART. I LOOK BEYOND THAT...
UMM UMM
...TO GET RID OF THE MATERIAL WORLD...
...AND CREATE ONE WHERE THE CONSCIOUS-NESS OF ALL WILL UNITE.
KRSHK KRSHK
ONE WHERE LIES AND CONFLICTS DO NOT EXIST.
THIS WORLD WAS CREATED BY SOMEONE...
...OUT OF COUNT-LESS REAMS OF DATA.
THE WATER, PEOPLE, TREES... EVEN THIS PLANET WAS COMPILED FROM THAT DATA.
AND...

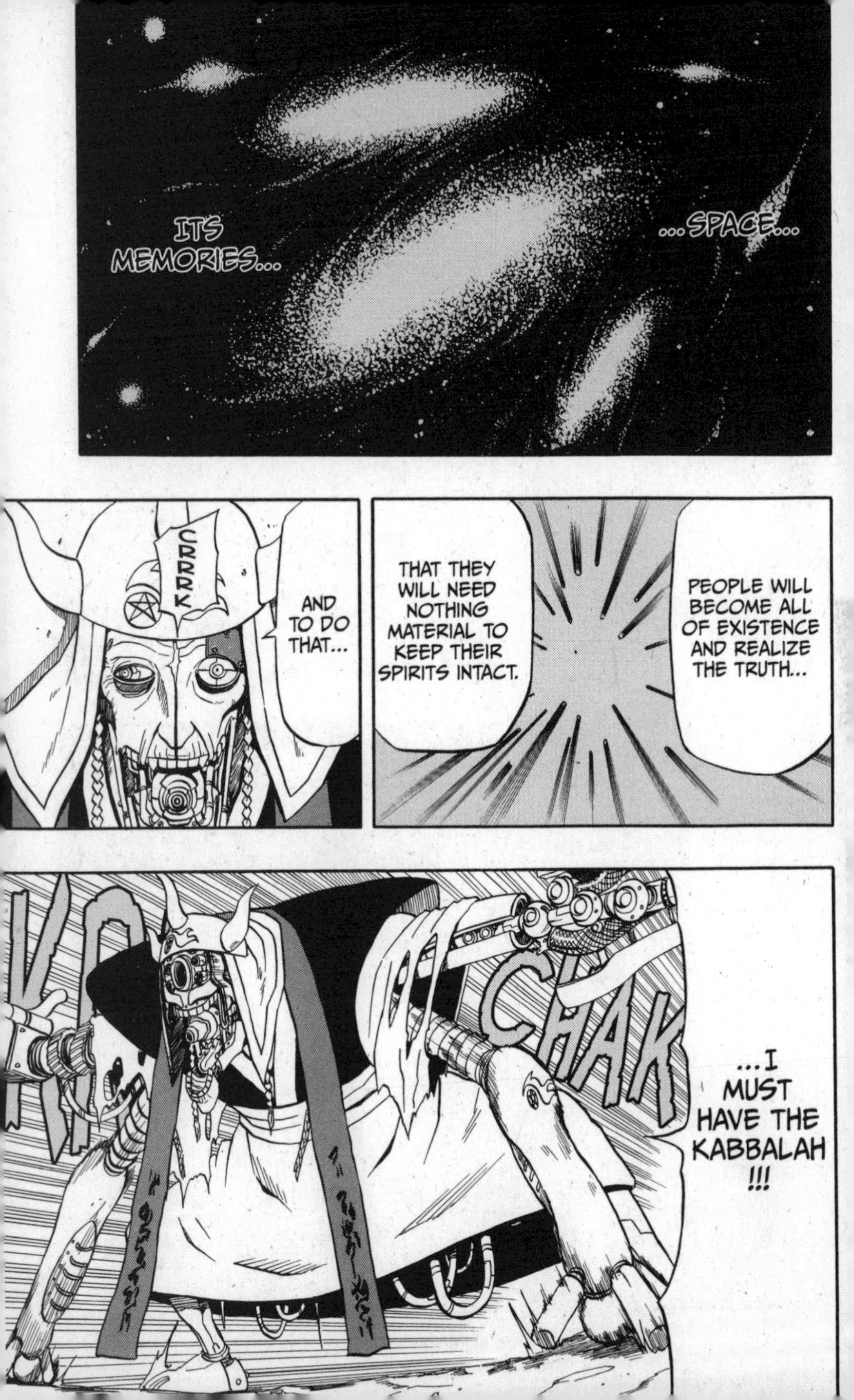
...SPACE...
ITS MEMORIES...
PEOPLE WILL BECOME ALL OF EXISTENCE AND REALIZE THE TRUTH...
THAT THEY WILL NEED NOTHING MATERIAL TO KEEP THEIR SPIRITS INTACT.
CRRRK
AND TO DO THAT...
CHAK
...I MUST HAVE THE KABBALAH!!!

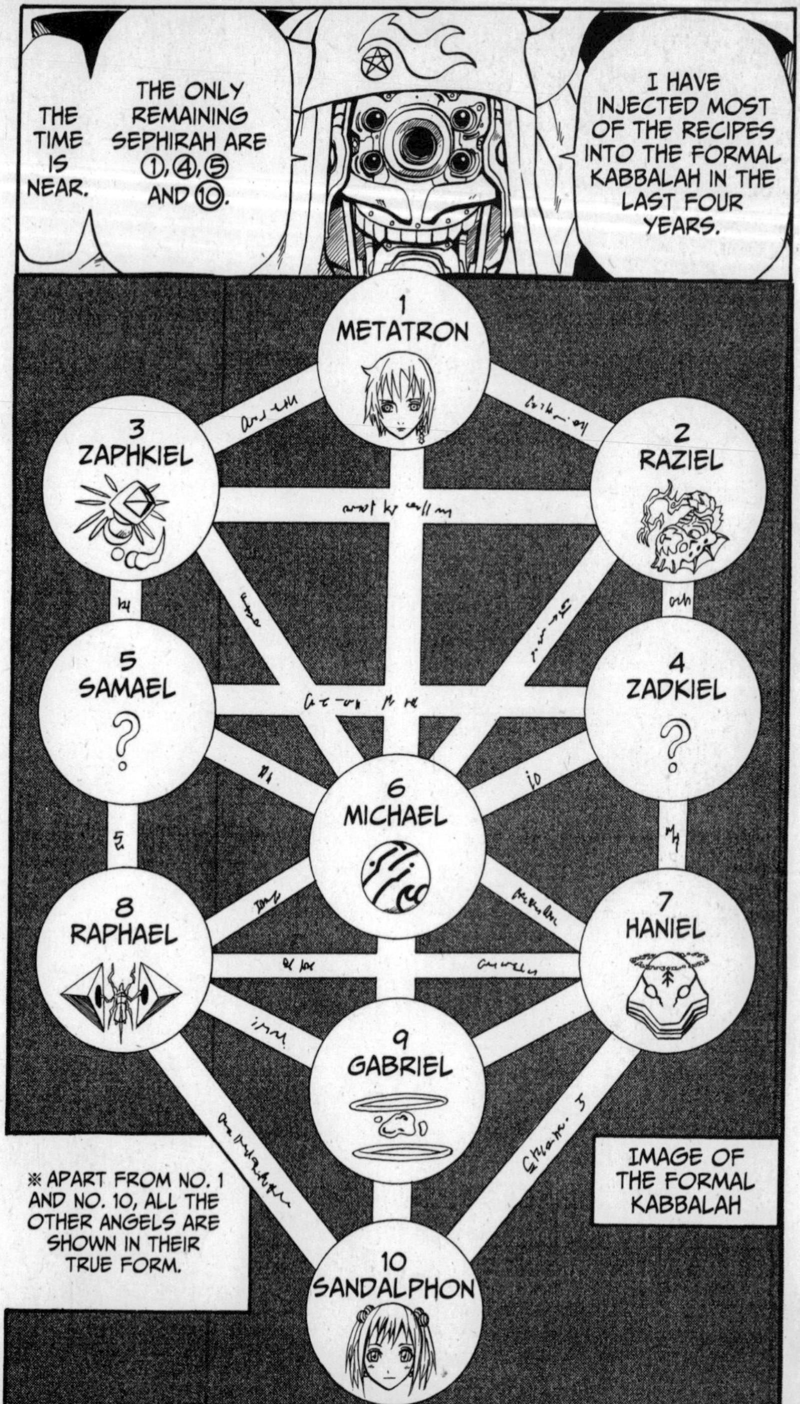
I HAVE INJECTED MOST OF THE RECIPES INTO THE FORMAL KABBALAH IN THE LAST FOUR YEARS.
THE ONLY REMAINING SEPHIRAH ARE ①, ④, ⑤ AND ⑩.
THE TIME IS NEAR.
1 METATRON
2 RAZIEL
3 ZAPHKIEL
4 ZADKIEL
?
5 SAMAEL
?
6 MICHAEL
7 HANIEL
8 RAPHAEL
9 GABRIEL
10 SANDALPHON
IMAGE OF THE FORMAL KABBALAH
※ APART FROM NO. 1 AND NO. 10, ALL THE OTHER ANGELS ARE SHOWN IN THEIR TRUE FORM.

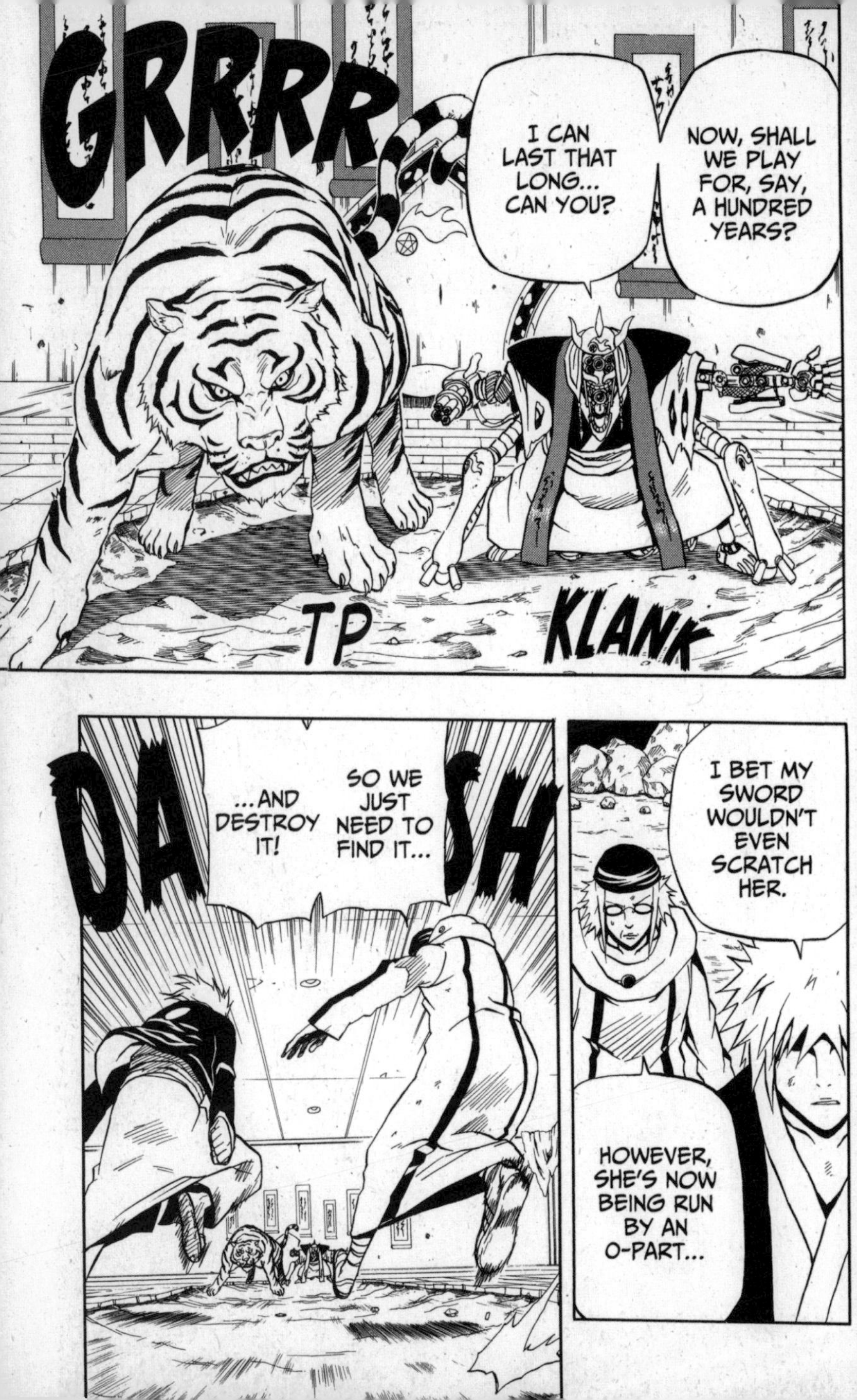
GRRRR
NOW, SHALL WE PLAY FOR, SAY, A HUNDRED YEARS?
I CAN LAST THAT LONG... CAN YOU?
TP
KLANK
I BET MY SWORD WOULDN'T EVEN SCRATCH HER.
HOWEVER, SHE'S NOW BEING RUN BY AN O-PART...
SO WE JUST NEED TO FIND IT...
...AND DESTROY IT!
DASH

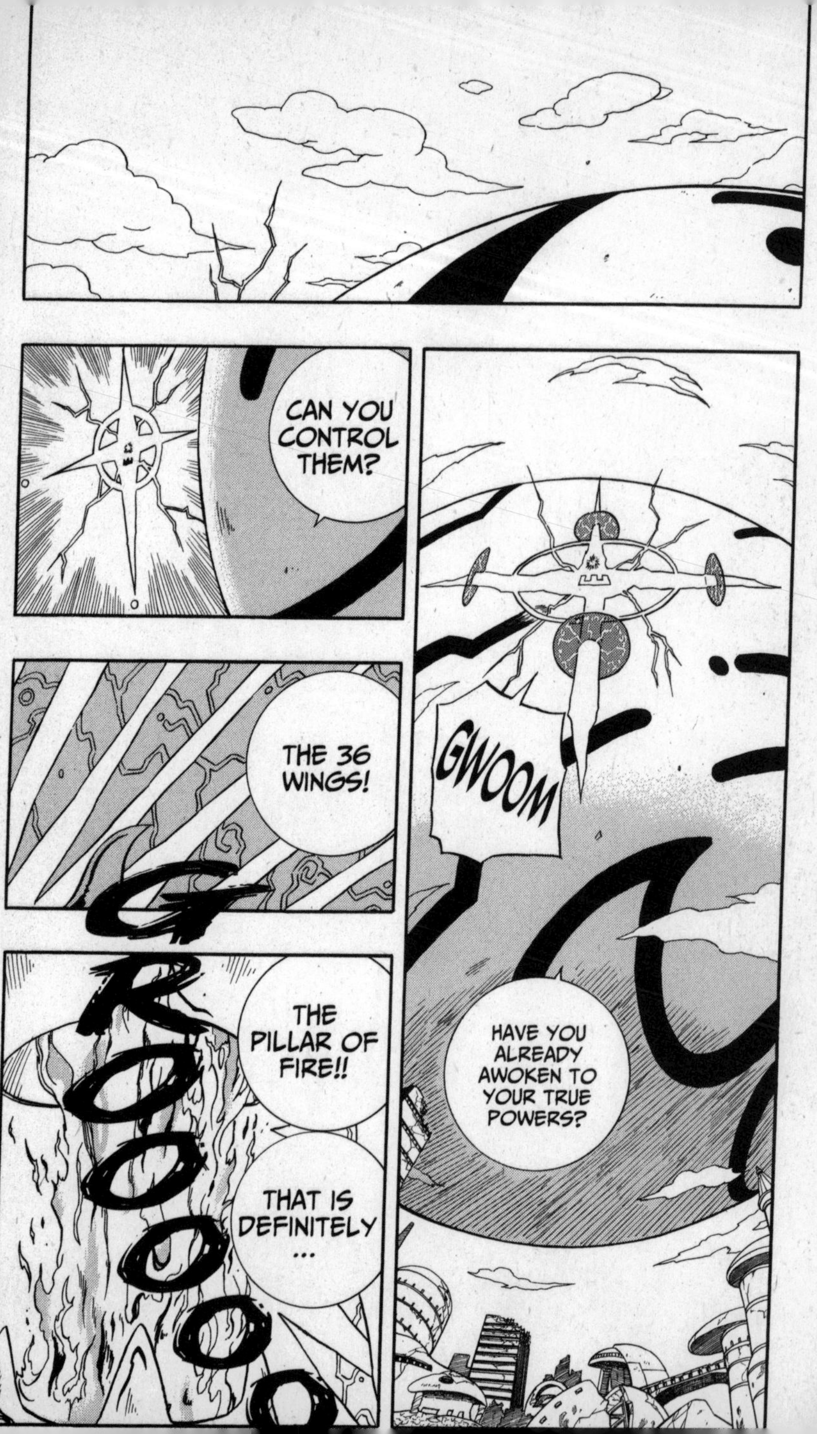
GWOOM
HAVE YOU ALREADY AWOKEN TO YOUR TRUE POWERS?
CAN YOU CONTROL THEM?
THE 36 WINGS!
GROOOOO
THE PILLAR OF FIRE!!
THAT IS DEFINITELY ...

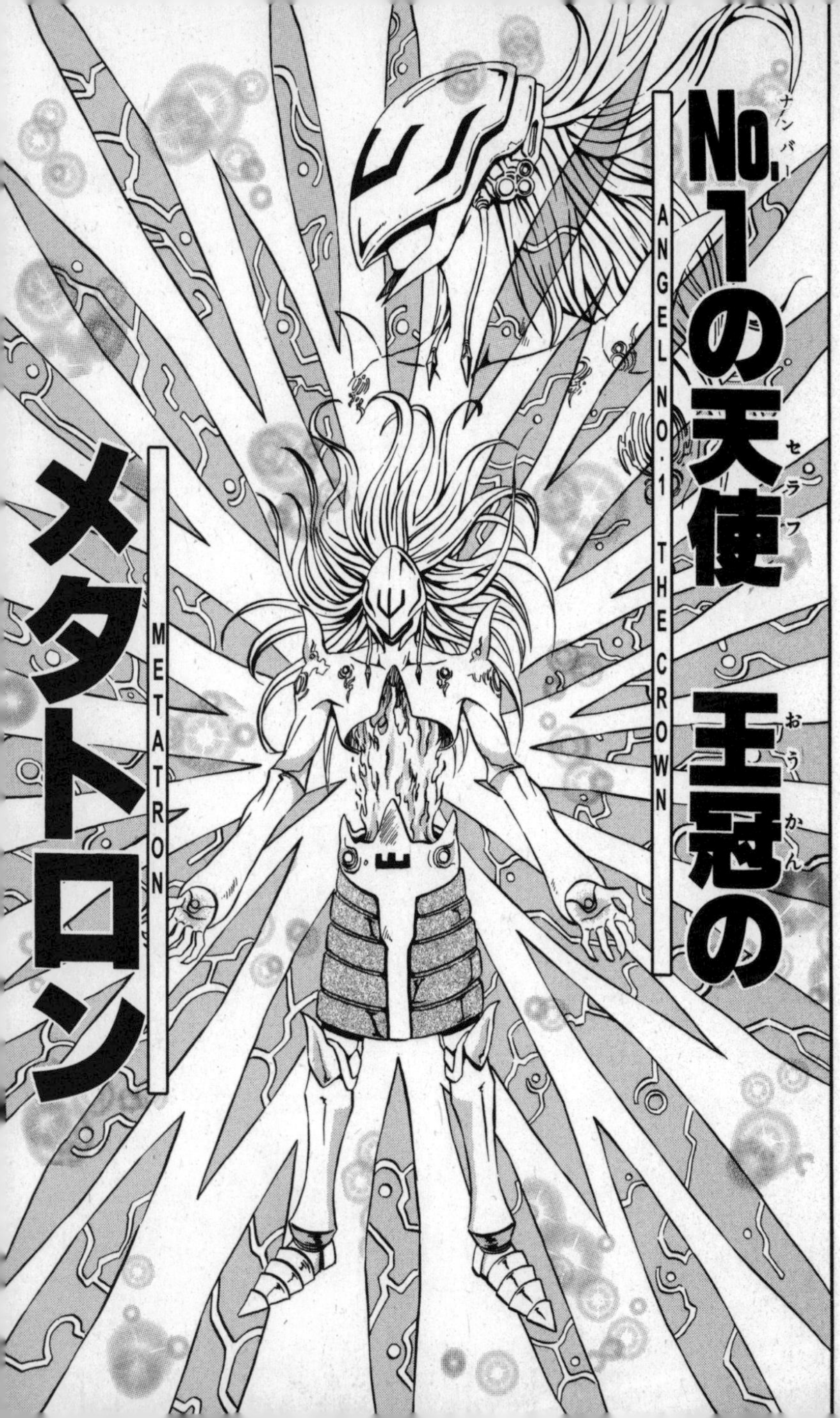
No.1の天使 王冠の
ANGEL NO.1 THE CROWN
メタトロン
METATRON

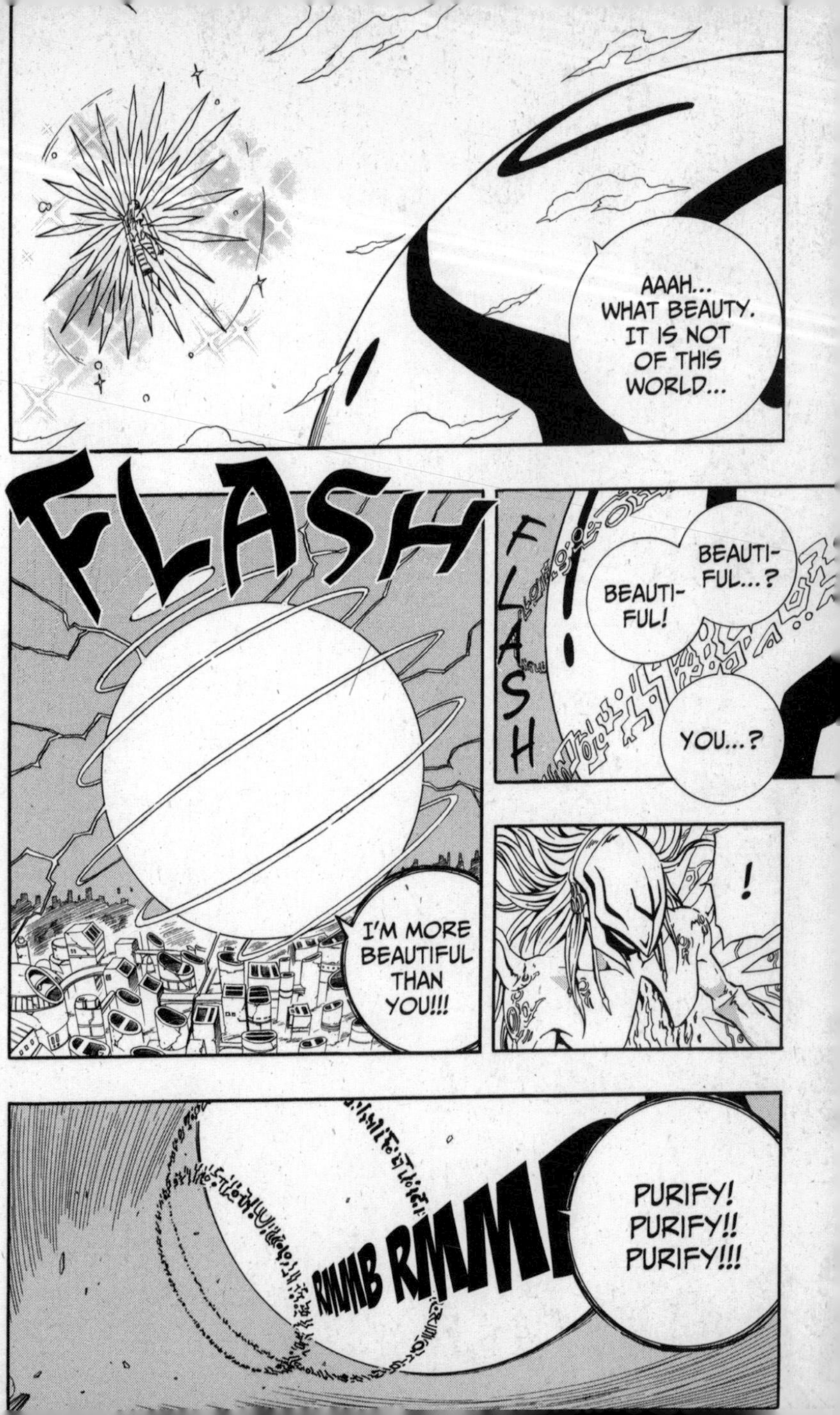
AAAH... WHAT BEAUTY. IT IS NOT OF THIS WORLD...
FLASH
BEAUTI-FUL...?
BEAUTI-FUL!
YOU...?
!
FLASH
I'M MORE BEAUTIFUL THAN YOU!!!
PURIFY! PURIFY!! PURIFY!!!
RMMB RMMM

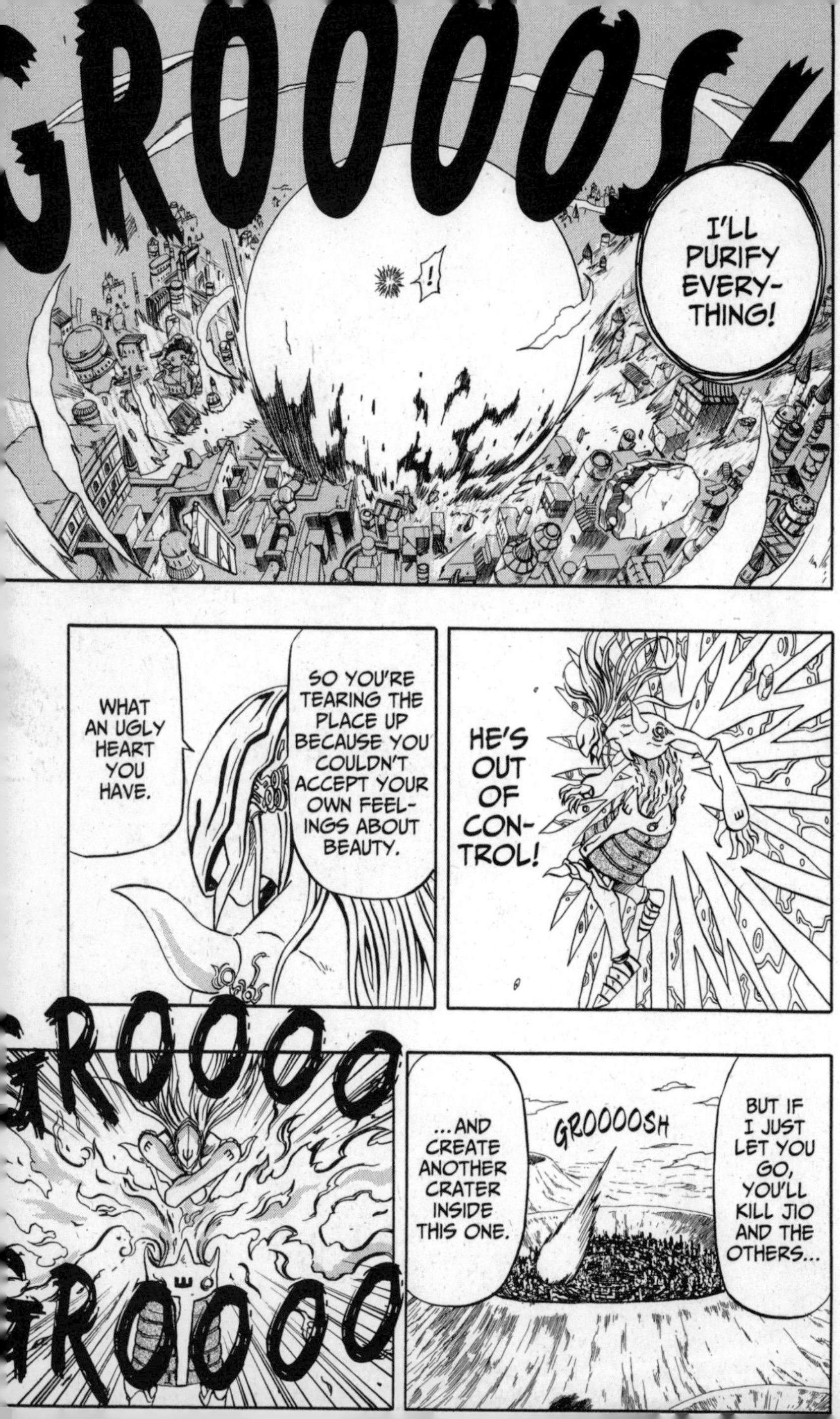
GROOOOSH
!
I'LL PURIFY EVERY-THING!
HE'S OUT OF CON-TROL!
SO YOU'RE TEARING THE PLACE UP BECAUSE YOU COULDN'T ACCEPT YOUR OWN FEEL-INGS ABOUT BEAUTY.
WHAT AN UGLY HEART YOU HAVE.
BUT IF I JUST LET YOU GO, YOU'LL KILL JIO AND THE OTHERS...
GROOOOSH
...AND CREATE ANOTHER CRATER INSIDE THIS ONE.
GROOOOO
TROOOOO

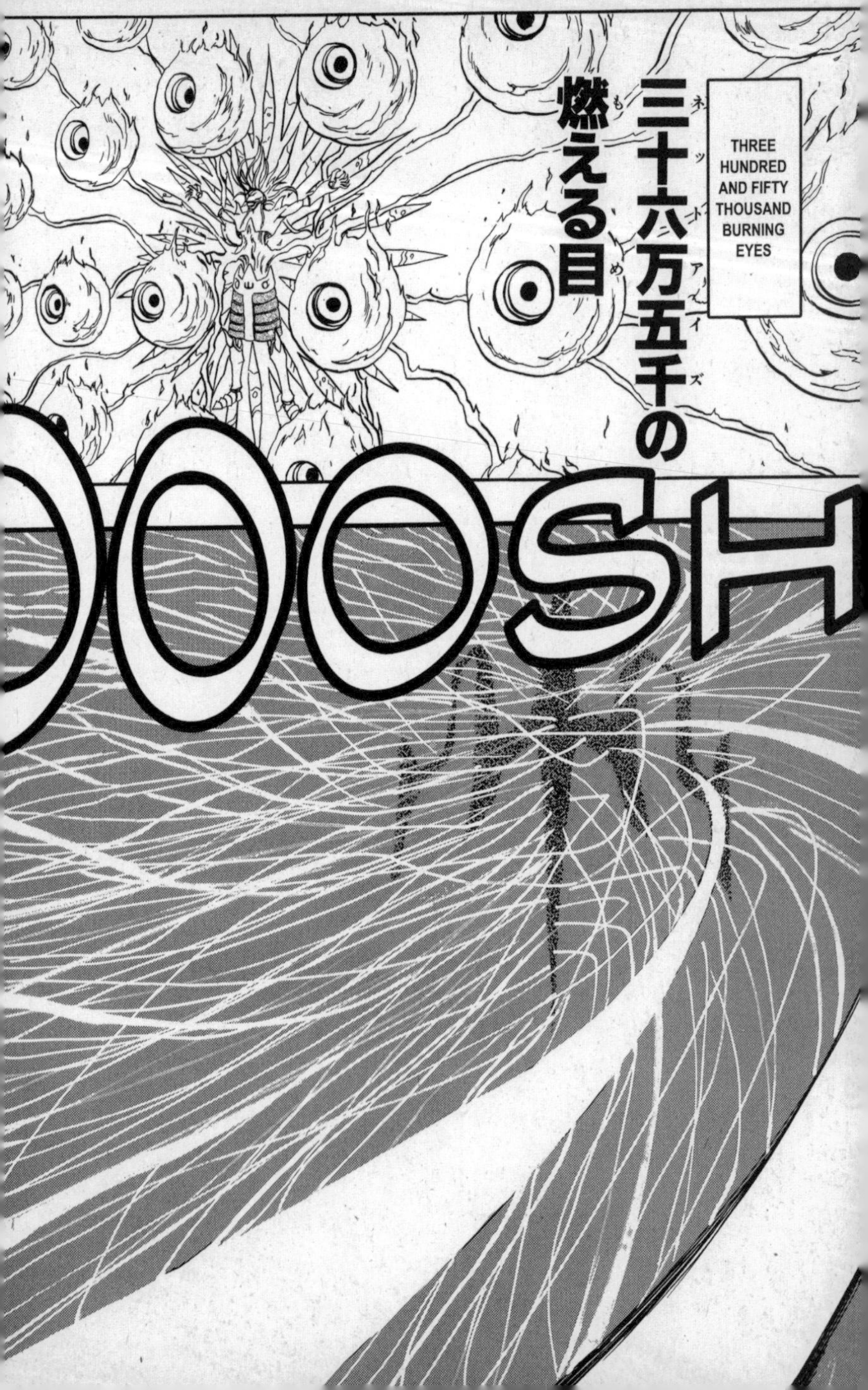
THREE HUNDRED AND FIFTY THOUSAND BURNING EYES
三十六万五千の燃える目
OOOSH

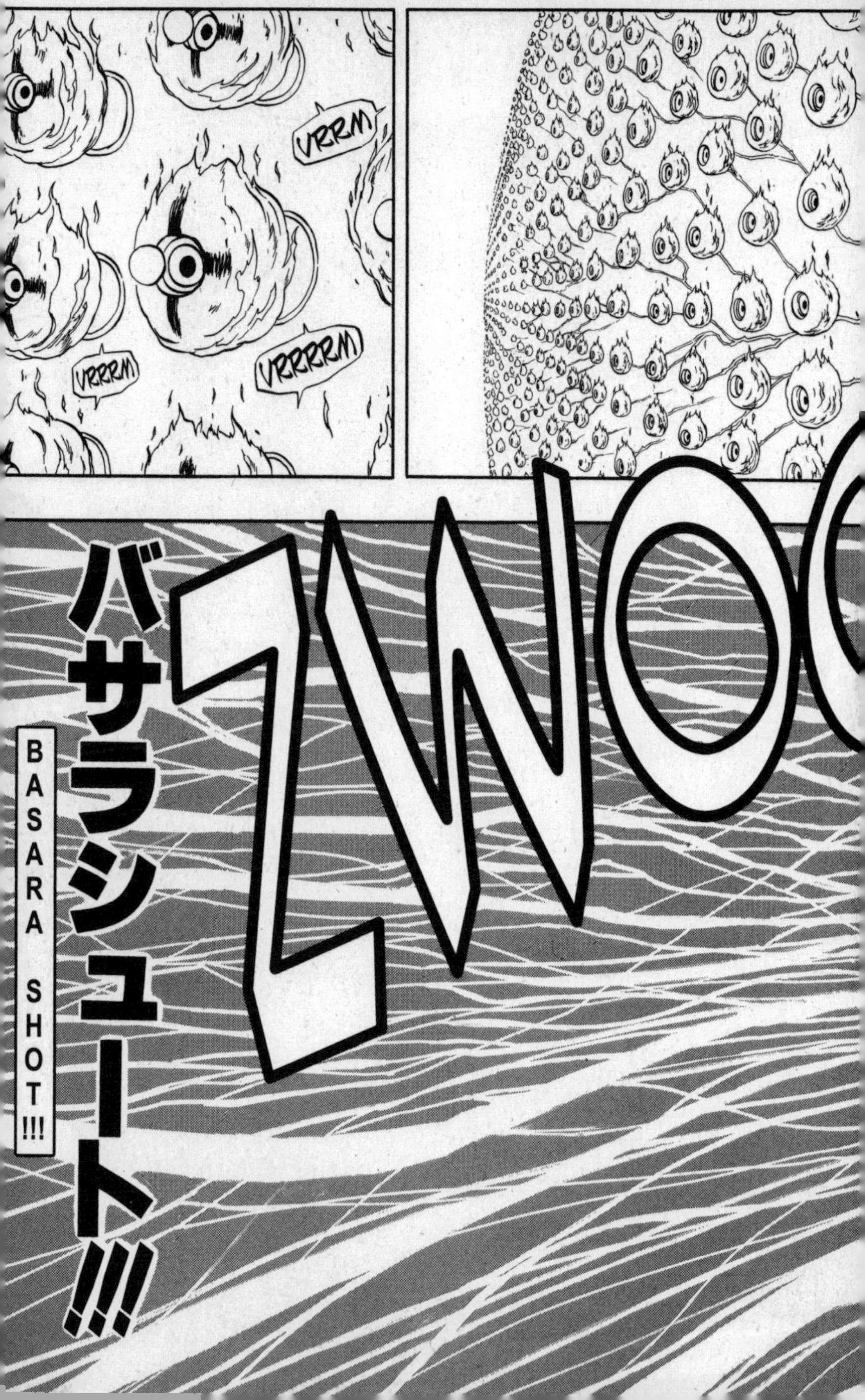
VRRM
VRRRRM
VRRRM
ZWOO
バサラシュート!!!
BASARA SHOT!!!

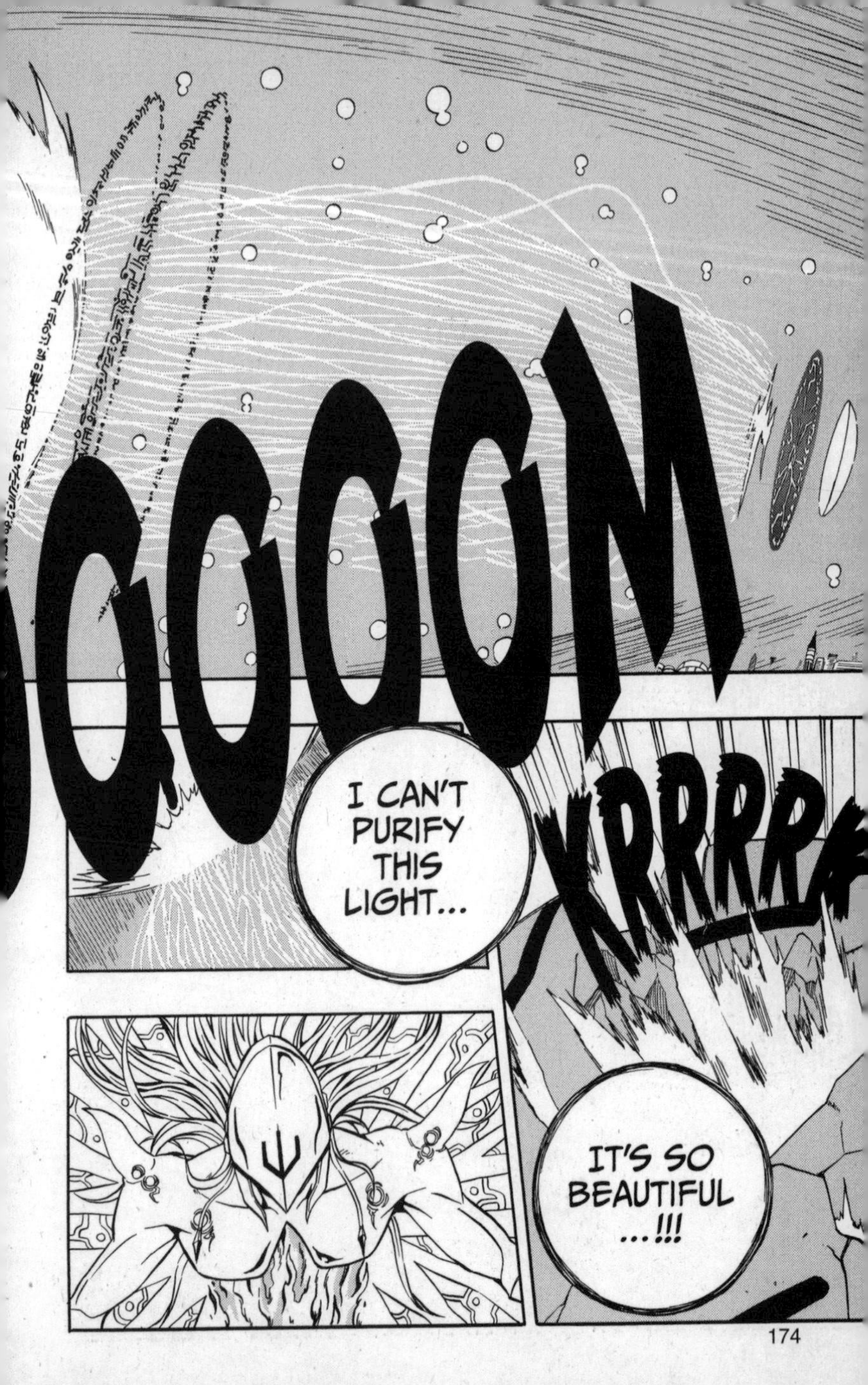
OOOOM
XRRRR
I CAN'T PURIFY THIS LIGHT...
IT'S SO BEAUTIFUL ...!!!

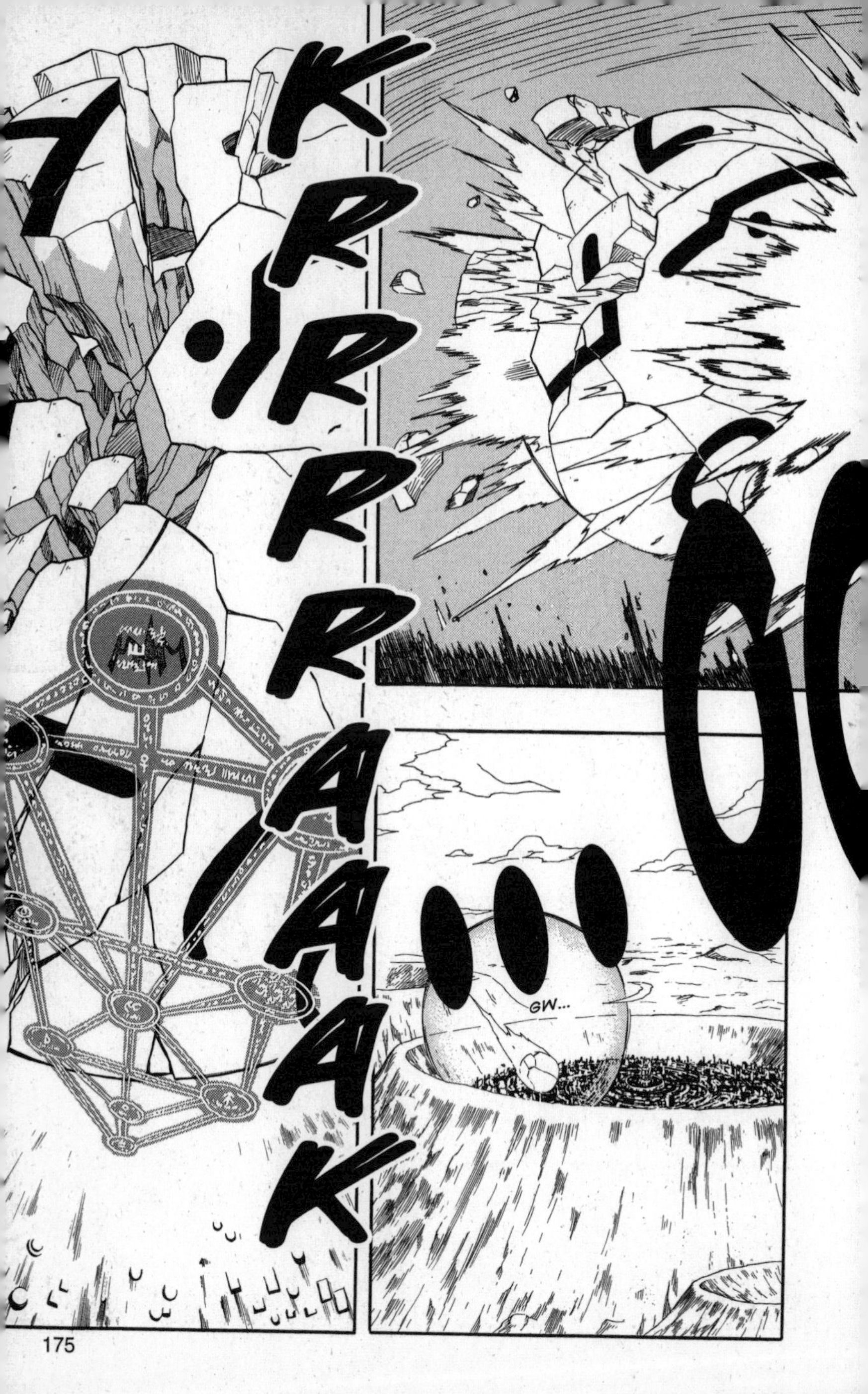
GO...
GW...
KRRRRRAAAAAK

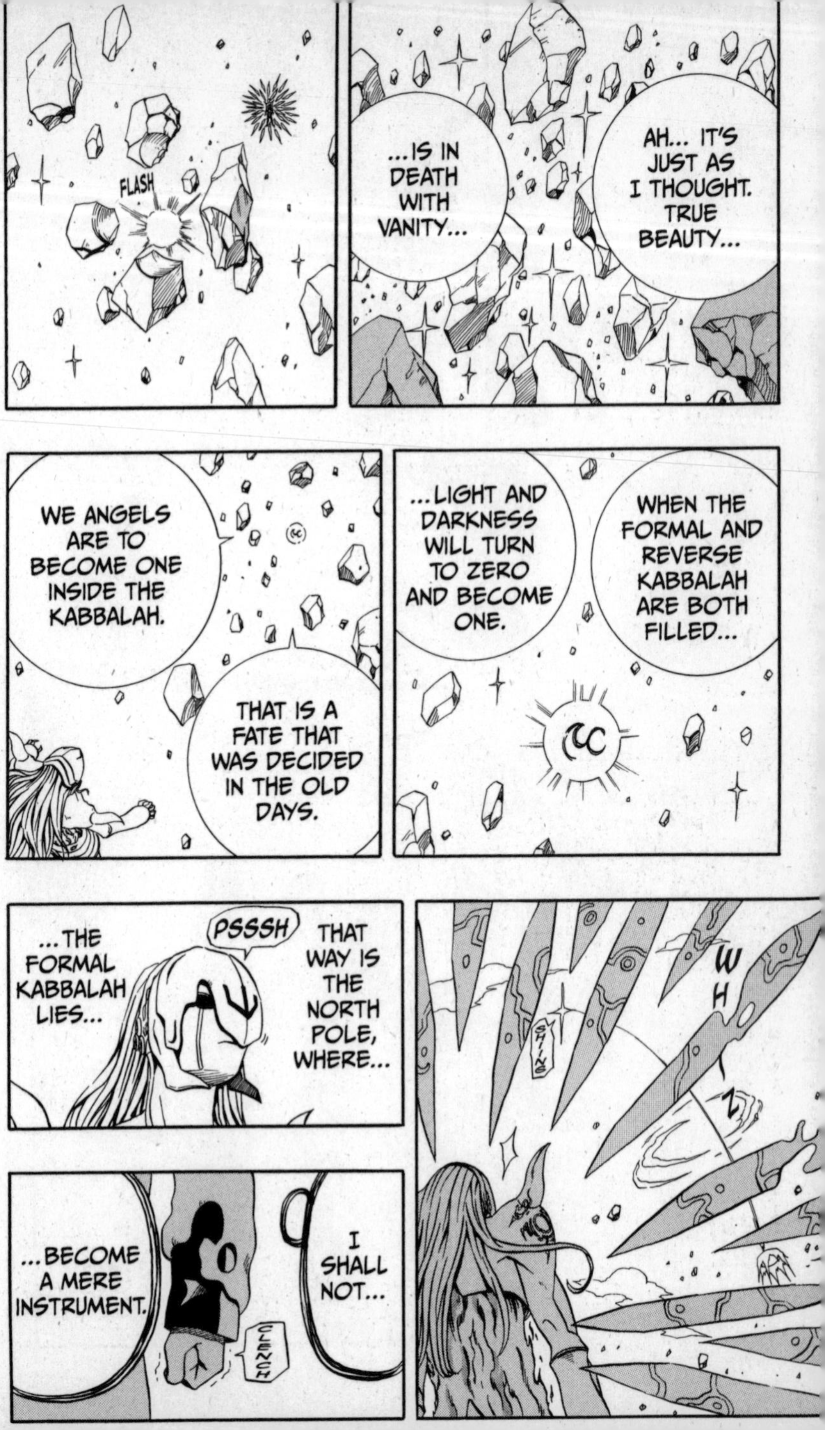
AH... IT'S JUST AS I THOUGHT. TRUE BEAUTY...
...IS IN DEATH WITH VANITY...
FLASH
WHEN THE FORMAL AND REVERSE KABBALAH ARE BOTH FILLED...
...LIGHT AND DARKNESS WILL TURN TO ZERO AND BECOME ONE.
WE ANGELS ARE TO BECOME ONE INSIDE THE KABBALAH.
THAT IS A FATE THAT WAS DECIDED IN THE OLD DAYS.
WHZ
SHING
THAT WAY IS THE NORTH POLE, WHERE...
PSSSH
...THE FORMAL KABBALAH LIES...
I SHALL NOT...
CLENCH
...BECOME A MERE INSTRUMENT.

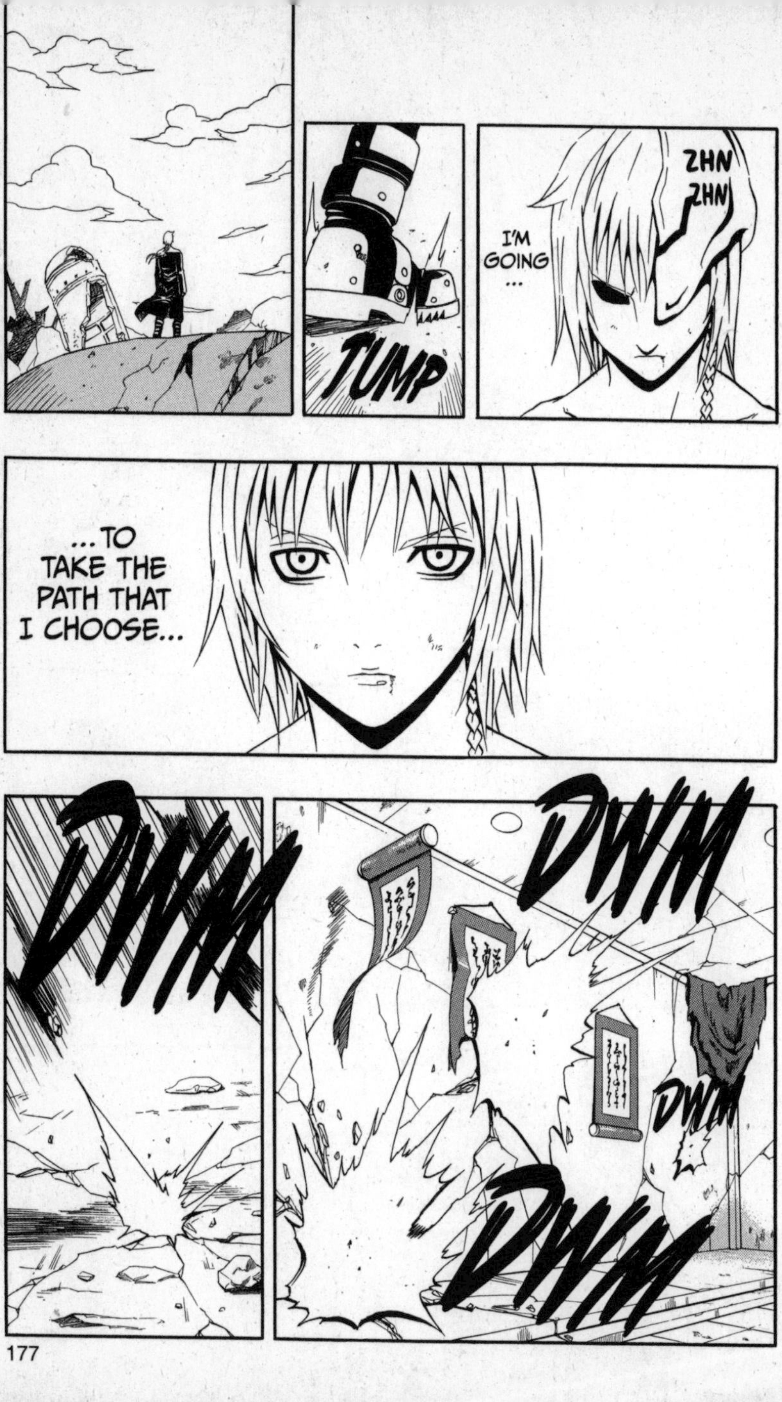
ZHN ZHN
I'M GOING ...
TUMP
...TO TAKE THE PATH THAT I CHOOSE...
DWM
DWM
DWM
DWM

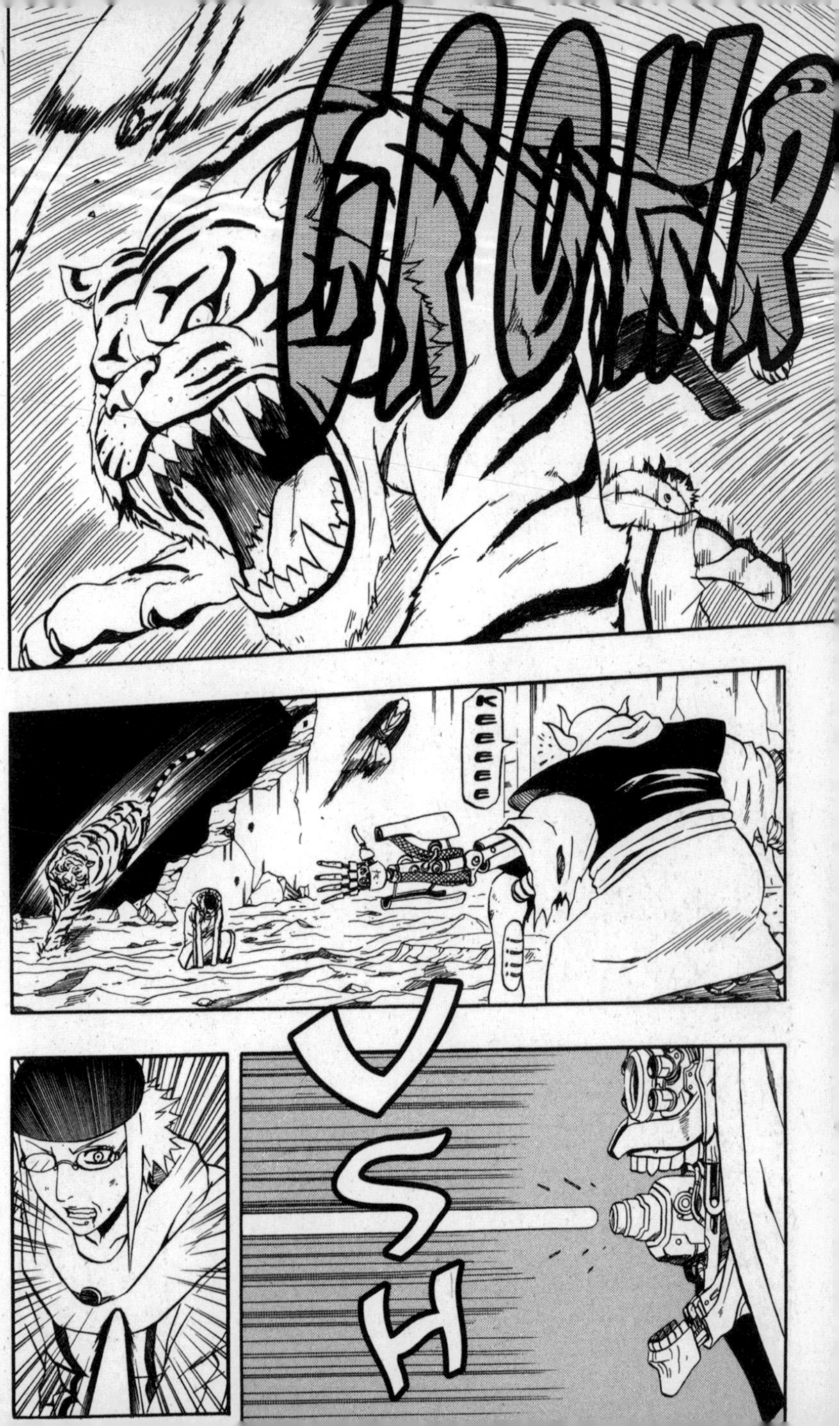
CHOMP
KEEEEEE
...

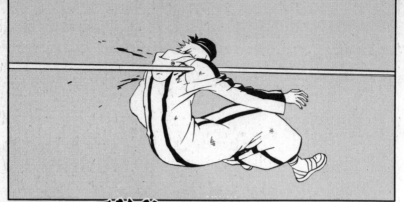

ZLISH ZLISH ZLISH

AMIDABA
!!!

CRUNCH

TAKES
ME DOWN
A PEG...

FSSS

TSK...

SHA

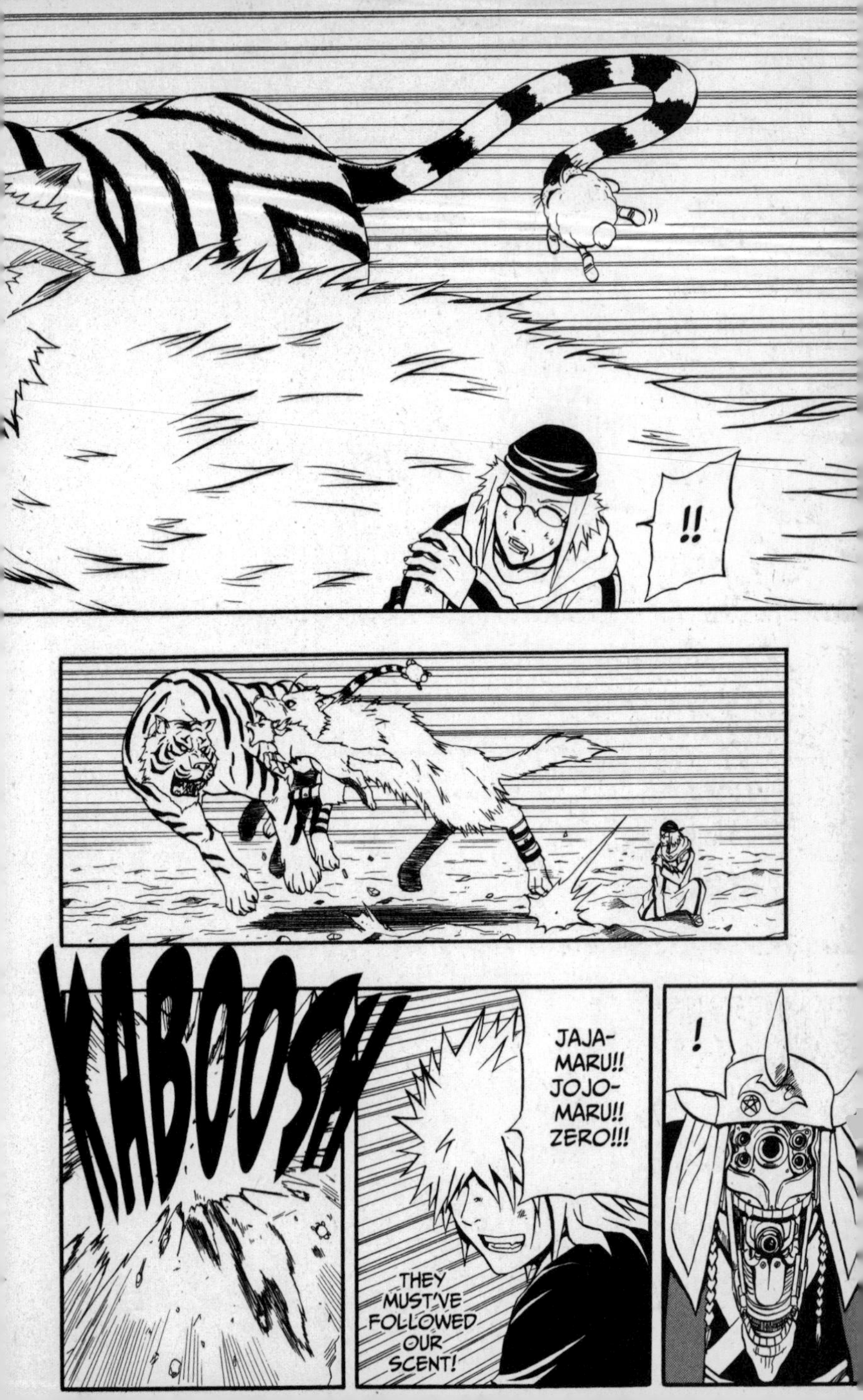
!!
!
JAJA-MARU!! JOJO-MARU!! ZERO!!!
THEY MUST'VE FOLLOWED OUR SCENT!
KABOOSH

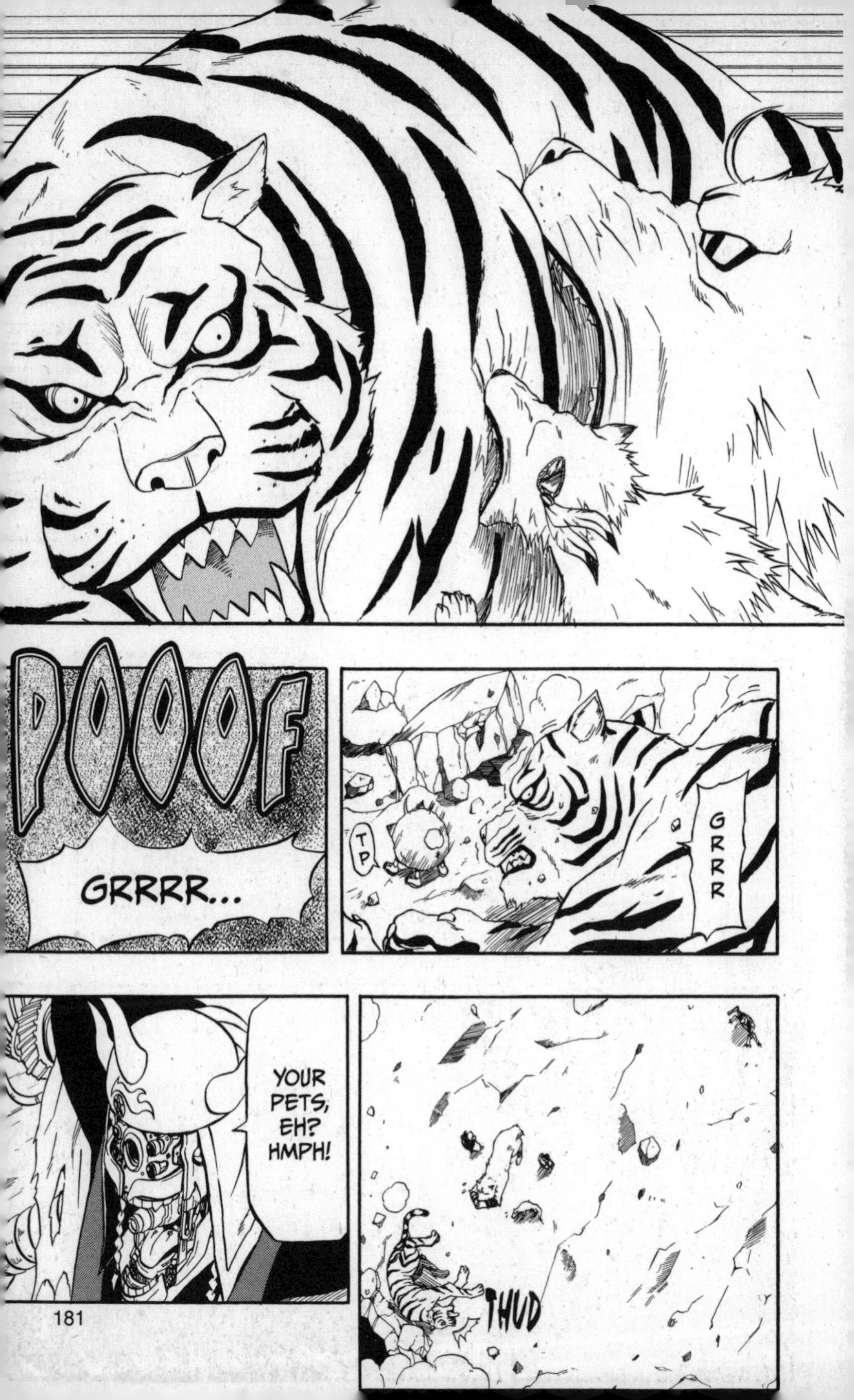
TP
GRRR
POOOF
GRRRR...
THUD
YOUR PETS, EH? HMPH!

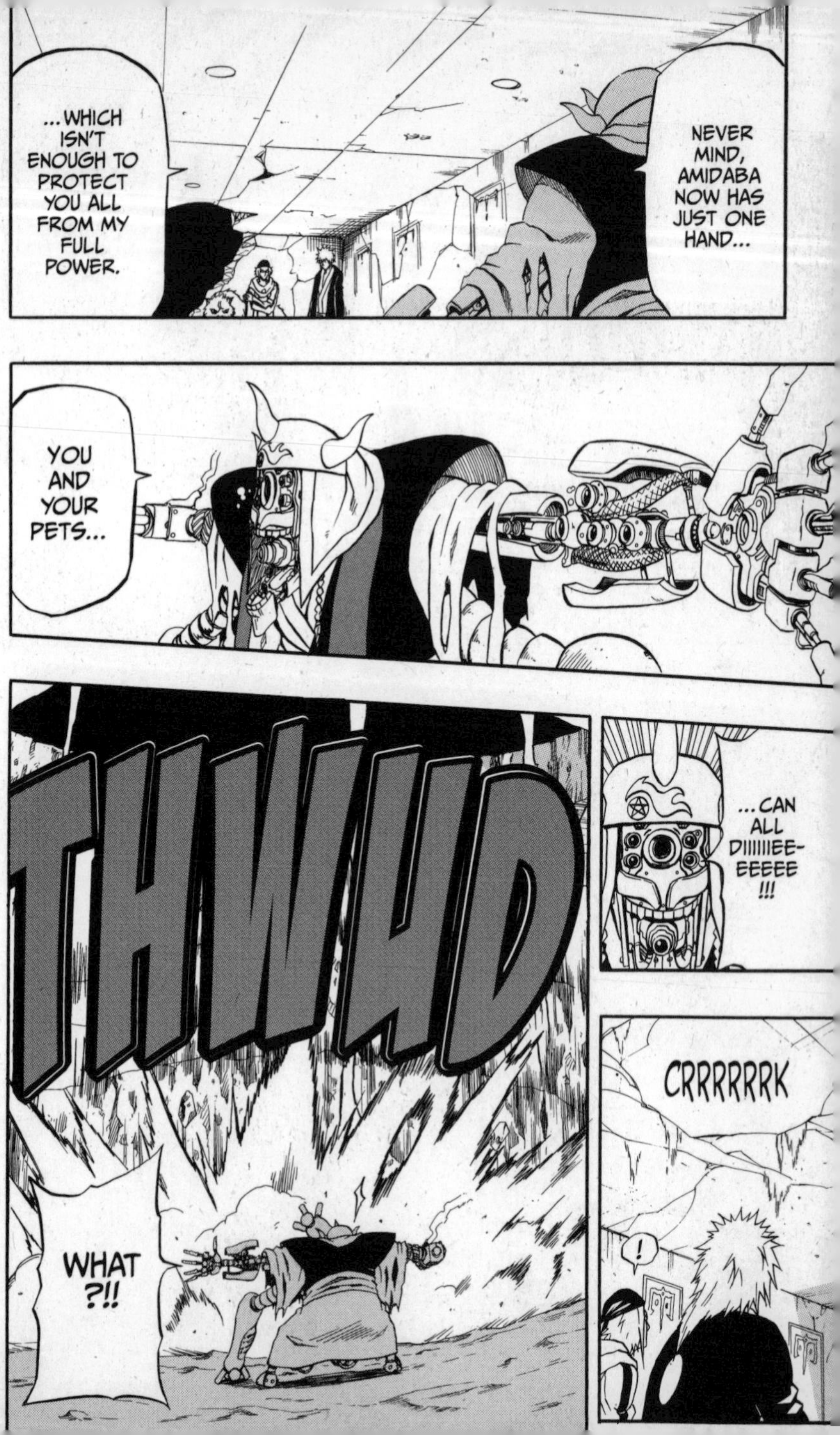
NEVER MIND, AMIDABA NOW HAS JUST ONE HAND...
...WHICH ISN'T ENOUGH TO PROTECT YOU ALL FROM MY FULL POWER.
YOU AND YOUR PETS...
...CAN ALL DIIIIIEE-EEEEE!!!
CRRRRRK
!
THWHD
WHAT?!!

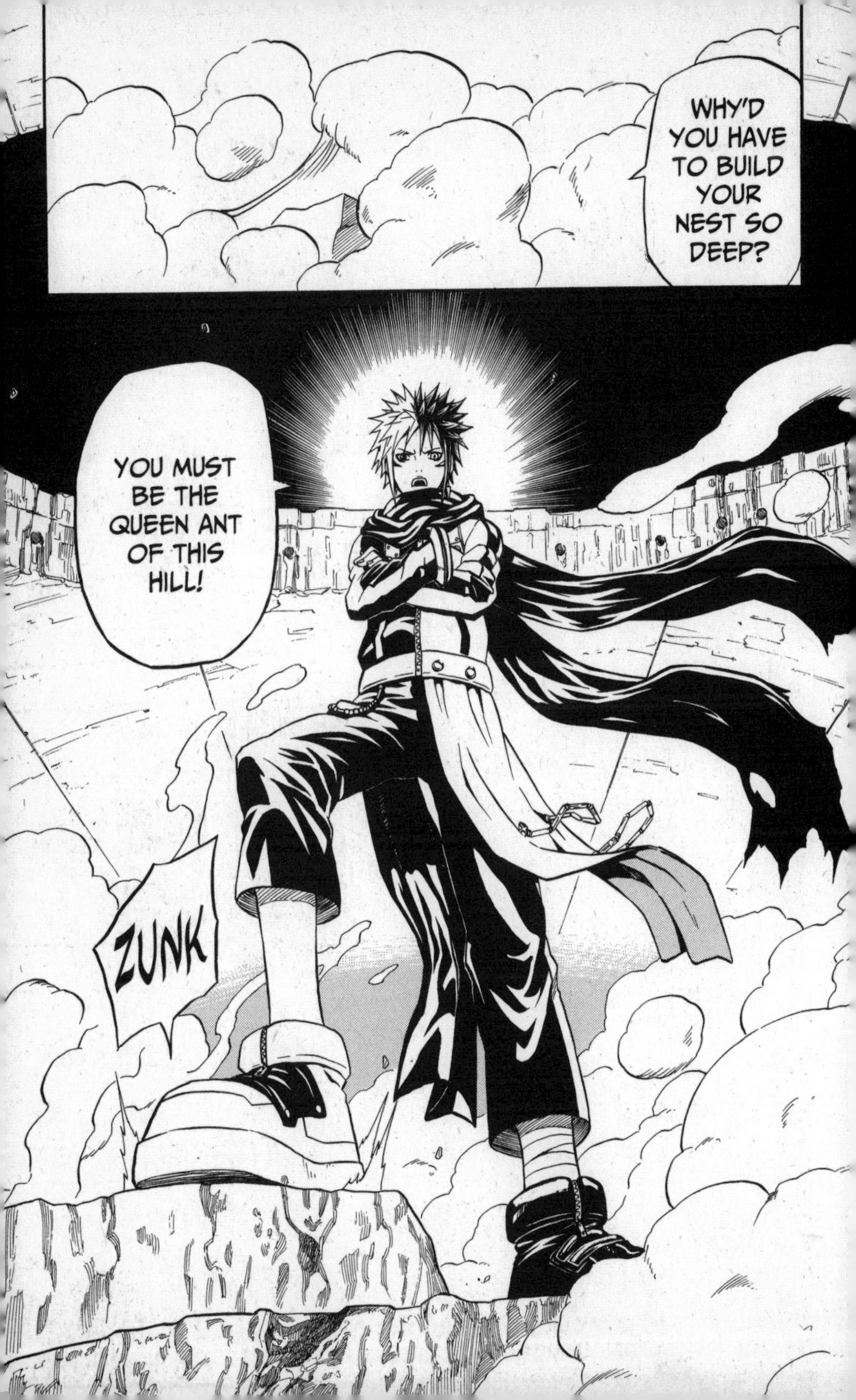
WHY'D YOU HAVE TO BUILD YOUR NEST SO DEEP?
YOU MUST BE THE QUEEN ANT OF THIS HILL!
ZUNK

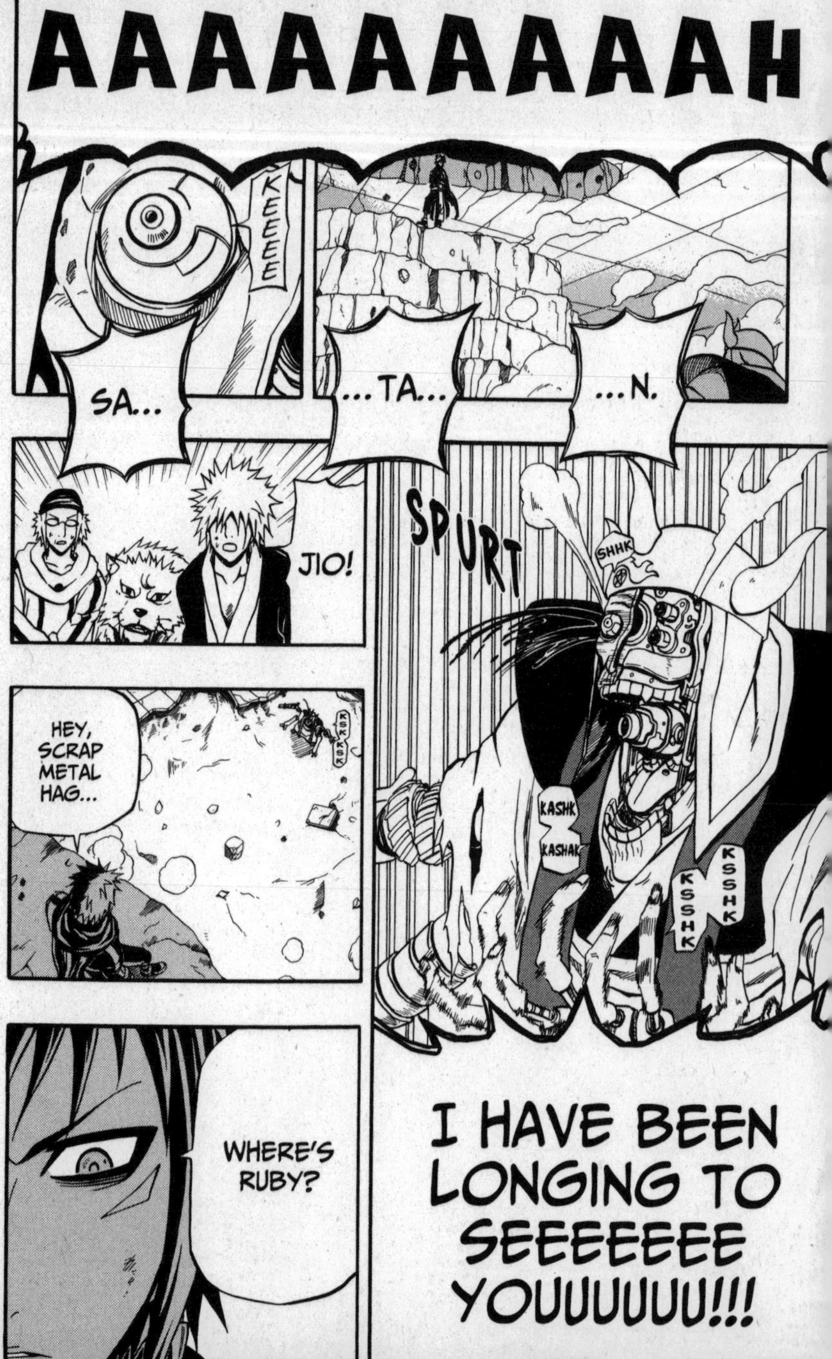
AAAAAAAAAH
KEEEE
SA...
...TA...
...N.
JIO!
HEY, SCRAP METAL HAG...
KSK KSK KSK
WHERE'S RUBY?
SPURT
SHHK
KASHK
KASHAK
KSSHK
KSSHK
I HAVE BEEN LONGING TO SEEEEEEE YOUUUUUU!!!

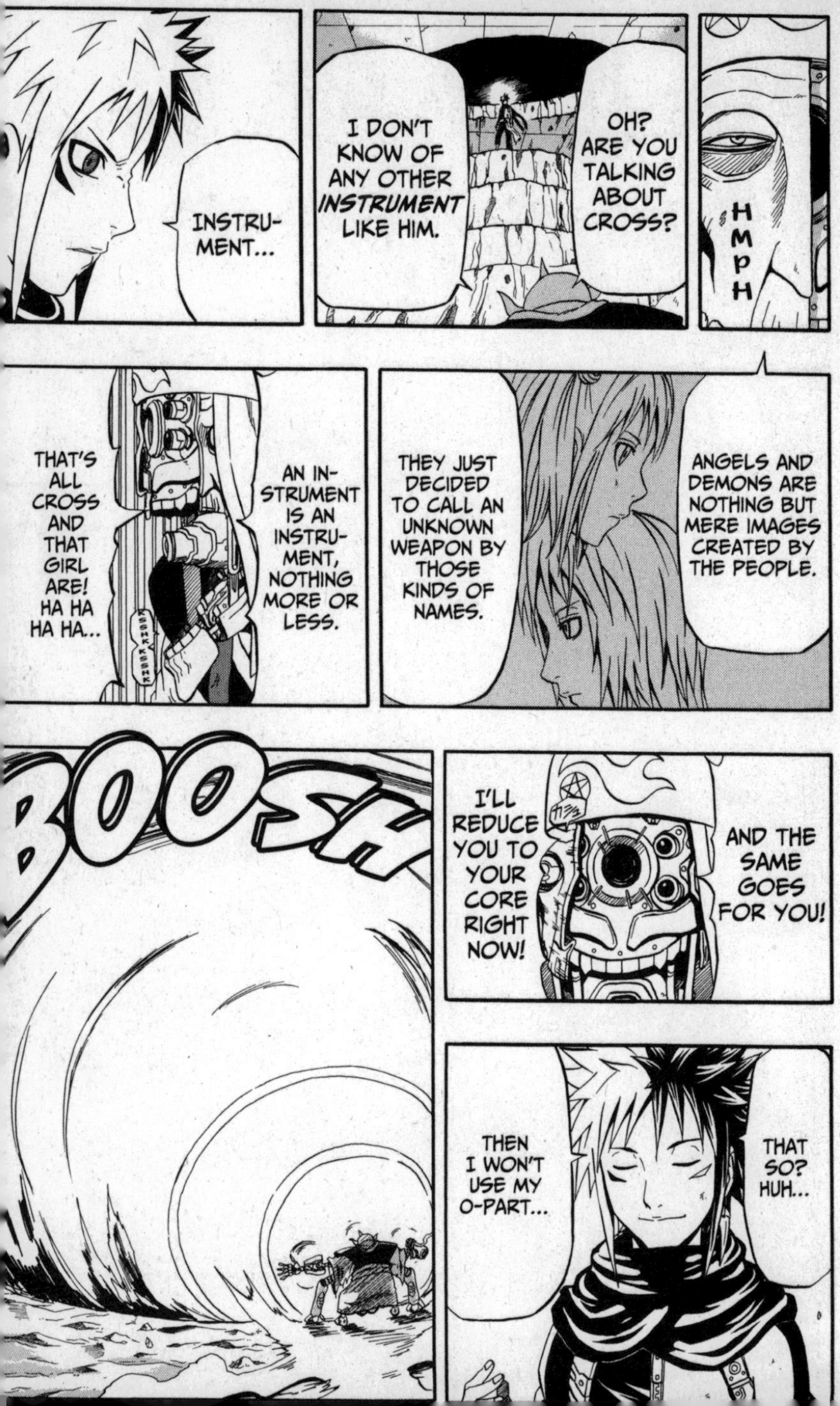
HMPH
OH? ARE YOU TALKING ABOUT CROSS?
I DON'T KNOW OF ANY OTHER *INSTRUMENT* LIKE HIM.
INSTRU-MENT...
ANGELS AND DEMONS ARE NOTHING BUT MERE IMAGES CREATED BY THE PEOPLE.
THEY JUST DECIDED TO CALL AN UNKNOWN WEAPON BY THOSE KINDS OF NAMES.
AN IN-STRUMENT IS AN INSTRU-MENT, NOTHING MORE OR LESS.
THAT'S ALL CROSS AND THAT GIRL ARE! HA HA HA HA...
KSSHK KSSHK
AND THE SAME GOES FOR YOU!
I'LL REDUCE YOU TO YOUR CORE RIGHT NOW!
THAT SO? HUH...
THEN I WON'T USE MY O-PART...
BOOSH

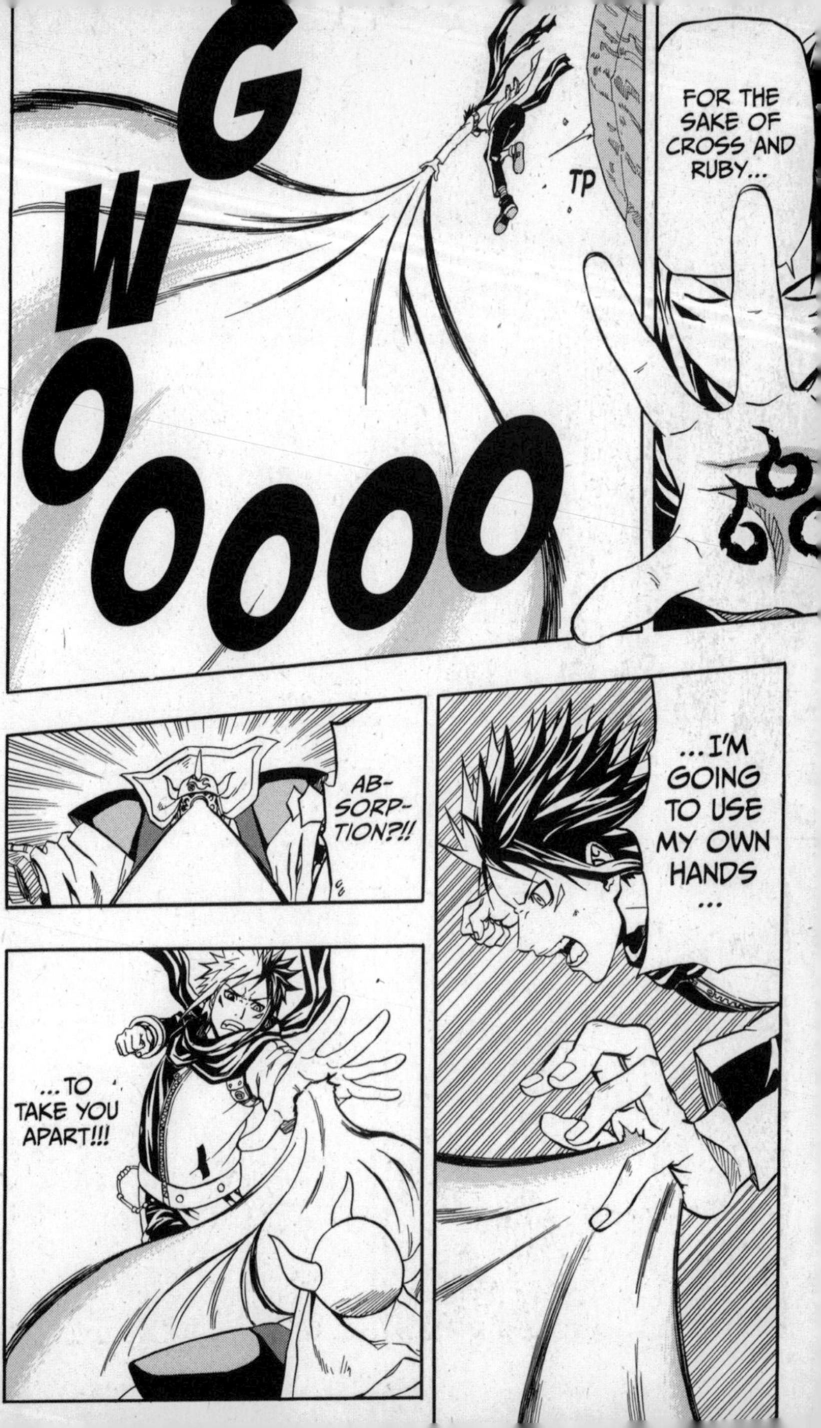
FOR THE SAKE OF CROSS AND RUBY...
TP
GWOOOOO
...I'M GOING TO USE MY OWN HANDS ...
AB-SORP-TION?!!
...TO TAKE YOU APART!!!

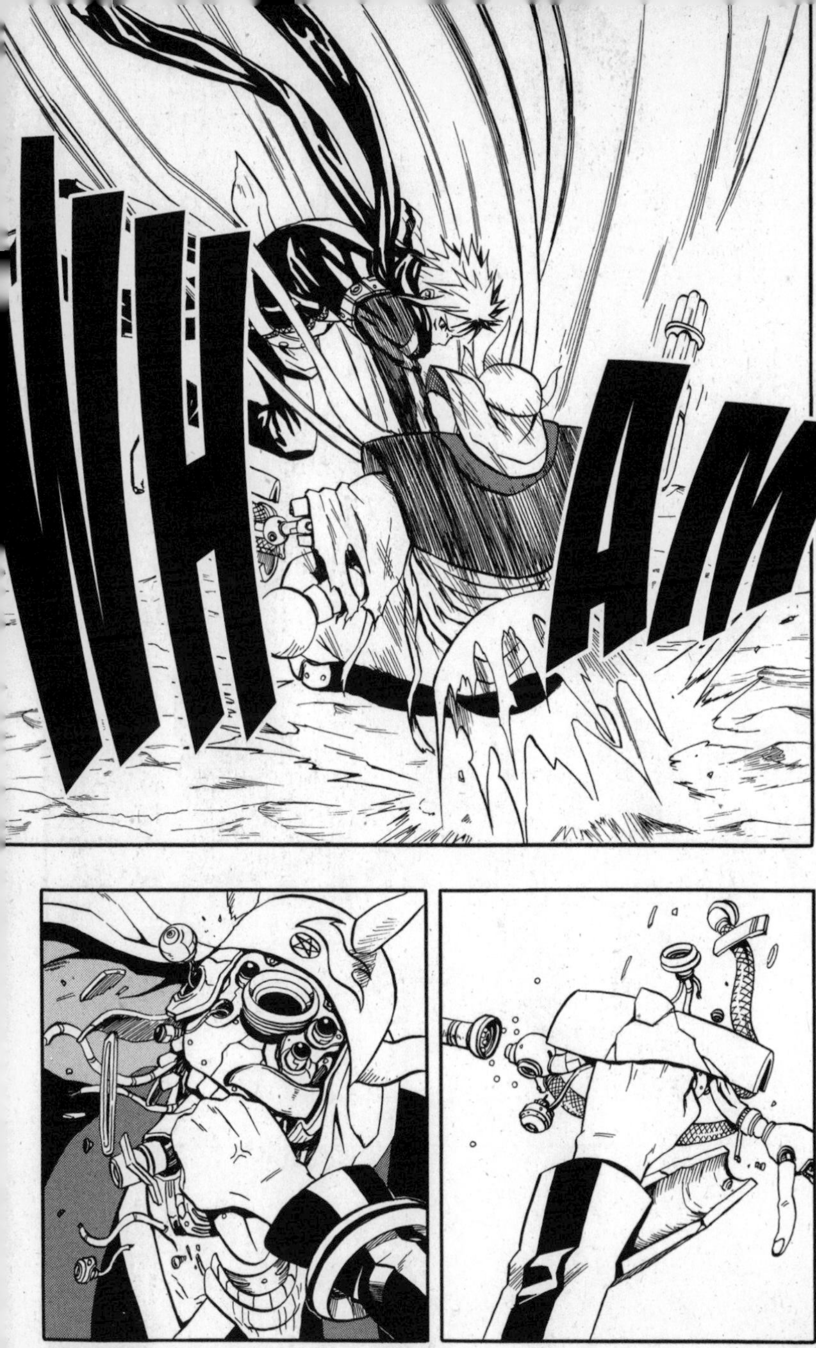
WHAM

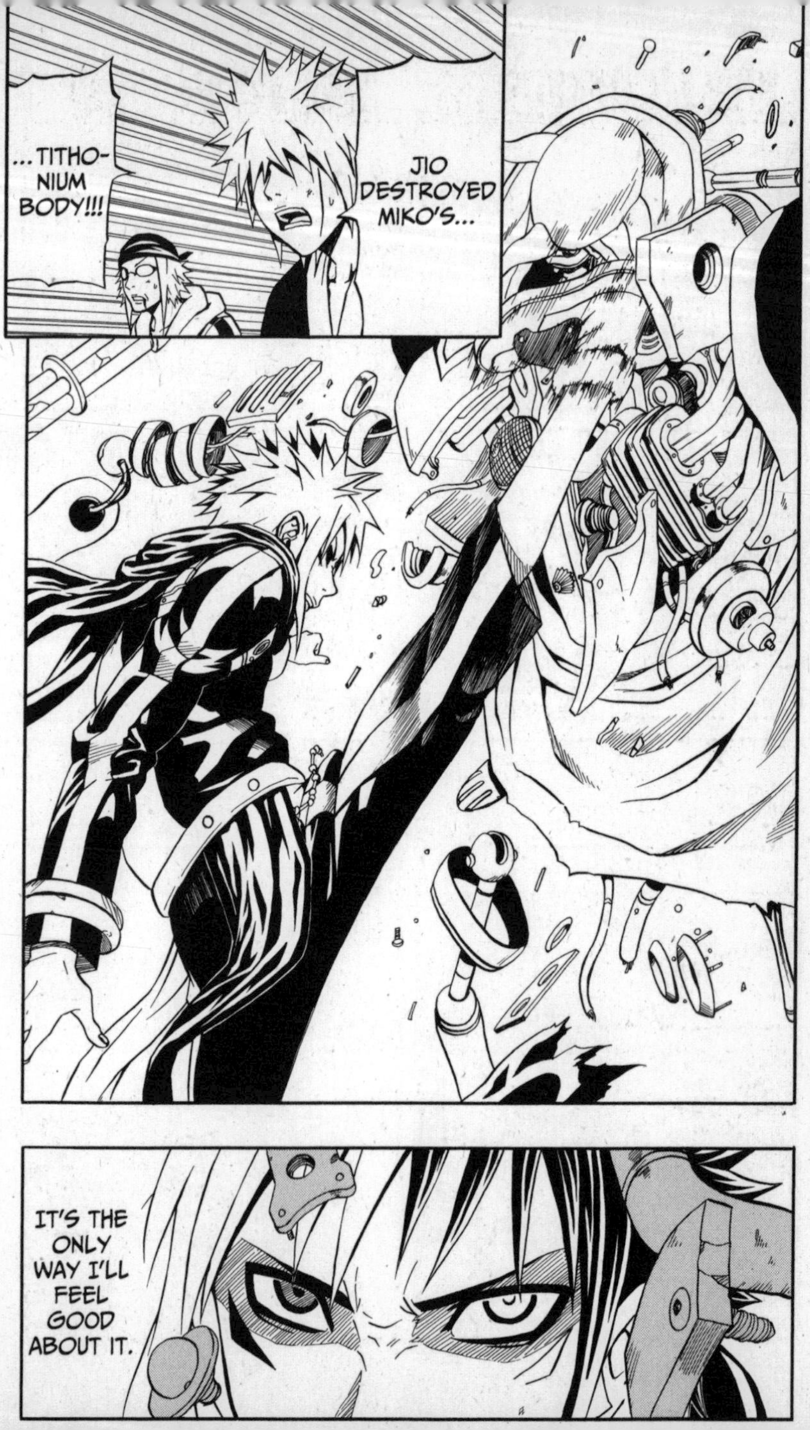
JIO DESTROYED MIKO'S...
...TITHO-NIUM BODY!!!
IT'S THE ONLY WAY I'LL FEEL GOOD ABOUT IT.

SEISHI AND ULT○MAN

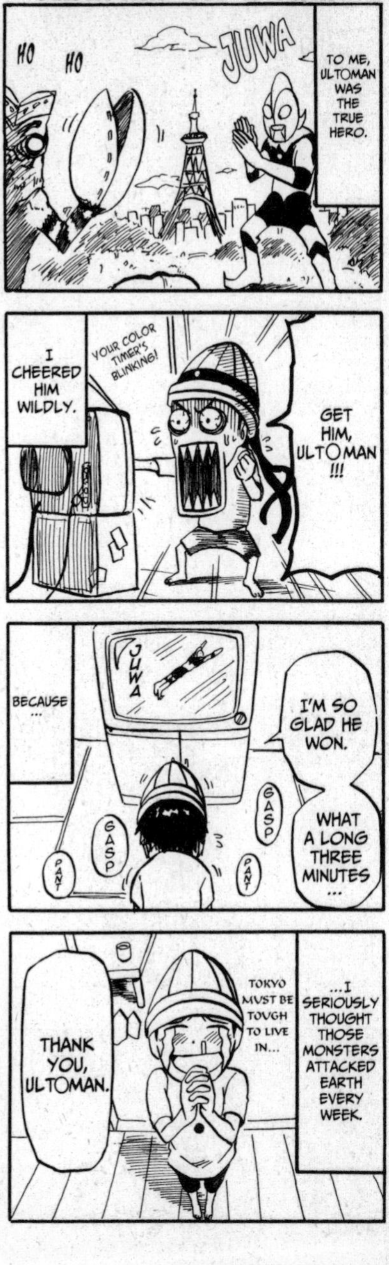
TO ME, ULT○MAN WAS THE TRUE HERO.
JUWA
HO
HO
GET HIM, ULT○MAN !!!
YOUR COLOR TIMER'S BLINKING!
I CHEERED HIM WILDLY.
I'M SO GLAD HE WON.
WHAT A LONG THREE MINUTES ...
GASP
PANT
JUWA
GASP
PANT
BECAUSE ...
...I SERIOUSLY THOUGHT THOSE MONSTERS ATTACKED EARTH EVERY WEEK.
TOKYO MUST BE TOUGH TO LIVE IN...
THANK YOU, ULT○MAN.

SEISHI AND THE CHEESE COD

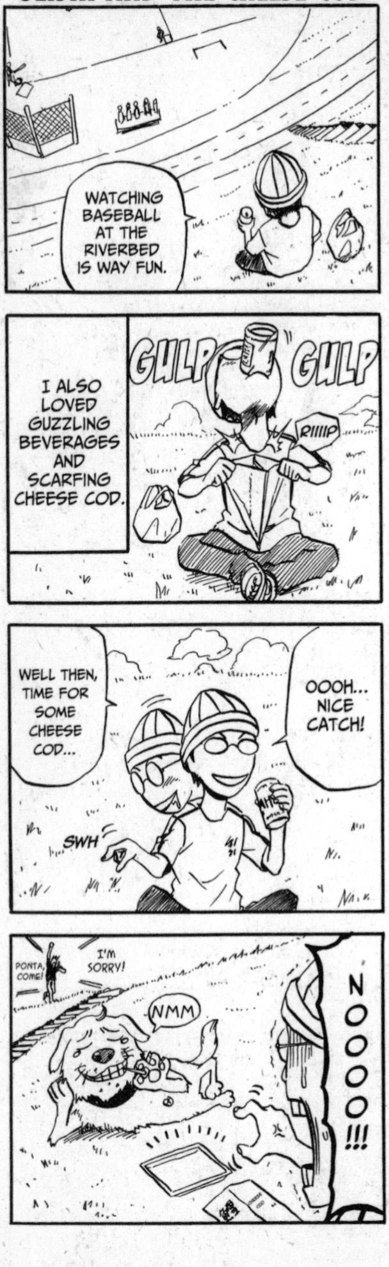
WATCHING BASEBALL AT THE RIVERBED IS WAY FUN.
GULP
GULP
RIIIP
I ALSO LOVED GUZZLING BEVERAGES AND SCARFING CHEESE COD.
OOOH... NICE CATCH!
WELL THEN, TIME FOR SOME CHEESE COD...
SWH
NOOOO!!!
NMM
I'M SORRY!
PONTA, COME!

O-Parts CATALOGUE⑮

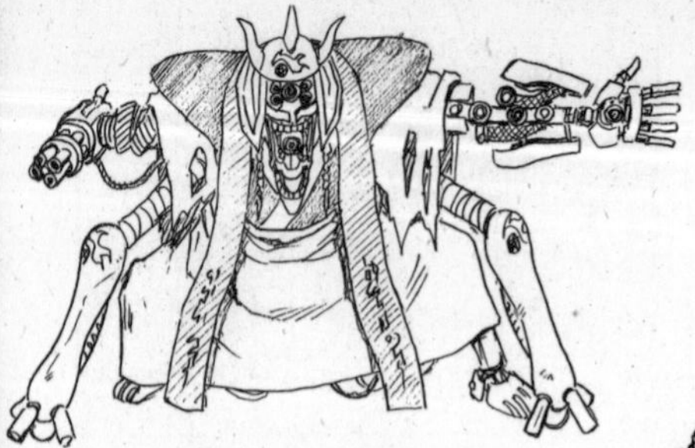

O-PART: TITHONIUM BODY
O-PART RANK: B
EFFECT: THE DENSEST METAL IN THE WORLD. ONLY MIKO KNOWS HOW TO PROCESS IT.

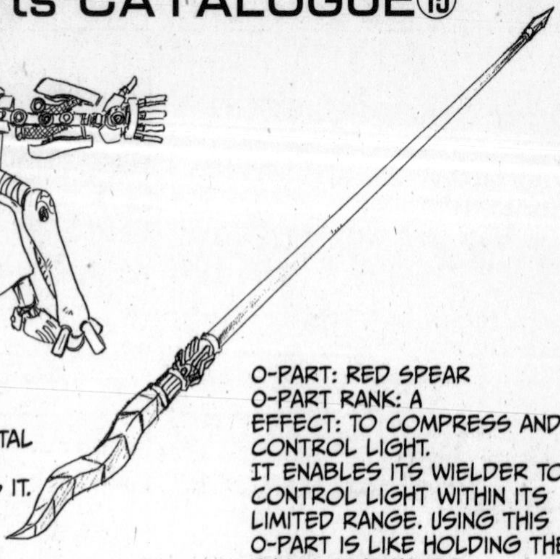

O-PART: RED SPEAR
O-PART RANK: A
EFFECT: TO COMPRESS AND CONTROL LIGHT.
IT ENABLES ITS WIELDER TO CONTROL LIGHT WITHIN ITS LIMITED RANGE. USING THIS O-PART IS LIKE HOLDING THE SUN IN YOUR HANDS.

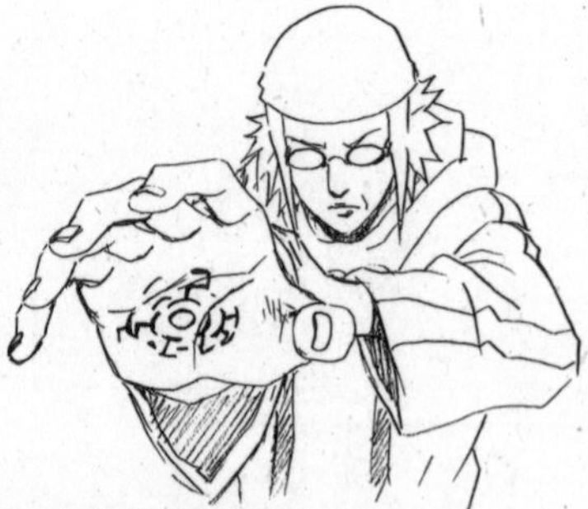

O-PART: RAINBOW (THE TATTOO ON HER HANDS)
O-PART RANK: B
EFFECT: FAVORITE TRICK (GRAVITY CONTROL)
THE SEVEN TATTOOS EACH HAVE A DIFFERENT POWER, AND SO THE NAME: THE SEVEN COLORED AMIDABA. HER FAVORITE TRICK IS GRAVITY CONTROL.

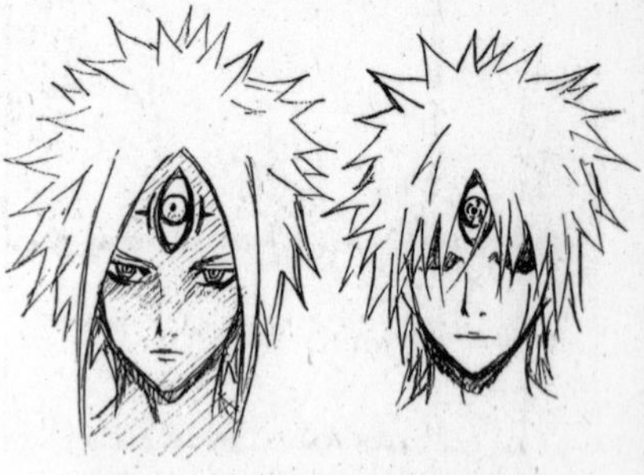

SPECIAL ABILITY: THE THIRD EYE
THIS ISN'T AN O-PART, BUT ITS POWERS ARE OVERWHELMING. IT ALLOWS YOU TO PROGRAM ANYTHING YOU SEE, EXCEPT HUMANS, AND CONTROL IT ANY WAY YOU LIKE. IT ALSO JACKS UP YOUR PHYSICAL ABILITY.

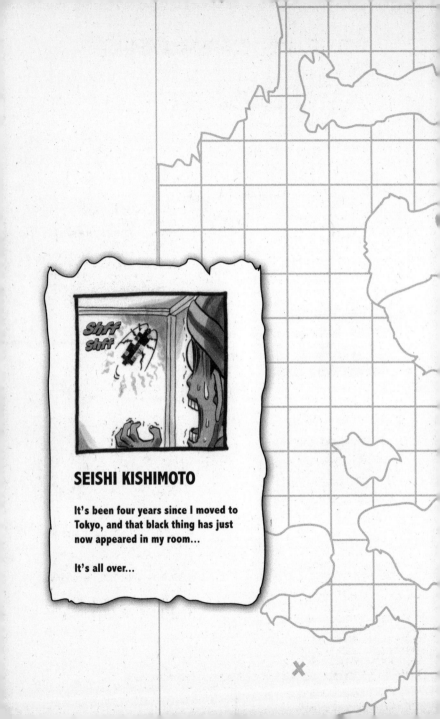

SEISHI KISHIMOTO

It's been four years since I moved to Tokyo, and that black thing has just now appeared in my room...

It's all over...

O-Parts HUNTER 15

VIZ Media Edition
STORY AND ART BY SEISHI KISHIMOTO

English Adaptation/David R. Valois
Translation/Tetsuichiro Miyaki
Touch-up Art & Lettering/HudsonYards
Design/Andrea Rice
Editor/Gary Leach

Editor in Chief, Books/Alvin Lu
Editor in Chief, Magazines/Marc Weidenbaum
VP, Publishing Licensing/Rika Inouye
VP, Sales & Product Marketing/Gonzalo Ferreyra
VP, Creative/Linda Espinosa
Publisher/Hyoe Narita

Printed in the U.S.A.

Published by VIZ Media, LLC
P.O. Box 77010
San Francisco, CA 94107

10 9 8 7 6 5 4 3 2 1
First printing, April 2009

viz media
www.viz.com
store.viz.com

PARENTAL ADVISORY
O-PARTS HUNTER is rated T+ for Older Teen and is recommended for ages 16 and up. This volume contains realistic and fantasy violence and adult situations.

RATED T+ FOR OLDER TEEN
ratings.viz.com